Social Studies

FOR CHILDREN

A Guide to Basic Instruction

John U. Michaelis

University of California, Berkeley

10th Edition

Allyn and Bacon
Boston London Toronto Sydney Tokyo Singapore

Managing Editor: Mylan Jaixen
Series Editor: Sean W. Wakely
Senior Editorial Assistant: Carol L. Chernaik
Production Administrator: Susan McIntyre
Editorial-Production Service: Ruttle, Shaw & Wetherill, Inc.
Cover Administrator: Linda Dickinson
Cover Designer: Design Ad Cetera
Composition Buyer: Louise Richardson
Manufacturing Buyer: Louise Richardson

Library of Congress Cataloging-in-Publication Data

Michaelis, John Udell
     Social studies for children : a guide to basic instruction / John
U. Michaelis.—10th ed.
        p.   cm.
     Includes bibliographical references and index.
     ISBN 0-205-13130-1
     1. Social sciences—Study and teaching (Elementary)—United
States.   I. Title.
LB1584.M43   1992
372.83′044—dc20   91-28888
                                                              CIP

Printed in the United States of America

10 9 8 7 6 5 4 3 2   96 95 94 93 92

6-25-93

To
Elizabeth Ann Michaelis
John Barry Michaelis
Susan Ann Michaelis

Contents

List of Plans, Study Guides, Activity Cards, Worksheets

Preface

This volume is a guide to instruction in grades K–8 that is needed to achieve excellence in citizenship education in a democracy. It is recognized that the role of teachers is enhanced by an understanding of the basic features of social studies instruction discussed in each chapter.

The first five chapters include guidelines and strategies for effective planning. Chapter 1 presents definitions, rationales, goals and objectives, and an overview of the curriculum. Chapters 2 and 3 focus on preparing plans and using multimedia. Chapters 4 and 5 contain a variety of group and individual learning activities.

Chapters 6, 7, and 8 suggest ways to incorporate content from disciplines, topics of social concern, and current affairs.

Specific teaching/learning strategies and activities are presented in the next five chapters. Chapter 9 is focused on development of concepts, generalizations and thinking skills. Chapter 10 describes expressive activities with emphasis on their use in developing creativity. Chapters 11 and 12 present teaching/learning strategies for applying and improving communication skills, and for developing map and globe concepts and skills. Chapter 13 discusses affective aspects of learning with emphasis on attitudes, values, and democratic behavior.

Chapter 14, on evaluation of learning, contains a variety of checklists, charts, test items, and other devices and techniques for appraising outcomes of instruction.

The order in which the chapters are studied may be varied to suit course requirements of instructors and needs of students. For example, some instructors follow the first three chapters with chapters 9–13 on teaching strategies so that students can incorporate them in plans for teaching. Whatever sequence is used, each chapter should be viewed as a source of ideas for teaching the social studies, just as social studies materials are used as data sources, not necessarily in a fixed order.

All chapters are structured to aid study. Each begins with an objective and related focusing questions that give an overview of content and serve as study guides. Practical teaching/learning strategies and activities are high-lighted and supplemented by charts, checklists, illustrations, and examples of teaching plans. End-of-chapter questions and activities are designed to provoke discussion, application, and evaluation of ideas. The critically selected references may be used to gain additional information and extend application of ideas presented in each chapter. Both the focusing questions and the suggested activities may be used for self-evaluation by students and for pre- and post-assessment by instructors in competency-based programs.

Grateful acknowledgement is made to the following who contributed ideas, materials, reviews, photographs, or suggestions included in this edition:

Charles Bahmueller, Francis Burke, Margaret Branson, Linda Castelli, Richard Clifford, Nina Gabelko, Jesus Garcia, Ruth Grossman, Virginia Lish, Sarah Madison, Victoria Mui, Albert Nelson, Eddie Ort, Haig Rushdoony, Richard Smith, Morrow Stough, Judith Wooster, Morris Lamb, Leroy Ortiz, and William Watkins. Special acknowledgment is made to instructors and their students whose suggestions continue to be a valuable source of ways to improve each edition.

Curriculum Overview and Historical Highlights

CHAPTER 1

Objective and Related Focusing Questions

To describe main features of the social studies curriculum and historical highlights of social studies education:

- What is included in definitions of social studies education?

- What is included in rationales for the social studies?

- What are major goals? How are related objectives stated?

- What is the conceptual structure of the curriculum?

- What three types of studies are included in the curriculum?

- How can conceptual, inquiry, and topical approaches be unified?

- What is included in the scope and sequence of the curriculum?

- What are highlights in the history of social studies education?

Definitions of the Social Studies

Definitions may be viewed in terms of the emphasis they place on one or more of the following orientations—subject matter, society, or students.[1]

The social studies may be defined as the area of the curriculum that:

Transmits basic aspects of our cultural heritage (subject matter-centered)

Is based on content and methods of study drawn from history, social sciences, and other disciplines (subject matter-centered)

Provides instruction on thinking and decision-making skills applied to social problems (society-centered)

Provides instruction to develop the competencies needed for social criticism and action (society-centered)

Develops students' potential for self-directed participation in group activities (student-centered)

Notice the inclusion of aspects of the above in a definition by a Task Force on Scope and Sequence (1989), which may be summarized as follows: The social studies is a basic subject that derives goals from the nature of a democratic society and links to other societies, draws content from the social sciences and other disciplines, is taught in ways that reflect the personal, social, and cultural experiences of students, and helps students transfer learning to life outside school. A Task Force on Early Childhood/Elementary Social Studies (1989) defined social studies as the study of political, economic, cultural, and environmental aspects of societies in the past, present, and future.

Implicit in all of the above is the study of human relationships and other elements of significance in current programs, as shown in Chart 1.1.

The foundations of the social studies are shown in Chart 1.1 because of their contributions to the program. From *social* foundations are drawn values, problems, concerns, trends, and mandated requirements. From *psychological* foundations are drawn findings and implications about child development and learning. From the disciplines—*history, social sciences, humanities,* and other sources—are drawn content and inquiry strategies needed to study human relationships. From *historical* foundations are drawn goals, strategies, and resources of proven value. From *philosophical* foundations are drawn the point of view, rationale, values, and beliefs that guide implementation of the program.

Social studies should not be confused with social competence or social education. *Social competence* is the ability to engage in group activities both in and out of school. *Social education* takes place in the school, family, church, and other institutions. Although social studies education contributes to both of these, it is first and foremost an area of the curriculum, as are the language arts and science education. Its significance as an area of the curriculum is discussed in the next section.

---

[1]For a detailed review, see Barr et al. (1977) and Brubaker et al. (1977).

The Social Studies
The study of human relationships to develop responsible citizenship in a democracy
↕

With a focus on:
Cultural heritage and content and methods from supporting disciplines
Social, political, economic, temporal, and spatial aspects of human activities in the past, present, and future
Application of thinking, valuing, and other skills to social problems, criticism, and action
↕

Based on foundations of the curriculum:
Social   Psychological   Disciplinary   Historical   Philosophical

---

Chart 1.1

Rationales for the Social Studies

The rationales for the social studies usually include the assumptions, reasons, beliefs, points of view, philosophies, or special characteristics underlying the curriculum. For example, assumptions or beliefs may be stated about the nature of the individual, society, values, knowledge, and learning: recognize students' learning styles; give attention to societal changes; consider the influence of ethical, moral, and spiritual values; build concepts and generalizations on a solid information base; relate instruction to students' developmental stages.

Many curriculum guides include goal-related reasons for the importance of social studies. A primary one is to develop understanding and appreciation of our democratic heritage. Another is to develop concepts and methods of study needed to understand human relationships and to deal with social issues and problems. A third reason is to develop reflective thinking skills and competence in social criticism and action to enable students to engage in decision making and participate in activities that improve the human condition. Other rationales are based on state and local requirements for instruction in state and national history, geography and government, the Constitution, our economic and legal systems, and observance of holidays and commemorations.

Some curriculum guides include a list of characteristics that are features of the program. Examples are emphasis on history, related literature, chronological sequence, integration of content from the disciplines, depth studies, multicultural perspective, ethical understanding, civic virtue, democratic values, principles from the Constitution, controversial issues, importance of religion in human affairs, critical thinking skills, active student participation in school and community service projects.[2] Another guide includes basic elements of knowledge, core democratic values, basic skills, social participation, and such characteristics as provision of K–12 instruction, emphasis on basic concepts, a structured curriculum, local translation of goals, clear

---

[2]*History-Social Science Framework.* Sacramento, CA: State Department of Education, 1988.

objectives and provision of related learning activities, use of a variety of media, supportive classroom climate, needs assessment, and evaluation.[3]

Some are brief and to the point. For example, A New York state guide offers the following rationale: Social studies education provides for citizenship education, the original rationale for public education; for development of critical thinking, problem solving, and decision-making skills; and for learning to live under law, interact with others, accept societal responsibilities, and deal with conflict.[4]

When no explicit statement of rationale is given, look for the following: philosophy, point of view, implications of child development and learning, societal changes and values, the nature of knowledge and knowing, characteristics of the program, and the reason stated goals, content, and other features of the program are important. Key reasons for social studies education also may be indicated in statements of contributions to goals of education and major goals of the social studies, as described in the next section.

Goals and Objectives

Goals are long-range desired outcomes of instruction that give a sense of direction to teachers at all levels. Objectives are related specific and measurable outcomes sought by teachers at each level. The goals and objectives of the social studies are related directly to our democratic heritage, views of citizenship, societal expectations, legislative mandates, and accountability programs.

Contributions to Goals of Education

Social studies contribute to goals of education in several fundamental ways. Students develop *self-realization* through experiences that foster each individual's growth in knowledge, skills, and values. Students better understand *human relationships* through multiethnic studies, the study of various cultures, the development of interpersonal skills, and analysis of intergroup problems. Students develop *civic responsibility* through civic activites in and out of school; they learn the concepts and main ideas of government and the legal rights of individuals; and they develop thinking and valuing processes that help them to deal with issues and make decisions. Students acquire *economic competence* as they explore concepts, attitudes, and skills related to good workmanship, career awareness, contributions of different workers, and use of resources. The social studies sharpen *thinking ability* through learning activities that involve students in critical and creative thinking and in decision-making activities. Students *learn how to learn* as they apply reading, study, and other skills; as they engage in independent study activities that emphasize self-direction and self-evaluation; and as they progressively develop the ability to use models of inquiry and processes of thinking. Other examples of contributions are given in the following section on social studies' goals.

[3]*Essential Goals and Objectives for Social Studies Education in Michigan (K–12)*. Lansing, MI: State Board of Education, 1989.
[4]*Supervision Manual: Social Studies Program*. Albany, NY: State Department of Education, 1982, 1–2.

Social Studies' Goals

Knowledge, skills, attitudes/values/appreciations, and social participation are goals that may be stated in many programs, with social participation sometimes included under skills. For example, California's *History—Social Science Framework* includes these goals as strands in the K–12 curriculum:

Knowledge and cultural understanding of historical, ethical, cultural, geographic, economic, and sociopolitical elements

Democratic understanding and civic values with emphasis on our national identity, constitutional heritage, civic values, and rights and responsibilities

Skills attainment and social participation with emphasis on study, thinking, and participation skills

Examples of the content of these goals are presented below to illustrate the emphasis of each.

Knowledge

To develop an understanding of content drawn from history, geography, social sciences, humanities, current affairs, and study of individual and social needs, including:

Historical, ethical, cultural, geographic, economic, and sociopolitical literacy

National identity, Constitutional heritage, civic values, rights and responsibilities

How people meet basic needs and are interdependent in communities, countries, and the world, here and now and in other times and places

Local, state, and national history, geography, and government

Relationships between people and their social and physical environments, and how they organize, adapt to, and change their environments

The impacts of science and technology on human relationships and conditions

Social institutions and social functions, such as government, education, communication, transportation, production, family life, and religion

World regions, their cultures, history, geography, contributions to civilization, economic and political systems, and relations with other areas

The diversity and influence of ethical and religious beliefs on ways of living, universal concern for ethics and human rights

The arts, literature, mythology, values, and ideals as a reflection of people's thoughts, feelings, and aspirations

Skills

To develop thinking, study, communication, and other skills needed for effective democratic citizenship, including:

Critical and creative thinking, problem solving, decision making, metacognition, and processes such as classifying, generalizing, analyzing, and evaluating

Detection and analysis of bias, stereotypes, prejudice, propaganda, assumptions, and opinions

Study, reading, writing, listening, and speaking skills needed to collect, process, and report information in oral, written, and graphic form

Interpretation of maps, globes, graphs, charts, diagrams, tables, time lines, cartoons, and illustrations

Construction of maps, graphs, charts, time lines, and other needed items

Use of computers, video and other electronic media, audiovisual and community resources, and mass media

Interpersonal and prosocial skills needed in group planning, discussion, evaluation, role taking, problem solving, decision making, and action

Attitudes/Values/Appreciations

To develop the attitudes/values/appreciations and related beliefs characteristic of those who have a firm commitment to democratic citizenship, including:

Positive attitudes toward others, diverse groups and cultures, and ethnic, racial, religious, and other differences

Commitment to unifying values—justice, equality, authority, participation, truth, and patriotism—and to pluralistic/individualistic values—freedom, diversity, privacy, due process, property, human rights (Butts, 1988)

Appreciation of Constitutional guarantees, democratic values and behavior, contributions of diverse groups to our culture, and the functions of social, economic, and political institutions in our society and in others

Competence in using valuing processes to analyze conflicts and make judgments in terms of justice, equality, and other democratic values

Social Participation

To develop the personal, group interaction, and social/political skills essential to civic competence in a democratic society, including:

Sensitivity to needs, feelings, problems, and goals of others, concern for rights and responsibilities of individuals and groups in multiethnic, cross-cultural, and cross-generational settings, forceful expression of reasoned personal convictions, adjustment of one's behavior to cooperate with others, recognition of need to eliminate stereotypes, prejudice, and bigotry

Constructive group interaction reflected in group planning, decision making, and acting, resolving conflicts, analyzing controversial issues, serving as a leader and follower, and using methods of persuasion and negotiation

Social and political action competence, including ability to identify needed action, to carry out civic responsibilities, to change one's role as circumstances change, to influence others to extend justice, equality, and other democratic values, and to accept and handle consequences of one's actions

Evaluation of quality of participation, contribution to improvement of human conditions, and processes of individual and group action

Instructional Objectives

This section presents procedures for translating goals of the social studies into instructional objectives. Statements of objective should indicate what students will learn and how they will reveal what they learn—how they will perform and what they will be able to do, say, write, make, or demonstrate. Four elements usually included are object, behavior (performance), performance level (criterion), and conditions, as shown in these examples:

Knowledge: To write [behavior] a definition of stereotype [object] similar to the one in the textbook [performance level], without referring to the textbook or a dictionary [conditions].

Thinking skill: Using information in the textbook [conditions], students will generalize [object] by writing [behavior] one [performance level] main idea about the role of governors.

Study skill: To make [behavior] a map of trails westward [object], using crayons and an outline map of the United States [conditions] to show three trails in different colors [performance level].

Value: To state [behavior] the extent to which justice was upheld [object] in a story read by the teacher [conditions], giving one [performance level] reason for the judgment.

Participation: To show sensitivity to feelings of others [object] by always [performance level] making constructive comments [behavior] in group discussion [condition].

Guidelines for Writing Objectives

When writing objectives, include only those elements necessary to make the objective clear. Conditions need not be stated when they are obvious. It is not necessary to state "given an outline map" as part of an objective that includes "to complete an outline map." Who will attain the objective need not be specified when it is obvious that all students should, as in the objective "to show respect for others during discussion."

Objectives can be kept to reasonable length by not repeating certain terms or phrases. For example, one may write "to describe" instead of "to be able to describe." As one teacher put it, "Why write *to be able to* over and over when we know it is implied." When listing objectives to be attained by the end of a unit, it is not necessary to repeat "at the end of the unit" for each objective. Nor is it necessary to repeat "by the end of the year" for objectives to be used in an accountability program. Keep in mind the following special points.

Object. State the knowledge, thinking process, skill, or value that is the intended object of instruction. This is a basic step to make one's intent clear, to provide a focus for instruction, and to indicate the desired student learning. For example, the intent may be able to develop such concepts as stereotype, justice, or public services; the ability to interpret or generalize; skill in reporting; or positive attitudes toward members of various ethnic groups.

Behavior. State what a student will be able to do after the objective is achieved, for example, to *explain* the meaning of stereotype, to *state* a generalization, to *write* a report, to *describe* contributions of ethnic groups. Use such verbs as

> Point to, group, sort, arrange, match, put in order, select, choose
> Describe, state, explain, tell, present, report, name
> Write, list, label, mark, circle, underline, outline
> Demonstrate, act out, show, role play, pantomime
> Make, draw, construct, prepare, produce, assemble, compose

To state objectives on increasing levels of cognitive complexity, use verbs such as[5]:

> *Knowledge:* define, describe, name, select, state, tell, write
> *Comprehension:* conclude, distinguish, interpret, summarize, state in own words
> *Application:* demonstrate, act out, apply, use, infer, predict
> *Analysis:* break into parts, distinguish features, separate into groups
> *Synthesis:* assemble, draw, create, make, plan, produce, prepare, write
> *Evaluation:* assess, judge, examine, apply criteria, distinguish

To write objectives on increasingly higher affective levels of internalization, use such verbs as

> *Receiving:* answer, follow, select, reply, identify, listen, watch
> *Responding:* answer, comply, describe, help, present, report, select
> *Valuing:* compare, complete, explain, initiate, judge, justify, propose
> *Organization:* adhere, defend, explain, integrate, organize, take a stand
> *Characterization:* act, influence, propose, question, use consistently[6]

Verbs expressing nonobservable behavior are sometimes used in statements of objectives. These verbs include *understand, know, appreciate, believe, develop insight into, enjoy,* and the like. Using such terms can create difficulties, as the following examples illustrate. The comment below each example shows how the objective can be clarified by using terms that express observable behavior.

> To *understand* the basic services provided by government [How will the student reveal understanding? It is better to use *describe, state, outline,* or *name.*]
> To *appreciate* the achievements of Afro-Americans in literature, art, science, medicine, education, and sports [How will students show appreciation? It is better to use *describe, report,* or *list.*]

Some teachers use such terms as *understand* and *appreciate* when it is not necessary to measure outcomes. If it is desirable to assess outcomes, the objective may be clarified by adding a phrase, as shown in these examples:

---

[5]For taxonomies of objectives on cognitive levels, see Bloom (1956) and Hannah and Michaelis (1977).
[6]For taxonomies of objectives on affective levels, see Krathwohl et al. (1964) and Hannah and Michaelis (1977).

To develop appreciation of the achievements of native Americans by choosing five examples from materials in the learning center and *presenting* them to the class

To demonstrate understanding of the rights guaranteed in the First Amendment to the Constitution by *explaining* the meaning of each one

Performance Level. When the acceptable standard of performance is not obvious, state a criterion, or desired level of achievement. For such an objective as "to describe achievements of native Americans," the standard may be "five or more," or another criterion depending on the capabilities of students and the available sources of information. Other phrases to use are "at least eight out of ten," "according to standards in the textbook," or "similar in quality to [a map, report, or other model used as a standard]."

Conditions. Note any special conditions that should be provided and are not obvious, such as materials, equipment, or restrictions. If special materials are needed or if students may not use references to demonstrate achievement of the objective, state these conditions—for example, "given a dictionary," "using notes," "without the aid of references," or "working in groups of three."

Other Elements. Two elements may be added when detailed statements are needed for accountability programs, specification of details for a competence-based assessment program, or clear communication of details to others. These two elements are *time* of attainment and *who* (which students) will attain the objective, as shown in these examples:

At the end of the unit [time] students without learning disabilities [who] will state [behavior] from memory [conditions] at least five [performance level] public services provided by cities [object].

By the end of the year [time] students reading at the fifth-grade level [who] will list [behavior] five or more [performance level] contributions of black Americans to science [object] without referring to reading materials [conditions].

Notice that all of the preceding examples focus on what students will learn, not on what the teacher will do. A mistake to be on guard against is writing such statements as the following:

The teacher will demonstrate interviewing techniques. Contributions of members of minority groups will be presented.

These statements focus on the teacher, not on students. To change any of them into an objective for students, the teacher must state what students will be able to do after instruction. For example, if ability to interview is the object, the teacher may select a key aspect and state an objective in this manner:

After a demonstration of interviewing [condition] students will write [behavior] a plan for an interview [object] that includes an introduction and five questions [performance level].

Both open and closed objectives are used in the social studies. Open objectives are useful to individualize instruction, provide choices, and tap students' creativity. Divergent thinking is emphasized, as shown in this example designed to elicit differing responses from students:

To develop creative thinking by finding and describing three or more new ways to save energy at home

Closed objectives are useful in making plans to develop concepts, skills, and values that all students should achieve. Convergent thinking is emphasized, as shown in this example designed to elicit similar responses from students:

To demonstrate respect for others in group work by helping to set and by adhering to group work standards

The Curriculum

Patterns of unit and course organization range from the widely used interdisciplinary approaches, in which disciplines are indistinguishable, to separate subject approaches, in which geography, history, and other disciplines are given primary emphasis. Interdisciplinary patterns are used, for example, in units on family life, community workers, communities around the world, improving the environment, and ethnic studies; in middle and high schools they are also found in such courses as career exploration, youth and the law, current problems, and international relations.

The separate subject approach is used in units on such topics as history of our community, geography of our state, and local government. Separate subject instruction is predominant in such secondary school courses as United States history, American government, and economics.

In between the interdisciplinary and separate subject approaches are multidisciplinary studies that bring the perspectives of different disciplines to bear on topics and problems in units on such topics as our state, the New England states, Canada, Latin America, and the Middle East. In multidisciplinary approaches the geographic, historical, economic, political, and sociocultural features of the area under study are considered and relationships among them highlighted. Each discipline is clearly visible, and the content is not brought together into an amalgam that renders the disciplines indistinguishable.

Conceptual Structure

Instruction may be structured around main ideas or generalizations, concepts and concept clusters, and themes. Terms critical to the conceptual structure of the social studies are defined below.

Vocabulary, or words such as *capital, Civil War,* and *urbanization,* encompasses the terms, names, or labels given to objects, events, qualities, or processes. Vocabulary can be used meaningfully by students only if they understand the concepts represented.

Concepts, represented by such terms as *cooperation, equality,* and *ethnic group* are abstractions that apply to a class or category of objects or activities that have certain characteristics in common.

Concept clusters, such as *natural resources* (water, soil, plants, animals, minerals), are sets of concepts subsumed under a major concept. All concepts within a cluster must be developed in a way that enables students to associate them with the major concept.

Themes, such as *growth of the community, the westward movement,* and *industrial growth in the South,* contain concepts in a phrase that indicates a topic, issue, or trend. Themes can be used to highlight an emphasis in a unit or part of a unit. Broad themes, such as *school and family, living in communities,* and *world cultures* are used to indicate the focus of instruction in various grades.

Facts, such as "The capital of New York is in Albany," are statements of information that include concepts, but they apply only to a specific situation. A set of related facts can form a generalization, such as "All states have a capital."

Generalizations, such as "People use resources to meet basic needs," are statements of broad applicability that contain two or more concepts and show the relationship between them. Generalizations are stated as main ideas, basic understandings, principles, laws, rules, and conclusions. *Descriptive* generalizations are based on what is, for example, "Members of minority groups have not had equality of opportunity." *Prescriptive* generalizations are based on what ought to be, for example, "Steps must be taken to extend equality of opportunity to minority groups." Additional examples are given in chapter 7.

Generalizing, Particularizing, and Decision-Making Studies

Three types of studies should be included in the curriculum. A single type of study is not adequate when one is learning about human relationships.

Generalizing Studies. Generalizing studies are designed to help the student to develop generalizations of broad applicability, to sharpen the process of generalizing, and to recognize sound generalizations. For example, if the objective is to develop a generalization about the public services that cities provide, then services in several cities should be identified and a general statement should be made about commonly provided services. Other examples of studies in which a single topic is analyzed in several settings are illustrated by these questions:

What are the basic needs of all families?

What is the primary role of mayors in large cities?

How does the level of technological development affect standards of living?

Students should learn that an adequate number of cases or situations must be studied to make a good generalization. They should also learn that it is sometimes wise to put limits on generalizations; for example, a generalization about the main role of mayors may be limited to "the mayor of our town." Then, as the role of mayors in other places is studied, students can extend their generalizations accordingly. This kind of learning helps students to avoid generalizing from a single instance or a few cases, and to avoid generalizing beyond the reasonable limits of the data they have collected. Furthermore, it helps them to identify faulty generalizations and to recognize prejudices, which are usually based on a lack of information that leads to biased judgments.

Particularizing Studies. Particularizing studies bring together (integrate or synthesize) particular characteristics of a person, place, or event, such as the distinctive characteristics of Chicago, the contributions of Martin Luther King, Jr., or the events that occurred at the Boston Tea Party. Other examples of studies that integrate particular characteristics are illustrated by these questions:

What is special about the families of members of our class?

What were the main periods in the development of our state?

What were the special contributions of Susan B. Anthony?

A key idea for students to learn is that every person, city, region, country, culture, or historical event has distinctive characteristics that set it apart from others—there is only one Abraham Lincoln, one New York, one New England, and one Japan; no other school, community, or state is just like our own; the American Revolution differs from other revolutions; and no two countries have identical histories (though some similarities in development may be identified). Therefore, to investigate a particular setting thoroughly it is necessary to do a comprehensive study that integrates key elements. A second key idea is that generalizations made in one situation do not necessarily hold up in others. To find out if they do, an adequate number of analytic multisetting studies must be made. A third key idea is that some concepts have special meanings and that terms such as the *Loop* in Chicago, the *French Quarter* in New Orleans, *carpetbaggers* and *muckrakers* in American history, the *caste system* in India, and *democracy* in China must often be defined in specific contexts. Finally, students should develop an appreciation of how art, music, literature, and other material from the humanities contribute to one's understanding of the particular features of the setting under study.

Decision-Making Studies. Decision-making studies are designed to develop students' ability to evaluate proposals and actions so that sound decisions or judgments can be made. For example, if the problem is to assure gender equality in school, the problem is defined, standards are considered, proposals are made, consequences of each proposal are pondered, and a decision is made about the proposal(s) that best meets the defined standards. Other examples of decision-making studies to develop evaluative abilities are illustrated by these questions:

Which plan is best to stop waste pollution at school?

Which proposal for urban renewal is best?

What should each of us do to eliminate prejudice against members of minority groups?

Students should learn that the issue or problem must be clearly defined first, after which related values must also be clarified. When students have different notions about an issue and use different values to appraise it, they make little progress. They must learn to interpret and analyze situations in which individuals arrived at different conclusions or decisions because of differing views of the problem and differing values. After clarifying the issue and the related values, students proceed to evaluate proposals, project consequences, and make a judgment, as noted in the section on evaluating in chapter 9 and the sections on valuing strategies in chapter 13.

What is special about each of these cities? Why are they so different? (Social Studies Workshop, University of California, Berkeley)

Unified Inquiry, Conceptual, and Topical Approaches

Some programs emphasize inquiry or conceptual approaches; others stress a topical approach. The advantages of all three approaches may be combined into an inquiry-conceptual approach to the study of topics. The procedure for doing so is simple and straightforward. Thinking skills and concepts are linked together and used to guide the study of topics.

A practical use of the inquiry-conceptual model is to generate questions that move thinking from recalling and observing to such higher cognitive levels as classifying and synthesizing. The procedure is simply to frame questions that include one or more concepts and that call for the use of a thinking skill. These examples for a unit on Canada are illustrative, with concepts shown in italics and thinking skills in brackets.

> What *natural resources* are shown in this filmstrip? [observing]
>
> Into what main groups can we place Canada's *natural resources?* [classifying]
>
> Which *natural resources* do you think are most important in Canada's *economy?* How can we find out? [hypothesizing]
>
> How should we organize and present our findings on Canada's use of *natural resources?* [synthesizing]

Other examples of questions that link concepts and thinking skills are presented in the following chapters, with all of chapter 9 on thinking skills. As you read them, notice how questions are used to move thinking to higher cognitive levels.

Scope and Sequence of the Curriculum

The scope, or breadth, of the curriculum includes the knowledge, skills, values, and students' experiences needed to achieve stated goals; it is usually defined by a theme for each grade. The sequence, or order, of themes and topics in many programs is based on a concept of the expanding environment; it usually begins with the immediate environment—family, home, school, neighborhood, and community—and moves outward to state, regional, national, and international environments. Comparative studies of families, schools, communities, regions, and other areas around the world help students develop a global perspective, and thus meet a main criticism of the expanding environment sequence.

The recommended criteria for a scope and sequence design are summarized below ("Ad Hoc Committee on Scope and Sequence," *Social Education,* 53 Oct. 1989, 375–387).

> State purpose and rationale of the program, be consistent with stated purpose and rationale, designate content for each grade, and recognize the cumulative nature of learning.
>
> Reflect a balance of local, national, and global content and a balance of past, present, and future.

Provide for understanding of the structure and function of social, economic, and political institutions, and emphasize concepts and generalizations from history and the social sciences.

Promote integration of skills and knowledge, integration of content across subjects, and use of a variety of methods and materials.

Foster active learning and social interaction, reflect a commitment to democratic beliefs and values, and reflect a global perspective.

Foster knowledge and appreciation of cultural heritage and diversity. Foster students' self-esteem, be consistent with research on how children learn, and be consistent with current scholarship in the disciplines.

Incorporate thinking and interpersonal skills, study of local, national and global problems, practice of skills of participation, and transfer of knowledge and skills to life, and be challenging and exciting.

The 1989 Report of the Ad Hoc Committee on Scope and Sequence noted above included the following:

Kindergarten—Awareness of Self in a Social Setting (from home to school)

Grade 1—The Individual in Primary Social Groups: School and Family Life

Grade 2—Meeting Basic Needs in Nearby Social Groups: The Neighborhood

Grade 3—Sharing Earth Space with Others: The Community

Grade 4—Human Life in Varied Environments: The Region

Grade 5—The People of the Americas: The United States and Its Neighbors

Grade 6—People and Cultures: Representative World Regions (focus on Eastern Hemisphere and Latin America)

Grade 7—A Changing World of Many Nations: A Global View (international, including Western Hemisphere)

Grade 8—Building a Strong and Free Nation: The United States

Grade 9—Systems That Make a Democratic Society Work: Law, Justice, Economics

Grade 10—Origins of Major Cultures: A World History

Grade 11—The Maturing of America: United States History

Grade 12—One-year course or courses required, selection from: Issues and Problems, Introduction to Social Sciences, Arts in Human Societies, Area Studies, Electives (Anthropology, Economics, Government, Psychology, Sociology), Supervised Community Affairs Experience

Outlines of three statewide K–12 programs are presented in Figure 1.1. Notice the similarities to the Task Force outline above and among the three state programs, for example, expanding environment through K–7, U.S. history in grades 5 (or 4), 8, and 11, world history and geography starting in grade 6, and required and elective courses in grade 12.

The local course of study and/or basic textbooks must be checked to identify specific units and topics for each grade. Examples of those found in many programs are presented below.

ILLUSTRATIVE K–12 PROGRAMS

	CALIFORNIA[1]	MICHIGAN[2]	NEW YORK[3]
K	Learning and Working, Now and Long Ago	Myself and Others	Self and Others
1	A Child's Place in Time and Space	School and Family	Self/Family/School
2	People Who Make a Difference (supply needs, many cultures)	Neighborhoods	U.S. Communities
3	Continuity and Change (local history, literature, holidays)	Communities: Urban, Suburban, Rural	World Communities
4	California: A Changing State (early times to modern times)	Michigan Studies	Local History and Government/American History
5	U.S. History and Geography: Making a New Nation (to 1850)	Western Hemisphere Studies: United States and Canada	United States/Canada/Latin America (geography/economics emphasis)
6	World History and Geography: Ancient Civilizations (to 500)	Western Hemisphere Studies: Mexico, Central and South America	Western Europe, Eastern Europe, Middle East (geography/economics emphasis)
7	World History and Geography: Medieval and Early Modern Times (500–1789)	Eastern Hemisphere Studies: Asia, Africa, Europe, Middle East	Grades 7 and 8: U.S. and N.Y. State history; references to Canada and Mexico
8	U.S. History and Geography: Growth and Conflict (1783–1914)	U.S. History, Michigan Studies: Exploration–Civil War	State/federal government included
9	Elective Courses in History—Social Science	Practical Law (one semester) Consumer Economics (one semester)	Global Studies: Africa, South Asia, East Asia, Latin America in 9
10	World History, Culture, Geography: The Modern World (1789–present)	Grades 10–12 include: U.S. History and Michigan Studies: Reconstruction–Present	Middle East, Western Europe, USSR, Eastern Europe, and World Today in 10
11	U.S. History and Geography: Continuity and Change in the 20th Century	Civics/Government (one semester) Global/Modern World Studies (one semester)	U.S. History and Government (chronological development)
12	American Government (one semester) Economics (one semester)	Electives: social sciences; ethnic, women's, urban-environmental studies; humanities; leadership	Economics/Participation in Government (one semester each)

[1] *History-Social Science Framework*. Sacramento, CA: State Department of Education, 1988.
[2] *Essential Goals and Objectives for Social Studies Education in Michigan (K–12)*. Lansing, MI: State Board of Education, 1989.
[3] *K–12 Social Studies Program*. Albany, NY: State Education Department, 1987.

Figure 1.1

Examples of Units and Topics

Kindergarten: Working, Learning, and Playing Together; Myself and Others; Our Needs; My Family: Other Families; Why Rules Are Needed; Using My Senses to Learn

Grade 1: How Families Meet Needs; Roles of Family Members; Our School; Other Schools; Roles of School Workers; Living in Neighborhoods; How We Depend on Others

Grade 2: Community Workers; How We Get Food, Shelter, and Clothing; Urban and Rural Communities; Groups People Form; Roles in Groups; Changes in Neighborhoods

Grade 3: Our Community; Other Communities; Local History; Community Groups; Cities and Towns; How Our Community Is Governed; How Communities Change; Future Communities

Grade 4: History and Geography of Our State; How Our State Is Governed; Links to Other States; Resources and Industries; Regions of the United States (or in grade 5); World Regions—Desert, Mediterranean, Mountain, Tropical, Grassland

Grade 5: Geography of North America; Regions of the United States—Northeast, Middle Atlantic, Southeast, North and South Central, Mountain, Pacific; Before Columbus; Exploration, Colonial and Pioneer Life; Beginning a Nation; Westward Expansion; Our Country in a Global Setting; Contributions of Individuals and Ethnic Groups; Our Neighbors—Canada and Mexico

Grade 6: The Earth's Geographic Features; Where People Live; Uses of Natural Resources; Western Hemisphere (if not in grade 5); Eastern Hemisphere (if not in grade 7); Early Civilizations, Greece, Rome, Middle Ages, Renaissance, and Other World History (if not in grade 7)

Grade 7: Prehistoric People; Beginning of Civilization; Ancient Egypt, Greece, and Rome; Middle Ages; Renaissance; Global Exploration; Industrialization; Western Europe; Eastern Europe and USSR; Middle East; Africa; Third World Countries; South Asia; East Asia; Oceania; State History and Government

Grade 8: Coming of Europeans; Winning Independence; Founding a New Nation; The Constitution; Building a Strong Nation; Civil War; Reconstruction; Industrial America; Contributions of Individuals, Women, and Ethnic Groups; Relations with Other Countries; Current Problems

Grades 9–12: Required and elective courses; U.S. History and Government (most frequently required); Economics; Psychology; Sociology; World History; World Geography; Ethnic Studies; Women's Studies; Asian Studies (and other area studies); Introduction to Social Sciences; Law

Not shown above are topics that recur throughout the curriculum—current affairs, special events, contributions of notable men and women, consumer education, and the American free enterprise system. Also included are multiethnic, sex-equity, career, law-related, global, environmental, and energy education. Futures studies are a part of many units, as illustrated in later chapters. Peace education is being included in global studies and special units in some programs (Reardon, 1988).

Instruction *about* religion in public schools may be a part of studies of families and communities, religious festivals and holidays, and various cultures. Such instruction should be academic and supportive of freedom of religion, as guaranteed by the Bill of Rights; it should develop understanding of diversity of religious beliefs, the impact on culture, arts, language, history, contemporary affairs, and social, economic, and political institutions. To be avoided are devotional activities, denigration of any religion, promotion of a religion, and attempts to promote or inhibit religious belief or disbelief. The significance of religious holidays and respect for those who observe them may be viewed as part of cultural diversity in a multicultural society (Haynes, 1990; National Council for the Social Studies, 1985).

To put various features of current programs in perspective, the historical highlights of social studies education are outlined in the next Section.

Historical Highlights

The historical highlights of social studies programs may be viewed in several overlapping periods.[7] Before the emergence of social studies was the introduction of geography, history, and civics. Next came recommendations of national organizations. The social studies movement began in 1916 and was followed by the shaping of modern programs in the 1920s–1950s. The reform movement of the 1960s–1970s included discipline-centered projects called the "new social studies" and demands for attention to social concerns. The late 1970s and the 1980s were marked by reports and projects that focused on "essentials" and on geography, history, and civics.

Introduction of Geography, History, and Civics

Colonial schools stressed the three Rs, religion, and morality. In the later colonial period some schools had courses in geography and history for older students. After the Revolutionary War, geography was the first addition to the three Rs. Among the first textbooks were Jedidiah Morse's geography book in 1784, John Mc'Culloch's U.S. history in 1787, and Noah Webster's grammar book in 1785 and reading and speaking lessons, which included stories on geography and history of the United States, in 1788. Many common schools had courses in geography and history prior to the Civil War.

Civil government (later called civics) was later added as part of history instruction in the upper grades, with a focus on the Constitution and forms of government. Philadelphia offered a separate course in 1888, a practice followed by others. Demands for Americanization of immigrants and inculcation of patriotism and a sense of duty led to increased instruction in civics and history in the late 1800s and after World War I. Many states passed laws requiring civics instruction.

Recommendations of National Organizations

National organizations published reports in the late 1800s and early 1900s that included specific content recommendations. In 1893 the Committee of Ten of the Na-

---

[7]Drawn from References on History of the Social Studies listed at the end of this chapter.

tional Education Association recommended biography and myths in grades 5 and 6, American history in 7 and 11, Greek and Roman history in 8, French history in 9, English history in 10, and one historical topic in depth and civil government in 12. Also suggested was civil government instruction in elementary schools as part of national history and local government, and the use of appropriate literature.

In 1895 the Committee of Fifteen of the National Education Association recommended that elementary schools provide oral lessons in history and biography for sixty minutes a week in grades 1–8, readings in U.S. history in 7 and the first half of 8, and lessons on the Constitution in the last half of 8.

In 1908 a committee of the American Political Science Association recommended instruction on civics in the middle grades and a course on government in high schools.

In 1909 the Committee of Eight of the American Historical Association recommended Indian life and stories about Thanksgiving and Washington in grade 1, same as 1 plus Memorial Day in 2, heroes, Indians, and Independence Day in 3, Colonial period events and people in 4, American history continued plus present great industries in 5, European backgrounds in 6, European backgrounds continued plus American history through the Revolution in 7, and American history since the Revolution plus selected events in European history in 8.

The Social Studies Movement

In 1916 the Committee on Social Studies of the National Education Association's Commission on Reorganization of Secondary Education made a report of historic significance. The label "social studies" was used to designate an area of the curriculum defined as "studies whose subject matter relates directly to organization and development of human society, and to man as a member of social groups." Social efficiency and good citizenship beginning in the neighborhood and extending to world society were cited as key purposes. Local development of the curriculum was recommended.

Many educators viewed as key goals those outlined in *Cardinal Principles of Secondary Education* (Commission on Reorganization of Secondary, 1918), such as citizenship, worthy home membership, and ethical character. World War I stimulated instruction on patriotism, loyalty, and and other aspects of "good citizenship."

Educators were involved in the scientific movement in education with studies of child development, analyses of human activities, statements of specific objectives, attacks on faculty psychology and mental discipline, and objective measures of achievement. Ideas drawn from progressivism, the writings of John Dewey, and the work of G. Stanley Hall, Francis Parker, and Edward Thorndike were quite influential. The Progressive Education Association, founded in 1919, became a force in shaping modern programs of instruction.

The influence of European educators continued to be evident, for example: Rousseau's ideas about child freedom and natural goodness; Pestalozzi's object lessons and use of observation; Froebel's emphasis on creativity and a rich learning environment; Herbart's emphasis on moral development and steps of instruction, adapted to include preparation, presentation, association, illustration and systematization, and application.

Shaping of Modern Programs

The 1920s through the early 1950s marked the design of programs with many features taken for granted today. Emphasis was given to planning in terms of the needs of society and students, as well as to the organization of subject matter. Growth of the whole child—intellectually, socially, emotionally, and physically—was stressed.

The National Council for the Social Studies, in its 1921 charter, stated: "Social studies is used to include history and the social science disciplines and those areas of inquiry which relate to the role of the individual in a democratic society, designed to protect his and her integrity and dignity and which are concerned with the understanding and solution of problems dealing with social issues and human relationships." The Council began publication of *Social Education* in 1937, and has published yearbooks, bulletins, how-to-do-it leaflets, position papers, and packets on a variety of issues and topics. The journal *Social Studies and the Young Learner* was launched in 1988.

In the early 1900s the National Society for the Study of Education published influential yearbooks on geography and history. These were followed by others on social studies, curriculum making, the activity movement, child development and the curriculum, audiovisual instruction, international understanding, measurement of understanding, and other topics.

Other significant volumes were those supported by the American Historical Association's Commission on the Social Studies, such as *A Charter for the Social Sciences in the Schools,* (Charles A. Beard, 1932), *Tests and Measurements in the Social Sciences* (Truman L. Kelley and August C. Krey, 1934), and *Methods of Instruction in the Social Studies* (Ernest Horn, 1937).

Social studies education at all levels was influenced by publications of the Educational Policies Commission: *The Purposes of Education in American Democracy* (National Education Association, 1938), which stated the purposes of education to be self-realization, human relationships, economic efficiency, and civic responsibility; *Learning the Ways of Democracy* (1940) and *Education for All American Children* (1948), which presented examples of practical ways to develop democratic values and behavior.

California's *Teachers' Guide to Child Development—Manual for Kindergarten and Primary Teachers* (1930) and *Teachers' Guide to Child Development in the Intermediate Grades* (1936) are illustrative of teaching guides based on progressive education principles that contained integrated content and comprehensive units of work.

Many school systems adopted recommendations of the Committee on American History in Schools and Colleges, directed by Edgar B. Wesley, in 1944: colonial and early national history in the intermediate grades; 1776–1876, the westward movement, and simple aspects of the industrial revolution in junior high; and the period since 1865, political and economic development, and foreign relations in senior high.

Major goals during this period included development of the democratic person, social attitudes such as concern for others, thinking, problem solving, study and group action skills, social concepts and generalizations, insight into democratic economic and political values, appreciation of contributions of various cultures and individuals, and responsibility to promote social progress.

Content, learning activities, and a variety of materials and community resources were organized in units of work, many them correlated or integrated with other subjects. Some state and local programs used basic social functions such as transportation, communication, production, consumption, religious and esthetic expression, education, and recreation to define the scope of the curriculum. The expanding horizons (expanding environment or communities) model, beginning with home, school, neighborhood, and community in early grades and moving to state, region, country, and world in later grades, was widely used to define the sequence of the curriculum. Major core concepts such as interdependence, adaptation, basic needs, use of resources, and social organization were brought to higher and higher levels of development as children moved from units on the immediate environment in early grades to the broader environment in later grades. Special attention was given to the development of unit-related concepts and generalizations. Current events were included and students' news weeklies were popular.

Activities, projects, problem solving, and learning by doing took precedence over memorization and recitation, providing what some now call "hands-on" learning. Cooperative group work, individual needs and interests, teacher-pupil planning, thinking skills, creativity, social attitudes, behavioral objectives, and democratic values and behavior were stressed. Evaluation was extended beyond testing to include a variety of informal techniques and pupil self-evaluation.

Following World War II there were studies and projects designed to improve citizenship education, applications of democratic values and beliefs to daily living, intergroup/intercultural/human relations education, and attention to world-mindedness and international understanding. Among the legal requirements in many states were American history, civics, the Constitution, observance of selected holidays, and state history and constitution. Many school systems gave special attention to air-age geography and to improved use of audiovisual resources. The formation of the Joint Council on Economic Education in 1949 was to have an impact on instruction at both elementary and secondary levels in the following decades.

A publication that had great impact on the social studies and other subjects in regard to framing objectives, questions, and test items on various cognitive levels was the *Taxonomy of Educational Objectives, Handbook I: The Cognitive Domain* (1956), edited by Benjamin S. Bloom. A companion volume, *Taxonomy of Educational Objectives: Affective Domain,* by David R. Krathwohl and others, was published in 1964.

Reform Projects and Social Concerns

Major reform developments during the 1960s and 1970s included history and social science curriculum projects and demands for instruction on social concerns. The projects highlighted conceptual structures and inquiry processes drawn from the disciplines. Bruner's *Process of Education,* published in 1960, offered this challenge: "Any subject can be taught effectively in some intellectually honest form to any child at any stage of development." Academicians in a variety of disciplines prepared instructional materials, some of which were called "teacher-proof." Although none of the projects gained a lasting place in the curriculum, they did have an influence on instruction, as evidenced by the inclusion of concepts and inquiry processes from the basic disciplines. Development of thinking ability was spurred by *The Central Purpose of American Education* (Educational Policies Commission, 1961).

Demands by individuals and groups for instruction on topics, issues, and problems of social concern had lasting effects. Provisions were made for black history, ethnic studies, women's studies, and exceptional children and for multicultural/multiethnic, career, global, environmental/energy, sex equity, law-related, values, moral, population, and peace education, as described in subsequent chapters.

The National Council for the Social Studies issued curriculum guidelines (1971 and 1979) related to rationale, goals, and key curriculum components and multiethnic education guidelines (1976) that stressed ethnic pluralism, positive interaction of groups, learning styles, and key values, knowledge, and skills.

Other emphases during this period included accountability, mainstreaming of exceptional students, simulation and games, learning centers, learning styles, thinking processes, social criticism and action, decision making, future studies, educational television, and computer-assisted instruction.

Emphasis on Essentials, Geography, History, and Civics

The late 1970s and the 1980s were noteworthy for pleas for an emphasis on basic knowledge drawn from the disciplines, democratic beliefs and values, and thinking, study, and participation skills. The National Council for the Social Studies issued a position statement, *Essentials of Social Studies* (1981), that noted the knowledge, democratic beliefs, thinking skills, participation skills, and civic action needed to function effectively in our democratic society and interdependent world.

Several projects in the late 1980s focused on the teaching of geography, history, and civics. The National Geography Society formed a foundation with alliances in many states. The Geographic Implementation Project proposed ways to implement guidelines for geographic education recommended by a committee of the National Council for Geographic Education and the American Association of Geographers. In 1988 CIVITAS was sponsored by the Council for the Advancement of Citizenship and the Center for Civic Education and proceeded to develop *A Framework for Civic Education* (1990).

More and earlier history instruction was recommended. For example, in 1988 California published *History–Social Science Framework* for grades K–12, which placed history in central focus and urged the integration of other content and related literature into history instruction. Also in 1988 the Bradley Commission on History in the Schools recommended a K–6 history-centered curriculum, more history in early grades, state, national, and world history in 4–6, and infusion of biography, geography, literature, and primary sources. The National Center for History in the Schools was set up the same year as a joint venture of the National Endowment for the Humanities and the University of California at Los Angeles.

In 1989 the National Commission on Social Studies recommended that history and geography serve as a framework for social studies and that concepts and main ideas from political science, economics, and other disciplines be integrated into the K–12 program. The Commission also recommended more content in the early grades, condensation of expanding environment studies, one year each of U.S. history, world history, and world geography in grades 4–6, local and oral history, courses in history, government, economics, anthropology, sociology, and psychology in secondary schools, and community service participation as an option.

There were several other projects and reports of note during this time (O'Neill, 1989). Attention to economic literacy was urged in a report by the Joint Council on Economic Education. *Education for Freedom* (American Federation of Teachers and others) set forth principles for including history, government, and geography in a more substantial and demanding curriculum. International education was recommended by a Task Force of the National Governors' Association, and global studies were recommended by a Study Commission on Global Education.

Recommendations from relevant projects and reports are presented as appropriate in following chapters.

Emphases in the 1980s included thinking skills, decision making, accountability, conflict resolution, peace education, computer, video and other electronic technology, cooperative and collaborative learning, futures studies, concerns for at-risk students, education of immigrant children, learning about religions, and the impacts of science and technology.

It is expected that the 1990s will see continued emphasis on the development of democratic citizenship as a basic goal; a central place for history, geography, and civics; infusion or integration of content from other social sciences and literature; more content in the early grades; continuing attention to impacts of science and technology on ways of living; the influence of religions on human affairs and to global, multicultural, gender equity, environmental, and other social concerns; use of multimedia and a variety of teaching/learning strategies; evaluation of both cognitive and affective outcomes; accountability programs; and staff development to keep abreast of new content and other changes.

Questions, Activities, and Evaluation

1. Examine a local curriculum guide or teacher's editions of adopted textbooks and note the following:
   a. How are the social studies defined? How does the definition resemble or differ from the definitions presented in this chapter?
   b. What rationale is given for social studies education? What changes, if any, do you think should be made in the rationale?
   c. What goals and objectives are identified? How do they resemble or differ from those presented in this chapter?
   d. What recommendations are there for including the following in the social studies: multiethnic studies, instruction on sex equity, career education, law-related education, global studies, peace education, environmental education, and futures studies?
   e. What themes and topics are recommended for each grade? How do they differ from the examples presented in this chapter?
   f. What topics discussed under Historical Highlights are included?

2. Write a set of instructional objectives for a unit of your choice. Write at least one objective for each of the following categories: knowledge, skills, values, and participation.

3. Review recent issues of the following magazines and note any articles that contain ideas you might use: *Social Education, Journal of Geography, The Social Studies, Early Years, Instructor, Learning,* and *Social Studies and the Young Learner.*

4. Examine these ERIC indexes and note items on a topic of your choice: *Current Index to Journals in Education,* and *Resources in Education.*

5. Indicate your position on the following by writing *A* if you agree, *D* if you disagree, and *?* if you are uncertain. Discuss your views with a colleague and explore reasons for any differences.

___ a. However the social studies are defined, primary emphasis should be given to transmission of the best of our cultural heritage.

___ b. Teachers in all grades should use the same rationale for the social studies.

___ c. In most situations, knowledge and skill goals should have priority over value and participation goals.

___ d. The writing of instructional objectives in performance or behavioral terms is well worth the time and effort.

___ e. Teachers should feel free to substitute topics they believe students need to study for those specified in the curriculum.

___ f. Generalizing studies should be emphasized over particularizing and decision-making studies so that students will develop main ideas of wide applicability.

___ g. Geography, history, and civics should have a central place in the K–8 curriculum.

References

Atwood, Virginia A., ed, *Elementary Social Studies: Research as a Guide to Practice.* Washington, D.C.: National Council for the Social Studies, 1986.

Banks, James A., "Citizenship Education for a Democratic Pluralistic Society," *The Social Studies,* 81 (September/October 1990), 210–13.

Barr, Robert D., James L. Barth, and S. Samuel Shermis, *Defining the Social Studies.* Washington, D.C.: National Council for the Social Studies, 1977.

Brubaker, Dale L., Lawrence H. Simon, and Jo Watts Williams, "A Conceptual Framework for Social Studies Curriculum and Instruction," *Social Education,* 41 (March 1977), 201–5. Five definitions of the social studies.

Bradley Commission on History in the Schools, *Building a History Curriculum.* Washington, D.C.: Educational Excellence Network, 1988.

Butts, R. Freeman, *The Goals of Democratic Citizenship: Goals for Civic Education in the Republic's Third Century.* Calabasas, CA: Center for Civic Education, 1988.

"Citizens for the 21st Century," *Social Education,* 52 (October 1988), 414–21. Series of articles in this and following issues on role of social studies.

CIVITAS: A Framework for Civic Education. Calabasas, CA: Center for Civic Education, 1990.

Geographic Education Implementation Project, *K–6 Geography,* and *7–12 Geography.* Macomb, IL: National Council for Geographic Education, 1987, 1989.

Ellis, Arthur K. *Teaching and Learning Elementary Social Studies* (4th ed.). Needham Heights, Ma: Allyn & Bacon, 1991.

Evans, Jack M., and Martha M. Brueckner, *Elementary Social Studies: Teaching for Today and Tomorrow.* Old Tappan, NJ: Allyn and Bacon, 1990.

Haynes, Charles C., "Taking Religion Seriously in the Social Studies," *Social Education,* 54 (September 1990), 276–301, 306–10. Special section.

History—Social Science Framework. Sacramento, CA: State Department of Education, 1988.

Jarolimek, John, *Social Studies in Elementary Education* (8th ed.). New York: Macmillan, 1990.

Keeping Up, News Bulletin from ERIC Clearinghouse for Social Studies/Social Science Education, Indiana Social Studies Development Center, 2805 East 10th Street, Bloomington, IN 47405.

National Commission on Social Studies in the Schools, *Charting a Course: Social Studies for the 21st Century.* Washington, DC: National Commission, 1989. Available from National Council for the Social Studies.

National Center for History in Schools, Moore Hall 231, 405 Hilgard Avenue, Los Angeles, CA 90024-1521. Write for newsletter.

National Commission on Social Studies in the Schools, *Voices of Teachers.* Dubuque, IA: Kendall Hunt, 1991. Current status of social studies.

National Council for the Social Studies, Position Statements in *Social Education:* "Revision of NCSS Curriculum Guidelines," 43 (April 1979), 261–73; "Essentials of Social Studies," 45 (March 1981), 162–4; "Including Study About Religions," 49 (May 1985), 413–4; "Science, Technology, Society and Social Studies," (April/May 1990), "Freedom to Teach and Freedom to Learn," 54 (October 1990), 189–211, 343; "Revised Code of Ethics," 54 (October 1990), 344–5.

O'Neill, John, "Social Studies: Charting a Course for a Field Adrift," *ASCD Curriculum Update,* 1989.

Reardon, Betty A., ed., *Educating for Global Responsibility: Teacher-Designed Curriculum for Peace Education, K–12.* New York: Teachers College Press, 1988. Also see related volume on *Comprehensive Peace Education.*

Report of Social Studies Syllabus Review and Development Committee, *One Nation, Many Peoples: A Declaration of Cultural Interdependence.* Albany, NY: State Education Department, 1991. Suggested multicultural perspectives.

"Science, Technology, Society, and the Social Studies," *Social Education,* 54 (April/May 1990), 189–211. Special section, policy statement.

Shaver, James P., ed., *Handbook of Research on Social Studies Teaching and Learning.* New York: Macmillan, 1990.

Task Force on Early Childhood Education, "Social Studies for Early Childhood and Elementary School Children," *Social Education,* 53 (January 1989), 14–23.

Task Force on Scope and Sequence, "In Search of a Scope and Sequence for the Social Studies," *Social Education,* 53 (October 1989), 376–87.

Van Cleaf, D.W., *Action in Elementary Social Studies.* Englewood Cliffs, NJ: Prentice Hall, 1991.

Sources of Objectives

Bloom, Benjamin S., ed., *Taxonomy of Educational Objectives, Handbook I: The Cognitive Domain.* New York: David McKay Co., 1956.

Hannah, Larry S., and John U. Michaelis, *A Comprehensive Framework of Objectives.* Reading, MA: Addison-Wesley Publishing Co., 1977.

Instructional Objectives Exchange, P.O. Box 24095, Los Angeles, CA 90024. Booklets of objectives and related test items.

Krathwohl, David R., Benjamin S. Bloom, and Bertram B. Masia, *Taxonomy of Educational Objectives: Affective Domain.* New York: David McKay Co., 1964.

References on History of the Social Studies

Barr, et al., 1977, cited above.

Bloom, Benjamin S., ed., *Taxonomy of Educational Objectives, Handbook I: The Cognitive Domain.* New York: David McKay Co., 1956.

Butts, 1988, cited above.

Cremin, Lawrence A., *The Transformation of the School: Progressivism in American Education, 1876–1957.* New York: Alfred A. Knopf, 1962.

Encyclopedia of Educational Research. New York: Macmillan, 1941, 1950, 1960, 1969, 1982. Historical review in social studies article in each edition.

Gibbons, Jimmie Lee, *Historical Development of the Social Studies Programs in American Elementary Schools.* Dissertation. Austin: University of Texas, 1953.

Grossman, Ruth H., *Development of the Elementary Social Studies Curricula in the Public Schools of New York City and San Francisco, 1850–1952.* Dissertation. Berkeley: University of California, 1964.

Hertzberg, Hazel W., *Social Studies Reform 1880–1980.* Boulder, CO: Social Science Education Consortium, 1981.

Jenness, David, *Making Sense of Social Studies.* New York: Macmillan, 1990.

Krathwohl, David R., Benjamin S. Bloom, and Bertram B. Masia, *Taxonomy of Educational Objectives: Affective Domain.* New York: David McKay Co., 1964.

Michaelis, John U., "New Directions in Social Sciences Education," *Influences in Curriculum Change,* Washington D.C.: Association for Supervision and Curriculum Development, 1966. Review of project impacts.

National Commission on Social Studies in the Schools, *Charting a Course: Social Studies for the 21st Century.* Washington, DC: National Commission, 1989.

Petrini, Glenda, and Dan B. Fleming, "A History of Social Studies Skills," *Theory and Research in Social Studies Education,* 18 (Summer 1990), 233–247.

Shermis, Samuel S., "World War I—Catalyst for the Creation of the Social Studies," *The Social Studies,* 80 (January/February 1989), 11–15.

Stanley, William E., ed., "Issues in Social Studies Education: A 50-Year Perspective," *Social Education,* 49 (January through December). Articles by various authors.

Tanner, Daniel, and Laurel Tanner, *History of the School Curriculum.* New York: Macmillan, 1990.

Tanner, Daniel, *Crusade for Democracy.* Albany, N.Y.: State University of New York, 1991. Impact of Progressive Education.

Tyron, Rolla M., *The Social Sciences as School Subjects.* New York: Charles Scribner's Sons, 1935.

Van Cleaf, D.W., *Action in Elementary Social Studies.* Needham Heights, MA: Allyn & Bacon, 1991.

Wesley, Edgar B., *American History in Schools and Colleges.* New York: Macmillan, 1944.

Wronski, Stanley P., and Donald H. Bragaw, eds., *Social Studies and Social Sciences: A Fifty Year Perspective.* Bulletin 78. Washington, D.C.: National Council for the Social Studies, 1986.

Preparing Plans for Instruction

CHAPTER 2

Objective and Related Focusing Questions

To describe planning guidelines and present formats and examples of plans for teaching:

- What approaches to planning may be used?
- What are main features of plans for lessons, modules, and units?
- What formats are used for lessons, modules, and units?
- What procedures are helpful in planning units?
- What introductory, developmental, and concluding activities may be included in plans?
- How can teaching/learning activities be sequenced to elevate thinking to higher cognitive levels?
- Where can sample units and other plans be obtained?

Planning guidelines and formats in this chapter provide a framework for placing strategies in the following chapters in useful and practical teaching plans. Long-range and daily plans are best made in the context of the course of study, available instructional media, and students' needs. Establishing an overview of work for the term should be followed by unit and lesson planning.

Useful sources of information for planning are: students' cumulative records; teacher's editions of textbooks containing background information, sample unit and lesson plans, group and individual activities, related media, and evaluation techniques; manuals for audiovisual media; school district units and guides; and teachers, principals, and supervisors who can give planning advice.

Review the appropriate chapter in this volume to get specific ideas on planning for the use of audiovisual and other learning resources, group work, individualized instruction, concept development, thinking skills, current events, and other topics.

Approaches to Planning

The *textbook-based* approach includes a review of the adopted textbook, and the related teacher's guide to note objectives and introductory, developmental, and evaluation activities. Many guides suggest supplementary materials and activities to enrich and individualize learning.

A *topic, problem,* or *thematic* approach begins with the selection of a unit from the course of study, textbook, or current affair. Objectives, learning activities and materials, and evaluation techniques are noted. Content, thinking, language and other skills, related art and music, and other elements may be integrated.

Teacher-guided group planning is the least formal approach. Tentative objectives, available materials, possible learning activities, individual and group work, and evaluation techniques are identified. A plan is made to guide students in a series of inquiry or problem-solving activities that will involve them in planning, implementing, and evaluating the unit of study. This approach may be incorporated into others or used with small groups and individuals to involve students more completely in the learning process.

Systematic planning based on mastery learning includes such phases as: specifying objectives, analyzing and sequencing learning tasks, considering students' capabilities; selecting activities, planning for anticipatory set or introduction; selecting input (telling) and modeling (showing) techniques; providing for appraisal of understanding and for guided practice; providing for reteaching as needed and for independent practice (Hunter, 1982).

Many teachers use a combination of approaches. As one teacher said, "Why use only one approach when there are good features in each one?"

Lesson Plans

Basic elements are illustrated in the following example, which is similar to plans in curriculum guides and in teacher's guides for textbooks.

FUTURES STUDIES

Objective

To identify reasons for engaging in futures studies

Materials

Checklist: "Reasons for Futures Studies"

Introduction

Ask students to brainstorm as many reasons as they can for why it is a good idea to study the future. Record their responses on the chalkboard.

Development

Give students copies of the following checklist and ask them to check reasons not already listed on the chalkboard.

Reasons for Futures Studies

_____ 1. Help us make plans for future changes

_____ 2. Clarify what future responsibilities may be

_____ 3. Identify various ways to achieve goals

_____ 4. Plan one's future, not let it just happen

_____ 5. Find ways to influence change

_____ 6. Identify effects of events on future activities

_____ 7. Anticipate impact of technologies on people and the environment

_____ 8. Extend one's time perspective into the future

_____ 9. Identify alternatives and ways to act on them

_____10. Improve skill in making decisions

Discuss any questions students have about each item. Discuss new reasons that they checked that were not listed on the chalkboard.

Ask students to make a complete list by combining the reasons listed on the chalkboard with those on the checklist and adding any new ones that were stimulated by discussion.

Conclusion and Evaluation

Ask students to select the three reasons they think are most important and to defend their choices. Evaluate by observing students in discussion.

Follow-up

Ask students to identify reasons in subsequent futures lessons.

Noting Thinking Skills in Plans

Chapter 1 discussed how concepts and thinking skills can be combined and applied to various topics. The following example shows how this may be done for lesson plans, to move children's thinking above the recalling level. The thinking skills used are noted in brackets. Additional examples are presented in the sample unit plan in this chapter and in later chapters.

CHARACTERISTICS OF A CITY

Objectives

To describe three characteristics of a city: population, area, and density
To express feelings aroused by listening to poems about cities

Materials

Textbooks: *Exploring Communities,* pages 77–78; *Towns and Cities,* pages 9, 44–45
Sources of poems: Baruch, *Stop-Go;* Hughes, *City;* Field, *Skyscraper*
Information on population and area of local community

Introduction

Tell the class that today they are going to learn three characteristics of cities that make them different from towns. Ask students what they think these characteristics are. [recalling, hypothesizing]

Development

Ask students to read pages 77–78 in *Exploring Communities.* After reading, ask students the following questions:

What characteristics did you find? [interpreting] Which characteristics were the same as those listed on the chalkboard? Which were different? [comparing, contrasting]

What about our community? Listen as I present information on population, area, and density or crowdedness. Do you think we should call our community a city? Why or why not? [analyzing]

Listen as I read some poems about cities. What special characteristics come to mind as you listen? Be ready to talk about them after I finish each poem. [observing]

Now that you have heard the poem, what characteristics did you notice? What feelings were aroused? [interpreting, inferring]

Conclusion and Evaluation

Ask students to state one characteristic of a city in their own words. Discuss each characteristic sufficiently to clarify the meaning of population, area, and density. [interpreting]

Ask students to look at the four outline maps of communities on page 77 of *Exploring Communities.* Which three are cities? Why? Which one is not? Why? [analyzing]

Ask students to express their feelings about those aspects of city life that they like best and why. Which aspects do they dislike? Why? [evaluating]

Follow-up

Ask students to look at pages 9 and 44–45 of *Towns and Cities*. Which pictures show parts of a city? Which do not? [analyzing]

Ask students to collect pictures from old magazines that show parts of a city and to make a collage. [synthesizing]

Other Formats

The preceding examples illustrate one format for lesson plans. Different formats may be available locally, as illustrated by this example.[1]

DAILY LESSON PLAN FORM

Date _____ Subject _____ Teacher _____
Unit Topic _____

Objectives (Behavioral)

Content to Be Considered	**Procedures and Materials**

Evaluation Techniques

Next Assignment, Follow-up, Reminders

Notes or Comments on Teaching This Lesson

[1]Provided by Professor Albert Nelson, Kansas Wesleyan, Salina, Kansas.

Double-Checking Plans

A sound procedure is to use questions such as these to be sure that key elements have been considered:

A. ___ Clear objectives? ___ Materials noted? ___ Needed equipment ready? ___ Room arrangement OK? ___ Time estimated for each part of lesson? ___ Individual needs noted?

B. ___ Introduction clarifies objectives? ___ Learning activities in order? ___ Concluding activities noted?

C. ___ Activities for gifted, less-able, others? ___ Activities for those who finish early?

D. ___ Directions and materials noted for groups? ___ Work space noted?

E. ___ Questions and directions double-checked for clarity?

F. ___ Evaluation procedures noted? ___ Follow-up activities noted?

Modules

Modules are referred to as individual study guides and individualized learning packages. They are designed to direct students' learning, are complete within themselves, and may be used alone or in conjunction with units, textbooks, and other media. Modules vary in length from those that can be completed in a single class period to those that require several hours. Some are based on a single source, such as a textbook; others are based on multimedia; and some are designed for use on microcomputers.

Some modules are designed to develop and assess performance of a skill such as map reading. A preassessment and a postassessment test may be included. Students who do well on the preassessment move to other activities. Other modules are similar to lesson plans in that they include objectives and other components; they are written with precise directions so that students can do them on their own.

The example that follows is designed to be used as an individual study guide. Most students will be able to complete it in one or two class periods. Time should be flexible, however, so that "time on task" can be varied to provide for individual differences and promote mastery learning. The module may be adapted to serve as a guide to making retrieval charts, building a dictionary card file, gathering information on past or current events, compiling information for a report, and organizing data on a variety of topics. An example of how modules may be used to develop geographic skills through individualized instruction is presented in chapter 5.

MAKING DATA BASE CARDS ON HISPANICS[2]

Our multiethnic data base includes information on the individuals and groups that make up our multiethnic society. We have added data cards as we have studied various periods and movements in the history of our country. We need to add cards on the roles, achievements, and contributions of Hispanics. Our textbook discusses several notable Hispanics. The librarian has

---

[2]Grateful acknowledgment is made to Dr. Jesus Garcia, University of Indiana, for suggestions on this module.

placed additional sources on a special shelf for our use. A list of people who are featured on tapes and filmstrips is posted by the listening and viewing centers.

Objectives

To add to the multiethnic data base by making cards on the roles, achievements, and contributions of Hispanics

To increase appreciation for the multiethnic makeup of our society and for the contributions of ethnic groups to American culture by describing activities of notable Hispanics

Procedures

1. Select the person you wish to investigate. You may choose one you have heard about, one you locate in our textbook or in another source, or one of the following:

Tony Bonilla	Ernesto Galarza	Julian Nava
Dr. Francisco Bravo	Hector Garcia	Michael Olivas
Vikki Carr	Henry B. Gonzalez	Tomas Rivera
Lauro Cavazos	Rodolfo Gonzales	Edward R. Roybal
Cesar Chavez	Ralph Guzman	Julian Samora
Henry Cisneros	Dolores Huerta	George I. Sanchez
Juan N. Cortina	Nancy Lopez	Roberto Segura
Marta Diaz	Zelma Martinez	Reies L. Tijerina
Richard Duran	Ricardo Montalban	Lee Trevino
Jose Feliciano	Joseph Montoya	

You may look for other prominent Hispanics in these books: Calihan, *Our Mexican Ancestors;* de Garza, *Chicanos: The Story of Mexican-Americans;* Meier and Rivera, *The Chicanos: A History of Mexican-Americans;* Nesmith, *The Mexican Texans;* Newlon, *Famous Mexican-Americans;* Pinchot, *The Mexicans in America;* Samora and Simon, *A History of Mexican-American People;* Trejo, ed., *The Chicanos: As We See Ourselves.* Also, find others reported in *Newstime.*

2. Be sure to follow the model we set up for data base cards. The following example shows what to include on the front and back of each card.

(Front)
Romana Acosta Banuelos

Born in 1925 in Arizona, she was appointed treasurer of the United States in 1971. She was the 34th treasurer and the sixth consecutive woman to serve as treasurer. She was the first Mexican-American woman appointed to such a high office.

When only 22 years old, she moved to Los Angeles and started a taco stand business with $400. Her business did very well and she later became head of a Mexican food company that earned about $5 million a year.

When she was 39 she started a bank in Los Angeles. This was the only bank that Mexican-Americans owned and operated.

(Back)
Who Am I?

1. I was appointed treasurer of the United States in 1971.

---

2. I founded a bank in 1964.
3. I ran a food business that earned about $5 million a year.
4. I started a taco stand with only $400.
5. I was born in Arizona in 1925.

(Note: Write *Who Am I?* questions that give good clues to use in a guess-who card game.)

3. Look up the person you selected in the index of your textbook. If he or she is in it, take notes.
4. Do the same for books in the reading center, using two or more sources.
5. If you cannot find a second source, go to the library. Or, see if the person you selected is portrayed on a tape or a filmstrip in the listening and viewing centers.
6. After you have taken enough notes on your subject, write a first draft of your data card. Proofread it for accuracy.
7. Bring your draft to me for approval. Then complete your card.
8. Proofread both sides of the card and place it in the file on my desk.

Activity Cards and Worksheets

Similar in design but shorter in length are individual activity cards and worksheets. As with modules they contain a clear statement of objectives, directions, and materials to use. Here is an example; others are in later chapters.

AFRICAN-AMERICAN INVENTORS AND SCIENTISTS

Objective: To identify contributions of inventors and scientists

Directions.   Use the references on African-Americans in the learning center to find the invention or field of study of the following as illustrated for Benjamin Banneker.

Benjamin Banneker: astronomy, mathematics, city planning _____

Lena Edwards: _____

Angella D. Ferguson: _____

Mathew Henson: _____

Lewis L. Latimer: _____

Jay Matzeliger: _____

Find two others and write their names and achievements:

_____ : _____

_____ : _____

Units of Study

Units are designed to study a topic, problem, or theme over an extended period of time, ranging from a few days to several weeks. They may focus on a region, a case study, concepts from disciplines, a chronological sequence of events, or a main idea. Teaching units are prepared for a particular class and are often in the form of a sequence of lesson plans. Resource units contain a variety of suggestions for general use; teachers select and adapt suggestions from them to fit individual classes. Main sections are:

1. *Title:* topic, problem, or theme, such as The Pacific States, How Can Acid Rain Be Stopped?, Living in Desert Regions
2. *Background information:* content, main ideas, key concepts
3. *Objectives:* knowledge, skills, attitudes/values/appreciations, social participation
4. *Initiation:* suggestions for beginning the unit
5. *Learning activities:*
   a. *Introductory* activities to focus attention on each main idea or problem to be investigated
   b. *Developmental* activities to provide for intake, organization, application, and expression of content
   c. *Concluding* activities to state main ideas, express ideas creatively, and culminate the unit
6. *Evaluation:* suggestions for assessment of learning
7. *Bibliography:* references for students and teachers

Although different terms may be used, the above are major sections of the typical unit. The following excerpts from the first part of a unit on Japan for middle/upper grades illustrate each section. This example on geography should be followed by similar sections on history, government, education, the economy, arts, family life, and other topics. For another example see the unit on North America in the 1988 edition of this volume.

Excerpts from Unit on Japan

Background Information

1. Located about 5,000 miles from the United States off the coast of China, in same latitude as eastern United States from Maine to Florida
2. Archipelago of about 3,000 islands more than 1,850 miles long with four main islands: Honshu (over one-half of the area and three-fourths of the population), Shikoku, Kyushu, and Hokkaido
3. Part of the "Rim of Fire" volcanoes located around the Pacific Rim

4. Area of about 145,800 square miles, slightly smaller than Montana or California, one-twentieth the size of the United States, with over 16,500 miles of coastline indented with bays and harbors

5. Forests on mountains that cover about 70% of the land, plains, and terraces

6. Variety of climates similar to those from Maine to Georgia; climate influenced by ocean currents and monsoons

7. Lack of resources for industry; forests, water resources, fishing

8. Major cities: Tokyo (capital), Osaka, Nagoya, Yokohama, Kyoto, Kobe

Main Ideas

Japan is a mountainous island nation with a variety of environmental features. The history of Japan is distinctive, yet it has been influenced by other people. Japan is a leading industrial nation with a variety of economic activities.

Concepts

Climate	Landforms	Population density
Culture	Physical features	Resources

What kind of questions might be stimulated by this display? What kind of display might you use to introduce a unit? (Tucson Public Schools)

Objectives

To describe the location of Japan in relation to the United States and other Pacific Rim nations

To describe the main natural features and the climate

To locate the four main islands and major cities

To make comparisons of population and population density between Japan and other areas

To identify Japan's limited natural resources

Needed Materials

Map of Japan, globe, world map, outline maps of Japan

Students' textbooks with section or chapter on Japan

Film, filmstrip, or videocassette on geography of Japan

Photographs, postcards, news stories, clippings on Japan

Initiation

Arrange a display that includes pictures, objects, news articles and other materials around a large map of Japan. Guide discussion of the display and pose such questions as: What comes to mind when you hear the word Japan? What have you seen on TV or read about Japan? What do you think we will find about the geography of Japan? [recalling, hypothesizing]

Learning Activities

Introductory Activities

Place the following question on the display set up to initiate the unit:

WHAT ARE THE MAIN FEATURES OF JAPAN'S NATURAL ENVIRONMENT?

Ask students to respond to the question. List student's responses on a chart or the chalkboard for future use. [hypothesizing]

Developmental Activities

1. Ask students to locate Japan on the globe and/or on a wall map. Discuss location and distance relative to the United States and other nations around the Pacific Rim. [interpreting]

2. Ask: Why is Japan called an island nation? What are the four main islands? Where is the Sea of Japan? What body of water is east of Japan? [interpreting]

3. Show filmstrip on geography of Japan and discuss the features that are shown. Compare them with features stated by students during opening activities. [interpreting, comparing]

4. Have students read pages 422–425 of their textbook and ask: What is an archipelago? About how many islands are included in Japan? Why are there so many

earthquakes? Where is the Kanto Plain? Why is it so important? [interpreting]

5. Discuss climate, guided by such questions as: How is the climate of northern Japan similar to that of Maine? How does it differ from the climate of southern Japan? What is the average annual rainfall? What are the effects of ocean currents and the monsoons on the climate? [comparing, analyzing]

6. Compare the population of Japan with the population of the United States, California, and other areas, using the latest World Almanac as a reference. Discuss population density of the same areas, highlighting the high density in Japan. Point out that in relation to arable land, Japan is the most densely populated major country. [comparing]

7. Have students locate and describe major cities, using their textbooks and books in the reading center. Discuss how they are located near harbors and plains. [interpreting, analyzing]

8. Show the film on Japan's human and economic geography. Discuss the statement: Human resources are Japan's greatest resources. Discuss the importance of forests, water resources, and fishing. Discuss the lack of mineral resources and the need to import raw materials. [interpreting]

9. Invite an expert on Japan to show slides, describe natural features, and respond to such questions as: Where are the main mountain areas? Active volcanoes? The Kanto Plain? Main harbors? Major cities? How are the seasons and the climate similar to and different from ours? How frequent and serious are earthquakes? [interpreting]

10. Arrange for individuals, teams, or small groups to investigate and report on such topics as: features of each of the four main islands; uses of water resources; uses of forests; fishing resources; Kanto Plain; Rim of Fire; ocean currents and monsoons. [synthesizing]

11. Have students write haiku and tanka poems that highlight features of the geography of Japan. [synthesizing] For example:
    Haiku with 17 syllables in 3 lines in a 5, 7, 5 pattern:

    Snow on Hokkaido   Northern cold climate
       Fallen during the cold night   Central temperate climate
          Greets the morning sun.   Warm southern climate.

    Tanka with thirty-one syllables in five lines in a 5, 7, 5, 7, 7 pattern:

    Mountainous islands   Lightning and thunder
    From Hokkaido in the north   Followed by a drenching rain
    South to Kyushu   And then a rainbow
    Sea of Japan on the west   Trees and plants dripping water
    The Pacific on the east.   A glistening green landscape.

Concluding Activities

1. Make a retrieval chart that includes information on Japan's natural environment: mountain ranges, major plains, natural resources, climate, and other features. [generalizing, synthesizing]

2. Have students complete outline maps on which they show the location of the four main islands, Kanto Plain, major cities, and other features. [synthesizing]

3. Guide students in creating a mural that shows main features of the natural environment. [generalizing, synthesizing]

4. Have small groups make and share box movie rolls or paper filmstrips that include photographs and/or drawings of landscape scenes. [synthesizing]

5. Have students share the main findings of individual and group reports and their haiku and tanka poems. [generalizing, synthesizing]

6. Discuss students' responses to: The most surprising thing I learned about Japan's geography is ＿＿＿＿＿＿. [analyzing]

Evaluation

1. Observe students during discussion and other activities to note development and use of concepts, application of thinking and other skills, and expression of attitudes and appreciations.

2. Examine students' completed outline maps, reports, and other written work.

3. Assess knowledge by use of such test items as:

   Which of the four main islands is the largest? A. Hokkaido B. Honshu C. Kyushu D. Shikoku

   Which of the four main islands has the coldest climate? A. Hokkaido B. Honshu C. Kyushu D. Shikoku

4. Examine students' responses to completion statements such as:

   Japan is called an island nation because ＿＿＿＿＿＿＿＿＿＿＿＿＿＿.

   The largest and most populated island is ＿＿＿＿＿＿＿＿＿＿＿＿＿.

   The capital of Japan is ＿＿＿＿＿. Other main cities are ＿＿＿＿＿＿.

   Japan is about ＿＿＿＿＿ as large in area as the United States, yet it has around ＿＿＿＿＿ the population of the United States.

Bibliography

Cogan, John J., and Donald O. Schneider, eds., *Perspectives on Japan: A Guide for Teachers.* Washington, D.C.: National Council for the Social Studies, 1983.

Cultural Atlas of Japan. New York: Facts on File, 1988.

Facts and Figures About Japan (updated annually) and *Geography of Japan.* Available from Japanese Information Center, Consulate General of Japan. Addresses in Wotjan reference below.

Reischauer, Edwin O., *The Japanese Today.* Cambridge, MA: Harvard Press, 1988.

Resource List for a Unit on Japan, 1990. East Asian Curriculum Project, East Asian Institute, 420 West 118 Street, New York, NY 10027.

SPICE, Stanford Program on International and Cross-Cultural Education, Stanford University, Stanford, CA 94305. Lessons, slides, and tapes on various topics.

Videocassettes such as Video Letter from Japan, The Asia Society, 469 Union Avenue, Westbury,

NY 11590. Titles include "My Day," "Tohoku Diary," "My Family," "Japanese Industry," "Living Arts," and "Our School."

Wotjan, Linda S., *Free Resources for Teaching About Japan.* Bloomington, IN: East Asian Studies Center, 1987. Description of various types of media available from centers, Japanese agencies, and other sources.

Other Formats

The preceding example illustrates one model for preparing unit plans. The following examples show multicolumn formats that may also be used.

Objectives	Learning Activities	Materials

Objectives	Content	Teaching Procedures	Materials	Evaluation

Generalizations and Concepts	Learning Activities and Materials	Evaluation

Guidelines for Unit Planning

The suggestions in this section focus on unit planning. Many of them, however, also apply to the planning of lessons and modules.

Selecting Units

The most widely used procedure is to refer to the course of study or teacher's guide for the textbook and select units that match the backgrounds and capabilities of students. If an optional unit of special interest to the teacher or students is to be selected, these criteria should be used:

What contributions will it make to social studies objectives?

Is it of equal or greater value than the unit it will replace?

Is it feasible in terms of time, available materials, and the students' abilities?

Building a Background and Reviewing Materials

Building a background of information for a unit requires reviewing textbooks, supplementary books, and other materials available to students. Most teachers review adopted textbooks and related teacher's guides first, noting main ideas, concepts, and background information. An outline of content is created and expanded as other materials are reviewed. If time permits, the following should be examined as suggested in the next chapter.

Printed materials: textbooks, booklets, references, pamphlets, children's periodicals, library resources

Nonprint materials: films, filmstrips, maps, transparencies, computer materials, video, and other audiovisual resources

Community resources: study trips, resource visitors, interviewees, museums, historical associations, local publications, and audiovisual materials

Stating Goals and Objectives

The models for lessons, modules, and units presented earlier in this chapter show ways of stating goals and objectives. Teacher's guides for textbooks include statements of goals and objectives for units and lessons, as do local resource units. Instructional objectives should indicate observable and assessable performance, as described in chapter 1.

Main ideas may be identified in various materials or generated when sources for them are not available. Teacher's manuals for textbooks and for audiovisual materials include main ideas under such headings as Major Understandings. Main ideas may also be generated by using key concepts and generalizations from the social sciences. For example, the concept of *interdependence* may be used to generate such main ideas as the following:

Interdependence

Community workers depend on each other for many goods and services.

The growing interdependence between our country and other countries is evident in trade and international relations.

Countries around the world have formed organizations to handle problems created by increasing interdependence.

In the following example, a generalization is used to derive main ideas: *Societies require a system of social control in order to survive.*

Communities have rules and regulations to provide for the safety and welfare of children and adults.

State and federal laws protect individual rights and promote the general welfare.

Both democratic and totalitarian systems of social control exist in various countries in Latin America.

Examples of main ideas for typical units are presented next. Others are given in chapters 6 and 7 for the social sciences and areas of special concern, such as multicultural and law-related education.

FAMILIES AROUND THE WORLD

Families differ in size and composition.

Families meet needs for food, shelter, clothing, and security.

Changes take place in homes and families.

Some members of the family produce goods and services.

COMMUNITIES AROUND THE WORLD

Ways of living are influenced by geographic conditions.

People work to meet needs for food, shelter, clothing, and health care.

Changes take place as new ideas are put to use.

Communities are alike in some ways but different in others.

GROWTH OF OUR STATE

Some ways of living brought by early settlers are still evident.

Many people have contributed to the growth of our state.

Industries have been set up to use resources, capital, and labor.

A high degree of interdependence exists between our state and others.

COLONISTS IN EARLY AMERICA

Many settlers came in search of a better life.

People from different countries came for different reasons.

Ways of living in colonies were related to beliefs, past experiences, and new problems.

The idea of self-government was expressed in several ways.

CANADA: A MAJOR COUNTRY IN NORTH AMERICA

Canada is a large industrialized and urbanized country with many resources.

Settlement patterns and transportation routes have been influenced by diverse physical features.

Ethnic diversity has been maintained by several groups, including the predominant English and French language groups.

There are many economic links between Canada and the United States.

Selecting and Sequencing Learning Activities

Checklist 2.1 is designed to serve as a master checklist of learning activities for use in making specific plans. Introductory activities are presented first and are followed by developmental and concluding activities. This sequence parallels the problem-solving and inquiry process in that it provides for defining the problem, collecting and organizing information, and using the information to answer questions, test hypotheses, and draw conclusions. It also provides for the movement of thinking skills from the recalling and interpreting levels to such higher levels as generalizing, analyzing, and synthesizing. The thinking skills used are noted in parentheses for each set of activities. Evaluation may be a part of all activities to diagnose needs during the introduction of a unit, to assess learning as a unit develops, and to appraise outcomes at the end of a unit.

Checklist 2–1
MASTER CHECKLIST OF LEARNING ACTIVITIES

INTRODUCTORY ACTIVITIES:

Observing, Recalling, Interpreting, Hypothesizing

____ Arrange a display
____ Link to past unit
____ Suggest a topic
____ Preassess content
____ Show new book(s)
____ Show audiovisual media

____ Pose questions
____ Elicit questions
____ Elicit hypotheses
____ Present an unfinished sentence, chart, time line, map, or story

____ Use a current event
____ Use a resource person
____ Show film without sound
____ Discuss a dilemma
____ Plan first activities

DEVELOPMENTAL ACTIVITIES:

Intake and Data-Gathering Activities: Observing, Recalling, Interpreting

____ Read
____ Listen
____ Observe
____ Ask
____ Use maps
____ Interview
____ Do a survey

____ Take a poll
____ Keep records
____ Use tables
____ Take notes
____ Outline
____ Make collections
____ Take field trips

____ Use graphs
____ Use indexes, tables of contents, headings, subheadings
____ Use library
____ Use data bases
____ Use learning centers

Organizing and Summarizing Activities: Comparing, Classifying, Generalizing

____ Find main ideas
____ Answer questions
____ Test hypotheses
____ Group items
____ Tape-record
____ Complete time lines

____ Outline
____ Diagram
____ Chart
____ Graph
____ Summarize
____ Complete contracts

____ Complete outline maps
____ Make data base cards
____ Make semantic maps

Applicative Activities: Inferring, Analyzing, Synthesizing, Hypothesizing, Predicting

____ Make maps
____ Make graphs
____ Make charts
____ Make checklists
____ Make time lines
____ Conclude

____ Reclassify
____ Judge
____ Predict
____ Report
____ Demonstrate
____ Take roles

____ Make plans
____ Debate
____ Participate in forums, panels, and action projects
____ Simulate

Creative and Expressive Activities: Interpreting, Analyzing, Synthesizing

____ Dramatize	____ Write pen pals	____ Make exhibits
____ Role-play	____ Write articles	____ Construct models
____ Pantomime	____ Write playlets	____ Create maps and
____ Simulate	____ Draw	charts
____ Brainstorm	____ Make murals	____ Process materials
____ Write poems and	____ Make collages	____ Compose songs
stories	____ Make dioramas	____ Create rhythms

CONCLUDING ACTIVITIES:

Generalizing, Analyzing, Synthesizing, Evaluating

____ State main ideas	____ Put on a program	____ Discuss ways to
____ Share projects	____ Take a field trip	improve
____ Have a quiz pro-	____ Have a panel dis-	____ Use charts, tests,
gram	cussion	and checklists
____ Review objectives	____ Complete booklets	____ Relate to next unit

Introductory Activities

Sometimes referred to as opening or initiating activities, introductory activities are used to initiate units and to introduce a main idea or another section of a unit. They build readiness, develop anticipatory set and interest, raise questions, explore what students know about the topic, identify misconceptions, recall relevant information, make plans, and set the stage for the first data-gathering activities. Many initiating activities grow out of the unit that preceded them. Some are based on an arrangement of pictures or other items that stimulate interest and questions. Others may be based on questions posed by the teacher, a stimulating current event, or photo essays or other introductory material in the textbook.

Developmental Activities

Developmental activities should grow out of opening activities to provide a smooth learning sequence. A complete series of developmental activities should flow from data-gathering or intake activities to data-organizing activities, to applicative activities, and on to creative and expressive activities. Data-gathering or intake activities provide the input needed to handle questions and hypotheses. Organizing activities help students structure and summarize information. Applicative activities extend learning and develop the ability to use concepts and skills. Creative and expressive activities enrich learning and develop the ability to improvise and apply learning in original ways.

Some activities overlap; and can be used to organize information, to apply learning, and to express ideas creatively. For example, a student may complete an outline map to organize information, make a map of an area with a key to apply map concepts and skills, and create a map to portray information gathered on transportation, resources, or other items.

Concluding Activities

Closely related to and flowing from expressive activities are concluding activities of two types. The first type are activities related to each main idea in the unit. The second are those culminating activities that encompass the entire unit and bring together the different main ideas. Culminating activities usually result in a presentation to parents or to other classes, with emphasis on educational outcomes rather than "putting on a show."

Planning Questions

Productive questions are related to objectives, tap important content, provoke thinking, and invite participation. They may be designed in a sequence to develop concepts, analyze information, and move thinking to higher cognitive levels as shown in later chapters. For example, these questions may be used in a variety of situations to move thinking from the knowledge level to the evaluation level:

Knowledge: What do you recall about this topic?

Comprehension: Can you summarize it in your own words?

Application: How can we use this information?

Analysis: What are the main parts? How is it organized?

Synthesis: How can it be organized in a new way?

Evaluation: How should it be rated in terms of the listed criteria?

Sequences also may be used to achieve specific objectives, such as to develop concepts, as shown by this example (Taba, et al., 1971):

What did you see? Hear? Note?

Which items can be grouped together? How are they alike?

What is a good name for this group?

A variety of questions may be used to elicit desired responses. For example, definitional questions focus attention on precise meaning—What is meant by gender equity? Empirical questions focus attention on what has been read, observed, or reported—What happened? Who did it? When? Where? Why? Evaluative questions elicit appraisals or judgments—To what extent was gender equity provided? Rhetorical questions emphasize an idea or suggest a response—Why is provision for gender equity fair and just? Open or divergent questions spark differing responses—How many ways can you think of to solve this problem? Closed or convergent questions elicit a desired correct response—What is the main idea in this report? Follow-up questions clarify ideas—What do you mean by that?

As a general rule, the following types of questions should be avoided or rarely used. Questions requiring a yes or no answer—Did John Adams serve as president? Questions that are ambiguous—What happened in Vietnam and Cambodia? Questions that are slanted or biased—Why should women be satisfied with the gains they have made? Questions with obvious answers—Should everyone work for gender equity?

Using Taxonomies

The taxonomies noted as sources of objectives in the preceding chapter may be used to plan objectives, activities, questions, and evaluation on various levels (Bloom, 1956; Hannah and Michaelis, 1977; Krathwohl, et al., 1964). The following examples on various levels of the cognitive domain are illustrative:

Unit on Early Civilizations

Knowledge Level
Objective: To name early civilizations in river valleys
Question: What civilizations arose in river valleys?
Activity: Study pp. 80–82 and list the described civilizations.
Evaluation: Civilizations that arose in river valleys were: _____

Comprehension Level
Objective: To describe early civilizations in one's own words
Question: Who can describe the river valley civilizations?
Activity: Guide discussion in which students describe early civilizations.
Evaluation: Write a paragraph description of one river valley civilization.

Application Level
Objective: To use information on early civilizations in studying later ones
Question: How were later civilizations alike and different from early ones?
Activity: Make a retrieval chart to compare early and later civilizations.
Evaluation: Make a summary of similarities and differences.

Analysis Level
Objective: To identify the main elements of early civilizations
Question: What were the main features of early civilizations?
Activity: Make an outline of the main elements of early civilizations.
Evaluation: Ask students to list main elements of early civilizations.

Synthesis Level
Objective: To create a mural that shows main features of early civilizations
Question: What features should we include in a mural on early civilizations?
Activity: Make drawings for a mural on early civilizations.
Evaluation: Guide development and application of evaluative criteria.

Evaluation Level
Objective: To rate quality of life in early civilizations
Question: How do you rate quality of life, using the criteria on page 92?
Activity: Do the rating on a scale of one for very good to ten for very poor.
Evaluation: List ways the rating system can be improved.

Integration of Instruction

Consideration should be given to integration of material from other subjects into the social studies and integration of social studies content into other subjects. For example, art and music activities should be a key part of some social studies units to clarify aspects of culture. At other times instruction in art and music can be related to holidays, festivals, and other social studies topics. At times science and social studies can be unified as climate, weather, environmental problems, impact of science and technology, and other topics are studied. Social studies content can be used to teaching outlining, writing, and other skills in the language arts program, and communication skills should be applied and improved in the social studies. The guiding principle is to identify meaningful relationships and then decide in which subject(s) that instruction should be provided.

Topics such as futures studies, teaching about religion in the social studies, multi-ethnic and sex equity studies, and law-related instruction also can be integrated into various units. For example, futures studies may be a part of units at all levels to help students identify trends, learn how to influence change, make forecasts, analyze possible, probable, and preferable changes, and weigh possible consequences of alternative actions. To aid planning, future changes may be differentiated as follows:

Value shifts related to work, quality of life, resource use, peace

Social changes in roles, careers, public services, group activities

Cultural diffusion of ideas, values, technology, the arts, leisure activities

Demographic changes in population, family structure, life span, rural-urban balance

Technological innovations, such as computers, robotics, information networks

Ecological changes in the environment, resource base, water and food supply

Systems changes in transportation, communication, economics, government

These and other changes are included in regular units, current affairs studies, and mini-units on alternative futures. Charts 2.1 through 2.3 suggest questions and items for use in futures studies.

Incorporating Teaching Strategies

Shown in Figure 2.1 are widely applicable teaching strategies that can be incorporated into plans. For example, the first—Expository Instruction—may be used for films, presentations by visitors, and other direct instruction. The Problem Solving strategy is helpful when studying environmental, community, state, or other problems. The Critical Thinking strategy may be used at many points when students are asked to make appraisals or judgments in terms of defined standards, facts, and reasons.

Evaluation Techniques

Evaluation is important in all phases of the unit, from initiation through concluding activities. A variety of devices may be used to appraise objectives of the unit. Some devices are prepared as a part of learning activities, for example, charts on work

Projecting Basic Trends	The Year 2000	Ways to Influence Change
What are the trends for these? Freedom and equality for all Changes in the family and other institutions Careers for women and men Conservation of resources and energy Quality of life and lifestyle Uses of science and technology Restoration of rainforests and wetlands Growth of democracy in other nations	What will be the most important? Community life Jobs for everyone Conservation Justice Education Leisure Environment Recreation Family life Wealth Health Food supply Housing Human rights Sex equity Cooperation Peace Creativity The arts Can you add others?	Know what we and others value Consider causes and effects Consider alternative proposals Consider consequences of actions Join with others to take action Make plans for the future now Evaluate action and plans Can you think of others?

Chart 2.1   Chart 2.2   Chart 2.3

standards, checklists for evaluating discussion and other activities, and standards for using materials. Many devices, such as tests and inventories, may be constructed ahead of time. The following list is illustrative of devices and procedures that may be used. Specific examples and a more detailed discussion appear in chapter 14.

Anecdotal records	Checking of written work
Attitude and interest inventories	Essay tests
Checking by a partner	Group discussion
Individual self-checking	Reviewing files of each student's work
Keeping logs or diaries	Student analysis of tape recordings
Objective tests	Teacher analysis of tape recordings
Rating scales and checklists	Teacher observation

Keeping a Log to Evaluate the Unit

An item that needs special comment is keeping a log. Teachers who have kept a log say that it is a great help in evaluating the unit and in gathering ideas to use in revising the unit. A satisfactory log is a brief running account of the unit and includes notes on strengths and weaknesses of instructional materials, changes to be made in learning experiences, and other ways in which the unit should be modified. Items are entered during or at the end of the day and kept in a folder. After the culmination of the unit, notes related to all main ideas or problems should be brought together and used as a basis for revising the unit.

Team Planning of Units

Many teachers find it helpful to work with a partner or a committee to prepare unit plans. Each team member's special talents can be tapped, responsibilities for review-

WIDELY APPLICABLE TEACHING STRATEGIES

EXPOSITORY INSTRUCTION

Introduction: Clarify objectives, create interest, set the stage.

Procedures: Follow sequence of steps to provide instruction.

Conclusion: Wrap up the lesson to bring closure.

Follow-up: Provide practice or application to clinch/extend learning.

INDUCTIVE-DISCOVERY

Observe and discuss specific examples.

Identify and describe common elements of features.

Discuss other examples and note common elements

State a main idea based on common elements and check it against new examples.

DEDUCTIVE-DISCOVERY

Present a main idea that can be checked against evidence.

Have students find supporting evidence or examples.

Have students state why the evidence is supporting.

Have students find other evidence or "proof."

PROBLEM SOLVING

Identify and define the problem.

Discuss key elements of the problem and propose a solution.

Collect and interpret related evidence.

Use the evidence to decide whether the proposed solution is warranted.

If so, use the solution to solve the problem.

If not, propose another solution and repeat the above phases.

DECISION MAKING

Define the issue or topic.

Clarify goals and values and note alternatives for achieving them.

Assess consequences of alternatives and prioritize them in terms of goals.

Choose the best alternative.

Evaluate the decision-making process, the decision, and any action taken.

CRITICAL THINKING

Define what is to be appraised or judged.

Define standards or values.

Use data to determine how well standards are met.

Consider emotional appeals, inconsistencies, and bias.

Separate facts from opinions and causes from effects.

Make judgment based on facts and sound reasons.

GROUP INQUIRY

Clarify topic or problem to be investigated.

State questions or hypotheses to guide study, using prior knowledge.

Plan and do small-group study to gather data to answer questions or test hypotheses.

Share, organize, and evaluate findings and use them to answer questions or test hypotheses.

State conclusions, note needs for more study, and evaluate procedure

INDIVIDUAL INQUIRY

Choose a topic or problem and define.

Recall prior learning and list questions you have.

Select reliable sources and gather, appraise, and organize needed information.

Use organized information to answer questions; gather more data if needed.

State conclusion, needs for more study, and evaluation.

CREATIVE THINKING

Think of a goal, activity, or topic to pursue in new ways.

Imagine new ways to use what you know.

Add new ideas and imagine new ways to express them.

Synthesize thoughts and feelings and express them freely.

Contemplate ways to improve creativity and make desired changes. Imagine modifications, novel applications, and original uses.

Figure 2.1

ing materials can be designated, best ideas drawn from past experience can be shared, and the work load can be divided. After the unit is prepared, each teacher has the responsibility of adapting the unit to educational needs and individual differences of students.

Moving from Textbook to Unit Instruction

Some new teachers, faced with the multiplicity of problems that typically arise, rely primarily on the adopted textbook for social studies instruction. It is possible to move from textbook to unit teaching in a series of steps as time permits. First, identify other reading materials on various levels of difficulty and audiovisual materials that complement textbook units. Note related field trips, resource visitors, and other community resources. In the beginning these materials may be used with chapters in the textbook and learning activities suggested in the accompanying teacher's manual. Next, make plans that are structured around main ideas, key concepts, and guiding questions that are central to the topic of study. Then list learning activities and instructional materials (including the textbook) under the main ideas, concepts, and questions as appropriate. Evaluation activities may also be planned to assess objectives related to all of the instructional materials used.

From Lesson Plans to Unit Plans

Another procedure that some teachers use to develop units, particularly in new areas of study, is to begin by making lesson plans related to new filmstrips, reading materials, or other resources. For example, a new filmstrip on energy conservation may be available or a new textbook may be adopted. The accompanying manuals are checked, ideas on needs of students are noted, ideas from past experience are drawn upon, and plans for using the new materials are made. After several plans are made, they are brought together, revised, and combined as a section of a unit clustered around a main idea or generalization. Then plans are made for other parts of the new textbook or other materials, clustering them around another main idea. A practical teaching unit is thus developed inductively by moving from daily planning to an overall plan that is a synthesis of specific plans.

Sources of Units

Preplanned units are available from local and county school districts, state departments, curriculum laboratories and media centers, and libraries in colleges and universities. Many have been placed in ERIC (Educational Resources Information Center) and are listed in *Resources in Education.* Some may be found in magazines such as *Instructor, Social Education,* or *Learning.* Teacher's manuals that accompany social studies textbooks contain unit plans directly related to the text and supplemented by a variety of activities and related materials. Other sources are noted in the references at the end of the chapter.

Questions, Activities, and Evaluation

1. Make a plan for a lesson similar to one presented in this chapter. Base it on a textbook or other resource. Ask a colleague to critique it.

2. Make a plan for a module similar to the one presented in this chapter. Ask a colleague to critique it.

3. Obtain a unit of instruction from one of the sources noted above and do the following:

   a. Note the contents of each major section. Does the unit include the same general sections noted in this chapter?

   b. How are the goals and objectives stated? What changes, if any, might be made to improve them?

   c. Summarize the introductory, developmental, and concluding activities that you believe to be most helpful.

   d. Note suggested techniques of evaluation.

   e. Note references that may be useful in your own future planning.

4. Plan a short teaching unit similar to the one in this chapter. Review as many related instructional resources as time permits. As you obtain ideas from subsequent chapters, add them to the unit.

5. Prepare a kit or box of materials that can be used with the unit you are planning. Include pictures, maps, free or inexpensive materials, songs, directions for arts and crafts, and other resources.

6. Arrange to visit a classroom where a unit of instruction of interest to you is in progress. Try to visit several times so as to observe the initiation, subsequent activities, and the culmination. Have questions ready to ask the teacher in charge.

References

Association for Supervision and Curriculum Development, *Curriculum Materials.* Washington, D.C.: The Association, annual. Listing of units and guides from school systems.

Banks, James A., and Ambrose A. Clegg, Jr., *Teaching Strategies for the Social Studies.* New York: Longman, 1990.

Banks, James, *Strategies for Teaching Ethnic Studies* (4th ed.). Boston: Allyn & Bacon, 1987. Sections on materials and procedures.

Barnes, Bruce, "Teaching about Native American Families," *Social Education,* 50 (January 1986), 28–30. Sample unit.

Berg, Marlene, ed., "Making the Connections," *Social Studies and the Young Learner,* 1 (January/February 1989), 3–18. Special section on integrating art and architecture, math and science, and language arts with social studies.

Bloom, Benjamin S., ed., *Taxonomy of Educational Objectives. Handbook I: The Cognitive Domain.* New York: David McKay, 1956.

Brophy, Jere, and Janet Alleman, "Activities as Instructional Tools: A Framework for Analysis and Evaluation," *Educational Researcher,* 20 (May 1991), 9–22. Principles for design, selection, and principles.

Commission on Schooling for the 21st Century, *Handbook for Conducting Future Studies.* Bloomington, IN: Phi Delta Kappa, 1984.

Communities Around the World. Albany, NY: State Education Department, 1989. Learning activities for 10 cities.

Ellis, Arthur K. *Teaching and Learning Elementary Social Studies,* 4th ed. Needham Heights, MA: Allyn & Bacon, 1991.

Future Survey, The Futurist, and *Future Survey Annual.* Bethseda, MD: World Future Society. Futures articles and sources of data.

Grossman, David, guest ed., "Teaching about a Changing China," *Social Education,* 50 (February 1986), 100–33. Articles on content, techniques, and materials.

Haas, John D., *Future Studies in the K–12 Curriculum* (2nd ed.). Boulder, CO: Social Science Education Consortium, 1988.

Hannah, Larry S., and John U. Michaelis, *A Comprehensive Framework for Instructional Objectives.* Reading, MA: Addison-Wesley, 1977. Sample objectives and how to write them for thinking skills, knowledge, skills, and attitudes.

Hunkins, Francis P., *Teaching Thinking Through Effective Questioning.* Norwood, MA: Christopher-Gordong Publishers, 1989. Variety of examples.

Hunter, Madeline, *Mastery Learning.* El Segundo, CA: TIP Publications, 1982.

Krathwohl, David R., Benjamin S. Bloom, and Bertram Masia, *Taxonomy of Educational Objectives, Handbook II: The Affective Domain.* New York. David McKay Co., 1964.

Michaelis, John U., and Haig A. Rushdoony, *Elementary Social Studies Handbook.* New York: Harcourt Brace Jovanovich, Inc., 1987. Sample unit and lesson plans.

New York State Department of Education, *K–6 Social Studies Program.* Albany NY: State Department of Education, 1982. Guides for each grade with learning activities.

Rogers, Vincent, Arthur D. Roberts, and Thomas P. Weinland, eds., *Teaching Social Studies: Portraits from the Classroom.* Washington, D.C.: National Council for the Social Studies, 1988. Reports by teachers.

Ryan, Frank L., *The Social Studies Sourcebook.* Boston: Allyn & Bacon, 1980. Activities that can be put into lessons and units.

Social Studies Grade 5—The Western Hemisphere. New York: City Board of Education, 1985, 1987. Learning activities for Planet Earth and countries in the Western Hemisphere.

Taba, Hilda, Mary C. Durkin, Jack R. Fraenkel, and Anthony H. McNaughton, *A Teacher's Handbook to Elementary Social Studies.* Reading, Mass.: Addison-Wesley, 1971. Planning units around main ideas; main and organizing ideas in appendix.

Identifying and Using Instructional Media

CHAPTER 3

Objective and Related Focusing Questions

To present principles and strategies for identifying and using a variety of media to improve teaching and learning:

- What criteria are used to select instructional resources?

- What guidelines are helpful in improving the use of textbooks, charts, data bases, literary selections, and practice materials?

- How can microcomputer, video, and the variety of other media be used to improve teaching and learning?

- What community resources are most useful? What guidelines are helpful in optimizing their contributions to learning?

- What general guidelines are helpful in planning, guiding, and evaluating all media?

- What sources are useful in finding needed materials that are not available in a school?

The development of media literacy is essential to living and learning effectively in the Information Age.[1] Electronic learning and teaching represented by such new technologies as computers, compact disks, and video are increasingly available in schools and in homes. Textbooks, films, recordings, and other print and nonprint media representative of older technologies continue to have a key place in instruction at all levels. Both technologies should be used selectively in terms of objectives, students' learning styles, strengths and limitations of each type of media, and the unique contributions they make to learning.

Critical Selection of Materials

Critical selection of materials is necessary to optimize learning and to avoid indiscriminate use of the variety of media currently available. The examples in Checklist 3.1 are used to select materials from instructional media centers, libraries, community agencies, and other sources. Forms for evaluating textbooks and other media are available in local school district offices. References at the end of this chapter include sample forms and procedures for estimating readability level.

Reading Materials

Reading materials are among the most widely used instructional materials in the social studies. Why? Because of the richness and variety of content, illustrations, graphics, and other features that make them a usable and effective tool of instruction. Checklist 3.2 provides a quick way to identify the types of reading materials that may be useful in a given unit, module, or lesson.

Textbooks

Textbooks serve as the core of instruction in many social studies programs, and they are used in several different ways. Some teachers use the adopted textbook as the basis of instruction, employing teaching procedures similar to those used in the reading program. Other teachers use a basic textbook as a general guide but supplement various chapters of the text with additional reading materials, audiovisual media, and other resources. This approach goes a step beyond reliance on the textbook and provides opportunities to use multiple data sources. In classrooms where multimedia and unit approaches are used, the textbook is one component of instruction along with a variety of other resources, all of which are viewed as sources of data for achieving the stated instructional objectives.

[1]For articles and a bibliography on media literacy, see "Focus on Media," *The History and Social Science Teacher,* 24 (Summer 1989), 185–215.

Checklist 3–1
EXAMPLES OF CRITERIA FOR SELECTING MEDIA

Applicable to All Media

___ Contribution to objectives?

___ Authentic, relevant content?

___ Fair treatment of gender and ethnic groups?

___ Good physical qualities?

___ Related to curriculum?

___ Significant, meaningful?

___ Absence of stereotypes, race, sex, and ethnic bias?

___ Useful teacher's manual?

___ Appropriate to students' maturity?

___ Positive recognition of cultural diversity?

___ Issues treated fairly?

Additional Criteria for Various Media

Reading Materials

___ Appropriate reading level?

___ Text-related illustrations?

___ Contribution to whole language development and to literary discourse?

___ Useful in diagnosis and individualized instruction?

___ Contribution to comprehension and other skills?

Free and Inexpensive

___ Reputable sponsor?

___ Free of objectionable advertisements?

___ No obligation incurred by use?

___ Material not available from other sources?

___ Accurate portrayal of labor, business, and other groups?

Computer Software

___ Good graphics, sound, color?

___ Good support materials?

___ Rate and sequence of presentation controllable?

___ Easy to use; user-friendly?

___ Contribution to interactive learning?

___ Effective feedback?

No matter which approach is used, teachers may use social studies textbooks to achieve such objectives as these:

To introduce a unit through photo essays and introductory sections that set the stage or give an overview

To develop new concepts and related vocabulary as students use picture and context clues, phonics, and structural analysis

To find main ideas and details related to topics and problems

To apply and extend learning, provide practice, and reinforce learning

To provide a background of ideas that students can use to make comparisons as they study media that present different information

To answer questions and "prove" points by having students locate and report relevant information

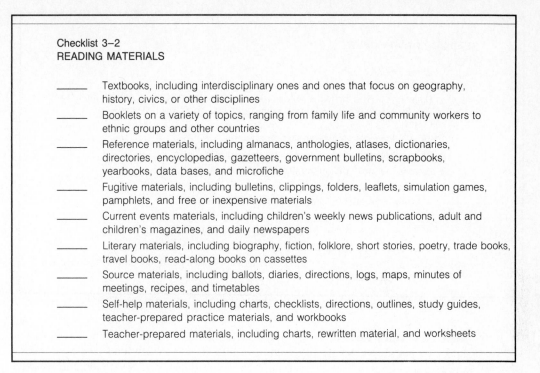

Checklist 3–2
READING MATERIALS

_____ Textbooks, including interdisciplinary ones and ones that focus on geography, history, civics, or other disciplines

_____ Booklets on a variety of topics, ranging from family life and community workers to ethnic groups and other countries

_____ Reference materials, including almanacs, anthologies, atlases, dictionaries, directories, encyclopedias, gazetteers, government bulletins, scrapbooks, yearbooks, data bases, and microfiche

_____ Fugitive materials, including bulletins, clippings, folders, leaflets, simulation games, pamphlets, and free or inexpensive materials

_____ Current events materials, including children's weekly news publications, adult and children's magazines, and daily newspapers

_____ Literary materials, including biography, fiction, folklore, short stories, poetry, trade books, travel books, read-along books on cassettes

_____ Source materials, including ballots, diaries, directions, logs, maps, minutes of meetings, recipes, and timetables

_____ Self-help materials, including charts, checklists, directions, outlines, study guides, teacher-prepared practice materials, and workbooks

_____ Teacher-prepared materials, including charts, rewritten material, and worksheets

To improve skill in reading, interpreting maps, charts, diagrams, illustrations, tables, and graphs, and using the table of contents, glossary, and index

To sharpen the ability to draw inferences, derive generalizations, predict outcomes, and use other thinking skills

To foster positive feelings and attitudes toward others as students read about other groups and cultures

Teacher-Prepared Material

One of the most useful types of material is that which has been rewritten by the teacher to fit the levels of students' reading ability. A sound approach is to imagine you are writing a letter or telling an exciting story to a child, keeping in mind that every idea must be expressed as simply and as clearly as possible. Choose vocabulary, phrasing, and sentences similar to those used by children, and keep sentences and paragraphs short, as they are in children's periodicals.

Other types of teacher-prepared material are charts, vocabulary lists and card files, practice exercises, and activity cards (such as the one that follows) that may be adapted for use with a variety of materials.

Booklets may be made of pictures and articles related to a topic, and folders may be organized to include materials on topics in a unit. Reports and scrapbooks prepared by students may be edited and revised for use by future classes.

READING ACTIVITY CARD

Wind Power

Directions.   Find the folder on wind power in the reading center. Answer the following questions as you read the one-page article entitled "What about Wind Power?"

1. What is the main idea in the first paragraph?
2. What is the main idea in the second paragraph?
3. What is the main idea in the third paragraph?
4. Complete the following:
    a. Three of the best places for using wind power are

    ———— ———— ————

    b. Three problems that are hindering the use of wind power are

    ———— ———— ————

5. What is your view of the future of wind power? Write a paragraph in which you include two or more reasons for your view.

Making and Using Charts. Charts are useful in units at all levels of instruction. They are especially helpful in developing reading ability in the social studies. For example, as concepts and generalizations and the related vocabulary are developed and used to make charts, children construct the meanings needed in a whole-language approach to reading and writing in the social studies.

The variety of charts that may be used include:

Experience charts based on field trips, interviews, and other activities

Question charts to guide individual and group study of topics

Vocabulary charts made up of special terms needed in a unit

Classification charts for recording specific items under such headings as fruits, vegetables, natural resources, and modes of transportation

Retrieval charts for recording data about cities, countries, and other topics

Organization charts that show committees, structure of government, economic or political systems, and organization of other groups

Direction charts to guide field trips, map making, and other activities

Sequence charts that show a series of events, processes or steps in producing various items, and the flow of materials from farm to city

Group standard charts to guide and evaluate discussion, committee work, role playing, and other activities

Progress charts to record the completion of individual and group work

The format of charts should be similar to that of the charts included in this volume. Make the lettering large enough for group use, use standard paragraph form, and leave adequate space between words and lines. Balanced placement of illustrations,

How new is wind power? What is its future? Social Studies Workshop, University of California, Berkeley

consistent use of standard letter forms, and margins similar to those on picture mats are other important elements of good charts.

Literary Materials

There is widespread agreement that children's literature provides a wealth of material for motivating students, enriching and individualizing instruction, and achieving affective objectives. Literary selections can heighten interest, deepen understanding, create mood and atmosphere, portray the diversity of ways of living and thinking among people in various cultures, stimulate imagination, give colorful backgrounds, promote more complete identification with others, create sympathy for the problems of others, improve attitudes toward others, build appreciations for other cultures, provoke creativity, and give vivid impressions of ways of living being studied in various units.

Factual material rarely kindles a feeling for the joys, sorrows, and problems of others; hence the importance of poetry, stories, biography, fiction, letters, legends, and travel literature to take children beyond facts to the spiritual and aesthetic qualities and values involved in human relationships. The following examples are illustrative of the ways in which literature can enrich the social studies program.

A primary group studying the community enjoyed Field's *General Store,* Clymer's *The Big Pile of Dirt,* and Chute's *Rhymes about the City.* A group studying new immigrants was sensitized to the problems of learning a new language, making new friends, and adjusting to a new school as they read Rosenberg's *Making a Home in America.* Insights into ways individuals and groups can work together despite differences were gained by those who read Davis's *Americans Everyone,* Eberle's *Very Good Neighbors,* and Sommerfelt's *My Name Is Pablo.* An upper-grade group developed deeper appreciation and understanding of our multiethnic society and the contributions of Afro-Americans as they read Davis's *Black Heroes of the American Revolution,* Bontemps's *Frederick Douglass: Slave—Fighter—Free Man,* Petry's *Harriet Tubman,* and Katz's *The Black West.* For more examples see "Bookwatching" in *Language Arts* and the April/May issue of *Social Education,* which lists trade books. Other sources are noted at the end of this chapter.

Care should be taken to distinguish fact from fiction and to discuss deviations from reality. Other guidelines to follow when using a literary selection are these:

Emphasize subjective outcomes, such as the enjoyment and excitement that children should experience as they read it or listen to it.

Enjoy it with the class; do not dissect it, and analyze it only if analysis increases enjoyment.

Share and discuss elements that children like; do not give tests or evaluate it as you evaluate factual materials.

Let the children discover moods, meanings, and values; do not moralize or overemphasize points of keen interest to you.

Use a variety of techniques and activities to share and enjoy literary works—book reports, card files of favorite poems and stories, choral reading, creative writing, dramatization, filmstrips, independent reading, films, oral reading by children or the teacher, programs and pageants, puppets and marionettes, radio and television programs, recordings, and storytelling.

Data Bases

Data bases may vary in size from "minibases" kept in the classroom and software on states, countries, and other topics, to large ones in libraries and media centers, and to even larger ones, such as *America Online, CompuServe, Delphi, FrEd Mail, Learning Link, Prodigy, The Source,* and others. Accessible local data bases can provide pictures, fact sheets, articles, summaries, reports, and other material for use in various units. When supplemented with almanacs, encyclopedias, video encyclopedias on compact discs, and other references, students have access to an abundance of information undreamed of a few years ago.

The making of data bases contributes to greater skill in locating, organizing, indexing, retrieving, and analyzing information. Data bases may be made on students and their families, the community, states, regions, countries, careers, notable people, and other topics. Children in primary grades can make mini-data bases that include drawings, pictures, charts, and local maps related to topics of study. Materials may be kept in folders or envelopes clearly labeled with such titles as Food, Shelter, Clothing, Workers, and Transportation. Students in middle and upper grades can create more detailed data bases with card file and cross-reference systems. Computer software for making data bases and filing data can be used to place information on diskettes for storage and retrieval as needed.

A practical approach is to involve students in making a data base for a particular unit, guiding them in such activities as the following:

Collect pictures, news reports, and articles related to a topic.

Prepare data sheets or cards on particular countries under study—for example, geography (physical features, climate, resources), people (population, urban centers, ancestry), economy (agriculture, manufacturing, mining, trade, transportation, communication), culture (education, traditions, customs, festivals, arts, values, religion), and government (national, other levels, branches, form, capital).

Make data sheets or cards that contain information on topics in a unit, such as achievements of members of minority groups, the views of W.E.B. Du Bois, and the Freedom March.

Make a chronology of key dates in a period or set of events, such as the exploration of the New World, settlement of the West, Afro-Americans in historical perspective, civil rights acts, and the struggle for sex equity.

Prepare biographical sketches of men and women included in a unit.

Prepare book reviews that may be used as guides to supplementary materials.

Make charts, diagrams, graphs, and tables on topics in a unit.

Make reference cards that indicate where to locate information in almanacs, encyclopedias, and other sources.

Organize data for computer use according to (1) *field*—a category such as capital and population of a country; (2) *record*—related fields, such as those for a country; and (3) *file*—a collection of records for several countries.

Practice Materials

Practice materials for individual and group use are needed to develop reading, mapping, and other skills and to correct specific problems that might arise. Multilevel materials that match students' reading levels and provide immediate feedback are helpful. Individualized practice is as necessary in social studies as it is in reading and other subjects. Excellent sources of practice materials are the teacher's guide that accompanies social studies textbooks, the end-of-chapter activities listed in textbooks, and the workbooks that accomany textbooks. Other sources are children's weekly news periodicals, booklets and instructional kits from publishers, computer programs, and activities in such magazines for teachers as *Instructor* and *Learning*.

Multimedia in Libraries

Modern libraries in schools, local and county school district offices, and the community contain a variety of media. Teachers in all grades and students investigating topics in middle and upper grades should take advantage of them. A worksheet to guide the search for useful media follows.

WHICH LIBRARY RESOURCES CAN YOU USE IN SOCIAL STUDIES?

Magazines: _____

Newspapers: _____

Picture file: _____

Pamphlets: _____

Videos: _____

Software: _____

Atlases and Maps: _____

Encyclopedias: _____

Dictionaries: _____

Thesaurus: _____

Yearbooks: _____

A-V Catalog: _____

Free Materials Guides: _____

Others: _____

Audiovisual Resources

Audiovisual materials are basic components of multimedia approaches to instruction. The different types are summarized in Checklist 3.3, which was developed to guide the search for locally available resources.

Checklist 3–3
AUDIOVISUAL MATERIALS

Realia and Representations of Realia

_____ Tools	_____ Art objects	_____ Facsimiles
_____ Utensils	_____ Coins	_____ Models
_____ Documents	_____ Textiles	_____ Exhibits
_____ Costumes	_____ Stamps	_____ Dioramas
_____ Dolls	_____ Collections	_____ Instruments
_____ Other: _____		

Sound and Visual Resources

_____ Films	_____ VCR	_____ Compact discs
_____ Television	_____ Camcorder	_____ Sound filmstrips
_____ Video	_____ Still video camera	_____ FAX machine
_____ Other: _____		

Microcomputer Resources

_____ Hardware	_____ Software	_____ Networks
_____ Printer	_____ Modem	_____ Scanner
_____ Graphics tablet	_____ Trackball	_____ Joystick
_____ Voice synthesizer	_____ Mouse	_____ Touch window
_____ Other: _____		

Pictures and Pictorial Representations

_____ Photographs	_____ Postcards	_____ Collages
_____ Drawings	_____ Study prints	_____ Murals
_____ Slides	_____ Albums	_____ Filmstrips
_____ Transparencies	_____ Scrapbooks	_____ Storyboards
_____ Other: _____		

Symbolic and Graphic Representations

_____ Maps	_____ Cartoons	_____ Chalkboard
_____ Globes	_____ Posters	_____ Bulletin board
_____ Atlases	_____ Diagrams	_____ Flannel board
_____ Charts	_____ Graphs	_____ Time lines
_____ Other: _____		

Projectors, Viewers, Players, Recorders

_____ Slide	_____ Film	_____ Overhead
_____ Tape	_____ Compact disc	_____ Video
_____ Other: _____		

Resources for Production of Media

_____ Lettering devices	_____ Slide making	_____ Duplicating
_____ Map outlines	_____ Chart making	_____ Map making
_____ Transparencies	_____ Picture mounting	_____ Photocopying
_____ Other: _____		

Realia, Exhibits, Dioramas, Panoramas

Realia are artifacts or real things, including objects, models, and items in exhibits, dioramas, and panoramas. Children cannot go back in time and space, but they can have experiences with real things or replicas of them. For example, colonial living can

What realia might you use in a unit? To achieve what objectives? Alameda County Schools

What research and planning are needed to make authentic dioramas? Berkeley Schools, California

be enriched by studying candle molds, muskets, cooking utensils, a spinning wheel, and clothing of the period. Questions for analyzing realia are:

1. What is it made of? What might it be used for? How does it resemble and differ from other objects we have studied?
2. Who might have made it? How was it used? What can we infer about the environment, work, and values of the people who made it?
3. Do the materials or the design suggest a relationship between this culture and other cultures? Why do you think so?

Social studies exhibits may include realia along with pictures, maps, and other items organized around a concept or theme, such as modes· of transportation or communication.

Dioramas show scenes such as Boonesboro or living in a log cabin in three-dimensional perspective. Panoramas depict a scene in broad scope, such as production of lumber or recreational activities in an area.

Demonstrations, Motion Pictures, Television

Demonstrations are used to show how to make maps, use a globe, card wool, operate microcomputers, and other hands-on activities. Motion pictures and television portray action, historical events, places around the world, and other topics. A forum technique is useful to get students to view selected TV programs. Three or four students are asked to report on a program and others are asked to be ready with questions. Critical viewing and listening skills can be developed by urging students to:

Be alert and note most important points.

Be ready to state main points and to raise questions.

Note any points with which you agree or disagree.

Note ideas we can use and ideas we need to learn more about.

Video Resources

Videodiscs and videocassettes are of increasing importance because they can be used as needed and are available on a variety of topics. For example, units on communities can be enriched by video materials on great cities such as Rome, London, and Athens. Camcorders and still video cameras can be used to create materials. Videotapes can be made of places in the community and of resource persons, thus reducing the need for field trips and interviews. The great storage capacity of compact discs can handle encyclopedias and other large masses of data. Material in the form of slides, films, graphs, and print can be stored, accessed, and retrieved readily. To locate videos and films on all subjects, see *Educational Film/Video Locator* (Bowker), *Film and Video Finder* (NICEM), *Films and Videos* (American Library Association).

Computer Resources

The advent of microcomputers and the development of social studies software have made possible electronic instruction that ranges from practice on skills and tutorials on skills, graphics, and programming to educational games, simulations, and creative expression, as shown in Chart 3.1. Among the benefits are providing quick feedback and self-pacing, developing linear thinking ability, individualizing instruction, and developing problem-solving and decision-making skills. Reading and expressive skills also can be improved, as noted in these comments of elementary students: "You better read and follow directions or you will get all fouled up," and "You can create maps, charts, graphs, drawings, puzzles—you name it."

Instruction in the social studies should be integrated into lessons and units and move beyond the development of computer literacy. The growing array of social studies software includes programs on map concepts and skills, time and seasons, exploration, colonization, states, countries, continents, notable men and women, and American history. Among the variety of simulations available are navigating to find the New World, sailing from New York to California, traveling to Oregon, fur trading, ruling an ancient kingdom, competing for a profit, living in ancient civilizations, and making governmental decisions. Examples of online information services that may be accessed are *American Online, CompuServe, Prodigy,* and others noted earlier in the section on Data Bases.

Programs are available for creating social studies word puzzles, dictionaries, task cards, posters, tables, graphs, drawings, charts, data bases, test items, music, and other materials. Software is available for word processing, desktop publishing and presenting, and programming materials that fit units of study. Integrated software contains several programs with one set of commands for easy coordinated uses—for example, data base, word processing, and graphics for preparing illustrated reports. Easy-to-use authoring software extends the range of items that can be created and enhances the development of problem-solving skills. Hypermedia (such as Hypercard) can be used to link text, pictures, and other materials.

Examples of other uses of computers are collaborative writing, sharing information via networks and bulletin boards, integrating text, sound, and graphics, using a scanner to display images on a monitor and to add images to reports, linking a computer and videodisc player to provide interactive learning systems, putting images from video cameras, photographs, and other items onto a computer, making slides and projectuals, sending/receiving electronic mail, aiding distance learning, and making

---

Using Our Computer in Social Studies

1. Make outlines, data bases, and spreadsheets.
2. Write, illustrate, edit, and revise reports.
3. Practice map, globe, study, and other skills.
4. Use tutorials to learn new content and skills.
5. Use simulations to improve decision-making skills.
6. Create graphs, posters, puzzles, and new programs.
7. Use integrated instructional and learning systems.
8. Do desktop publishing and presenting of material.
9. Use online services, networks, and bulletin boards.
10. Can you think of others to add to our list?

Chart 3.1

multimedia presentations.

The use of computers by special students may be aided by providing a voice synthesizer, powerpad, touch window, other devices, and selected software (Sloan, 1989).

Sources such as the following contain information on useful software: *Electronic Learning, Teaching and Computers, Instructor, Social Education, Media & Methods, Educational Technology, The Computing Teacher, Education Software Report, The Educational Software Selector,* and directories or catalogs from Bowker, Scholastic, Social Studies School Service, and other distributors.

Combining Microcomputer, CD-ROM, and Video Technology

Linking these technologies makes possible the creation of a single package that may include films, slides, text, video, audio, and other elements (Beardslee and Davis, 1989). With available videodiscs that can store thousands of frames of visual material and other information that can be readily accessed, the computer can be said to retrieve single pictures, a set of pictures, text, and other items as needed for decision making, problem solving, reporting, or other purposes. Interactive video lessons can be created to achieve various objectives. Original video and CD-ROM disks can be created, containing text, images, animation, graphics, and other features.

Recordings

Recordings are made and used for many different purposes in social studies. They provide background and sound effects for dramatic activities, programs, choral readings, and rhythmic expression. They may be made of speeches, school visitors, students' reports, interviews, and songs related to a unit. Recordings made of students' reports may be played back to encourage self-evaluation and help identify ways to improve.

Pictures

Of all visual materials, pictures are the most widely used. Pictures and study prints can introduce topics, raise questions, clarify concepts, illustrate reports, show steps in sequence, and be made into collages and scrapbooks. They can also clarify map symbols, show how tools are used, and develop visual literacy—recognizing and naming objects, interpreting what is seen, analyzing objects and activities that are portrayed, and inferring the feelings of people who are shown. Guidelines for effective use of pictures are presented in Charts 3.2 and 3.3.

Filmstrips, Slides, Overhead and Opaque Projections

Filmstrips and slides cover a variety of topics in all grades, are accompanied by helpful manuals, and enable teachers to use them as needed and to stop and discuss what is shown as long as desired. Overhead projections enable teachers to write on transparent plastic and to point to items on maps, diagrams, and the like while facing the class. Relationships can be shown by using overlays, for example, placing a population map transparency over a relief map transparency to show settlement/landform relationships. Opaque projections are used to present a nontransparent picture, map, or other item to the class and thereby eliminate the need to pass it around the room or duplicate it. Enlargements also can be made of maps, diagrams, and other items.

Interpreting Pictures of Landscapes	Interpreting Pictures of Human Activities
Where is the scene located?	Where is the activity located?
What items stand out? Hills? Valleys? Rivers? Others?	What are the people doing?
How high, large, or small are they?	Is individual or group work emphasized?
Is natural vegetation shown?	What tools and materials are being used?
Are crops or gardens shown? If so, what is being raised?	How are their ways of working like ours? How are they different?
Are there indicators of the weather? Wind? Temperature? Amount of rainfall? Snow?	What kind of clothing are they wearing?
Are there roads? Canals? Railroads? Buildings?	What homes or other buildings are shown?
	How are activities and buildings adapted to the climate?
	What values seem to underlie their activities?

Chart 3.2   Chart 3.3

Be a photo detective. How many different cultural features can you find? How many different natural features? Social Studies Workshop, University of California, Berkeley

The Bulletin Board

The bulletin board is useful for initiating units, stimulating new interests, clarifying problems, posting children's work, and displaying materials. In initiating units, display materials that evoke interest and stimulate questions about those topics that come first in the unit. By changing and rearranging materials to stimulate new interests, the teacher can guide the development of the unit in sound directions. Related materials, such as posters, drawings, charts, maps, or graphs, should be posted as they are needed. Children's work may be displayed to share and summarize learning.

Interactive bulletin boards that invite student participation may be arranged by providing captions, questions, and space for students' contributions. Students may bring pictures, postcards, clippings, and other items that they can share, describe, respond to questions about, and be guided to arrange on the bulletin board.

A variety of arrangements are useful, as shown in Figure 3.1.

ILLUSTRATIVE BULLETIN BOARD ARRANGEMENTS

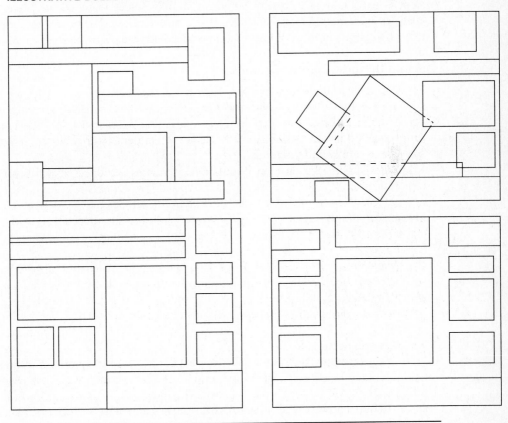

Figure 3.1

The Storyboard

A storyboard guides the making of a film, filmstrip, videotape, or photo essay; it consists of sketches or pictures arranged in a sequence to portray a story, theme, or topic. To make a storyboard, follow these basic steps: (1) Select a topic; (2) use a flannel board or make sketches or select pictures to tell the story; (3) place the sketches or pictures in sequence; (4) add notes for making the photo essay, film, or tape; (5) make the resource; and (6) evaluate. Some teachers find that making a storyboard is itself a rewarding experience because of the contribution it makes to the development of visual literacy.

The Chalkboard

The chalkboard is a basic and versatile visual tool. Use it to list suggestions during group planning, sketch illustrations, list reading materials, note assignments, copy suggestions for charts, note facts under main ideas, summarize a discussion, record group-dictated stories or letters, and give chalk talks. Many teachers increase the effectiveness of chalkboard use by adding simple stick figures to illustrate points, by using colored chalk to emphasize key ideas, and by using rulers, compasses, and stencils to obtain neat, artistic effects. Carefully select materials to place on the chalkboard, remembering that slides, charts, and duplicated materials are more effective when large amounts of information or detailed data are to be presented.

Symbolic and Graphic Materials

Posters convey a single idea in a way that can be grasped at a glance. They are used to sway people to a course of action and are often used in campaigns for safety, energy conservation, or other topics of concern. Space, line, form, and color direct attention to the desired action. Making posters acquaints students with ways of presenting a single idea simply and forcefully.

Tables summarize data on population, resources, products, exports, and other topics in succinct form. The first tables interpreted by students may simply be a list of figures headed by a title—for example, Classroom Attendance or Population Growth in Our Community. Tables with two or more columns are then introduced, and the teacher directs attention to the title, the column headings, comparisons between columns, and changes and trends to be identified.

Graphs are visual presentations of data. In the early grades they are used to show such information as daily temperature, enrollment, attendance, books read, and other items familiar to children. In later grades they are used to show population growth, resources, exports, and other items originally organized in tables. In all grades the interpretation and construction of graphs must be related to instruction in the mathematics program.

Cartoons are designed to convey an idea by means of caricature, humor, stereotype, oversimplification, exaggeration, and satire. Such symbols as Uncle Sam, John Bull, and the dove of peace may be used. The meaning of the symbol must be clear and an understanding of the situation, issue, or problem must be developed if students are to interpret cartoons. This is why so many cartoons that amuse adults have little or no impact on children. When cartoons are encountered in reading and other materials they must be analyzed to help students understand the symbols used, the situation or problem portrayed, and the purpose of the cartoonist.

Learning activities and questions that help students learn to interpret symbolic and graphic material are presented in chapter 11.

Time Charts and Time Lines

Time charts and time lines are used to clarify time relationships, to relate events to major time periods, and to relate events in one country to those in another. In the early grades charts may be made to show events of the day, major events during the week, events related to the growth of the community, changes in transportation, changes in farming, and changing ways of providing food, shelter, and clothing. In later grades charts and time lines may be used to show events during major periods of the history of the state or the nation, the development of transportation or communication, and the like.

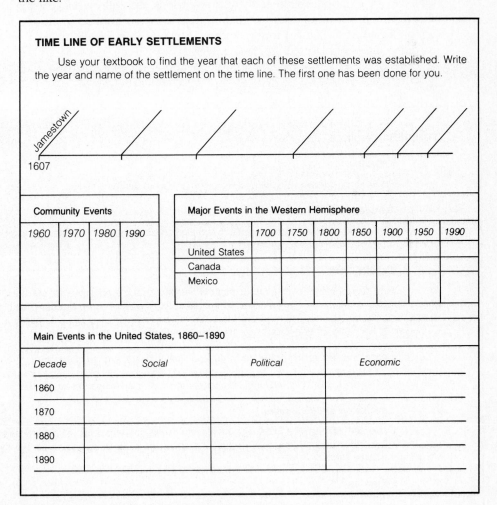

Figure 3.2

Children should be guided to develop a time base or frame of reference for interpreting time periods and time relationships. Many teachers have children use their own age for this purpose. For example, the following time periods were charted by a group of ten-year-olds:

Decade—10 years, equal to my age, about one-third my parents' age

Generation—33 years, a little more than three times my age, about the same as my parents' age

Century—100 years, ten times my age, about three times my parents' age

Time charts and time lines take many different forms, as shown in Figure 3.2. The most common form is simply a sequence of events listed on paper with space between the events scaled to show elapsed time. A wire can be strung across the room and cards representing events hung at appropriate intervals. Large envelopes can be attached to the wall under a line showing time periods, and children can place appropriate pictures or names of events in them. Events in two or more regions or countries can be arranged in parallel form, either vertically or horizontally, to show what occurred in different places at the same time.

The following lesson plan illustrates how futures time lines may be made:

FUTURES TIME LINES

Objective

To make personal and community (or state or nation) futures time lines.

Introduction

Review time lines in children's textbooks that show past events. Tell students that they are going to learn to project a time line into the future.

Development

First, ask members of the class to make a personal time line on a time horizon of their choice, explaining that "time horizon" refers to the period of time to be used. Discuss possible events that may be included, such as birthdays, promotion to a higher grade, completion of elementary school, and other events of special interest, such as a trip or a vacation.

After completion and discussion of the personal time lines, ask students to make one for their community (or state or nation) over the same time period. Discuss possible events to include, such as legal holidays, elections, changes in transportation, new buildings, renewal projects.

Conclusion and Evaluation

Share and discuss time lines, with attention to events students think will actually happen and to those they hope will happen. Evaluate by observing students in discussion and by checking their time lines.

Follow-up

Ask students to continue to add to and revise their time lines.

Learning Centers

An effective way to make instructional materials available for individual and small-group use is to set up learning centers. Examples are shown in Figure 3.3. Illustrative guidelines for using learning centers are shown in Figure 3.4. Additional examples are presented in later chapters.

EXAMPLES OF SOCIAL STUDIES LEARNING CENTERS

NEIGHBORHOOD/COMMUNITY	DRAMATIC PLAY	CONSTRUCTION
Photographs of main places, such as school, homes, stories	Small table and chairs, hats and clothes, dolls, crib, other items for role playing family activities	Construction paper and pieces of cardboard, wood, dowel
Picture or simple map of the community or neighborhood	Table for counter, shelves, canned goods, other items for role playing shopping for groceries	Saws, hammers, nails, C-clamps, T-square, scissors, sandpaper
Reading materials on other neighborhoods and communities		Models of airplanes, trucks, other items students may make
Cards with names of fire station and other places to place on map	Models of airplanes, space marked for runway and control tower, baggage trucks, other items for airport play	Low flat-top sawhorse or work bench
Outline maps for labelling main streets, school, other items		Templates or simple diagrams to guide the cutting of materials

ART	VIEWING	READING/LIBRARY
Drawing and construction paper	Picture file of cutouts from magazines	Trade books and other library materials on various reading levels
Scissors, compass, rulers	Photos, slides, filmstrips	
Crayons, colored chalk, white chalk, charcoal, paste	Projectors for individual or small-group viewing	Pamphlets, brochures, leaflets, other fugitive materials
Easels, brushes, poster or other needed paints	**LISTENING**	Student and adult newspapers and magazines
Clay, block-printing, stenciling materials	Headphones and recording player, tapes, records	A file of clippings related to topics under study
Unit-related pictures, prints, slides, filmstrips	Study guides to direct listening activities	Dictionary and other references

MAP AND GLOBE SKILLS	CURRENT EVENTS	PIONEER LIFE
Large globe, wall map, atlas for reference use	World newsmap, state and national maps for locating events	Books from library on various reading levels
File of highway, state, resource, population, other maps	Current newspapers, clippings, space to post news events	Pictures of flatboat, house raising, cabin, other items
Map games and puzzles	**HISTORY**	Map showing trails used by the pioneers
Worksheets, task cards, outline maps to guide research, mapping, other activities	Historical maps and atlas	Task cards to direct research on settlements, food, other items
	Books, photos, filmstrips, word puzzles, timelines	

U.S. HISTORY	STATES OF THE UNITED STATES	PRESIDENTS
Pictures and books on explorers, colonists, pioneers	Atlas, almanac, encyclopedias, library books	Books, with articles and pictures
Historical wall map and atlas	Worksheets for study of each state's geography, history, landmarks, resources, products, population, capital, flower, nickname, other items	Outline maps to show home state
Worksheets and outline maps to organize data on explorations, colonial life, early cities, other items		Task cards directing students to find term of office, political party, main achievements, main events during presidency, other information

---

Figure 3.3

GUIDELINES FOR USING LEARNING CENTERS

COMPUTER USES

You may work alone or with a small group.

Follow procedures and rules for use.

Use tutorials, drill/practice, games, simulations, data bases, word processing.

Make graphs, tables, puzzles, spreadsheets, puzzles, slides

USING LEARNING CENTERS

Go to a center where work space is available.

Follow the procedure and rules posted in each center.

Work without disturbing others.

Use available worksheets and task cards.

Return materials to their place when finished.

USING THE WORLD CULTURES CENTER

Select a country of your choice in the region we are studying.

Find material on your country in the books, atlas, picture file, clipping file, and other sources.

Use the worksheets to note information on your country.

Organize your notes and be ready to report to the class.

LITERATURE CENTER

Choose a story or poem and answer these questions:

What meaning does it add to our social studies unit?

What is its literal meaning?

What is a deeper, below-the-surface, meaning?

How do you rate it? Good? Fair? Poor?

What new (creative) ideas did it stimulate?

Should others read it?

MATCHING ACTIVITIES

Look for these matching activities in learning centers:

Pictures of people or objects and names of them on cards

Names of workers and the tools they use

Resources and products made from them

Map symbols and pictures of what they represent

News events and their location on a map

COLLABORATIVE LEARNING

Be cooperative and positive as you work with others.

Follow directions and help others do so.

Explain procedures to anyone not sure of them.

Take turns as you talk about any problems that arise.

Evaluate yourself as you work and make needed improvements.

Tactfully help others evaluate and make improvements.

Figure 3.4

Community Resources

The community can be a social studies laboratory where geographic, historical, economic, and other concepts can be developed in a realistic setting. Changing conditions can be studied as they take place, and factors that produce them can be explored. Holidays, special events, and commemorations can be experienced with others. Field trips can be taken, local experts can be interviewed, historical sites can be visited, and other resources can be tapped, as shown in Checklist 3.4.

The Community Survey

In many social studies programs the community is the focus of study, and the topics chosen for study are determined by the curriculum and the maturity of the students.

Checklist 3–4
COMMUNITY RESOURCES

_____ Study (or field) trips (industries, museums): _____

_____ Field studies (housing, pollution, transportation): _____

_____ People to interview (travelers, police): _____

_____ Resource visitors (panel or individuals): _____

_____ Service and other organizations (Red Cross, clubs): _____

_____ Service projects (safety, cleanup): _____

_____ Local current events (campaigns, drives): _____

_____ Recreational resources (parks, marinas): _____

_____ School resources (collections, teachers): _____

_____ Publications, visual media (newspapers, bulletins): _____

_____ Television, radio (travel programs, news): _____

_____ Other: _____

Topics can include:

Communication	Health services	Residences
Conservation	History	Resources
Ecology	Mass media	Sanitation services
Education	Museums, theaters	Social services
Ethnic groups	Occupations	Sports facilities
Future plans	Pollution	Transportation
Geography	Population	Urban renewal
Government	Recreation	Utilities

Many educational benefits can be gained from a community survey. As students conduct their survey—perhaps checking safety hazards, type and location of residence, housing conditions, the business and industrial sections, or museums—their observation skills are sharpened. As they talk with old-timers, business people, school workers, public officials, and other community workers, they improve their interviewing techniques. As they examine pictures, letters, newspapers, reports, and other local documents, they develop skill in content analysis.

Daily Experiences

Everyday experiences in the community constitute one of the student's most valuable resources. As children see buildings under construction, watch changes in the season, see workers in action, observe holidays and celebrations, enjoy radio and television, hear and discuss current events, buy articles in stores, use the transportation system, attend churches, and engage in a host of other activities, they make discoveries and are stimulated to raise questions. Sharing, discussion, individual reporting, and journal writing may be used to capitalize on daily experiences.

Study Trips

Listed here are examples of study trips. As a substitute, videotapes can be made and used as needed.

Airport	Farms	Police station
Bakery	Firehouse	Post office
Bank	Historic homes	Sawmill
City hall	Library	Stores
Courtroom	Mission	Telephone exchange
Dairy	Museum	Television station

Short informal walks taken in the immediate neighborhood are valuable study trips. Children may see a house being built, changes in the season, a neighborhood fire station or library, a historic home, soil erosion, or various people at work. Also useful are trips with parents to places in the community, especially when guided by questions raised in class. Informal walks and trips with parents require a minimum of organization and make children more critical observers of their environment.

Planning Study Trips. The one great difference between a study trip and just going somewhere is that a study trip has educational objectives. Key points for a teacher to keep in mind are presented in Checklist 3.5.

It is sound procedure to summarize specific plans on charts, the chalkboard, or duplicated sheets of paper so that each student clearly understands objectives, procedures, and behavior standards. When many questions are to be raised, they may be divided into sets and assigned to committees. Each member may pose a question as directed by the teacher or tour guide.

Resource Persons

Community studies are enriched when fire fighters, police, journalists, and other workers are interviewed or meet with the class to discuss problems and questions. In units about foreign countries such as Mexico or Japan, individuals who are natives or who have visited the country can share their experiences with the class. The showing

Checklist 3–5
GUIDE FOR THE PLANNING OF STUDY TRPS

First Considerations

_____ Have adequate backgrounds, ideas, and objectives been developed?
_____ Are related materials—films, books, pictures—available?
_____ Are there profitable follow-up activities?
_____ Other: _____

Preliminary Arrangements

_____ Has administrative approval been given?
_____ Has the approval of parents been secured?
_____ Are eating and toilet arrangements satisfactory?
_____ Has the time schedule been prepared?
_____ Has the guide been advised on problems, needs, and maturity of the group?
_____ Have travel arrangements and expenses been arranged?
_____ Are assistants needed to help supervise the group?
_____ Has a list been made of the names, telephone numbers, and addresses of those children who are going?
_____ Other: _____

Group Planning

_____ Are questions prepared and understood?
_____ Are recording procedures and assignments clear?
_____ Have behavior standards been developed?
_____ Have safety precautions been considered?
_____ Have the time schedule, travel arrangements, and expenses been clarified?
_____ Has attention been given to appropriateness of dress?
_____ Are monitorial assignments clear?
_____ Other: _____

Follow-up Plans

_____ Do experiences that follow contribute to objectives?
_____ What summaries and records should be made?
_____ Is attention given to the development of charts, maps, diagrams, displays, murals, models, scrapbooks, construction, dramatic activities, and floor layouts?
_____ Are procedures in mind to discover and clarify misconceptions?
_____ Are letters of appreciation to be sent?
_____ How is learning to be evaluated?
_____ Other: _____

of realia, pictures, and slides along with the discussion enhances the contributions of resource visitors.

A sound procedure is to organize a file of resource persons who can make valuable contributions to the social studies program. A simple card system can be used by noting the following information on index cards:

Contribution _____

Name _____Telephone _____

Hours available _____

Will come to school? _____

Children may visit at home or office? _____

Comments _____
_____

Examples of resource persons to invite to the classroom, or to videotape at work, are as follows:

Airport employees	House builders	Old-time residents
Authors	Industrial workers	Police
Business people	Lawyers	Social workers
City officials	Librarians	Traffic safety specialists
Consuls of foreign nations	Merchants	Travelers
	Musicians	

Interviewing Resource Persons. When a resource person cannot come to school, when essential materials must be kept on the job, or when seeing the person in a working situation is more beneficial, a student or a small group can interview the person at work. Interviews require the same kind of planning as done for resource visitors. Interviewing guidelines to follow are:

Introduce yourself. State questions clearly and listen attentively.

Let the expert talk. Ask questions on any points that are not clear.

Take notes on difficult ideas or technical points.

Do not waste time. Express thanks when finished.

Guidelines for Using Media

All media should be viewed as sources of information for achieving instructional objectives. Media on differing levels of abstractness should be included, ranging from objects, models, and pictorial materials to maps, charts, graphs, and reading materials. The classroom should be viewed as a laboratory—a planned learning environment—

where materials are arranged and used in learning centers, in individual activities, and in class and small-group activities. A multimedia approach is generally more effective than the traditional textbook approach; it may be facilitated by arranging the materials in a kit in the sequence in which they will most likely be used. Finally, materials should be evaluated not only before use but also during and after use to identify strengths and weaknesses and to plan for future improvements. A summary of general and specific guidelines for using various media is presented in Checklist 3.6. Later chapters contain additional guidelines on reading resources, maps, globes, and other media.

Checklist 3.6
GUIDELINES FOR USING VARIOUS MEDIA

General Guidelines for All Media

____ Get useful ideas from accompanying manual or teacher's guides.

____ Clarify objectives, new concepts, and questions or comments to guide utilization.

____ Note relationships to unit or lesson topics and ways to stimulate interest.

____ Clarify students' activity during use and prepare related directions.

____ Identify ways to use content to answer questions and achieve other objectives.

____ Note critical-thinking comparisons to make with information from other media.

____ Detect and correct gender, ethnic, other bias and stereotypes, and misconceptions.

____ Review, repeat, or reshow any parts that are not clearly understood.

____ Double-check to be sure materials and equipment are in place and in working order.

____ Follow-up with group and/or individual applications to unit or lesson activities.

____ Evaluate in terms of objectives and reactions of students.

Realia	Exhibits and Displays	Pictures
____ Use models, specimens, and other objects in daily lessons, dioramas, exhibits, displays, demonstrations.	____ Involve students and discuss the following:	____ Guide students from enumerating and describing items to interpreting and inferring.
____ Respond to questions and suggest research on how they are used.	____ Central focus, background, color scheme, labels	____ Discuss setting and main items.
____ Discuss relationships to concepts and ideas from pictures and other media.	____ Placement of key items	____ Discuss human activities, homes, clothing, and tools.
	____ Avoidance of clutter and distracting elements	____ Relate to text in print materials.

(continued)

Checklist 3.6 *(continued)*

Motion Pictures

___ Note meaning added by movement and sound.

___ Discuss examples of cooperation, responsibility, and other democratic behavior.

___ Detect and correct time, space, size, or other distortions.

Slides

___ Arrange in desired sequence.

___ Present each slide with related comments.

___ Adjust tempo to students' needs and respond to their questions.

___ Use pointer to focus attention on key items.

Television, Radio, Recordings

___ Use as sources for current events, holidays, and inaugurations.

___ Urge students to observe relevant programs before and after school.

___ Record desired programs for use at appropriate time.

___ Have students give simulated broadcasts.

Textbooks

___ Improve reading skills and use:

___ Photo essays and introductory sections to initate units.

___ Picture and context clues to develop concepts and vocabulary.

___ Text, maps, tables, graphs, and diagrams as data sources.

___ Practice exercises to improve reading/ study skills.

Maps

___ Use to introduce, summarize, and review topics.

___ Clarify purpose each map is designed to serve.

___ Clarify symbols and scale.

___ Compare with globe to detect shape and size distortions.

___ Use A-V media to add meaning and reality.

Computers

___ Clarify procedures and rules for individual and small-group use.

___ Use unit-related tutorials, simulations, games, drill/practice, and data bases.

___ Use to make charts, graphs, maps, word puzzles, slides, and tests.

___ Use to make outlines and write, edit, and revise reports.

Making Critiques of Media

Students as well as teachers should critique media to note strengths, weaknesses, bias, and other elements. Specific attention should be given to purpose, underlying values, motives, feelings that were aroused, images of people, stereotypes, emotional appeals, use of persuasion and propaganda techniques, fallacies of thinking (noted in chapter 9), the subtle nature of bias, and the impact of various media on thinking and acting. For example, questions for appraising and critiquing TV, film, and video media are:

What is the central theme, purpose, or motive?

What positive, negative, or mixed feelings were aroused?

What images of people were presented? Any stereotypes?

Evaluating the Treatment of Women	Evaluating the Treatment of Ethnic Groups
Are women shown in a variety of activities and jobs?	Are a variety of contributions presented?
Are a variety of contributions reported?	Are they shown in a variety of roles and jobs?
Are girls portrayed as passive, fearful, and changing their minds?	Are any groups portrayed as problems, primitive, lazy, savage, dull, or slow?
Are boys portrayed as active, more mature, and larger?	Are the values of cultural diversity presented?
Are boys shown making things and earning money, while girls are shown sewing, cooking, or playing with dolls?	Is there treatment of evils of discrimination, prejudice, or stereotypes?
What changes should be made?	Are equality, justice, and concern for others clarified?
	What improvements should be made?

Chart 3.4   Chart 3.5

What special effects were used—music, color, lighting, other?

What is the text message—factual, opinionated, explicit, other?

What should be changed—images, special effects, text, other?

Critiques of the treatment of women and ethnic groups may be guided by questions in Charts 3.4 and 3.5.

Sources of Information

When needed media are not available in a school, check the following sources. Most are available in instructional media centers and college libraries.

1. The catalog of materials in the school system's media center.
2. Catalogs and lists from the county schools office, the state department of education, state universities, colleges, and other agencies from which your school district obtains materials.
3. The NICEM (National Information Center for Education Media) indexes (Los Angeles: University of Southern California).
4. Detailed analyses of materials: *Curriculum Materials Data Book* (Boulder, CO: Social Science Education Consortium); *Educational Product Report* (New York: EPIE Institute).
5. Guides to free or inexpensive materials (also check special sections in the magazines listed in item 7): *Educator's Guide to Free Social Studies Materials, Elementary Teacher's Guide to Free Curriculum Materials,* and *Educator's Guide to Free Films* (Randolph, WI: Educator's Progress Service); *Vertical File Index* (New York: H. W. Wilson); *Economic Education* (New York: Joint Council on Economic Education); *Selected United States Government Publications,* Superintendent of Documents, Government Printing Office, Washington, D.C. 20402 (ask to be put on the

mailing list); and *Free Ed Guide* (502 Woodside Avenue, Narbeth, PA 19072).

6. Latest editions of guides to reading materials: *Basic Book Collection for Elementary Grades, Subject Index to Books for Primary Grades,* and *Subject Index to Books for Intermediate Grades* (Chicago: American Library Association); *Best Books for Children, Children's Books in Print* (New York: R. R. Bowker Company); *Bibliography of Books for Children* (Washington, D.C.: Association for Childhood Education); *Children's Books to Enrich the Social Studies for the Elementary Grades* (Washington, D.C.: National Council for the Social Studies); *Reading Ladders for Human Relations, Adventuring With Books* (Urbana, IL: National Council of Teachers of English); *The Horn Book Guide* (Boston: The Horn Book Inc.).

7. Periodicals: *AIT Newsletter, Booklist, Bulletin of the Center for Children's Books, Learning, Social Studies Review, Textbook Letter, Instructor, Social Education, Media & Methods, Educational Technology, Electronic Learning, Teaching and Computers, Classroom Computer Learning, The Computing Teacher, Social Studies and the Young Learner, The Reading Teacher.*

8. Detailed source lists in professional textbooks on learning materials, such Heinich et al., (1989).

9. Information on materials related to ethnic groups: African-American Institute, 1390 19th Street, NW Washington, D.C., Anti Defamation League of B'nai B'rith, 823 United Nations Plaza, New York, NY 10017 (also, Holocaust materials); Asia Society, 469 Union Avenue, Westbury, NY 11590; Association for the Study of Negro Life and History, 1538 Ninth Street, N.W., Washington, D.C. 20001; *Afro-Am Educational Materials,* 819 Wabash Avenue, Chicago, IL 60605; Council on Interracial Books for Children, 1841 Broadway, New York, NY 10023; Social Studies School Service, 10,200 Jefferson Boulevard, Culver City, CA 90232

Questions, Activities, and Evaluation

1. Visit an instructional media center or check the center's catalog to identify materials for use in a unit of your choice. Use the checklists in this chapter to guide your search.

2. Examine a textbook and make notes detailing how you might use it in a unit. Which of the objectives noted in the first part of this chapter might you achieve?

3. Make a sketch of a chart you might use in a unit. Indicate what type of chart it is and how you would use it.

4. Select and preview a film or a filmstrip. Make a plan for using it in a unit, following the guidelines in Checklist 3.6, "Using Instructional Materials."

5. Examine one or more of the guides to free or inexpensive materials listed at the end of this chapter. Request materials that appear suitable for a unit you plan to teach. Appraise items that you receive in terms of the criteria in the first part of this chapter.

6. Identify two community resources you might use in a unit and note the objectives you would hope to achieve.

7. Obtain magazines that contain pictures related to a unit you plan to teach. Cut out and mount useful pictures and organize them in a picture file. Indicate how they may be used to develop interpreting, classifying, and other thinking processes as well as concepts and related vocabulary.

8. Visit a local school and note the following:
   a. Microcomputer and video resources and how they are being used
   b. Library resources for use in the social studies, including encyclopedias, almanacs, other references, literary selections, periodicals, other resources

9. Write to three or more of the following to obtain materials on civic education.

ACCESS: A Security
Information Service
1730 M St., N.W., Ste. 605
Washington, DC 20036

Center for Civic Education
5146 Douglas Fir Rd.
Calabasas, CA 91302

Council for the
Advancement of
Citizenship
1724 Massachusetts Ave.,
N.W.
Washington, DC 20036

National Institute for Citizen
Education in the Law
711 G St., S.E.
Washington, DC 20003

American Federation of
Teachers
555 New Jersey Ave.
Washington, DC 20001

Close Up Foundation
1235 Jefferson Davis
Highway
Arlington, VA 22202

Foreign Policy Association
1726 M St., N.W., Ste. 800
Washington, DC 20036

National Issues Forums
100 Commons Dr.
Dayton, OH 45459–2777

American Newspaper
Publishers Association
Foundation
P.O. Box 17407 Dulles
Airport
Washington, DC 20041

Constitutional Rights
Foundation
601 S. Kingsley Dr.
Los Angeles, CA 90005

National Council for the
Social Studies
3501 Newark St., N.W.
Washington, DC 20016

A Presidential Classroom for
Young Americans
441 N. Lee St.
Alexandria, VA 22314–2346

References

Beardslee, Edward C., and Geoffrey L. Davis, *Interactive Videodiscs and the Teaching-Learning Process.* Bloomington, IN: Phi Delta Kappa, 1989.

Brunesco, Marci, "Adaptive Technology," *Electronic Learning,* 10 (October 1990), 20, 22. Adaptations for the disabled, such as keyboard software, replacement and emulation, voice input, adaptive cards.

Data Book of Social Studies Materials and Resources. Boulder, CO: Social Science Education Consortium. Annual review.

Ellis, Arthur K. *Teaching and Learning Elementary Social Studies* (4th ed.). Needham Heights, Ma: Allyn & Bacon, 1991.

Fitzpatrick, Charlie, "Computers in Geography Education," *Journal of Geography,* 89 (July–August 1990), 138–39.

Fry, Edward, *Fry Readability Program.* Providence, RI: Jamestown Publishers, 1982. Manual and computer program for estimating readability level.

Heinich, Robert, Michael Molenda, and James Russell, *Instructional Media and the New Technologies of Instruction* (3rd ed.). New York: Macmillan, 1989.

Horn, Royal Van, "Educational Power Tools: New Instructional Delivery Systems," *Phi Delta Kappa,* 72 (Mar., 1991), 527033.

Laughlin, Margaret A., H. Michael Hartoonian, and Norris M. Sanders, eds., *From Information to Decision Making.* Bulletin 83. Washington, D.C.: National Council for the Social Studies, 1989. How to deal with the Information Age.

Lockard, James, Peter D. Abrams, and Wesley A. Many, *Microcomputers for Educators* (2nd ed.). Glenview, IL: Scott Foresman/Little, Brown, 1990.

Margeau, Therese, "Redefining the Textbook," *Electronic Learning,* 10(Feb.1991), 14–18.

"Notable Children's Trade Books in the Field of Social Studies," annual review, *Social Education* (April/May).

Richie, Mark L., "Interactive Instructional Systems," *Media & Methods,* 26 (March/April 1990), 12–14.

Roberts, Nancy, et al., *Integrating Telecommunications into Education.* Englewood Cliffs, NJ: Prentice-Hall, 1990. Section on social studies.

Robinson, Cynthia, "Making Good Use of Museum Resources," *Social Studies and the Young Learner,* 3(March/April 1991), 9–11.

Sloan, Eydie, "Technology—the Equalizer," *Instructor,* 98 (April 1989), 34–36. Uses of voice synthesizer, powerpad, touch window, and other devices by special students; list of software.

Van Cleaf, D.W., *Action in Elementary Social Studies.* Needham, MA: Allyn & Bacon, 1991.

Warger, Cynthia, ed., *Technology in Today's Schools.* Alexandria, VA: Association for Supervision and Curriculum Development, 1990.

White, Charles S., "Directing the Software Evaluation Process: A Guide for Evaluators," *Social Education,* 53 (January 1989), 67–68.

Wishnietsky, Dan H. *Using Electronic Mail in an Educational Setting.* Bloomington, IN: Phi Delta Kappa, 1991.

Young, M. Jean, and Charles M. Riegeluth, *Improving the Textbook Selection Process.* Bloomington, IN: Phi Delta Process, 1988. Procedures and criteria.

Planning and Guiding Group Learning Activities

CHAPTER 4

Objective and Related Focusing Questions

To present guidelines and strategies for whole-group and small-group learning activities?

- What are the values and limitations of group learning activities?

- What growth in skills may be noted as students move from beginning to intermediate to advanced levels?

- What guiding principles are helpful in improving discussions?

- How can questions be used to guide and enrich discussion?

- What guidelines are helpful in improving learning in small-group activities?

- How can study guides be prepared and used to improve learning in small groups?

The quality of learning in the social studies is directly related to the skill with which teachers provide group learning activities. The core of instruction is provided in whole-class and small-group activities. Many individual and committee activities emerge from planning, discussion, and evaluation done by the class. As a student stated, "We really learn a lot by working together!"[1]

Values and Limitations

The class as a whole and small groups may be used to provide firsthand learning about interpersonal and group participation skills. Objectives can be set, questions can be raised, concepts can be clarified, and problems can be discussed. Being part of a group fosters feelings of belonging, mutual respect, and responsibility. Interaction with others stimulates thinking as ideas are shared. Attitudes and behavior patterns such as open-mindedness, responsibility, cooperation, creativity, and concern for others can also be developed.

The limitations of group activities should be recognized. For example, group activities should be limited to ones that are guided by objectives shared by all group members; that can be done better by a group than by individuals; in which constructive working relationships can be maintained. Groups such as panels and round tables should not be used until students have developed the prerequisite skills, and they should put to use the diverse talents of members.

Whole-Group Activities

In many learning situations the class works together as a single group. All students may participate in such whole-group activities as

Planning dramatizations, things to make, displays, use of materials, murals, maps, charts, arts and crafts projects, stories, simulation games, ways to obtain information, individual and small-group work, interviews, field trips, programs, group action projects, and evaluation standards.

Observing demonstrations, films and other audiovisual resources, people and activities on field trips, role playing, committee reports, changes in the neighborhood and community, and resource persons.

Discussing observations, interpretations, generalizations, classifications, inferences, hypotheses, predictions, analyses, syntheses, and evaluations based on data gathered from reading materials, community resources, and audiovisual materials.

Evaluating plans, projects, use of materials, displays, dramatic activities, discussion, demonstrations, group behavior, sources of data, role playing, and interviewing and other data-gathering techniques.

[1]Grateful acknowledgment is made to Dr. Ruth Grossman, City University of New York, City College, and Dr. Victoria Mui, California State University, Hayward, for suggested revisions in this chapter.

The following may be used to present information, analyze cases, provide feedback, and give instructional cues.

Minilectures to clarify concepts and themes, present advance organizers or background information, give directions for an activity, introduce a unit, explain a procedure such as how amendments may be made to the Constitution, or round out ideas presented in a film or other source of information.

Demonstrations of how to outline a topic, prepare a bibliography, use encyclopedias or other references, find great circle routes and measure distance on a globe, conduct an interview, or use a loom.

Case analysis of issues, problems, events, or situations, with attention to description of the issue, review of evidence or facts, identification of values involved, such as equal rights, various positions and consequences of each, and reasons for a judgment or decision.

Feedback to aid learning and achieve desired standards of performance by reviewing standards, making suggestions in oral and written form, discussing difficulties that arise, suggesting corrective procedures, providing worksheets, and having students help each other in collaborative learning activities.

Instructional cues to direct learning, including verbal cues such as directions, suggestions, questions, and explanations and nonverbal cues that call for the use of tactile and visual senses such as models, photographs, drawings, sketches, diagrams, and maps.

Discussion Guidelines

One of the most valuable group activities is discussion. Discussion is used to clarify objectives, introduce topics, answer questions, make plans, formulate work standards, analyze issues and problems, make decisions, and evaluate learning. Students observe social amenities, share thoughts and feelings, delegate responsibilities for individual and group work, and learn to respect the rights of others to express themselves. Teachers can observe originality of contributions, sharing of ideas, respect for the opinions of others, consideration of differing points of view, and shyness, boldness, and the like, and can give special help as individual needs arise.

The teacher has a crucial role in group discussion. A supportive atmosphere is essential so that all children will feel that their contributions are valued by the teacher and the group. Shy children should be encouraged, and children who tend to monopolize the discussion should be guided in learning to share discussion time with others. The topic to be discussed should be clarified and kept in focus. The teacher should also call for questions, illustrations, and comments as particular items need clarification and should allow adequate time for thinking about the points made and questions raised. The group should avoid such pitfalls as not sticking to the point, failing to clarify the topic, wasting time on side issues and repetitious comments, failing to listen, embarrassing participants by rejecting their contributions, and allowing a few individuals to dominate discussion. Guidelines such as those in Charts 4.1 through 4.3

What planning is needed for this group activity? What questions should guide students' observation? Alameda County Schools

are useful in various grade levels. The importance of listening should be stressed, as noted in Chart 4.4.

Discussion should not be limited to interaction between the teacher and a few individuals. Chart 4.5 illustrates a pattern of discussion that limits interaction. The teacher raises a question and a student responds. The teacher comments or raises another question and calls on another student. The same question-answer recitation pattern continues. Although this pattern is useful at times—as in eliciting information needed for an activity, reviewing key ideas, or achieving other objectives that require close teacher direction—it should not be used all the time.

In sharp contrast is discussion characterized by interaction among group members, as shown in Chart 4.6. Here the teacher or discussion leader raises a question or makes a comment and several participants respond before the leader intervenes. This pattern brings out a variety of ideas and stimulates questions. It encourages initiative and enables children to build on each other's contributions.

Students need to develop skill in leading and taking part in small-group discussions, particularly in intermediate and upper grades. The objective may be to brain-

Discussion in Primary Grades	Discussion in Intermediate Grades	Discussion in Upper Grades	Listening in Discussions
1. Take turns. 2. Help make plans. 3. Listen to others.	1. Help state the problem. 2. Give your ideas. 3. Consider other ideas. 4. Listen carefully. 5. Help to make a plan.	1. State problems clearly. 2. Stick to the point. 3. Be a good listener. 4. Make a contribution. 5. Weigh the evidence. 6. Ask questions on issues. 7. Help in making decisions. 8. Help in summarizing.	1. Get the topic clearly in mind. 2. Raise your hand if you cannot hear. 3. Note points made by others. 4. Make your points when they fit in. 5. Listen to others as you want them to listen to you.
Chart 4.1	Chart 4.2	Chart 4.3	Chart 4.4

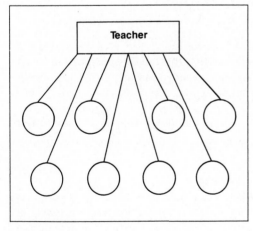

Chart 4.5

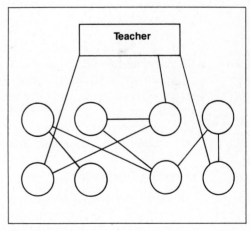

Chart 4.6

storm ideas, explore an issue in a buzz session, plan a panel or round-table presentation, or find ways to solve a problem.

Using Questions to Improve Discussion

The following general guidelines should be followed as questions are used in discussion. The attention of the class is held by asking the question and then calling on a student. A question is not repeated but may be rephrased if a student cannot respond, or another student may be asked to answer it. Individual differences are considered so that each student is challenged to think but no one is pushed beyond his or her capabilities. Efforts are made to call on as many students as possible, and interaction among students is encouraged. Students are encouraged to add comments to each others' contributions and to raise questions for the group to consider. Getting side-tracked is avoided by planning for a sequence of questions that will move the discussion in desired directions yet take account of students' questions and their need for elaboration or further development of aspects of the topic. Unwarranted and excessive praise after each response is avoided because repeated use of such expressions as "excellent" and "very good" is self-defeating. Cuing may be used to help a student who has a partial answer; for example, the teacher may ask the student to recall a similar event, give a hint, suggest a synonym for a needed term, or point to a picture or a chart that provides a clue. Sufficient wait-time is provided so that students can reflect before responding and thereby improve the quality of their contributions to discussion.

Questions may be sequenced according to cognitive levels, as noted in chapter 2 and as shown by these examples.

Knowledge: What do you recall about early settlements in Ohio?

Comprehension: Who can summarize the main features of early settlements?

Application: How can we use this information to study western settlements?

Analysis: What are the main parts of this reading on western settlements?

Synthesis: How can we portray western settlements on a mural?

Evaluation: What were the best and poorest features of western settlements?

Three types of questions should be used to guide discussion, as shown in Figure 4.1.[2] Questions related to *content* are basic in the sense that they are designed in terms of concepts and main ideas under study. Questions related to the *structure* of discussion are designed to guide concept formation, interpretation of data, and use of high-level thinking skills. Questions related to *students' comments* are designed to develop a positive classroom climate and give support and encouragement to students. Additional examples are given in the following chapters.

Evaluating Discussion

Both the teacher and the group should evaluate discussion, giving specific attention to points and problems as they arise. The teacher should keep in mind both the essential elements of effective discussion and the maturity of students. The discussion itself can be appraised in terms of the items listed in charts in the preceding sections. Evaluation can be sharpened by taping a discussion and having students listen to the playback.

In addition to group evaluation, the teacher should do ongoing evaluation and follow-up with individual guidance. Checklist 4.1 includes key points to keep in mind in appraising students' discussion skills. Many students in middle and upper grades can use the checklist for self-evaluation.

---

[2]Adapted from Helen McGinnis, Director, *Retrieval: A Social Sciences Handbook for Teachers,* Social Science Project, Area III Superintendents (Sacramento, CA: County Office of Education, 1972).

PLANNING QUESTIONS TO GUIDE DISCUSSION.

QUESTIONS RELATED TO CONTENT

Open-ended questions invite participation and elicit divergent responses: What do you remember about _____? How many different ways can you think of to _____? What parts of _____ will be most interesting?

Specifying questions focus attention and elicit convergent responses: What steps were taken to _____? How are _____ and _____ alike? Different? What were the main reasons for (or causes of) _____?

Probing questions call for additions, explanations, alternatives, and deeper thinking: What are other possible reasons for _____? What is a another explanation for _____? What are possible underlying motives for _____?

Clarifying questions focus on the meaning of terms and statements: What do you mean by _____? What are examples of _____? Who can state it in your own words?

QUESTIONS TO STRUCTURE THE DISCUSSION

Focusing questions guide thinking step-by-step: What did you find? Which items can be grouped together? Why? What is a good name for the group?

Refocusing questions bring students back to the topic: What is the point we are discussing? Who can state the focus of this discussion? Can we wait on that and get more examples of _____?

Lifting questions shift thinking from recalling to higher levels: What do you recall about _____? How can we group (classify) _____? What is likely to happen if _____? What is your evaluation of _____?

QUESTIONS RELATED TO STUDENTS' COMMENTS

Accepting questions or comments help students who repeat items or wander: Interesting point, Ben. Can we come back to that later? Have we already listed that? Let's check. You seem to agree with what Joe said?

Supporting questions help shy children and those who make errors or have difficulty in making a point: Can we look that up later? Can you tell us more about _____? What is your own feeling about it?

Encouraging questions bring silent students into the discussion: Has anyone else something to say about _____? Can someone who hasn't had a turn add to that? Who has a question about any points made so far?

Figure 4.1

Small-Group Activities

Small-group activities are needed to carry out work planned by the whole group and to meet special needs and interests of students. Examples are:

Investigating topics, problems, questions, and hypotheses raised in class discussion through interviews, library research, and use of materials in study centers

Collecting pictures, stories, articles, postcards, objects, and other items related to questions under study

Making maps, charts, graphs, labels, dioramas, murals, clay and papier-mâché figures, instruments, objects needed in dramatizations, booklets, displays, corner arrangements, and plans for reporting and sharing

---

Checklist 4–1
GROWTH IN DISCUSSION SKILLS

Note: Check each child two or three times during the term to see if growth is taking place.

Behaviors to Be Checked   *Names of Children*

Helps define the topic				
Sticks to the topic				
Is an interested and willing listener				
Interjects ideas at appropriate points				
Considers ideas contrary to his or her own				
Tries to clarify, not "win" arguments				
Does not repeat ideas given by others				
Gets to the point without delay				
Speaks so all can hear				
Uses appropriate language				
Uses concepts accurately				
Helps evaluate discussion				

Small-group activities are usually coordinated so that each group makes a contribution to the work of the class. On field trips, for example, the class may be divided into four or five groups to obtain information on different questions. Several groups may be set up to interview different individuals. Parts of murals, time lines, bulletin board arrangements, scrapbooks, and other projects may be handled by designated groups.

Growth in Group-Work Skills

The growth and development of group-work skills from a beginning phase to an advanced phase is shown in Chart 4.7.[3] Items in the beginning phases should be

[3]Grateful acknowledgment is made to Dr. Ruth Grossman, City University of New York, City College, for this chart.

Developing Group Work Skills: A Continuum of Skills

	Beginning Phase	Intermediate Phase	Advanced Phase
Objectives	Brief, specific	→ Longer, yet directed	→ Long, more complex
Planning	Planned primarily by the teacher	→ Planned jointly by the teacher and pupils	→ Planned primarily by pupils
Duration	Short, one or two days	→ Longer, several days	→ Several days to several weeks
Materials and Sources of Data	Use of single source or few sources	→ Varied sources and materials	→ Variety of media and materials
Organization, Interaction	Informal, parallel activities, little interaction	→ Chairperson selected, tasks varied and assigned, some interaction	→ Chairperson or coordinator, much interaction in all phases
Reports	Parallel reports, or one student reporting with others filling in	→ Each member reports, or pupils share in reporting pooled information	→ Synthesis of information in one report; planned and given by the group
Evaluation	Informal, emphasis on sharing of best ideas	→ Attention to both content and procedures, self-evaluation	→ Emphasis on self-evaluation of activity in greater depth

Chart 4.7

emphasized in the early grades with all students and in later grades with students who are inexperienced in group work. Students should be guided to move to the intermediate and advanced phases by being given instruction on the necessary skills. By the time children reach the middle and upper grades they should be able to work at the advanced phase.

Space Arrangements for Group Work

Group work of all types is most productive when space arrangements can be made to accommodate groups of varying sizes. Open-space schools provide an unlimited number of arrangements. Single classrooms with moveable furniture can also provide a high degree of flexibility, as Chart 4.8 shows. Notice the spaces provided for learning centers, storage of unit materials, and group activities.

Guidelines for Small-Group Activities

Initiating Small-Group Work

Guidelines for organizing and starting committees and forming other small working groups are as follows:

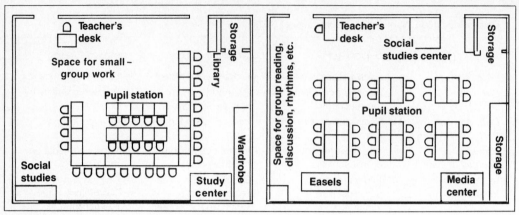

Chart 4.8

1. Make two analyses before starting group work. First, identify individuals who can work well together so that the first attempt at group work will be successful and serve as a model for other groups. Second, identify specific needs for productive small-group work directly related to the unit under study. Be sure to provide sufficient materials that each member can use, including audio and pictorial resources for those unable to use reading materials.

2. Plan to begin with one group. Clarify the task, directions to be followed, materials to be used, and working space. Select a recorder whose role is to note the group's task and what each member is to do. At the end of the work period the recorder should note what was accomplished and what still needs to be done. By reviewing the recorder's notes the teacher can monitor progress and identify students who are and are not staying on task, how materials are being used, and other needs.

3. After the rest of the class is busy at work, take the small group to the work area, clarify what is to be done, and see that they are off to a good start. Provide supervision as needed during the work period.

4. After the task is completed, guide the sharing of the group's efforts with the class. Discuss procedures used as well as outcomes, giving attention to any problems that arose and suggesting ways to prevent them in the future. Summarize standards that similar groups can use.

5. Make plans for other working groups in a similar fashion. Move from one group to two or more as needs for group work became clear and children assume the necessary responsibilities. Have worthwhile independent activities ready for children who become overstimulated in small-group work and are not ready to assume a role in group activities.

6. Move from group to group as needed to supervise and direct. Note ideas that provide more effective ways of working together for the follow-up evaluation.

7. As the class members develop group-work skills, provide them with more freedom to work on their own. Arrange groups so that children who are advanced in group-work skills can assume leadership in helping others and in keeping the

group moving in profitable directions. Give close supervision to any children who continue to have difficulty working with others.

Organizing Cooperative Learning Groups

To organize effective groups the teacher must consider not only the job to be done but also needs of individual students to develop leadership and followership, their readiness for the activity, and compatability among students. Many teachers, therefore, assign students to small groups. However, students should be allowed to select groups at times when interest in an activity is a key factor and students are ready and able to handle group tasks. When special topics are to be researched in reading materials, it is wise to use reading groups and to provide materials on different reading levels.

A variety of teams may be used to serve such purposes as helping each member of the team, preparing and sharing reports, having periodic tournament games, and motivating learning through constructive competition. Emphasis should be given to positive team rewards, individual accountability, and equal opportunities for all team members to succeed.

Examples of cooperative learning groups are: Students Team-Achievement Divisions (STAD), in which students complete worksheets and are tested and scores are determined by each student's performance; Teams-Games-Tournament (TGT), which is like STAD except weekly tournaments replace quizzes; Jigsaw, in which students become "experts" on a topic and teach it to others and team members are tested individually; Group Investigation, in which members plan, complete, and report on a topic; Learning Together, in which assignment sheets are completed; Coop-Coop, in which there is cooperation between groups as well as within groups; Taking Turns, in which members take turns in making written or oral reports; and many variations of the preceding examples (Slavin, 1990). Other examples are given in Figure 4.2 and in chapter references. Charts 4.9 and 4.10 contain guidelines and questions to discuss with students.

Cooperative Learning	Learning Together
Clarify the group's goal so that every one knows what is to be done.	What is our goal? What are the main parts of our task?
Relate individual goals to the group's goal.	How can we think together about ways to proceed?
Discuss ways to use critical and creative thinking skills.	What critical/creative and other thinking skills can be used?
Clarify rules and procedures to be followed.	What can each individual do to help achieve our goal?
Discuss each person's role and how members depend on each other.	How can thinking aloud and thinking about our thinking help?
Evaluate continuously and on completion of the task.	How can we evaluate and make improvement as we work?

Chart 4.9   Chart 4.10

The groups summarized in Figure 4.2 are used to report to the class on selected topics.

Illustrative rules to guide brainstorming and buzz sessions, and sample questions for brainstorming, are presented in Figure 4.3.

SYMPOSIUM

The chair introduces the topic and each of the five or six speakers. Each speaker has three to five minutes on one aspect of the topic. The audience is invited to ask questions after the last speaker.

PANEL DISCUSSION

The chair explains the topic, identifies issues involved, calls on panel members, directs discussion, and summarizes ideas.

Each panel member informally presents ideas on the problem and a point of view on each issue as it is raised by the chair.

The chair sees to it that all panel members participate, that no one takes too much time, and that all points of view are expressed.

After summarizing key points and different views, the chair invites questions from the class.

ROUND TABLE

The chair introduces the topic, invites discussion, and summarizes main ideas and differences in points of view.

The three or four participants talk about the problem, challenge each other on differences in views, and state their own positions.

The chair asks for clarification of views and requests evidence or reasons for positions, viewpoints, or conclusions.

The audience is invited to put questions to participants, limiting them to the topic under discussion.

BUZZ GROUP

The class is divided into five or six groups to discuss a question, analyze a problem, brainstorm ideas, or clarify an idea or issue.

Each member of the group expresses thoughts and feelings freely and informally, adhering to standards on working quietly and taking turns.

A member of each group is selected to report to the class on ideas generated by the group.

PROBLEM SOLVING GROUPS

The problem is described and five or six groups are set up to propose solutions.

A leader and recorder are appointed, or each group chooses them.

Each group proposes one or more feasible solutions and lists them in order of priority.

Recorders report to the class for discussion and evaluation of proposals and for placing them in order of priority.

Figure 4.2

BRAINSTORMING RULES	WHAT SHOULD WE BRAINSTORM	BUZZ SESSION RULES
Listen to and obey the chair!	Possible solutions to a problem?	State your ideas when called on by the chair!
State whatever you think!	Differing points of view on an an issue?	Stick to the topic assigned to your group!
Do not criticize any ideas!		State your ideas clearly!
Be brief and to the point!	Variety of alternatives? Realistic possibilities? Best choices?	Listen to others and do not repeat their ideas!
Give the note taker time to record your ideas!	Steps to take to do a task?	Help to summarize best ideas!
Give others a chance to state their ideas!	Groups of items as very interesting, interesting, not interesting?	Think of ways to improve!
	A list of other brainstorming possibilities?	

Figure 4.3

Planning

Initial planning is carried out in group discussion, and special attention is given to questions, problems, and responsibilities. Replanning is necessary as new needs arise and as special problems surface. Attention may well be given to such items as stating goals, devising ways to secure data, setting up work standards, deciding on procedures, considering ways to secure and use materials, overcoming obstacles, helping others, clarifying roles, evaluating proposals, asking for help, and assigning places to work. Guidelines are:

1. Encourage everyone to take part so that the best ideas of each member are secured and a feeling of responsibility for completing the activity is developed.
2. Consider problems and questions expressed by students. Bring to their attention any problems they have overlooked.
3. Obtain constructive suggestions for work standards, use of materials, and roles of group members. Redirect negative comments into positive suggestions.
4. Guide planning to assure success, anticipate difficulties that may arise, and clarify what each member is to do.
5. Make records for use in group action, such as charts of work standards, directions, worksheets, study guides, and diagrams.
6. At the end of planning discussions, check to see that each student understands what to do, where to do it, how to proceed, materials to use, work standards to follow, and how to get help if needed.

Guiding Activities

As children engage in group activities, the teacher should gather information to use in group evaluation, observing such behavior as acceptance of responsibilities, cooperation, courtesy, and self-control. During group work the teacher has many opportunities to move about and to give help as needed. One child may have difficulty locating material in a given reference; another may have difficulty using tools and materials. By giving judicious assistance, the teacher can make sure that effective learning takes place.

Attention should also be given to the various materials being used, techniques that need to be improved, and misconceptions or erroneous ideas that arise. For example, in a unit on pioneer life, the teacher noticed during a research period that several youngsters were having difficulty using the table of contents; others were not sure of the topics to locate in the index. Notes were made for use in a later discussion that centered on skills involved in the location of materials.

The teacher should also note how children use the work standards that they have helped to set. Commendation may be given to those who carry out group-made standards and who help others to do so. Occasionally the teacher will have to ask a child to stop an activity for a few minutes and consider whether his or her behavior conforms to the group standard. In a few instances some children must be excluded from the group until they realize that they must accept all the responsibilities involved in the activity. Following the work period, time should be given to a careful reconsideration of the group standards and how well each member of the group helped maintain them.

Particular attention must be given to those few youngsters who appear unsure of what they should do in an activity. If the planning period has been carefully organized, few children will lack a clear sense of purpose. During the work period children who do not have clear purposes in mind may need further guidance. Classmates frequently volunteer to help others who are not sure of what they should do to complete an activity. This is a good indication of cooperative behavior and should be encouraged. More important, however, is careful planning at the beginning of the work period to assure that all members of the group participate.

Several techniques may be used to deal with conflicts that arise within groups. Standards of work and conduct can be reviewed, explanations can be given to clarify misunderstanding of rules or roles, and direct suggestions can be made to correct obvious infractions of standards. Time may be taken to discuss a difficulty, to role-play or negotiate a "fair" solution, or to work out a compromise. In serious cases, a "cooling-off" period may be needed during which students do independent work. The group activity is not resumed until the conflict is resolved.

Other ways to improve behavior in group work are: provide extra rewards to winning teams; give extra points for cooperativeness and other good behavior; switch partners or change team membership if poor behavior continues; and commend team members who work well with others (Slavin, 1990).

Evaluation

Group evaluation is essential, from initial definition of problems to appraisal of the effectiveness of group work. During evaluation, the group answers such questions as these: Is each individual doing his or her part? Are the plans effective? Are leadership responsibilities being carried out? Are our objectives being achieved? Are additional resources needed? What steps should be taken next? In making appraisals, the group may use discussions and charts or checklists, as in Checklist 4.2, refer to a log or diary

Checklist 4–2
WHICH OF THESE DO YOU DO TO IMPROVE GROUP WORK?

___ Share leadership	___ Help clarify points	___ Encourage others
___ Take turns	___ Compromise as needed	___ Consider feelings
___ Set standards	___ Stick to standards	___ Stick to the task
___ Cooperate	___ Take responsibility	___ Help evaluate

of activities, get assistance from the teacher, examine work materials, or use other evaluative procedures. Committees and other small groups may use "quality circles" to evaluate participation, suggest improvements, and develop self-evaluation skills.

Committees

Committees should be congenial working groups interested in the job to be done and balanced in terms of needed abilities and talents. The leader may be selected by the group or the teacher after due consideration of needed qualifications. Necessary materials and a place to work should be provided. Some teachers demonstrate committee work to indicate guidelines for students to follow, either by selecting four to six students or by using the class as a committee with the teacher as leader. Standards should be developed and listed, as shown in Figure 4.4.

Games

A variety of games may be used, as illustrated here, ranging from social studies bees to computer-based games. How might you adapt them for use in a unit? What other games might students prepare for small groups?

COMMITTEE MEMBERS	COMMITTEE LEADERS	COMMITTEE REPORTS
1. Know what to do.	1. Keep the main job in mind.	1. Stick to the questions.
2. Divide the work.	2. Get ideas from all members.	2. Use pictures, objects, and maps.
3. Do each job well.	3. See that each member has a job.	3. Be ready to answer questions.
4. Discuss problems quietly.	4. Be fair and do not talk all the time.	4. State ways to improve.
5. Plan the report carefully.	5. Urge everyone to do his or her best.	
	6. Say *our* committee, not *my* committee.	

FIGURE 4.4

GAMES FOR SMALL GROUPS

Social Studies Bees

Have small groups of four to five students select social studies words for a spelling bee. Or have a defining bee, in which words are presented and members of teams are asked to define them, or a geography bee with questions on places being studied.

Fruits and Vegetables in Alphabetical Order

Arrange four teams and tell them that each member will have a turn to name one fruit or vegetable, beginning with the letter *A*. Record responses for each team. A member who cannot think of one may pass. After no one can think of any more names to add that begin with the letter *A*, move on to *B*. Continue through other letters of the alphabet. Variations are to name states, capitals, notable people, or other items in alphabetical order.

Who Am I?

Have members of teams respond to such questions as

I help build houses by putting in pipes. Who am I?
I help build houses by putting in wires. Who am I?
I draw plans for houses. Who am I?
I make fireplaces. Who am I?

Similar questions can be asked for other workers, including police officers, firefighters, postal service workers, city employees, and office workers. In later grades questions can be asked about explorers, colonists, pioneers, scouts, presidents, and notable men and women.

Computer-Based Games

Arrange pairs or teams of students to use such computer programs as the following in a game in which individual or group scores are kept.

U.S. Map	*Uncle Sam's Jigsaw*	*Game of the States*
U.S. Cities	*Regions of the United States*	*Continents*
History Star	*Thirteen Colonies*	*Meet the Presidents*
Oregon	*Geography Search*	*Transcontinental Railroad*
Lincoln's Decisions	*Trailwest*	*The Match Game*
Lemonade	*Factory*	*Market Place*
States & Traits	*Road Rally, USA*	*Cross Country USA*
Voyages of Discovery	*Countries and Capitals*	*European Nations & Locations*

Study Guides for Cooperative Learning

Study guides enable cooperative learning groups to be more productive. Several types of study guides can be used, ranging from those that contain questions on a single source of information to those created by students themselves.

Guide for a Single Source of Information

The following example illustrates an easy-to-prepare study guide based on readings about the expansion of U.S. territory. Groups had been set up to find out about acquisition of the Louisiana, Florida, Oregon, and other territories. The same format may be used for a film, a filmstrip, or some other data source.

STUDY GUIDE FOR THE ACQUISITION OF LOUISIANA

A. Answer the questions listed below as you read pages 114–17 in *The Country*.

　　1. Who had claimed the territory first?
　　2. Who had it when the United States wanted it?
　　3. Why did the United States want it?

　　　　Does the group agree on each member's answers to the above questions? If so, proceed to the next questions. If not, reread the section and find out who is right.

B. Discuss these questions in your group and write the answers that members agree are the best.

　　1. Why did some people support acquisition of this territory?
　　2. Why were some people against it?
　　3. How was the territory finally acquired?
　　4. Was it a "good deal" for the United States? Why or why not?

Guides Based on Retrieval Charts

Another type of study guide is based on a retrieval chart. The chart is discussed with the class before teams go to work, and each team is assigned responsibility for one section of the retrieval chart. For example, Chart 4.11 was designed for use in a unit on Latin America. In using such charts, teams of three to five students are set up to gather information on each country. Work may be divided in several ways; some students might gather data on the first three topics, others on agriculture and other economic activities, and so on. Or a team of two to three may find information on economic activities in one country, another team may collect data on education, art, and music, and so on. As the teams report their findings, the information is pooled and displayed on large wall charts.

Retrieval Chart on Latin American Countries

Topics	Argentina	Brazil	Chile	Colombia	Ecuador	Peru
Population						
Area						
Main Regions						
Agriculture						
Manufacturing						
Mining						
Trade						
Transportation						
Education						
Art						
Music						
Form of Government						
Capital						

Chart 4.11

Semantic Maps or Webs

Groups can make a semantic map or web around a concept, question, or other item, as shown in these examples.

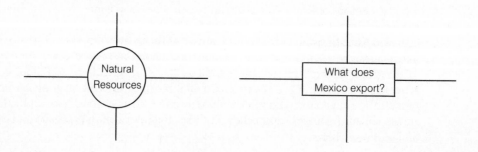

Study Guides Combining Independent and Small-Group Study

A more detailed type of study guide can be used to combine aspects of independent study and small-group study, as illustrated in the sample study guide for lifestyle that follows. Each member of a team or group receives a copy of the guide, uses it to collect information, compares information and answers with other members, makes revisions after small-group discussion, and submits a final report to the teacher. Such a study guide combines the benefits of interacting with others and getting ideas from them with the benefits of independent study. Several small-group sessions may be needed. The groups that used the following study guide held four sessions: one to compare notes on the materials to read, one to discuss and revise responses to the questions, one to compare notes and discuss the follow-up activity, and one to sharpen ideas on evaluation.

STUDY GUIDE FOR LIFESTYLE

Objectives

To state the meaning of lifestyle

To describe the effects of one's lifestyle on the environment

To state changes that may be made in one's lifestyle to improve the environment

Materials

Read one or more of the following books: *At Home around the World*, *People Use the Earth*, *Population, Production, Pollution*, and *The Social Sciences*. Use the index to find the pages on which lifestyle is discussed. Take notes on the filmstrip *Using Our Forest Wisely* when it is shown to the class.

Questions and Activities

1. What do you think *lifestyle* means?
2. Find and write the meaning of lifestyle in one of the readings. How is the meaning like and different from yours?
3. Describe your own lifestyle by completing the following:
   Foods I eat are _____
   Clothes I wear are _____
   Things I do to have fun are _____
   The way I treat other people is _____
   Other aspects of my lifestyle are _____
   Things I do that cause waste pollution are _____
   Things I do that cause noise pollution are _____
   Other things I do that hurt the environment are _____
   Things I do that do not hurt the environment are _____
4. How is your lifestyle like the lifestyle of people described in the reading material? How is it different?

---

5. Which changes in lifestyle noted in the reading materials do you think are most important to help the environment? Why?
6. Which changes in lifestyle do you think are most important in the filmstrip on forests? Why?
7. What changes in your lifestyle should be made to help the environment? Why? Do you think that you will make them? Why or why not?

Follow-up Activity

During the next three days keep a record of your activities, following the form below. (Examples are given in the first box.)

Activities	Energy or Resources Used	Helps the Environment	Hurts the Environment	Type of Pollution
Example: Family picnic	Car and food	No	If we litter	Waste
1.				
2.				
3.				

Using Models as Study Guides

Models of decision making, problem solving, case-study analysis, and other sets of processes may be used by committees set up to consider proposals, solve a problem, analyze a case, or tackle a particular issue. The use of models in groups is most effective after students have considered them in class discussions directed by the teacher. Examples of decision-making and case-analysis models follow. They outline the procedure for a group to follow, focus discussion on key points, and serve as guides for preparing oral and written reports. They may be applied to a variety of issues, proposals, problems, and dilemmas that arise in social studies units.

DECISION-MAKING MODEL

Clarify the Issue or proposal

Discuss and list values (justice, equality, etc.) that are important in this issue.

Discuss alternative decisions and reasons for them.

Discuss the consequences of each alternative.

Select the best alternative in terms of consequences and values.

Summarize reasons for the decision. If there is disagreement, make a minority report.

CASE-ANALYSIS MODEL

Discuss the Issue to be resolved

Determine the facts (evidence) in the case.

Double-check reliability of the facts.

List the facts pro and con (for and against).

Make a decision or judgment after discussing pros and cons.

List reasons for the decision—how justice will be served.

The following lesson plan illustrates one way to guide students to consider alternatives as a part of decision making.

CHARTING ALTERNATIVES

Objective

To describe ways to reach a goal by charting alternatives.

Introduction

Present a problem that can be solved in different ways, such as playground litter cleanup, collecting materials for recycling, or reduction of noise pollution. After the problem is clarified ask the group such questions as these: How can a problem such as this be handled in different ways? Why should different ways be considered?

Development

Select one problem and write it on the chalkboard. Draw a chart such as the one shown below. Ask students to fill in the chart by describing different ways the problem may be solved, evaluating each suggested option and concluding with the expected results.

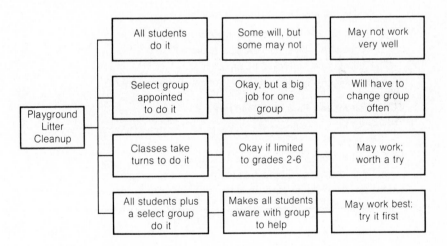

Conclusion and Evaluation

Discuss the value of considering alternative ways to solve problems. Ask students to suggest other problems that might be handled in a similar way. Observe to assess learning.

Follow-up

Ask individual students or committees to apply the procedure to a new problem.

Student-Prepared Guides

A most valuable learning activity is to have students develop their own study guides. Before students begin, the general plan should be discussed with the class; then teams go to work to develop their own detailed plan. Each team answers the questions listed below, then presents the resulting study plan to the teacher or the class for review and improvement. Think of the skills that students must use and the extra learning they may achieve as a result of sharing ideas and creating their own guide!

PLANNING A STUDY GUIDE

Beginning

1. What is the topic of study?
2. What questions should be answered?

Identifying Sources of Information

1. What reading materials in the classroom may be used?
2. What library materials may be used?
3. What people may be interviewed?
4. What other sources may be used?

Collecting and Organizing Information

1. How may note taking and outlining be used?
2. What information should be put on charts?
3. What information should be put on maps?
4. What other ways of organizing information may be used?

Sharing and Reporting Findings

1. What are the main parts? Can the report be organized around questions stated at the beginning?
2. In what order should the parts be placed?
3. What ideas should be put on cards for an oral report?
4. How can pictures, maps, or other items be used to improve the report?

Questions, Activities, and Evaluation

1. Which of the values and the limitations of group work skills do you believe to be most significant? Why? What do you think are some dangers in overemphasizing them at the expense of independent study skills?

2. Note four or five whole-group activities you might use in a unit of your choice. Do the same for small-group or committee activities.

3. Visit a classroom and use the following questions to observe and analyze the teacher's role in guiding discussion. Was the initiating question clear? How did it

give a focus to discussion? Note how each of the following types of questions was used:

   a. Open-ended, specifying, clarifying, and probing questions related to content of the discussion

   b. Focusing, refocusing, and lifting questions related to the structure and flow of discussion

   c. Accepting, supporting, and encouraging questions related to students' comments

On what level(s) was the discussion held? How did students respond to any shifts that were made to raise the level?

4. Select one small-group activity and make a plan for using it in a unit of your choice. Specify how you would select students, initiate the activity, guide it, and evaluate it.

5. Make a plan for a study guide that you might use to improve learning in small-group work, relating it to a unit of work.

6. Mark your position on the following by writing A if you agree, D if you disagree, and ? if you are uncertain. Discuss your views with a colleague and explore reasons for any differences.

   _____ a. Small groups used for instruction in reading should also be used in the social studies.

   _____ b. Students who do not follow group standards for committees should be given individual assignments.

   _____ c. In general, a teacher should assign students to groups to assure compatibility among members.

   _____ d. The chair for a committee should be chosen by committee members.

   _____ e. A teacher should have good discipline and control of whole-class activities before starting small-group work.

   _____ f. The same care that is given to planning lessons based on textbooks and other materials should be given to planning group activities.

   _____ g. Teachers who are serious about "back to basics" should give little or no time to small-group activities.

References

Adams, Dennis M., and Mary E. Hamm, *Cooperative Learning.* Springfield, IL: Charles C. Thomas, 1990. Guidelines and examples.

Barnes, Buckley, and Gail O'Farrell, "Cooperative Learning Strategies," *Social Studies and the Young Learner,* 2 (January/February 1990), 4 pp. Pull-out section.

Boschee, Floyd, *Grouping = Growth.* Dubuque, IA: Kendall/Hunt, 1990. Objectives and strategies.

"Cooperative Learning, "*Educational Leadership,*" 47 (December 1989, January 1990), 4–67. Special section: articles; bibliography; variety of examples.

Curwin, Richard L., and Allen N. Mendler, *Discipline With Dignity.* Alexandria, VA: Association for Supervision and Curriculum Development, 1989, Guidelines.

Ellis, Arthur K. *Teaching and Learning Elementary Social Studies* (4th ed.). Needham, MA: Allyn & Bacon, 1991.

Hilke, Eileen V., *Cooperative Learning.* Bloomington, IN: Phi Delta Kappa, 1990. Basic procedures.

Johnson, David W., and Roger T. Johnson, *Learning Together and Alone* (2nd ed.). Englewood Cliffs, NJ: Prentice-Hall, 1986. Specific suggestions.

Slavin, Robert E. *Cooperative Learning: Theory, Research, and Practice.* Englewood Cliffs, NJ: Prentice-Hall, 1990. Guidelines for various groups.

Steinbrink, John E., and Robert M. Jones, "Team Learning in Social Studies," *Social Studies and the Young Learner,* 2 (January/February 1990), 3–5.

Van Cleaf, D.W., *Action in Elementary Social Studies,* Needham, MA: Allyn & Bacon, 1991.

Welton, David A., and John T. Mallan, *Children and Their World.* (3rd ed.). Boston: Houghton Mifflin, 1988. Chapter on group-based activities.

Planning and Providing Individual Learning Activities

CHAPTER 5

Objective and Related Focusing Questions

To describe guidelines and strategies for providing instruction that is individualized and enhances each student's learning:

- What strategies are useful in identifying individual needs and differences, and in making plans to accommodate them?

- How can learning centers, contracts, activity cards, modules, worksheets, reports, and other independent study activities be used to enhance learning?

- How can social studies reading and reporting be individualized?

- What procedures may be used to teach children to individualize for themselves?

- How can special needs of gifted, less able, disadvantaged, learning disabled, emotionally disturbed, and physically impaired students who are mainstreamed into a classroom be met?

Individual learning activities are needed to achieve objectives, accomodate individual differences among students, and personalize students' learning. Students can be challenged and guided to achieve levels consistent with their capabilities. Questions and problems that flow from group learning activities can be pursued in depth and shared with others. As a student said, "It's great to study a topic and report back to the class."

Point of View

Teachers who truly value differences and recognize the unique characteristics of each child are the ones who excel at providing individual learning activities. They care deeply about all children and can see the unique characteristics of each child, whether average, physically impaired, disadvantaged, less able, or gifted. They believe that each child's maximum growth is more important than minimum standards for the group, that some children can go far beyond grade standards, whereas others can make substantial progress only if instruction is geared to their needs. They use diagnostic evaluation to identify needs, set attainable expectations, critically select media and activities, vary time and supervision, recognize differences in learning styles, and assess outcomes in terms of students' abilities.[1]

Mainstreaming

The mainstreaming of students in need of special educational services has further highlighted the value of planning to provide for individual differences. When children with special needs are placed in regular classes, the learning of all students is enriched. Schools that mainstream students foster democratic attitudes and positive self-concepts and discourage negative labeling of others, problems that often arise when children with special needs are isolated in separate classes. Those who are mainstreamed benefit from acceptance and from the variety of role models they are exposed to. They also benefit from more positive expectancies on the part of teachers, parents, and other students. The social studies provide special opportunities because of the variety of activities and materials available for individual learning.

Individualized Education Programs (IEP) are prepared for students mainstreamed into classrooms as required by PL 49-142 and school district regulations. The IEP for each student should include objectives, activities, materials, and evaluation procedures that are selected and adapted to meet individual needs. Strategies in this chapter may be incorporated into an IEP, using forms provided by local schools. The assistance of specialists is available in many schools districts.

[1]For a review of individualized systems of instruction, see James A. Kulik, "Individualized Systems of Instruction," *Encyclopedia of Educational Research* (5th ed.). New York: Macmillan, 1982, 851–58. For planning based on the concept of mastery learning, see Benjamin S. Bloom, *Human Characteristics and School Learning.* New York: McGraw-Hill, 1976.

Planning Guidelines

Various approaches to individualized instruction commonly follow guidelines that include management and instructional planning—two components of effective teaching. Checklist 5.1 summarizes guidelines for planning individual learning activities. Notice the flow from needs assessment and diagnostic evaluation, to a variety of strategies, to evaluation of learning. Also note that both management and instructional aspects of teaching are included.

Checklist 5–1
PLANNING TO ACCOMMODATE INDIVIDUAL DIFFERENCES

Needs Assessment and Objectives

What special needs have been identified in terms of social studies objectives?

_____ Knowledge   _____ Skills   _____ Attitudes   _____ Participation
_____ Other: _____

Diagnostic Evaluation

What are individual needs, strengths, weaknesses, and achievements?

_____ Interests   _____ Capabilities   _____ Reading level
_____ Problems   _____ Talents   _____ Learning style
_____ Other: _____

Use of Multimedia Materials

What instructional materials are available for individual use?

_____ Reading materials on different levels   _____ Activity cards
_____ Learning kits or packages   _____ Practice materials
_____ Rewritten material   _____ Community resources
_____ Library materials   _____ Individual contracts
_____ Audiovisual materials   _____ Taped material
_____ Study guides and modules   _____ Computer programs
_____ Other: _____

Classroom Environment

How should the classroom environment be organized?

_____ Learning centers   _____ Classroom library   _____ Viewing station
_____ Listening post   _____ Computer station   _____ Interest centers
_____ Other: _____

(continued)

Checklist 5.1 *(continued)*

Use of a Variety of Learning Activities

What intake, organizing, applicative, and creative activities should be used?

_____ Reading   _____ Listening   _____ Word processing

_____ Writing   _____ Reporting   _____ Making charts

_____ Dramatizing   _____ Role taking   _____ Mapping

_____ Drawing   _____ Interviewing   _____ Making webs

_____ Other: _____

Organization of Collaborative Learning Groups

What groups should be organized to promote individual learning?

_____ Reading groups   _____ Groups needing special instruction

_____ Interest groups   _____ Groups to make maps and other items

_____ Committees   _____ Groups of two or three for team learning

_____ Other: _____

Provision for Individual Study

What variations and adjustments can be made in individual study activities?

_____ Topics to investigate   _____ Use of computer   _____ Type of report

_____ Sources of data   _____ People to interview _____ Use of library

_____ Individual contracts   _____ Worksheets   _____ Activity cards

_____ Other: _____

Provision for Individual Tutorial

How can selected students be provided with individual tutoring?

_____ By the teacher   _____ By a teacher aide   _____ By worksheets

_____ By a parent   _____ By a student   _____ By computer

_____ Other: _____

Teacher Guidance and Supervision

What variations and adjustments should be made in the role of the teacher?

_____ Questions   _____ Individual help   _____ Evaluation of
                                                    learning
_____ Directions   _____ Assistance to
                           groups   _____ Parental help
_____ Explanations
                     _____ Class discusssion _____ Home visitation
_____ Discipline

_____ Other: _____

(continued)

Checklist 5.1 *(continued)*

Allocation of Time

What variations in time should be made for individuals and groups?

_____ Introducing   _____ Developing   _____ Completing
       topics   readiness   activites

_____ Making maps or   _____ Preparing oral and   _____ Making models
       other items   written reports   or other items

_____ Other: _____

Standards and Evaluation

What variations and adjustments should be made in evaluation of learning?

_____ Vocabulary   _____ Concepts   _____ Main ideas

_____ Thinking skills   _____ Study skills   _____ Values

_____ Self-evaluation   _____ Testing   _____ Rating devices

_____ Other: _____

Key Aspects of Individualizing

Identifying Individual Needs

Diagnostic evaluation should include such techniques as observing students, using rating devices, reviewing portfolios of work, and giving tests. Cumulative records should be reviewed and needs informally diagnosed during actual classroom activities. For example, as children engage in group planning, discussion, and evaluation, the teacher can identify interests, difficulties, language skills, and levels of understanding about selected topics. As children observe and interpret pictures, maps, graphs, and other resources, the teacher can identify those who need special help and those who have attained adequate achievement levels. As students prepare reports, make murals, dramatize activities, and engage in other experiences, the teacher can detect interests, needs for further study, and misconceptions.

Data obtained from tests should always be interpreted with caution. It is well known that intelligence tests do not give an accurate assessment of the ability of students from disadvantaged homes and neighborhoods, and that they are culturally biased. Because tests and inventories designed to measure personality, attitudes, and social adjustment are even less reliable than achievement and intelligence tests, their data should be interpreted in light of continuing direct study of children as they work in the classroom.

The limiting of learning because of labels and classifications of students should be avoided. For example, a student who is classified as less able, disadvantaged, or otherwise handicapped may thereafter be presumed to have all the characteristics of that classification, and as a consequence instruction is shaped to fit the classification rather than the individual. Expectations may be set too low, with no challenge to move to higher levels of development or attainment. In one school district, a minority child from a disadvantaged neighborhood was placed in a fourth-grade classroom after the school psychologist and the teacher had used intelligence and achievement test data to establish what seemed to them to be reasonable expectations. But because of the ways he responded to questions, selected materials in the library corner, and participated in group discussion, the teacher realized that the child could reach higher levels in reading and other activities. Had the teacher not been alert, the student could have continued indefinitely at a low level of learning.

Give special attention to "at-risk" students—those who may fail or drop out, feel inadequate, have low self-esteem, and are from impoverished or disadvantaged homes. These students need activities that they can complete with success, cooperative work with supportive peers, continuing encouragement by the teacher, and guidance in setting realistic objectives.

Diagnostic evaluation may include self-evaluation by students, supplemented by teacher observation and evaluation. The following examples of devices may be modified as needed to encourage self-evaluation of interests, background knowledge on a theme or topic, and other items.

WHICH SKILLS CAN YOU USE WELL IN OUR UNIT?

Underline the ones on which you need help.

Listening	Following directions	Outlining	Using the computer
Reading	Discussing topics	Taking notes	Using the library
Speaking	Investigating topics	Reporting	Making maps
Writing	Working in groups	Interviewing	Making graphs

WHICH ONES CAN YOU USE TO AID LEARNING

Underline the ones hardest for you to use.

Individual project	Partner learning	Picture file
Learning center	Interview	Article file
Library research	Computer resources	Microfiche
Field study	Listening post	Reference center
Tutor or aide	Viewing station	*Reader's Guide*

WHICH MODES OF AESTHETIC EXPRESSION CAN YOU USE IN OUR UNIT?

Underline the ones you are best at using.

Drawing	Sculpting	Photography	Weaving	Woodworking
Painting	Making mosaics	Creative writing	Quilting	Stitchery
Modeling	Making murals	Dramatizing	Basketry	Knitting

Learning styles may be identified by using locally available inventories and by observing and questioning students. Questions to discuss with students and suggestions for expanding learning styles are listed below.[2]

Notice the variety of ways to learn that can be used to tailor activities to various learning styles. A key point is to help students use a variety of styles and not be limited to a single one.

WHAT IS YOUR FAVORITE WAY OF LEARNING?

Visual? Seeing pictures, illustrations, demonstrations?
Auditory? Listening to others, hearing recordings?
Kinesthetic? Touching things, doing hands-on activities?
Reading? Getting main ideas, details, answers to questions?
Combination? Using all of the above plus other ways?

EXPAND YOUR LEARNING STYLE!

Learn visually by getting ideas from photos, drawings, demonstrations, and other visual materials.

Learn by listening to others, hearing recordings, and using other auditory materials.

Use both visual and auditory ways of learning as sound films and filmstrips, videocasettes, and other audiovisual materials are used.

Learn by handling models, making things, and other hands-on activities.

Learn through reading by getting an overview, finding main ideas, noting details, and finding answers to questions.

Learn by working with others in various group activities, discovering how others get ideas, and sharing ways you get ideas.

Learn by working on your own, defining the task, sticking to it, and evaluating how well you did it.

Use a combination of the above, sometimes using one or two, other times using several of them to learn new ideas and solve problems.

Some teachers use systems specially designed to accomodate learning styles. For example, the *4MAT System* (McCarthy, 1990) includes four major types of learners: imaginative, analytic, common-sense, and dynamic. Attention is given to use of both hemispheres of the brain—the analytic, serial, and rational left, and the global, visual, and holistic right. Provision is made for concrete experience, reflective observation, abstract conceptualization, and active experimentation. Emphasis is given to personal meaning, content and curriculum, usefulness of learning, and creativity.

[2]For various views of learning styles, see articles in "Learning Styles and the Brain," *Educational Leadership,* (October 1990), 3–80.

Teacher Guidance and Supervision

Variations in teacher guidance range from varying the amount of time to complete individual work to providing different kinds of assistance. For example, one child may need help in settling down to work, another may need help in completing an outline, and a group working on a map may be puzzled about the location of particular items. By moving about the room and observing children at work, a teacher can give guidance when it is needed. Because each child is a unique person, the teacher should tailor his or her approach to fit emotional as well as intellectual needs. A smile, an encouraging comment, or an understanding nod may be just right for one child, whereas another may need a thought-provoking question, a specific suggestion, or direct assistance on a problem.

At times a child may need and should receive a direct answer to a question—how to find a booklet, how to complete an outline, or where to locate particular items on a map. At other times the best answer is another question—Have you checked the study guide? Will the outline form on the chart be useful? Do you think the atlas will be a good source? If a student needs to move ahead, then direct assistance may be given, but if the objective is to improve thinking skills and to help students become more self-directive, then a question or a comment may actually be more helpful.

Also helpful for clarifying meaning is a dialogue between the teacher and a student. Key points may be noted, ideas can be summarized, questions and difficulties can be addressed, and predictions of what may be coming next may be made.

Differing Levels of Conceptualization

There are differences in the cognitive levels at which students raise questions, interpret maps and reading selections, draw inferences, and state generalizations. One student may respond to the questions given in Charts 5.1 and 5.2 by describing activities and obvious features or relationships. Another student may go beyond description to explain complex relationships between items. The questions in Charts 5.1 and 5.2 begin at basic observing or recalling levels and move to interpreting, classifying, and other higher-level processes. One individualizing technique is to ask ques-

---

Interpreting the Map of Mexico
What does each symbol in the key stand for?
Where is the capital? What is its name?
Where are other large cities located?
Where are the main roads?
What relationships can you find between the location of cities and roads?
How are the locations of cities, roads, and mountains interrelated?

Chart 5–1

Main Ideas about Mexican Industries
What data did you find on each industry?
Which facts seem to go together?
What is common or general about them?
Have the common facts and ideas been grouped together?
What can we say in general about each industry?
Do our general statements fit the facts? Are changes needed?
What is the order of importance of the industries? Why?

Chart 5–2

tions on different levels of complexity and accept responses that fit the individual student's capabilities. The teacher may also vary the number of questions or items to be deliberated and vary the depth of analysis expected from students. The important point is to find a way to challenge each student.

The same principles can be applied in adjusting expectations related to using concepts and making generalizations. Varied responses should be expected and accepted from students as they bring facts together and state main ideas. For example, compare the following generalizations, which vary in complexity and generality: (1) People in the home have different jobs. (2) Work is divided in the home and neighborhood. (3) Division of labor helps to get more work done. By accepting generalizations that fit the facts the student has collected, the teacher is recognizing and making an important adjustment to each child's ability.

Providing Different Learning Activities

The variety of learning activities presented in chapter 2 should be reviewed to select those needed to accommodate individual differences. Two approaches are helpful. First, provide activities that students can handle successfully in group work, making contributions to planning, discussion, and evaluation. Second, provide a variety of independent and team activities to meet special needs. Too frequently some students do a single activity over and over because they are good at it. Students who always choose drawing and painting, for example, may miss other needed learning activities.

Learning Centers and Stations

Setting up learning centers and stations helps to individualize instruction and also provides study and work centers for general use. A learning center that includes a variety of materials may be arranged and the materials changed for each unit. Learning stations may be set up to listen to tapes and records, to view slides and filmstrips, to make maps, to construct objects or process materials, to engage in games and simulation, to research and prepare reports on selected topics, or to use computer programs. Reading materials on different levels, task cards, individual activity cards, study guides, and other items designed to meet individual needs of students should be included. Students should be introduced to the materials in each center or station and given procedures for using them and rules to follow. Illustrative guidelines are presented in Charts 5.3 through 5.6.

Choosing and Using Materials

Choose materials you want to use.

Use one item at a time.

Identify ideas to share.

Return the item to its place.

Choose another item. Return it when you are finished.

Chart 5–3

Did You Choose Well?

What ideas did you find?

Which ideas were most interesting? Most useful?

Which ideas should be shared?

Did any problems arise in using materials?

What can you do to avoid or solve them?

Chart 5–4

Using the Listening Center

Have you listened to the following?

Story of what two children did about pollution at home

Report on kinds of waste pollution

Report on steps taken to halt waste pollution in our city

Story of what one group did to help prevent waste pollution

Chart 5–5

Using Materials in the Reading Center

Top shelf: materials for the transportation committee

Middle shelf: materials for the urban renewal committee

Bottom shelf: materials for the pollution committee

On the table: city map for the mapping committee

Chart 5–6

How might you use a learning center to stimulate individual study? Richmond Schools, California

Developing Learning Contracts

One practical means of varying time, providing for choices, and using the other guidelines noted earlier to meet individual needs is to develop learning contracts. A learning contract is an agreement between a student and a teacher stating what the student will do and when it is to be completed. Some teachers use a standard form, while others simply list key items in the contract, as illustrated in these examples.

LEARNING CONTRACT FORM

We do hereby agree that you will do the following by _____.

1. _____
2. _____
3. _____
4. _____
5. _____

_____   _____   _____
Student's Signature   Teacher's Signature   Date

MY LEARNING CONTRACT

I, _____, agree to do the following by _____.

    1. To find information on shipbuilding in Japan in *Japan,* by Cuban and Greenblatt; *Japan,* by Pitts; and *The World Almanac*
    2. To prepare a report on shipbuilding in Japan
    3. To present the report to the class

_____   _____   _____
Student's Signature   Teacher's Signature   Date

Learning contracts may be prepared cooperatively by a student and a teacher, prepared by the teacher to meet a particular need, or prepared by a student to pursue a special interest. Whichever procedure is used, the student should fully understand what is expected and the teacher should be sure that the activities of the contract have value for the student and are not busywork. The following form may be used to guide students' planning.

PLANNING A LEARNING CONTRACT

1. My objectives are (state specific things you plan to accomplish):

2. I will use these materials (list textbooks, references, and other sources):

3. I will find answers to these questions (list questions you plan to answer):

4. I will complete these activities (list mapping, chart making, interviewing, and so on):

5. I will complete the contract by _____.

Signature: _____

Providing Individual Activity Cards or Worksheets

The preceding guidelines can also be applied by preparing a set of individual activity or task cards, as shown in Figure 5.1

Jobs at Home	Neighborhoods	Communication
Who does each job at home?	Which of these are shown in the picture on page 26?	Which of these forms of communication are shown on page 32?

Jobs at Home

Who does each job at home?

Cooking _____
Dusting _____
Vacuuming _____
Making beds _____
Putting toys away _____
Mowing lawn _____

Neighborhoods

Which of these are shown in the picture on page 26?

____ School   ____ Houses
____ Bank   ____ Cars
____ Store   ____ Bakery
____ Boys   ____ Men
____ Girls   ____ Women

Communication

Which of these forms of communication are shown on page 32?

____ Television   ____ Newspapers
____ Radio   ____ Magazine
____ Telephone   ____ Speech
____ Satellite   ____ Signals
____ Telegraph   ____ Signs

Where Are These Located?

Look at the map on page 38. On what streets are these?

Bank _____ City hall _____
Park _____ Hospital _____
School _____ Library _____
Church _____ Post office _____
Bakery _____ Fire station _____

Crops and Industries

List the crops and industries in or near our community.

Crops	Industries
_____	_____
_____	_____
_____	_____
_____	_____

Comparison of Two Communities

Compare our community and our state capital on the following:

Features	Community	Capital
Population	_____	_____
Area	_____	_____
Industries	_____	_____
Recreation	_____	_____

Complete These Sentences

Read pages 62–63 and complete the following:

Adaptation means _____
An artifact is _____
Archeologists study _____
Customs are _____
Traditions are _____

Choose the Best Answer

Archeologists find artifacts by
(a) asking natives
(b) using maps
(c) reading books
(d) digging ruins.

First Americans came from
(a) Africa (b) Asia
(c) Europe (d) Mexico

True or False?

Study the table on page 88 and circle *T* for true and *F* for false.

T F 1. The Pacific Ocean is the deepest ocean.

T F 2. The Atlantic Ocean is the largest ocean.

T F 3. The Indian Ocean is the smallest ocean.

Write Sentences

Use these words to write sentences:

Landforms Plain Plateau Elevation Slope Incline Region Province Country Altitude Latitude Longitude

Interpret a Graph

Study the graph on page 67. Answer these questions:

What is the wettest month in San Francisco? In Los Angeles?

What is the driest month in San Francisco? In Los Angeles?

Which Source Should Be Used?

____ 1. Climate maps
____ 2. Word meaning
____ 3. Article on Incas
____ 4. Current facts on Canada
____ 5. Population of a city
____ 6. Word spelling

a. Almanac
b. Atlas
c. Dictionary
d. Encyclopedia

What Is Your Cognitive Style?

____ Objective   ____ Analytical
____ Subjective   ____ Integrative
____ Factual   ____ Realistic
____ Opinionative   ____ Idealistic
____ Concrete   ____ Reflective
____ Abstract   ____ Impulsive

What Happened on These Dates?

1607 _____
1620 _____
1642 _____
1648 _____
1680 _____
1733 _____

Locate Cities on an Outline Map

Amsterdam	London
Athens	Madrid
Berlin	Moscow
Copenhagen	Paris
Helsinki	Rome

Figure 5.1

More detailed than activity cards are worksheets that present a task or objective, directions, and materials to use, as shown in these examples.

WORKSHEET ON EXPLORERS

Objectives:

To use the index to locate information
To summarize information on explorers

Materials:

Textbook

Directions:

Use the index of your textbook to find information on the explorers listed below. Complete this worksheet by filling in the blanks as shown for the first explorer.

Name of Explorer	Sponsoring Country	Year(s) of Exploration	Area Explored
Jacques Cartier	France	1534–1535	St. Lawrence River
Samuel de Champlain			
Henry Hudson			
William Baffin			
Robert de La Salle			

A variety of types of activities may be used in activity cards and worksheets, ranging from writing and labeling to making or completing items. The following examples are drawn from teaching guides and various media.

Write: name of school, community, state, country, places studied; descriptions of people, objects, activities, rural and urban scenes; answers to questions; conclusions, main ideas and details, causes and effect; notes, outlines, definitions, letters, editorials, reports

Label: places on community, state, regional, country, and world maps; oceans, continents, and mountain ranges; poles, equator, and other features on hemi-

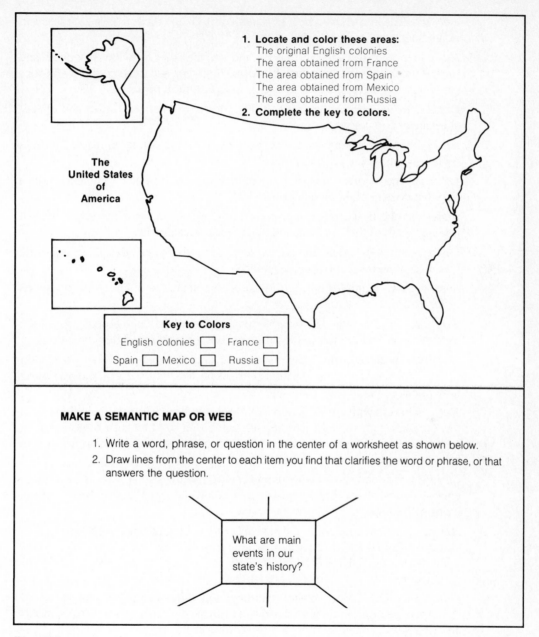

1. **Locate and color these areas:**
   The original English colonies
   The area obtained from France
   The area obtained from Spain
   The area obtained from Mexico
   The area obtained from Russia
2. **Complete the key to colors.**

The
United States
of
America

Key to Colors

English colonies ☐   France ☐

Spain ☐   Mexico ☐   Russia ☐

MAKE A SEMANTIC MAP OR WEB

1. Write a word, phrase, or question in the center of a worksheet as shown below.
2. Draw lines from the center to each item you find that clarifies the word or phrase, or that answers the question.

What are main
events in our
state's history?

Figure 5.2

sphere maps; features on drawings and diagrams; travel routes; U.S. territorial acquisitions

Copy: fire drill and other basic rules; selected parts of documents such as the Declaration of Independence and the Constitution; dates of main events

Rewrite: ideas in own words; false statements to make them true; main ideas and related details in correct order

List: community workers and goods and services they provide; resources and related products; steps in making bread, making steel, and other processes; historical events and dates in sequence; items in alphabetical order

Outline: main ideas and related details; ideas for a report; causes and effects; alternatives and consequences

Fill in: blanks in statements and paragraphs; names of places on maps; blanks in outlines; names of states and capitals

Cross out: the incorrect answer to an item; items that do not belong in a group; a step that does not belong in a process

Underline: the best answer; a preferred position on an issue; items in a list that belong together; the word needed to complete a statement

Circle: pictures or words for goods, service, needs, wants, and other items; the best answer; items that belong together

Answer: essay, multiple-choice, true–false, completion, and Who Am I? questions or items

Find information: atlas; dictionary; glossary; thesaurus; encyclopedia; gazetteer; card catalog; almanac; yearbooks; airplane, bus, or train schedules; directories

Compute: distances using map scale; great circle routes on globe; population density; per capita income; time between events B.C., B.C. into A.D., and A.D.; travel time to places via air, bus, train, and ship

Match: workers with goods or services they provide; words with definitions; state or countries with capitals; people with achievements; branches of government with activities; map symbols with what they represent; needed information with best source; places with description

Classify: goods and services; needs and wants; resources and products; causes and effects; duties of executive, legislative, and judicial officials; places by climate; crops by regions; past and present events

Number in order: sequence of events in bread making or other process; events in chronological order; cities, states, or countries by area, population, or income; items by value; activities, values, and points of view by interest, concern, or agreement

Draw: pictures of food, shelter, clothing, and other needs; pictures of wants; changes in seasons and seasonal activities; modes of transportation; map symbols and what they represent

Make: maps; charts; diagrams; tables; graphs; time lines; word puzzles; analogies; models

Trace: maps; travel routes; dots or numbers to make letters, words, maps, or names of places; equator, prime meridian, and other lines on hemisphere maps

Solve: riddles; wordsearch, crossword, and other word puzzles; scrambled words and phrases

Complete: sentences and paragraphs; outline maps; time lines; retrieval charts; stories; graphs; worksheets

Providing Modules

Modules are more extensive than worksheets. They enable students to work at varying rates and to achieve specified objectives. The following example may be modified to develop such skills as finding main ideas and related details in reading materials and interpreting maps, tables, diagrams, and other media.

IDENTIFYING FEATURES ON THE GLOBE AND GLOBAL MAPS

Objective

To identify and name hemispheres, continents, and oceans shown on the globe and global maps

Directions

Go to the map center and use the globe and global maps in folder A to complete this module.

Part A: Western Hemisphere

Take the global outline map that shows the western hemisphere and place it by the globe turned to show the western hemisphere. Do the following:

1. Find the North Pole on the globe. Print North Pole on the global map.
2. Find the South Pole on the globe. Print South Pole on the global map.
3. Find North America on the globe. Print North America on the global map.
4. Find South America on the globe. Print South America on the global map.
5. Find Antarctica on the globe. Print Antarctica on the global map.
6. Find the Pacific Ocean on the globe. Print Pacific Ocean on the global map.
7. Find the Atlantic Ocean on the globe. Print Atlantic Ocean on the global map.
8. Find the Arctic Ocean on the globe. Print arctic Ocean on the global map.

Part B: Eastern Hemisphere

Take the global outline map that shows the eastern hemisphere and place it by the globe turned to show the eastern hemisphere. Do the following:

1. Find the North Pole on the globe. Print North Pole on the global map.
2. Find the South Pole on the globe. Print South Pole on the global map.
3. Find Europe on the globe. Print Europe on the global map.
4. Find Asia on the globe. Print Asia on the global map.
5. Find Africa on the globe. Print Africa on the global map.
6. Find Australia on the globe. Print Australia on the global map.
7. Find Antarctica on the globe. Print Antarctica on the global map.
8. Find the Atlantic Ocean on the globe. Print Atlantic Ocean on the global map.
9. Find the Pacific Ocean on the globe. Print Pacific Ocean on the global map.
10. Find the Indian Ocean on the globe. Print Indian Ocean on the global map.

Part C: Completion Items

Complete the following items. You may refer to the globe and the global maps.

1. Continents in the western hemisphere are _____
2. Continents in the eastern hemisphere are _____
3. The ocean west of North America is _____
4. The ocean west of South America is _____
5. The ocean east of North America is _____
6. The ocean east of South America is _____
7. The ocean west of Europe is _____
8. The ocean west of Africa is _____
9. The ocean east of Asia is _____
10. The ocean west of Australia is _____

Planning for Differences in Reading and Other Skills

The wide range of reading ability that exists in every class calls for the same care in planning for reading in the social studies as in the developmental reading program. Information on children collected as part of the developmental reading program can be used to individualize reading in the social studies. It may be supplemented by observation of students as they read social studies materials. Particular attention should be given to students' ability to read maps, time lines, graphs, diagrams, and such reference materials as atlases and encyclopedias. Teachers should also observe students' use of the table of contents, index, and glossary in social studies textbooks. Social studies tests and study skill assessment also provide useful data.

Locating Needed Materials

One of the best sources of information is the list of materials in school district units of study and teaching guides. Some media centers provide kits of materials on varying readability levels that have been assembled for different units. Catalogs from local media centers and the list of additional reading materials in social studies textbooks and accompanying teacher's guides are other good sources of information. School and community libraries are excellent sources of reading materials for both students and teachers. Many teachers share their room libraries with each other, thus making books on different levels available. Guides to books and free and inexpensive materials are listed in the references at the end of chapter 3, "Identifying and Using Instructional Media."

Grouping for Instruction

Small-group instruction is most effective for meeting needs that several children have in common. Groups may be organized on the basis of

Achievement level, in which those who read on approximately the same level are grouped together and materials on the appropriate level are provided for them.

How might you use partner or group-leader study to develop map-reading or other skills?
Walnut Creek, California

Special needs, in which students are given instruction in using the index, interpreting material, or other basic skills.

Assigned topics, in which students are given a topic or a problem to investigate in depth.

Common interest, in which those who have chosen a topic or a problem read materials related to it.

Partner or group-leader study, in which one child assists a partner, or two or three children, in reading selected materials.

A form for making a block plan for three groups is presented in Chart 5.7. Notice that provision is made for each group to work with the teacher, to read an assignment, and to do a worksheet or independent study.

Using Self-Directed Reading Strategies

The self-directed reading strategies that follow are designed to help students in upper grades read on their own. A widely used one is SQ3R, adapted from Robinson (1970).

S (Survey). Get an overview; check the organization; read headings.

Q (Question). Have questions to answer based on heading or topic sentences.

R (Read). Find answers to questions.

R (Recite). State or write answers to questions.

R (Reread). Clinch key ideas, check answers, reread key parts.

Group A	Group B	Group C
Instruction by teacher:	Worksheet or independent reading:	Reading by students:
Reading by students:	Instruction by teacher:	Worksheet or independent reading:
Worksheet or independent reading:	Reading by students:	Instruction by teacher:

Chart 5–7

A helpful and creative activity is to guide students to create their own self-directed reading strategy, as illustrated by the following example:

Prove

   P (*Purpose*). Set a purpose or questions to guide reading.

   R (*Read*). Achieve your purpose or answer your questions.

   O (*Organize*). Place details under main ideas.

   V (*Vocabulary*). Note new concepts and words you mastered.

   E (*Evaluate*). Did you achieve your purpose?

Encouraging Independent Reading

Provide individualized reading so that students can select and read unit-related materials on different reading levels, keep logs of their reading, share ideas related to unit topics, and recommend favorites to others. Guide them to volumes available from children's book clubs, articles and stories in children's magazines, and library resources.

Arrange special times for all students and the teacher to read silently, using DEAR (Drop Everything and Read), SSR (Sustained Silent Reading), WIERD (We're Involved in Enthused Reading Daily), DIRT (Daily Independent Reading Time), or SQUIRT (Super Quiet Undisturbed Reading Time) for students' reading of literature related to social studies instruction. Provide time for conferencing, in which children share ideas, read selected parts orally, raise questions, respond to questions raised by the teacher and others, and make plans for future reading (Wiseman, 1991).

Preparing Reports

Oral and written reports are an effective means of individualizing instruction in accord with differences in expressive skills. Students may work on a topic of special interest or on an assigned topic at a pace and a level consistent with their capabilities. The variety of topics is vast indeed, as the following sampling from a few social studies units shows.

Home and Family: How Work is Divided; Care of Pets; Workers Who Come to the Home; How Our Family Saves Energy; How Our Family Has Fun; How Families Have Fun in Other Cultures; Future Families

Our Community: How Our Community Got Its Name; The First Buildings; The First School; Our Water Supply; Parks with Playgrounds for Children; The City Center Renewal Projects; Ethnic Groups in Our Community; The Future of Our Community

Our State: The First Americans; The First European Settlers; The First Town; Early Travel Routes; Main Transportation Routes Today; How the Capital Was Chosen; Our State's Nickname; The Story of Our State Flag; Products We Send to Other States; Our State's Largest City; Our State Parks; Environmental and Pollution Problems; Future Plans to Meet Problems

Living in Early America: The Plymouth Colony; Town Meetings; What Early Schools Were Like; Games Children Played; Help from Native Americans; How Clothing Was Made; Candle Making; The Saugus Ironworks; Being a Slave on a Plantation; Some of Ben Franklin's Inventions

Living in Other Cultures: Family Life; Foods They Eat; Family Recreation; A Day in the Village of _____; Places to Visit; Special Customs and Holidays; Ways that We and the People of _____ Are Alike; Their Schools; Art and Music; Main Problems They Are Facing; Future Plans

Other subjects for reports may be found in students' textbooks and identified in discussions of unit topics. Guidelines to use in choosing a subject and exploring ideas for a report are listed in Charts 5.8 and 5.9.

After a subject is selected and explored, a plan should be made and steps should be taken as noted in Charts 5.10 and 5.11. Reading, interviewing, and other skills may be used to gather information. Various forms of reporting should be considered, as shown in Chart 5.12. (See chapter 11 for guidelines on the preparation of written reports.)

Choosing a Subject for a Report

Why is the subject important? How is it related to our unit?

Why do you find it interesting? Why will others be interested?

Where can you find information on it? What sources of information do we have in our room?

Can you finish the report in our time limits?

Chart 5–8

Exploring Ideas for a Report

Think of questions that your report should answer.

List the main topics that you think should be included.

Find information related to each question or topic.

Look for new questions or topics that you may have overlooked.

Chart 5–9

Social Studies Reports	Preparing a Report	Various Ways to Report
The subject is _____ _____ Sources of information are _____ Main parts in order are: Introduction _____ _____ Development _____ _____ Conclusion _____ _____	State the subject in the title and clarify it in the introduction. Develop the subject by putting main ideas and related details in order. Use or make drawings, maps, charts, or other materials to present ideas and hold interest. State a short conclusion. Give the sources of information.	Pretend to be a newscaster, interviewer, tour guide, or public official. Make a movie box roll to show as you report. Give a chalk talk. Use a hand puppet. Ask questions and give answers as in a TV quiz program. Can you think of other ways to report?
Chart 5.10	Chart 5.11	Chart 5.12

Independent Study Habits

Good study habits are essential to the completion of learning contracts, activity cards, reports, and other individual activities. Because of the variety of opportunities for individual study, the social studies program is particularly well suited to developing effective study habits and encouraging their use at home and in the library. The foundations for good study habits are established in the early grades and are refined as students advance. Desirable habits and procedures are listed in Charts 5.13 and 5.14.

Good Study Habits	Improving Home Study
Know your purpose and keep it clearly in mind: *Stop.* Stop other activities so that you get clear directions. *Look.* Watch the teacher so that you understand each point. *Listen.* Note the details on what to do. *Ask.* Raise questions if you do not understand any part. Proceed to do it: *Organize.* Arrange materials and plan the steps to take. *Concentrate.* Stick to your job and ignore distractions. *Finish.* Complete the job before starting other activities. *Check.* Review your work to be sure it is complete and well done.	Know exactly what you are to do. Be sure to take needed materials home. Plan study time so that you will not have to stay up late. Study in a place where you can work without interruption. Arrange the study materials so that you can use them effectively. Finish the job once you have started it. Do your own work. (You may get advice on hard parts.) Review your work and make any changes that will improve it. Be ready to ask questions the next day on any parts you need help on. Get tips from *Homeworker, The Homework Solution, Deskmate,* or *A-Plus* in the computer center.
Chart 5.13	Chart 5.14

Teaching Children How to Individualize

This strategy is used to provide instruction that enables students to individualize on their own. When the teacher also takes steps to individualize, each child's chances of getting tailored instruction are greatly improved. The guiding principle is to teach students specific ways in which they can vary materials, activities, time, individual work, group work, and standards to fit their own needs. If the goal of learning how to learn is to be achieved, children themselves must be able to identify and apply guidelines and techniques of individualization appropriate to their level of development. Charts 5.15 through 5.18 illustrate ways in which this can be done.

Because We Are Different We vary the time on some activities. We work as a class on some projects and in small groups on others. We have projects each of us can do alone. We find materials we can use. We give help on some things and get help on others.

Chart 5–15

Use Free Time To work on individual projects. To listen to tapes and records related to our unit. To view slides and filmstrips related to our unit. To find ideas in the picture file. To find materials in the reading center.

Chart 5–16

Do You Know How To use the materials in the listening center? To find materials in the library corner? To get ideas from pictures, maps, and charts in books too hard to read? To find books you can use in the school library and the local library?

Chart 5–17

Help Yourself to Learn By raising questions when you are not sure of something. By asking for help when you need it. By finding and using different materials. By getting clear directions for activities and home study.

Chart 5–18

Planning for Exceptional Students

Checklist 5.2 summarizes recommendations by experts in special education regarding ways to enhance the learning of exceptional students. The items in the checklist are suggestions for individualizing instruction, not for isolating students in special groups. Nor should the labeling of students as "exceptional" or "special" lead to an overemphasis on drill and remedial work for a student categorized as less able, to the neglect of critical and creative thinking, and to an overemphasis on creative activities for gifted and talented students, to the neglect of basic social studies instruction. All students need well-rounded instruction along with individual adjustments that improve learning.

View the following as suggestions for adjusting instruction to meet students' special needs. Do not view them as prescriptions; rather, view each item in the context of each student's unique background and needs. Additional suggestions are presented in the end-of-chapter references.

Checklist 5–2
SUGGESTIONS FOR MEETING NEEDS OF EXCEPTIONAL STUDENTS

ALL EXCEPTIONAL STUDENTS

_____ Obtain useful background information from IEPs and other records, maintaining the confidentiality of records and reports.

_____ Build on each student's strengths and work for well-rounded growth—intellectual, social, emotional, and physical.

_____ Use suggestions made by school psychologists, special education experts, and reading specialists; seek their advice as problems arise.

_____ Use available learning materials, computer and other equipment, and "resource room" facilities.

_____ Provide individualized home study and obtain home cooperation in finding and using the services of libraries, service agencies, and other organizations recommended by the special education department.

_____ Identify and develop talents and special abilities in all areas, including academic, creative, social, and physical.

_____ Emphasize development of self-esteem, positive attitudes toward differences, respect for others, and prosocial behavior.

_____ Look for discrepancies between learning potential and achievement, and make plans to overcome underachievement.

THE GIFTED OR TALENTED STUDENT

_____ Look for the variety of abilities and talents that exist in all ethnic and socioeconomic groups.

_____ Extend learning by means of additional opportunities to formulate hypotheses, draw inferences, state generalizations, synthesize main ideas, and evaluate ideas and materials.

_____ Provide many opportunities for independent inquiry, use of library and community resources, and synthesis of data from several sources.

_____ Encourage individual initiative and planning, leadership, concern for others, sharing, teamwork, and appreciation for different types of contributions.

_____ Extend learning through wide reading of materials that take students far beyond basic and supplementary texts.

_____ Emphasize positive traits and attitudes, such as individualism without being overbearing and self-criticism without being overly critical of others.

_____ Emphasize creative expression in individual and group work, oral and written reports, mapping, designing computer programs, and other activities.

_____ Avoid reviewing, drilling, and reteaching items that may be needed by some students but not by gifted students.

THE LESS ABLE STUDENT

_____ Prepare concrete and specific questions, directions, and suggestions for individual activities.

_____ Provide review, extra practice, and additional study time to ensure learning.

(continued)

Checklist 5.2 *(continued)*

_____ Prepare simplified study guides based on pictures, charts, and diagrams.

_____ Adjust the number of concepts to be learned and the level of development to challenge but not frustrate the student.

_____ Provide creative activities as suggested in chapter 10 to motivate learning and enable the student to experience the thrill of self-expression.

_____ Identify and use special talents and provide opportunities for the less able student to contribute to discussion and other activities, such as reporting findings obtained from pictures, maps, computer programs, or other sources.

_____ Plan team-learning activities to gather data, prepare reports, use computer programs, make maps, create murals, and complete other activities.

_____ Provide regular feedback on progress, commend the student for effort, and guide student self-evaluation in order to provide motivation.

THE ECONOMICALLY DISADVANTAGED STUDENT

_____ Encourage participation in question raising, planning, discussion, role playing, and other activities.

_____ Use language that clarifies objectives and directions for learning activities, giving attention to students' language patterns as appropriate.

_____ Develop language power, using bicultural-bilingual materials as needed.

_____ Develop positive self-concepts through growth of personal competence and appreciation of one's own heritage.

_____ Provide opportunities for constructive and rewarding interaction with students of differing backgrounds, stressing respect for each individual.

_____ Utilize special talents and backgrounds of students to develop self-esteem and enrich the learning of all students.

_____ Provide special units and learning activities that meet identified needs, including appropriate multiethnic, law-focused, and career education, as presented in chapter 7.

THE LEARNING DISABLED STUDENT

_____ Adapt and use in the social studies the reading, writing, and other activities designed to overcome disabilities.

_____ Give precise directions and clarify work standards for each learning activity.

_____ Provide unit-related computer programs that the student can use alone or with a partner to improve reading, interpreting maps, and other skills.

_____ Use whole-language and corrective/remedial strategies to improve communication skills.

_____ Adjust instruction on graphs, tables, and other quantitative material for the student with math disabilities.

_____ Help students keep their desks well organized so that needed materials can be readily retrieved.

_____ Provide tape-recorded material and talking software for students with reading disabilities.

_____ Break assignments into short segments and give the student one segment at a time.

(continued)

Checklist 5.2 *(continued)*

THE EMOTIONALLY DISTURBED STUDENT

_____   Provide stability, structure, and consistency in work standards, daily routines, and behavior expectations.

_____   Anticipate changes in classroom routines and activities, prepare the student for them, and clarify expected behavior.

_____   Set clear standards of conduct and consistently maintain them, explaining why they must be followed and how they benefit the student.

_____   Provide immediate feedback and encouragement as standards are met and improvement in self-control is exhibited.

_____   Avoid involving the student in situations or activities that create frustration, hostility, feelings of inferiority, and overstimulation.

_____   Provide a learning station or cubicle in which the student can work independently without distractions.

_____   Develop skill in interpersonal relationships by beginning with partner activities and moving gradually to small groups of three or four compatible students.

_____   If unmanageable problems arise, seek help from the principal, the school psychologist, and other support personnel.

THE PHYSICALLY IMPAIRED STUDENT

The Hearing-Impaired Student

_____   Speak in a normal voice with clear enunciation to aid speech reading.

_____   Face students and keep your hands away from your face.

_____   Get attention by touching a student or using an inconspicuous gesture.

_____   Introduce new vocabulary both orally and in writing.

_____   Provide written instructions for assignments and detailed directions.

_____   Use visual materials, closed caption TV, and audio loops.

_____   Avoid writing and speaking simultaneously while at the chalkboard.

_____   Have a classmate provide assistance when a situation arises in which a child cannot hear a speaker or a recording.

_____   Encourage and supervise the proper use of hearing aids.

The Visually Impaired Student

_____   Provide the best possible lighting and eliminate glare and shadows.

_____   Arrange seating for ease of seeing and hearing the teacher and members of discussion groups.

_____   Avoid exacting and extended visual tasks, hard-to-read worksheets, minute outline maps, and intricate construction and art activities.

_____   Provide recommended materials such as widely spaced and heavily lined paper, worksheets and books with large type, raised relief maps and globe magnifiers, and talking computers that use voice synthesis software.

_____   Provide rest periods to reduce eye strain and tension.

(continued)

Checklist 5.2 *(continued)*

The Orthopedically Impaired Student

_____ Arrange seating for ease of entrance, exit, and participation in activities.

_____ Emphasize independence in using crutches, braces, and other devices.

_____ Provide assistance as needed to use scissors, references, and other materials.

_____ Provide a computer system modified for use by the impaired student, or appoint a computer partner.

_____ Make necessary modifications so that children can participate in group activities.

_____ Provide substitute activities in situations that demand physical capabilities children do not possess.

The Blind Student

_____ Orient the child to the layout of the classroom, seating arrangements, work centers, teacher's desk, own work station, and other features.

_____ Provide "talking books," Braille translation software, and Braille materials obtained from the library and special teacher.

_____ Have an aide serve as interpreter to transmit messages to and from the student.

_____ Provide models, objects, and other realia that the student can feel, touch, and manipulate.

_____ Use raised relief maps and globes to locate mountain ranges and other surface features by feeling them.

The Student with Speech Difficulties

_____ Use activities suggested by the speech therapist and encourage children to apply newly developed skills in social studies activities.

_____ Guide students to choose activities in which they feel secure, such as giving a chalk talk, using puppets, or participating in choral speaking.

_____ Call on those children who volunteer to contribute to discussion and give them time to respond without pressure or interruption.

_____ Avoid situations that create tensions and feelings of insecurity.

Questions, Activities, and Evaluation

1. Visit an elementary-classroom and note the following:
   a. Differences among children in the use of language, work habits, involvement in activities, and the like
   b. Techniques and activities used by the teacher to accommodate individual differences and to mainstream special students in the social studies
   c. Learning centers in the classroom and materials that might be used to accommodate individual differences
   d. Forms used to prepare an IEP
2. How might the basic strategies and techniques for accommodating individual differences be put to use in a unit you are planning? Which are easiest to use? Which are hardest?

3. Prepare the following for use in a unit of your choice:
    a. A learning contract, an individual activity card, or a module
    b. A plan for teaching a self-directed reading strategy to students
    c. A plan for teaching students to individualize for themselves
    d. Adaptations you might make in a unit for disadvantaged, gifted, or other exceptional students discussed in this chapter.

References

Bristow, Diane, et al., "Technology Reaching Out to Special Education Students," *Media & Methods* 26 (May/June 1990), 38–40.

Devine, Thomas G., *Teaching Study Skills* (2nd ed.). Boston: Allyn & Bacon, 1987. Basic skills; tips on individualization.

"A Guide to Special Education Resources," *Electronic Learning*, 9 (February 1990), 26–27. Media for exceptional students.

Hargis, Charles H., *Teaching Low Achieving and Disadvantaged Students.* Springfield, IL: Charles C. Thomas, 1989.

Haring, Norris G., and Linda McCormick, eds., *Exceptional Children and Youth.* Columbus, OH: Merrill, 1990. Coverage of all types of exceptional students.

Hill, Howard D., *Effective Strategies for Teaching Minority Students.* Bloomington, IN: National Educational Service, 1990. Practical strategies.

Kirk, Samuel A., and James J. Gallagher, *Educating Exceptional Children* (6th ed.). Boston: Houghton Mifflin, 1989. Suggestions for both regular and special education teachers.

McCarthy, Bernice, "Using the 4MAT System to Bring Learning Styles to Schools," *Educational Leadership,* 48 (October 1990), 31–37.

Margolis, Howard, Patrick P. McCabe, and Elliot Schwartz, "Using Cooperative Learning to Facilitate Mainstreaming in the Social Studies," *Social Educations,* 54 (February 1990) 111–14.

Marzano, Robert J., et al., *Reading Diagnosis and Instruction.* Englewood Cliffs, NJ: Prentice-Hall, 1987. Strategies and activities.

Milgram, Roberta M., *Teaching Gifted and Talented Students in Regular Classrooms.* Springfield, IL: Charles C. Thomas, 1989. Guidelines and strategies.

Robinson, Francis P., *Effective Study.* New York: Harper & Row, 1970. Procedures for improving study habits.

Salend, Spencer, J., *Effective Mainstreaming.* New York: Macmillan, 1990. Guidelines and techniques.

Van Cleaf, D. W., *Action in Elementary Social Studies.* Englewood Cliffs, NJ: Prentice-Hall, 1991.

Wiseman, Donna L., *Reading Instruction: A Literature Based Approach.* Englewood Cliffs, NJ: Prentice-Hall, 1991. Chapter on independent reading.

Ysseldyke, James F., and Bob Algozzine, *Introduction to Special Education* (2nd ed.). Boston: Houghton Mifflin, 1990.

Incorporating Content from Basic Disciplines

CHAPTER 6

Objective and Related Focusing Questions

To identify substantive and process knowledge of enduring value and to give examples of discipline-based questions, study guides, and learning activities:

- What are primary sources of content for the social studies?

- What content is recommended in recent reports on geography, history, and civic education?

- What substantive knowledge—concepts, concept clusters, themes, generalizations—are drawn from key disciplines?

- How can concepts and themes be used to generate questions and improve thinking and learning?

- What are examples of discipline-based study guides and learning activities?

- What process knowledge—values, attitudes, models, methods of inquiry—may be used to improve learning?

Social studies education is based on substantive and process content drawn from various disciplines. Geography and history have a central place and have been given increased emphasis in recent years. Content is also drawn from economics, political science, and the behavioral sciences—anthropology, sociology, and psychology. Philosophy, the arts, literature, and other humanities provide content and activities that enrich learning. Content from current affairs and from ethnic, gender equity, environmental, law-related, and futures studies is also significant.

Recommendations in recent frameworks and reports illustrate the central place of history and geography as a matrix of time and place for the study of human relationships (California, 1988; Bradley Commission, 1988; National Commission on Social Studies, 1989). The integration of content from other social sciences and the humanities is also urged. The importance of content from many disciplines is highlighted in the goals of a framework that urges development of six types of literacy (California, 1988).

> *Historical literacy:* sense of historical empathy; meaning of time and chronology; cause and effect; continuity and change; history as memory with political implications; importance of religion, philosophy, and other major belief systems in history
>
> *Ethical literacy:* sanctity of life and dignity of the individual; how societies have tried to resolve ethical issues; how ideas affect behavior; universal concern for ethics and human rights as aspirations in every time and place
>
> *Cultural literacy:* complex nature of culture—history, geography, politics, literature, art, drama, music, dance, law, religion, philosophy, architecture, technology, science, education, sports, social structure, economy; relationships among parts of a culture—mythology, legends, values, and beliefs; literature and art as reflection of inner life of people; multicultural perspective that respects dignity and worth of people
>
> *Geographic literacy:* awareness of place; locational skills and understandings; human and environmental interaction; human movement; world regions and their historical, cultural, economic, and political characteristics
>
> *Economic literacy:* economic problems confronting all societies: comparative economic systems; economic goals; performance and problems of our society; international economic system
>
> *Sociopolitical literacy:* relationships between social and political systems; relationships between society and law; comparative political systems

The Core Disciplines

History and geography are primary sources of content. Content is also drawn from political science, economics, anthropology, sociology, and psychology. These disciplines are interrelated by concepts and methods of investigation as well as by their focus on human relationships. Geography and history draw freely from a variety of disciplines but do so with reference to the space and time dimensions of human relationships. All the disciplines have their own historical dimensions, and all are concerned with the study of various aspects of human behavior.

A few points about the general nature of each discipline should be noted. Regional geography, social history, and cultural anthropology are highly integrative disciplines. Regional geography provides a well-rounded view of cultural and physical elements in areas under study. History provides an integrated view of significant past events in a time framework. Cultural anthropology provides a holistic view of ways of living in selected cultures. These three fields of study are used extensively to synthesize content: geography in a spatial context, history in a temporal context, and anthropology in a cultural context.

Political science and economics are policy sciences that study processes and decision making in two realms of human activity. Material from these two disciplines may be included in units based primarily on geography or history, or in separate units on local, state, and national government or economic activities. Political science is a key source of content for civic education, as shown later in this chapter.

Three behavioral sciences—anthropology, sociology, and psychology—are sources of concepts such as roles, groups, institutions, and processes of social interaction. These fields contribute to the study of social problems, social change, and human interaction in a variety of cultures and societies.

Not listed above, but discussed later in this chapter, is philosophy. Philosophy provides definitions, critiques of the methods of study and conclusions of other disciplines, and methods of reasoning and analysis. Inferring, critical thinking, valuing, using criteria to make judgments, finding fallacies in statements, and examining the grounds for claims and beliefs all call for reasoning and logical analysis.

Geography

Geography bridges the social and natural sciences. It provides information on the spatial variation of the cultural and physical elements that make each place on earth unique. Content selected for the social studies enriches understanding and appreciation of the earth as the home of people, of variations in human habitats and cultures, and of human interaction with the natural and cultural environments. People-land relationships are studied, with attention to the past, present, and future uses of resources, population growth, the impact of technology, adaptation to the environment, and global interdependence.

The social studies program draws from the two main branches of geography—physical and human. *Physical geography* provides information on landforms, water bodies, climate and weather, and plant and animal life that is relevant to the study of human activities in various settings. *Human geography* provides information on the interaction of people with their physical and cultural environments, ranging from ways of living in selected cultures to historical, demographic, urban, economic, political, and other aspects of human settlement of the earth.

Regional and topical studies along with spatial analysis are included in the social studies. Regional studies reveal the unique features of a particular region, such as mediterranean, tropical, and desert areas. Topical studies provide data on a single

How are *adaptation* to and *use* of the environment shown in this photograph? International Society for Study of Education, Tokyo

element, such as climate, population, resources, and land use. Spatial analysis is used to identify patterns made by distributions of surface features, associations of elements that tend to be located near one another, and interaction among elements and between areas.

Such special fields of study within geography as urban, economic, political, and historical geography are also drawn upon to enrich learning. Concepts from urban geography—zones of a city, specialized cities, and central places—are used to study communities, to classify manufacturing, commercial, and other specialized cities, and to identify settlement patterns that range from village and town to metropolis and megalopolis (for example, the area stretching from north of Boston through New York to south of Washington, D.C.). Major cities such as New York, Chicago, Los Angeles, London, and Tokyo are studied as central cores that serve large areas. Urban sprawl is studied in cities that have mushroomed outward in concentric circles, strips, or other patterns. The internal structure of a city may be analyzed, beginning with streets in the neighborhood and extending to land use in inner, middle, and outer zones for business, industrial, residential, recreational, and other uses.

Concepts from economic and political geography are used to study relationships between communities, states, and nations, changing boundaries, use of resources, and trade. Wise use and conservation of resources are stressed in units on energy and resource use, beginning with the local community and extending to examination of countries and regions around the world. The importance of resources along with capital, labor, and know-how (a central concept cluster in economics and economic geography) is used to analyze economic activities in different regions. Of particular importance is the concept of interdependence that begins to emerge in local studies and is extended through regional and international studies to lead to the concept of global interdependence.

Historical geography considers spatial changes over time and is clearly evident in units on growth of the community, rural to urban population shifts, early settlements in the home state, growth of cities, and territorial changes. Maps and content on exploration and colonization, westward expansion, the growth and decline of the Roman Empire and other great domains, and the emergence of early civilizations in different parts of the world may be found in middle and upper grades.

A major contribution of geography is instruction on globes and maps, as shown in chapter 12. The following examples of conceptual components illustrate substantive contributions to the social studies.

Concepts

Adaptation, interdependence, culture, conservation, spatial distribution and differentiation, spatial association and interaction, land use, continent, country, region, state, community, maritime, coastline, polar, temperate, tropical, elevation, equator, poles, latitude, longitude, resources, products, rural, urban, capital, central city, metropolitan

Concept Clusters

The environment: natural, cultural, spheres (hydrosphere, lithosphere, atmosphere, biosphere or life layer), human elements (people and their cultures), physical elements (land, water, climate), biotic elements (plants, animals)

Earth-sun relationships: source of energy, rotation, revolution, inclination and parallelism of axis, circulation of atmosphere, seasons, night and day

Environmental concerns: acid rain, pollution, ozone layer, wetlands, rainforests

Major landforms: plains, hills, plateaus, mountains

Water bodies: rivers, lakes, bays, straits, seas, oceans

Natural resources: water, soil, animal life, plant life, minerals, climate

Population: size, distribution, centers, density, composition, growth rate, movement, prediction, control, problems, productive potential

Settlement patterns: isolated, village, town, suburb, city, metropolis, megalopolis

Urbanization: growth of urban centers, central cities, location, functions, internal structure (residence, business, industry), interaction with other places, accessibility, changing occupancy patterns, migration, invasion, segregation, desegregation, redevelopment

Specialized cities: manufacturing, commercial, transport, port, government, other

City structure: inner, middle, outer zones; central business district; residential, industrial, suburban, exurban areas

Generalizations

Every community has special features that make it different from other communities.

People use resources to meet their needs in ways that are shaped by their culture and influenced by their environment.

Each region of our country interacts with other regions and makes unique economic contributions.

Urbanization has taken place in countries around the world.

Human activities and natural forces cause changes on the earth's surface.

Fundamental Themes and Related Questions[1]

Location: position on the earth's surface; absolute and relative location to indicate positions of physical and cultural features

> Where is it? What is its location by degrees of latitude and longitude?
> What is its location in relation to our community? Our state? Our country? [interpreting]

Place: physical and human characteristics; description of characteristics that distinguish a place from other places

> What landforms, water bodies, and other physical features are characteristic of this place?
> What are distinctive human features, such as settlement patterns and population density? [interpreting]

Human-Environment Interactions: relationships within places; how people modify and adapt to the environment; consequences of changes in the environment

> How have people used resources in their environment? How has climate affected ways of living?
> How have people changed their environment? What are the consequences of changes? [analyzing, synthesizing]

Movement: movement of people, goods, services, and ideas; local to global interdependence; interaction by means of communication and transportation

> How do people in our community and other places depend on each other? In our country and others?
> How do networks of communication and transportation speed movement of ideas, people, and goods? [analyzing, synthesizing]

---

[1] Adapted from reports of Geographic Education National Implementation Project, 1987, 1989. For information on related materials from Geography Alliances set up in states around the country, write to Geographic Education Program, National Geographic Society, 17th and M Streets, Washington, D.C. 20036.

Regions: how they are defined by unifying features of the physical or human environment; how they are formed and changed for geographic study; types of physical and cultural regions

> What criteria are used to define mountain regions? Desert regions? Other physical regions?
> What are unifying features of the Corn Belt? The Middle East? Other human regions? [analyzing, synthesizing]

Illustrative questions, study guides, and learning activities follow.

WHAT DIRECTION IS IT?

Look at the map on page 28.

Is the school facing north or south?

What direction is it from the school to the library?

What direction is it from the library to City Hall?

In what direction is the school bus going?

What park is south of City Hall?

HOW FAR IS IT?

Look at the airways map on page 88.

How far is it from Chicago to:

	Miles	Kilometers
Boston	____	____
New York	____	____
Miami	____	____
Denver	____	____
Seattle	____	____
San Francisco	__	__

WHERE ARE MAJOR URBAN AREAS?

List the cities shown in these areas on page 29.

Northeast

Middle Atlantic

Southeast

Great Lakes

South Central

North Central

Pacific Coast

LANDFORMS AND WATER BODIES

Look at the drawing on page 44. What landforms are shown?

_____

_____

_____

What water bodies are shown?

_____

_____

_____

CONTINENTS AND OCEANS

Use the maps on pages 16–17 to answer these questions.

What continents are in the Western Hemisphere?

What oceans are in the Western Hemisphere?

What continents are in the Eastern Hemisphere?

What oceans are in the Eastern Hemisphere?

LIVING AND NONLIVING RESOURCES

Read pages 256–258 and look at the map on page 257.

List the living resources:

_____

_____

_____

List the nonliving resources:

_____

_____

_____

(continued)

WHAT TIME IS IT?

Examine the map that shows time zones in the United States.

What time is it in the zones below when it is 1:00 p.m. in New York City?

Central ____ Mountain ____

Pacific ____ Alaska ____

Hawaii ____

WHAT STATES ARE IN THESE BELTS?

Read the article on Belts in the geography center.

List the states in each Belt.

Corn Belt _____

Wheat Belt _____

Rust Belt _____

Sun Belt _____

Ice Belt _____

WHAT STATES ARE IN MAIN REGIONS?

New England _____

Middle Atlantic _____

Southeast _____

North Central _____

South Central _____

Great Plains _____

Rocky Mountain _____

Pacific _____

MAKE A STATE RETRIEVAL CHART

Name of state _____

Capital _____

Population _____

Landforms _____

Water bodies _____

Resources _____

Products _____

Unique features _____

NORTH AFRICA AND THE MIDDLE EAST

What countries are on the map of North Africa and the Middle East?

Which country is largest?

Which one is smallest?

Which country is farthest east? Farthest north? Farthest south?

How far is it across the area shown from west to east? From north to south?

HOW TO DESCRIBE A PLACE

Give location in relation to a known place.

State main physical and cultural features.

Describe human-environment interactions.

Note urban, suburban, and exurban growth.

List distinctive features.

RETRIEVAL CHART ON U.S. REGIONS

Region	States	Major Cities	Economy	Special Features
New England				
Middle Atlantic				
Southeastern				
North Central				
South Central				
Southwestern				
Midwest				
Pacific				

(continued)

DATA BASE ON THE NEW ENGLAND STATES

Objective:

To make a data base on key features of the New England states

Procedure:

Select one of the New England states. Print the name of the state at the top of a 3 × 5 card. Record information on the following:

Area	Population	Capital	Key cities
Landforms	Water bodies	Vegetation	Minerals
Agriculture	Industries	Resources	Other items

GEOGRAPHY PROGRAMS IN THE COMPUTER CENTER

Use these programs to make a data base on places being studied:

AppleWorks   Bank Street Filer   pfs:File   Easy Working   Data Manager

Use these programs to find information on places being studied:

World Atlas Facts   See the USA   States and Continents   Dataquest: The Fifty States   Continents and Countries   United States Database   World GeoGraph   Crosscountry USA   Where in _____ is Carmen Sandiego?

COMPARISON OF CANADA, THE UNITED STATES, AND MEXICO

Use sources in the reference center to make a comparative chart on Canada, the United States, and Mexico that includes:

Population   Area   Political divisions   Branches of government

Main ethnic groups   Major landforms   Major water bodies   Resources   Products

Exports   Imports   Main trading partners   Distinctive or unusual features

CAUSES AND EFFECTS OF FRAGILE ENVIRONMENTS

Use pages 278–285 in your textbook and the articles labelled "Stress Zones" and "Fragile Environments" to find the causes and the effects of changes made by people in the following:

Rainforests   Wetlands   North slope of Alaska   Taiga

STUDYING AND COMPARING COMMUNITIES

Where are the following located? Which items tend to be near each other? What relationships (interactions) can we find?

Landforms	Major zones	Population	Transportation
Water bodies	Industries	Ethnic groups	Recreation
Climate	Trade	Shifts to suburbs	Education
History	Government	Urban problems	Special features

(continued)

STUDYING AND COMPARING POPULATION

Where do the people live? Why do they live there? What people lived there first? What people have come from other places?

Number	Distribution	Areas of concentration
Density	Ethnic makeup	Settlement patterns
Growth rate	Immigration	Population shifts
Forecasts	Emigration	Central and other cities

STUDYING AND COMPARING REGIONS

Focusing Questions

How is the area defined as a region? What characteristics or criteria were used? Where are the items below located? What patterns of distribution are there? Which items tend to be together? What patterns of association are there? What are the relationships between items? What patterns of interaction are there?

The Physical Setting

Space: area, relative size, shape, natural and political boundaries, neighbors

Landforms: plains, hills, plateaus, mountains; effects on ways of living

Water: underground, rivers, lakes, bays, straits, coastline; uses

Climate: average temperature and precipitation; effects of latitude, elevation, ocean currents, land and water distribution, mountain barriers

Resources: soil, water, vegetation, animal life, minerals; uses

The People—Human Activities

Population: number, density, growth rate, shifts, settlement patterns, cities

Culture: history, links to others, values, social classes, institutions, art, music, literature, architecture, crafts, changes

Political system: type of government, administrative units, relation to other areas

Economics: agriculture, fishing, industry, trade, transportation, communication, relation to other areas

Future: plans for solving problems—economic, political, health, education, urban, ecological, other

Pitfalls to Avoid. Because so much information is available on various regions and cultures, it is easy to overemphasize facts at the expense of higher-level learning. It is better to study a selected area in depth and to use facts to develop concepts, answer key questions, test hypotheses, and develop understanding and appreciation of human uses of the environment. Facts take on more meaning when structured around concepts and main ideas; students should use facts to explain adaptations to the environment, and areal differentiation, why cities have developed in some places and not in others, the impact of technology, and so on. A related pitfall is to overemphasize the bizarre and exotic features of various lands and peoples. The inevitable outcomes of this approach are stereotypes and misconceptions.

Develop clear distinctions between such concepts as weather and climate, physical and cultural regions, and country and continent. For example, *weather* refers to the atmospheric conditions—temperature, precipitation, air pressure, and wind—that prevail at a given time in a given place. Ask students to note weather reports on television and in newspapers, looking for changes during the week. *Climate* refers to temperature and other conditions over a period of years. Ask students to note references to climate in textbooks, films, and other sources—for example, a warm tropical climate, a hot dry climate, or a continental climate with cold winters and hot summers. Provide for study of factors that control climate, such as latitude, elevation, mountain barriers, ocean currents, and land and water features—for example, how surfaces of water heat up and cool off more slowly than land surfaces. Guide students to discover that cities at high elevations near the equator have climates different from those of cities at low elevations near the equator, and that ocean currents, mountains, and other controls have an impact on climate that is sometimes quite surprising. For example, the Gulf Stream has a moderating effect on the climate of the areas it passes.

In the middle and upper grades a curricular issue is the value of a depth study of selected cultures in an area versus an overall study of cultures in the area. The issue has been resolved in some schools by giving an overview of a large region or area followed by an intensive study of one or more representative cultures or countries within the area. Be sure that students do not generalize about all countries within the area on the basis of the single country studied in depth. Although certain common geographic, economic, political, and cultural characteristics are to be found among countries in the Middle East, in Africa, or in Latin America, specific differences exist that can be grasped only by studying each country in detail. When representative countries are studied, pupils should understand that the purpose is to get a view of certain characteristics that are generally typical of the area, but that may be manifested differently in other countries. For example, many countries in Africa aspire to improved standards of living, better educational and health services, increased industrial output, and stable government, but the specific ways and means employed to attain them vary greatly from country to country.

The outmoded concept of environmental determinism has been rooted out of most new materials and should be rooted out of instruction. Geographers take the position that although environmental conditions are key factors to consider as ways of living are studied, they are not *the* factors that *cause* ways of living. If this were so, all people in desert areas, for example, would live the same way. Students can quickly

---

Low, Middle, and High Latitudes

1. Low latitudes are between 23½ degrees north and south of the equator; this area is sometimes called the torrid zone.

2. Middle latitudes are between 23½ and 66½ degrees north, and between the same degrees south; these areas are sometimes called temperate zones.

3. High latitudes are between 66½ degrees north and the North Pole, and between 66½ degrees south and the South Pole; these areas are sometimes called frigid zones.

Chart 6-1

discover differences in ways of living in similar environments and interpret them in terms of differences in culture. And they can discover how interaction with the environment changes as changes occur in a people's culture by studying their own community, state, and nation as well as Eskimos, Nigerians, and people in other lands.

When referring to places relative to the equator, the terms *middle latitudes, high latitudes,* and *low latitudes* should be used. The terms *temperate, frigid,* and *torrid zones* are climatic rather than locational terms, and they are not accurate descriptions of climatic conditions in the particular zones they are used to designate. Since some writers still use the terms, however, children should become acquainted with them and understand the inaccuracies and limitations that exist in their usage. An example of how one group of children in the sixth grade handled this problem is shown in Chart 6.1.

History

Historical content is evident at all levels, including family life from colonial times to the present, community and state history, background on current and special events, and American and world history. Oral history is receiving increased attention. Students interview key individuals, record their accounts, and replay and interpret them. Also used are taped accounts such as *Geronimo: His Own Story, Hard Times,* and *The Immigrant.* Local or community history has been enriched by the development of sourcebooks and active local historical associations. For example, *The Worcester Sourcebook, The Small Town Sourcebooks I* and *II,* and the *Guide to Small Town Sourcebooks* are replete with teaching suggestions, photos, drawings, and other source materials.[2] The sourcebooks are useful in comparative studies of the growth of communities and as models for developing materials on any community. A variety of computer programs may be used to simulate trekking westward, making decisions, exploring, trading, ruling ancient kingdoms, and other events. Examples are *Oregon, Trailwest, Westward—1847, Lincoln's Decisions, Fur Trading, Voyageur, Hammurabi, Kingdom,* and *Sumer.* Folksongs for different historical periods may be used to enrich

---

[2]Available from New England Bookstore, Old Sturbridge Village, Sturbridge, MA 01566.

What historic sites are in your community to make history live for children? Social Studies Workshop, University of California, Berkeley

learning.[3] A variety of books and historical literature may be used at all levels to nurture empathy, feelings, and nuances that cannot be obtained in other ways.[4]

Habits of Mind

Habits of mind that are useful in making thoughtful judgments are stressed as a principal aim of history instruction (Bradley Commission, 1988). Checklist 6.1 was

[3]For examples, see music textbooks and issues of the following in a library: Lawrence I. Seidman, *Folksongs in the Classroom*. Also, use audiocassettes of folksongs about Colonial, Revolutionary, Civil War, Moving West, and other events and periods.
[4]*Recommended Books and Historical Literature for the History-Social Science Framework*. Sacramento, CA: California State Department of Education, 1990.

Checklist 6.1
WHICH HABITS OF MIND DO YOU USE IN HISTORICAL STUDIES?

____ Know significance of past to yourself? ____ To our society? ____ To other societies?

____ Separate the important from the inconsequential? ____ Use discriminating memory to make judgments?

____ Have historical empathy? ____ View past events as involved people did? ____ Avoid present-mindedness?

____ Comprehend diversity of cultures?____ Shared humanity?

____ Understand how things happen and change? ____ How intentions matter? ____ How means affect consequences? ____ How purpose and process are intertwined?

____ Comprehend the interplay of change and continuity? ____ Recognize that both are to be expected?

____ Prepared for uncertainties? ____ Unfinished business? ____ No solutions for some problems?

____ Understand complexity of causation? ____ Respect particularity? ____ Avoid excessively abstract generalizations?

____ Appreciate tentative nature of judgments about the past? ____ Avoid "lessons" of history as cures for present problems?

____ Recognize the importance of individuals? ____ The significance of character for good and ill?

____ Appreciate the force in history and human affairs of the nonrational? ____ The irrational? ____ The accidental?

____ View history and geography as a matrix of time and place? ____ As a context for events?

____ Read widely and critically? ____ Distinguish fact from conjecture and evidence from assertion? ____ Frame useful questions?

Which habits of mind are easiest to follow? Most difficult? How can you improve?

designed for use by teachers in planning, guiding, and evaluating instruction and for use in upper grades for self-evaluation by students.

Many of the conceptual elements used to interpret and synthesize historical information are drawn from other disciplines. For example, role, division of labor, and cultural borrowing may be used to explain changes in family life, communities, and nations in different periods of time. Time, process, and organizing concepts are also widely used in historical materials, and special emphasis is given to events and themes, as the following summary shows.

Concepts

Time concepts: time, day, week, month, season, year, decade, generation, century, millennium, B.C., A.D., period, epoch, age, era, prehistoric, ancient, medieval, Middle Ages, modern

Process concepts: criticism, analysis, and synthesis of primary and secondary sources; reconstruction of events; interpretation; periodization

Organizing concepts: event, theme, period, place, movement, trend, chronology

Events and Themes

Events and themes in local history: first settlers, homes, school, church; beginning as a town; growth of population, transportation, communication, business, education, public services, the arts; contributions of individuals and groups; problems of growth

Events and themes in U.S. history: discovery and exploration, living in the colonies, gaining independence, establishing a government, living on the frontier, the westward movement, growth of sectionalism, the Civil War, the period of reconstruction, growth of agriculture and industry, becoming a world power, growth of cities, contributions of ethnic groups

Interpretations and Generalizations

History helps to answer such questions as: How did the present come to be? Who am I? Who are we? Who are they? What caused that to happen?

Social problems and institutions of today have roots in events of the past.

Ideas about self-government were strengthened on the frontier.

Multiple causes and consequences must be considered in studying events.

Time and space provide a matrix within which events can be placed.

Six Vital Themes and Related Questions

The following summary of themes is drawn from the report of the Bradley Commission (1988). The questions under each theme have been added to illustrate how aspects of each theme might be studied.

Civilization, cultural diffusion, innovation: evolution of human skills and means of exerting power over nature and people; centers of power; flowering of civilizations; social, religious, and political patronage of the arts; importance of the city

How are basic needs for food, shelter, and clothing provided in our community? How were they provided in early communities? How did early cities serve as centers of transportation and communication? [interpreting]

How did early civilizations emerge in river valleys? How did ideas spread among societies? What are significant contributions of ancient Greece and Rome? [analyzing, synthesizing]

Human interaction with the environment: geography/technology/culture relationships and their effects on economic, social, and political developments; choices made possible because of climate, resources, and location and the effect of culture and beliefs on choices; gains and losses of technological change; role of agriculture; effects of disease and disease-fighting on people, plants, and animals

What adaptations have been made to climate in our community? How did early settlers adapt to the environment? [interpreting]

How did early settlers use resources in their environment? How has the use of

resources changed? How has the environment been modified because of agriculture? The growth of cities? The growth of industry? [analyzing]

Values, beliefs, political ideas, institutions: religions and ideologies; political and
social institutions at various stages of industrial and commercial development;
interplay among ideas, material conditions, moral values, and leadership, especially in democratic societies; tensions between aspirations for freedom and security, liberty and equality, distinction and commonality

How did the values and beliefs of colonists in New England influence their ways
of living? What values were held by leaders of the Revolution? [interpreting]
What has been the impact of religious beliefs in the United States on the
making of laws? On politics? On ideas about right and wrong? [analyzing,
synthesizing]
What has been the impact of religions and ideologies in China? In Japan? In
Middle Eastern countries? What has been the impact of European ideologies
such as Marxism? Nationalism? Others? [analyzing, synthesizing]

Conflict and cooperation: causes of war and approaches to prevention and peace
making; relations between domestic affairs and ways of dealing with the outside
world; contrasts between international conflict and cooperation and between
isolation and interdependence; consequences of war and peace for societies and
their cultures

What were the causes of the American Revolution? The French Revolution?
What were the immediate consequences? The long-range consequences? [in-
terpreting]
What were the origins and effects of the two world wars? What war-prevention
strategies have been proposed? What individuals have won Nobel Peace prizes?
What did they do to win them? [interpreting]

Comparative history of major developments: revolutionary, reactionary, and reform periods across time and place; imperialism; comparative instances of slavery
and emancipation, feudalism and centralization, human successes and failures,
wisdom and folly; comparative elites and aristocracies; role of the family, wealth,
and merit

How are families today alike and different from families in colonial times? How
has the role of women changed? [comparing]
How did ways of living differ in New England, Middle, and Southern Colonies?
What were key reasons for the differences? [analyzing]
What foundations of western ideas can be traced to the ancient Hebrews and
Greeks? To the ancient Romans? To the Renaissance? [analyzing, synthesizing]

Patterns of social and political interaction: changing patterns of class, ethnic,
racial, and gender structures and relations; immigration, migration, and social
mobility; effects of schooling; new prominence of women, minorities, and common people in study of history and their relation to political power and influential
elites; characteristics of multicultural societies; forces for unity and disunity

How has the status of minority groups changed since the Civil War? What has
been the impact on politics? On business? On freedom and justice? [analyzing]
What have been the contributions of immigrants to our multicultural society?

What distinctive aspects of culture have some groups maintained? What are common or shared aspects of culture? What are their roots? [interpreting] What are primary forces of unity? Of disunity? How well have various forces been managed in the past? What improvements are needed? [evaluating]

Information on teaching guides and essential understandings related to the above may be obtained from the National Center for History in the Schools, Graduate School of Education, University of California, Los Angeles, CA 90024.

Illustrative study guides and learning activities follow.

MODERN AND COLONIAL FAMILIES	**ORAL HISTORY INTERVIEWS**	**INVESTIGATING COLONIES**
Compare them on:	Outline the topic or event to be investigated.	What colonies were established in these areas?
Kinds of food and ways of getting it	Prepare questions and list them in order.	New England
Kinds of clothing and ways of getting it	Have the recorder ready.	The Middle Atlantic
Kinds of shelter and ways of getting it	Ask questions in order. Ask about unclear points.	The South
Recreation, games, playthings	Give the interviewee time to elaborate and add ideas.	Who were the leaders in each of the colonies?
Work of men and women and boys and girls	Ask for information to fill in gaps between events.	What were the main economic activities in each colony?
School and religious activity	Ask if anything has been overlooked in your questions.	What states were eventually formed in New England, the Middle Atlantic, and the South?
Transportation and communication	Express thanks sincerely.	
MODERN AND EARLY COMMUNITIES	**INVESTIGATING STATE HISTORY**	**HISTORICAL LITERATURE**
Compare them on:	First explorers and reasons for exploring	Read and share a review of one the following:
Provision of food, shelter, and clothing	First settlement and names of famous settlers	*The Long Road to a New Land*
Schools, churches, and public buildings	First main highway, railroad, and telegraph	*Clipper Ship* *Wagon Wheels*
Transportation and communication	Date of statehood and reasons for location of capital	*Franklin's Autobiography*
Industries and trade	First schools and university	*Daniel Boone* *Johnny Tremain*
Health and medical services	First governor and other leaders	*I'm Deborah Sampson*
Recreation and sports	Growth of industry and agriculture	*By Wagon and Flat Boat*
Work of men, women, and children	Other significant events	*Waiting for Mama* *Call Me Ruth*
The surrounding environment		*The Oregon Trail* *Going West*
		Little House on the Prairie

(continued)

LOCAL HISTORY QUESTIONS

When was our community founded? Who settled here first?

Where was the first school? Church? General store? Post office? What were they like?

What buildings were on Main Street? Other streets? When were streets first paved?

Who was the first mayor? Teacher? Sheriff? Members of the council? How long did they serve?

What sites have been preserved?

INVESTIGATING EXPLORERS

Note sponsoring country, dates, area explored, and gains for any five of these explorers.

Balboa	De Soto
Cabot	Dias
Cartier	Drake
Champlain	Ericson
Columbus	Hudson
Coronado	Magellan
Cortes	Pizarro
Da Gama	Verrazano
De Leon	Vespucci

PRIMARY OR SECONDARY SOURCE?

Write P for primary source and S for secondary source.

___ Novel   ___ Diary

___ Biography ___ Letters

___ Textbook ___ Editorial

___ News article

___ Minutes

The main features of primary sources are: _____

The main features of secondary sources are: _____

INVESTIGATE A NOTABLE PERSON

Investigate and report on one notable person who is included in our unit. Use materials in the history learning center. Include the person's name, major contribution(s), location, dates of activity, and other information of special interest.

WRITE A DIARY OF AN EVENT

Select an event such as the Lewis and Clark Expedition and imagine that you are there. Write a diary of the event that includes what happened and your feelings related to each entry in the diary.

WHO WAS PETER ZENGER?

Use references in the history center to learn about Peter Zenger. Who was he? What was his job? Why was he put on trial? What was the outcome of the trial? Why was this an important event?

CREATE A HISTORY CARD GAME

Create a card game on selected events or people we are studying. Put the name of the person or event on one side of the card. Put a question and the answer to it on the other side.

(continued)

INTERPRET A TABLE OF POPULATION GROWTH

Use the table Population Growth in the Colonies, page 106, to answer these questions:
What years are shown in the first column? What colonies are shown across the top?
Which colony had the smallest growth in 1680 and the largest growth 80 years later?
Which colony had the smallest population in 1760? Which had the second largest in
1760?
In general, what can be said about population growth in this period?

REASONS FOR GOING TO THE NEW WORLD

Write two or more reasons why explorers from the following countries went to the New
world.

        England   France   Spain

MAKE A TIME LINE

First, find and write the date for the first settlement or colony in:
___ Carolina   ___ Maryland   ___ Georgia   ___ Jamestown   ___ Plymouth
___ Rhode Island   ___ Connecticut
Second, make a time line that includes the name and date of each of the above.

READ AND SHARE HISTORICAL LITERATURE

Choose one of the following or one book in the history center and be ready to share
interesting parts with the class.

Sewell, *The Pilgrims of Plimoth*   Scarf, *Meet Benjamin Franklin*
Siegel, *Fur Trappers and Traders*   Akers, *Abigail Adams*
Davis, *Black Heroes of the American Revolu-*   Forbes, *Johnny Tremain*
tion

TERRITORIAL EXPANSION OF THE UNITED STATES

Read the text and study the map in today's assignment. Write the name of the area
acquired by the United States on these dates:

1803 _____   1818 _____
1818 _____   1846 _____
1848 _____   1853 _____

(continued)

HIGH REGARD FOR LAFAYETTE

Objective:

To identify ways that Americans have expressed admiration for and appreciation of the contributions of Lafayette.

Materials:

Article by Samuel Sifton, "Lafayette, You Are Here," *American Heritage,* 40 (July/August 1989), 45–51.

Directions

Read the article on Lafayette in the history center and answer these questions:

Why has Lafayette been so highly regarded by Americans?

How many towns and counties have been named Lafayette? Is one near your community?

What kinds of home furnishings bear his portrait? Have you seen any?

What other items have been erected, named, or produced to honor him?

Which of the ways of showing regard are most surprising? Give a reason for your choice.

THE WEST INDIES

Objectives

To identify and list the areas included in the West Indies

To name the capitals of Cuba, Haiti, Dominican Republic, and Grenada

To identify areas controlled by the United States, Great Britain, and France

To describe selected events during periods between 1492 and the present

Material:

West Indies, National Geographic Map, November, 1987

Directions

Use the West Indies map in the history center and answer these questions:

What areas are shown in the central part of the map, from Cuba to Grenada?

What are the capitals of Cuba, Haiti, Dominican Republic, and Grenada?

What are the names of areas controlled by the United States? By Great Britain? By France?

Who were the first explorers to land on islands in the West Indies?

What main events occurred during 1492–1625? During 1625–1763? During 1898–1945? From 1945 to the present?

Political Science and Law

Current programs go beyond content on civics to include such concepts as power and authority in the family, the school, and the community. Early-grade instruction is given on making rules, carrying out rules, and the settling of disputes in situations familiar to children. Later these concepts are extended to legislative (rule-making), executive (rule-applying), and judicial (rule-adjudicating) processes of local, state, and national government. Attention is given in community studies to the mayor, the city council, teachers, police, and other public employees; to public services such as education, protection, and recreation; to city planning and redevelopment; and to metropolitan planning to solve transportation and other cross-community problems. State and national studies include such concepts as authority, separation of powers, due process and equal protection of law, and processes of government. Historical studies include material on contributions of the Greeks and the Romans to government, the Magna Carta, changes in laws in England, law and government in early America, case studies of struggles for justice, and great documents such as the Declaration of Independence and the Constitution.

Examples of key conceptual components follow.

Concepts

The Constitution, Bill of Rights, separation of powers, political systems, levels of government, legal system, rules, laws, regulations, rights, civil liberties, due process, equal protection, justice, responsibility

Concept Clusters

Tasks of government: external security, internal order, justice, public services, freedom (under democracy)

Processes: rule making (legislative), rule applying (executive), rule adjudicating (judicial)

Public services: police, fire, postal, education, health, welfare, sanitation, conservation, recreation, labor, business

Due process of law: protection against arrest without probable cause, unreasonable search and seizure, forced confession, self-incrimination, and double jeopardy; right to public trial, counsel, fair judge and jury, habeas corpus, knowledge of accusation; right to confront and cross-examine witnesses, to have witnesses for one's defense, to the assumption of innocence until proven guilty

Sources of law: the Constitution, statutes, common law, administrative rulings, decrees

Generalizations

Rules are needed to guide individual and group activities.

Due process of law is needed to provide equal opportunity, protection, and justice for all individuals and groups.

Laws provide for social control and stability; they limit behavior that endangers life, liberty, and property.

Conflicts arise when individuals and groups have competing goals, apply different standards of conduct, and interpret laws differently.

Laws are nonviolent means of handling conflicts.

A proposed framework for civic education (CIVITAS, 1990) states that effective participation requires moral deliberation, knowledge, reflection, and commitment. Citizens should understand the nature of politics and government, politics and government in the United States, and the role of the citizen. Civic virtue—including such dispositions as civility, self-discipline, open-mindedness, and respect for diversity; a commitment to such values as individual rights, the common good, justice, equality, diversity, truth, and patriotism; and a commitment to such principles as popular sovereignty and constitutional government based on rule of law, separation of powers, checks and balances, minority rights, civilian control of the military, and power of the purse—should be nutured. The following are exmaples of learning activities for grades K–9 related to instruction on "The Nature of the State."

K–3: Students role play and discuss how members of government agencies serve various purposes of government, for example, crossing guards protecting lives, sanitation workers controlling waste, police officers maintaining order and protecting citizens.

4–6: Students investigate and report on key figures and events important in the evolution of constitutional democracy in Great Britain and the United States, including growth of suffrage and the extension of individual rights under the Fourteenth Amendment, judicial decisions, and Civil Rights laws.

7–9: Students use excerpts from the U.N. Declaration of Human Rights as a set of criteria to identify and collect news clippings on situations in several nations to determine to what degree they are meeting the criteria. Then students stage a "meet the press" TV show on situations related to issues of freedom of religion, the right to political dissent, and due process of law.

Other examples are given in the next chapter, in the section on law-related education.

Main Topics and Related Questions

The following examples are drawn from a project based primarily on political science and law (CIVITAS, 1990). The questions under each topic have been added to illustrate ways to guide study.

The Nature of Politics and Government: political power and authority; sources of authority; purposes and types of government; ethics and politics; religion and public life; economics; race/class/ethnicity; gender issues; human rights; purposes of law; legal systems

What is political power? What is political authority? How do they differ? [interpreting]

What are the purposes of government? What is constitutional government? What are other types of government? [interpreting]

What is the place of ethics in government? What are problems of morality in politics and government? How has religion impacted government? [interpreting, analyzing]

Politics and Government in the United States: fundamental values—common good, individual rights, justice, equality, diversity, truth, patriotism; fundamental principles—popular sovereignty, constitutional government, rule of law, separation of powers, checks and balances, minority rights, civilian control of the military, separation of church and state, power of the purse; conflicts over rights, between individuals and groups, between liberty and equality, between diversity and unity, and between liberty and authority What is meant by "the common good"? What are rights of the individual?

What is justice? How can justice and equality be maintained? [interpreting, analyzing]

Why is truth essential to decent and effective government? How can it be identified? [analyzing]

What is patriotism? Why is it important? What is the place of dissent? [interpreting]

How does separation of powers work? How does the principle of checks and balances work? [analyzing]

How did separation of church and state evolve? [interpreting]

How can minority rights be preserved? [interpreting, analyzing]

How can conflicts between individual and societal rights be resolved? How can conflicts between liberty and authority be resolved? [interpreting]

What are the best ways of handling conflicts between diversity and national cohesion? [evaluating]

What are the functions of Congress? The executive branch? The judicial system? [interpreting]

How do the following influence citizens and government? Political parties, Interest groups, Mass media, Public opinion, Citizen action [analyzing]

The Role of the Citizen: responsibilities of citizens, rights of citizens, formation of policy, civic and community action, civil disobedience

What are citizens' responsibilities in the classical tradition? In the tradition of liberal democracy? [interpreting]

What are citizens' rights? What are American's legal rights? [interpreting]

What are forms of citizen participation? How can citizens help to form public policy? [interpreting, analyzing]

How effective have civic and community action been? [evaluating]

How effective have various forms of civil disobedience been? [evaluating]

Civic Virtue: Dispositions—civility, self-discipline, civic-mindedness, open-mindedness, compromise, respect for diversity, patience and persistence, compassion, generosity; commitments, values—right to life and liberty, personal, political, and economic freedom, right to pursuit of happiness, the common good, justice, equality, diversity, truth, patriotism; commitments, principles—popular sovereignty; constitutional government—rule of law, separation of powers, checks and balances, minority rights, civilian control of the military, separation of church and state, power of the purse

What civic dispositions are of key importance in American democracy? [interpreting] How can they be put to productive use? [analyzing]

To what fundamental values should citizens be committed? [interpreting]
How can differences in views regarding individual rights and the common good be resolved? [analyzing]
What are effective means of assuring justice and equality for minority groups? [evaluating]
To what principles of constitutional government should citizens be committed? [interpreting]

Illustrative questions, study guides, and lesson plan follow.

FOCUSING QUESTIONS TO GUIDE STUDY

How are public services like and different from private services? [comparing]
What concepts are used in the computer programs on *Decisions?* [interpreting]
What branches of government are common at local, state, and federal levels? [generalizing]
Which ideas for equity for all groups in our community are best? Why? [evaluating]

RULES, RIGHTS, AND RESPONSIBILITIES	**LOCAL GOVERNMENT**	**STATE GOVERNMENT**
What rules are required in our school for safety? Discussion? Personal property? Other rules?	How is our community governed? What is the role of the mayor? What is the role of city council members?	How is our state governed?
What rules must we follow in our community for safety? Property? Bicycles? Other rules?	What public services are provided? For health? Education? Fire and police? Other services?	What is the role of members of the executive branch? The governor? Treasurer? Others?
What rights do all have in our community? To speech? To education? To religion? To property? To other activities?	What is the role of judges and others in local courts?	What is the role of members of the legislative branch?
What responsibilities do all have to make sure rules are followed? That the rights of all are respected? What happens when we fail to do so?	How are other communities governed?	What is the role of members of the judicial branch? What is the highest court? What are other courts?
	How is county government different from city government? What are the main services of county government?	What are the main state boards and agencies or departments?
		What services do they provide?
		How are state and local services related?

(continued)

FIND AND WRITE THE MEANING	FOUNDATIONS OF GOVERNMENT	CONCEPTS IN COMPUTER PROGRAMS
Democracy Authority Republic Political power Executive Representative Government Legislative Judicial Due process Rights Majority rule Freedoms Equal protection Responsibilities Rule of law	How were early colonies governed? What ideas about government emerged? What rights and freedoms were stressed? What branches were set up in the Constitution? What rights were guaranteed by the Bill of Rights?	List and define the concepts used in these programs: Bill of Rights Jury Trial Lincoln's Decisions U.S. Constitutional Learning Machine The Constitution Congress U.S. Constitution Tutor

Use your textbook and learning center materials to complete this retrieval chart.

COMPARISON OF BRANCHES OF LOCAL, STATE, AND FEDERAL GOVERNMENT

Branches	Local	State	Federal
Legislative			
Executive			
Judicial			

LESSON PLAN: RULES
Objectives

To name rules students must follow at home and in school
To state why rules are needed and must be followed

Materials

Textbook, pages 72–73
Filmstrip on Rules

(continued)

Introduction

Ask: Who can give an example of a rule that must be followed at home? Who can give an example of a rule that must be followed at school?

Development

1. Ask students to find as many rules as they can as they watch the filmstrip on Rules. List their responses on the chalkboard under these two headings:
   Rules at Home   Rules at School
2. Tell students to look at pages 72–73 in their textbooks. Ask them to tell what rule is being followed in each picture. Add any new ones to the list on the chalkboard.
3. Ask students to think of other rules, for example, for games, for safety, for watching TV.
4. Discuss why rules are needed at home and in school. Ask what happens when rules are broken.

Conclusion

Have students summarize rules under such headings as family rules, school rules, personal rules, safety rules, play rules, and property rules.

Follow-up

Have students keep a record for a week of rules that are easiest and hardest to follow.

Economics

There have been many advances in economics education in recent years. Newer instructional materials include a clearly defined set of concepts and main ideas drawn from economics. Concepts such as division of labor are introduced in the beginning grades as children compare the production of favors or other items on an "assembly line" with individual production. The differences between producers and consumers and between goods and services are discovered as children study roles of family members, community workers, and people in other places who produce goods and services. Price, cost, supply, market, production, and other concepts may be noted in such computer programs as *Sell Apples, Lemonade, Markets, Factory,* and *Market Place.* The opportunity-cost principle is used as students consider such questions as "What does Joan give up if she spends her allowance for candy?" "What does a family give up when they take a trip instead of spending the money for other things?" The world of work, roles of various workers, and careers in different fields of work are included in some units.

Concepts

Conflict between wants and resources, scarcity, costs, benefits, trade-offs, division of labor, specialization, interdependence, economic system, trade, production, consumption, distribution, producers, consumers, goods, services, market, supply, demand, price, money, credit, saving, spending, investing

Concept Clusters

Basic economic problem: conflict between wants and resources, need to make choices, need for an economic system to allocate resources to alternative uses

Specialization: division of labor by occupations, technological applications, and geographic situation; resulting interdependence

Productive resources: human (workers, managers, know-how), capital (tools, machines, factories), natural (soil, water, climate, minerals, forests)

The market: means of allocating resources; interaction of supply and demand; use of money, transportation, and communication; modification by policies related to economic goals

Economic goals: equity, growth, stability, security, freedom, employment, efficiency

Career clusters: agriculture, communication, education, health, recreation, transportation, and so on

Generalizations

Members of families, people in communities, and societies meet the basic economic problem by finding answers to these questions: What shall we produce? How shall we produce? How much shall we produce?

How shall we distribute what we produce?

Division of labor increases production and leads to interdependence among individuals, communities, states, and nations.

In our system the government provides certain goods and services, such as highways, schools, protection, and welfare services.

Illustrative questions, study guides, and lesson plan follow.

FOCUSING QUESTIONS TO GUIDE STUDY

How is their use of resources like and different from ours? [comparing]
What changes in use of resources are shown in this graph? [interpreting]
What does the future hold for exhaustion of mineral resources? [predicting]
What appear to be their most valuable resources? [evaluating]

WHAT DO THEY PRODUCE?		FIND AND DEFINE THESE CONCEPTS		BENEFIT-COST ANALYSIS
Author	Carpenter	Needs	Benefits	What are the benefits?
Baker	Cartographer	Wants	Costs	Who gets the benefits?
Bus Driver	Farmer	Goods	Supply	What are the costs?
Dentist	Painter	Services	Demand	Who pays the costs?
Doctor	Pilot	Producers	Market	What will be gained?
Nurse	Plumber	Consumers	Labor	What will be given up?
Librarian	Teacher	Resources	Capital	Do benefits exceed losses?

(continued)

ARE YOU A WISE CONSUMER	CONSUMER CHECKLIST	ECONOMIC DECISION MAKING
Distinguish needs from wants.	Why should I buy it?	Define the situation.
Know what you really need.	Why do I need it?	Clarify and prioritize goals.
Know what is given up if you buy something.	How reasonable is the price?	Clarify alternatives or choices.
Control influence of ads.	How good is the quality?	Analyze consequences of alternatives.
Recognize sales pitches.	Should I wait for a sale?	Make decision in light of goals.
Evaluate goods and services.	Am I just following a habit?	Evaluate decision in terms of goals and consequences.
Get advice from consumer reports.	What are reasons for and against buying it?	

FIND AND LIST EXAMPLES OF DIVISION OF LABOR

Housing Construction _____

_____

Supermarkets _____

_____

Airports _____

_____

LESSON PLAN: THREE ECONOMIC SYSTEMS

Objective

To identify three economic systems and describe how they work

Materials

Students' textbooks, pages 446–448, and activity books, pages 201–202

Introduction

Ask students to recall the basic economic questions that all countries must answer (what to produce, how much to produce, how to distribute what is produced).

Explain that an economic system is the way people in a country produce and use goods and services. State that today we are going to identify three systems and find out how they work.

Development

1. Direct students to read pages 446–448 of their textbooks and take notes on the main features of each economic system.

(continued)

2. Write the following on the chalkboard:

        TRADITIONAL   MARKET   COMMAND

3. Ask students to report the features they noted for each economic system. List the features of each system on the chalkboard.

4. Discuss the main differences among the three economic systems. Include attention to who decides what and how much to produce, choices of consumers, how prices are set, and who gets the profits.

Conclusion and Evaluation

1. Ask students to state which system they think is most efficient and to give reasons for their choice.

2. Discuss advantages and disadvantages of each system. Include attention to situations in which a command economy may be needed and how some features of a market economy may be used in a command economic system to improve production.

3. Ask students to take the test on Economic Systems, pages 201–2 of their workbooks.

Follow-up

Read the following statements and ask students to identify the related economic system:

1. It may be referred to as free enterprise. (Market)
2. The government decides what to produce. (Command)
3. There is little or no surplus. (Traditional)
4. People produce and use what they need. (Traditional)
5. Supply and demand determine price. (Market)
6. The government takes the profits. (Command)
7. Competition among producers keeps prices down. (Market)
8. The government sets the pay scale of workers. (Command)
9. The economy has been the same for generations. (Traditional)

Cultural Anthropology

Knowledge of both universal and particular traits of the diverse peoples of the world is provided by cultural anthropologists, who study the wholeness or totality of human cultures. From this rich storehouse of knowledge is drawn content ranging from beliefs, values, traditions, and customs to technology, tools and the ability to use them, institutions, social organization, and aesthetic and religious expression. The all-inclusive "culture" concept brings together the foregoing and other learned behavior to give a unified view of ways of living. Examples of social studies units rooted in cultural anthropology are comparative studies of families, villages, communities, early civilizations, and prehistoric peoples. Specific units on Eskimos, native Americans, peoples of Africa, Aztecs, Incas, Mayas, and other groups include anthropological material on food, shelter, clothing, tools, arts, crafts, rituals, ceremonies, folklore, and other aspects of culture. This material is used to answer such key questions as: What is their culture? Why is it like that? How was it changed by interaction with others?

Concepts

Culture, society, community, social organization, civilization, traditions, customs, cultural change, technology, beliefs, values

Concept Clusters

Culture: learned patterns of behavior; ways of living; arts, crafts, technology, religion, economic activities, language, other learned behaviors

Processes of cultural change: invention, discovery, diffusion, adaptation

Food-getting activities: gathering, hunting, fishing, herding, gardening, agriculture

Societies: folk or preliterate, preindustrial, transitional, industrial

Characteristics of civilization: writing, accumulation of food and other goods for managed use, division of labor, government, arts, sciences, urbanization, trade

Generalizations

Culture is socially transmitted in all societies, differs from society to society, and is a prime determiner of behavior.

Families around the world have common needs, but they meet those needs in different ways.

Major differences among people are cultural, not biological.

The culture of modern societies has evolved from the culture of earlier societies.

Illustrative questions and study guides follow.

FOCUSING QUESTIONS TO GUIDE STUDY

What can we learn about their culture by examining these objects? [inferring]

What might have been the main causes for the shift from hunting to herding? [hypothesizing]

In general, what conditions were necessary for the rise of civilization? [generalizing]

Which concepts in the computer program *Archeological Search* are most useful in our study of early Egypt? [evaluating]

COMPARING FAMILIES	COMPARING COMMUNITIES	COMPARING CULTURES
How are they alike and different on the following? Food Cooking Clothing Homes Rooms Furnishings Health care Safety Roles of children	How are they alike and different on the following? Physical environment Climate Population Ethnic groups Type of government	How are they alike and different on these ways of living? Family life Kinship systems Community life Social activities

Roles of adults Rules for children Recreation Holidays Other important features	Main economic activities Recreation Transportation Urban problems Urban renewal Shifts to suburbs Main zones Other distinctive features	Economic and political systems Response to the environment Science Technology Resource use Arts Crafts Literature Customs Values Cultural borrowing/contributions Other significant features

How can artifacts such as these be used to develop concepts and appreciation of aesthetic expression in cultures under study? San Diego City Schools

Mark X by the Items Below that are Artifacts.

___ acorns	___ canoes	___ pots
___ aprons	___ clothing	___ sandals
___ baskets	___ corn	___ spoons
___ berries	___ fish	___ trees
___ blankets	___ ladles	___ wagons

Sociology

Concepts and key ideas from sociology are included in many units of study. The family and school, two basic social institutions, are usually studied early in the program. The positions and roles of members of the family, the teacher, and other school personnel are included. Values and expectations of children, parents, teachers, and community workers are considered in the context of children's relationships to each other and to adults. Norms and sanctions and their relation to social control are discovered through the children's own experiences and in units that include material on customs, regulations, rewards, punishments, and laws in communities and other places near and far away. Understandings of processes of social interaction, such as cooperation, competition, and conflict, are also developed. Historical and geographic studies centered on the community, state, nation, and other places typically include such sociological concepts as role, groups, institutions, values, and social change.

Concepts

Society, socialization, group behavior, population, social problems, norms, roles, status, expectations, social processes, social control, group structure, group interaction, minority groups, social class

Concept Clusters

Values: personal, social, economic, political, religious, aesthetic

Social institutions: family, economic, political, educational, scientific, religious, recreational, welfare, aesthetic

Processes of social interaction: cooperation, competition, conflict, assimilation, accommodation

Groups: primary, secondary, reference, ethnic, minority

Social control: dependency, rewards, sanctions, norms, laws

Generalizations

The family is a basic social institution in all societies.

The work of society is done by organized groups.

One's role in a group is related to the expectations of others.

Societies need a system of social control in order to survive.

Social institutions are shaped by societal values and norms.

Illustrative questions and study guides follow.

FOCUSING QUESTIONS TO GUIDE STUDY

What are the differences between ethnic and racial groups? [comparing]

What means of social control will we find in democratic countries? [hypothesizing]

Which urban renewal proposals stress social values? Which one do you favor? Why? [analyzing, evaluating]

What should we include in our plan for litter cleanup? [synthesizing]

CAN YOU DEFINE THESE TERMS?		CAN YOU ANSWER THESE QUESTIONS?	HOW SHALL WE INVESTIGATE IT?
Role	Status	How do groups shape people's behavior?	Interview experts?
Cooperation	Competition		Conduct a survey?
Innovation	Institution	What is the difference between ethnic and minority groups?	Do a case study?
Leadership	Followership		Do a content analysis Trace its history?
Customs	Traditions	How do families, education, and other institutions shape the behavior of people?	Do an experiment?
Norms	Values		Some other way? Several ways?
Ethnic	Minority		
Society	Socialization	What are the main institutions in our society?	

Psychology

Concepts and key ideas from psychology are embedded in units of study at all levels of instruction. For example, the concept of individual differences is important in studies of families, schools, community workers, and people in other places. How the senses—seeing, hearing, touching, and others—help one to observe and to learn may be included early in the program. The importance of attitudes, motives, and interests as key factors in human behavior is brought home in both contemporary and historical studies of people near and far away. How to control feelings and what happens when feelings are not controlled are considered in the context of children's own experiences and in studies of others. Students are taught effective ways of learning; they are taught how to remember and use what is learned and how to improve critical thinking and problem solving.

Concepts

Learning, senses, remembering, self-concept, intergroup relations, personal-social needs, individual differences, attitudes, feelings

Concept Clusters

Using our senses to learn: seeing, hearing, smelling, touching, tasting, balancing

Learning and remembering: clear purposes, meaning, practice, use, review, application, grouping around main ideas, contrast, comparison, concentration, knowledge of results, ideas in own words

Personal-social needs: acceptance, belonging, security, achievement, self-expression, interaction with others, learning, self-actualization

Individual differences: appearance, personality, role, attitudes, beliefs, family, customs, learning, abilities, habits

Social roles: leadership, followership, aggression, submission

Generalizations

Individual differences exist among members of families, children in schools, and people in communities.

Perceptions of others vary from individual to individual and are conditioned by motives, attitudes, and other factors.

Both individual and group needs may be met through group action.

Learning and remembering can be improved by concentrated effort.

An individual takes different roles in different groups and situations.

Illustrative questions and study guides follow.

FOCUSING QUESTIONS TO GUIDE STUDY

What does this picture show about individual differences? [interpreting]
What does that kind of behavior show about their values? [inferring]
What do you think will happen if leadership is changed? [predicting]
How can we show individual differences in our class? [synthesizing]

FINDING INDIVIDUAL DIFFERENCES		FEELINGS AND THEIR CONTROL	LEARNING ABOUT HOW WE LEARN
Height	Weight	What makes you angry? How do you control it?	How do we use seeing, hearing, and other senses to learn?
Appearance	Personality	What makes you excited? How do you control it?	What study habits help us to learn?
Likes	Dislikes	What makes you afraid? How do you control it?	How can we improve short-term and long-term memory?
Hobbies	Sports	What makes you sad? How do you control it?	How do we learn attitudes and values? How do they affect our behavior?
Attitudes	Interests	On which do you need help?	
Customs	Habits		
Beliefs	Values		
Skills	Others		

Philosophy

Although it is one of the humanities, philosophy is included in this chapter because conceptual elements related to values, inquiry, and reasoning are part of the social studies. Understanding of such values as freedom, equality, responsibility, loyalty, and patriotism is emphasized along with the positive attitudes and feelings needed to make them enduring qualities. Students should also understand the nature of logical fallacies, the meaning of the spirit of philosophical inquiry, and the processes involved in making judgments. The following value-related elements are found in most social studies materials.

Concepts

Rights, duties, moral conduct, loyalty, freedom, justice, equality, self-interest, common good, ethical behavior, free society, free inquiry, responsibility, cooperation, creativity, open-mindedness, concern for others

Concept Clusters

The spirit of inquiry: longing to know and understand, questioning of all things; search for data and their meaning; demand for verification; respect for logic; consideration of premises, causes, and consequences

Logical fallacies: appeal to force, argument from ignorance, appeal to pity, emphasis on false cause, snob appeal, neglect of all causes, false premises

Making judgments: clarifying what is to be judged, defining related criteria, analyzing in terms of criteria, making the judgment, checking the judgment with others

Generalizations

The basic value of human dignity underlies our way of life.

Criteria should be defined in terms of values and used to decide what is good or ought to be.

Ideas and proposals must be subjected to critical examination if their value is to be determined.

Illustrative questions and study guides follow.

FOCUSING QUESTIONS TO GUIDE STUDY

What values should we use to judge treatment of minority groups? [recalling]

How does enlightened loyalty differ from blind patriotism? [comparing]

What action should be taken to improve equality of opportunity for this group? [analyzing, synthesizing]

DO YOU AVOID LOGICAL FALLACIES?	DO YOU MAKE SOUND JUDGMENTS?	IS IT TRUE?
Can you give examples of these?	Clarify what is to be judged.	Is it true by definition?
Appeal to force Snob appeal	Define the criteria to use.	Is it true based on observation?
Appeal to pity Mass appeal	Apply all the criteria.	Is it true based on criteria?
False cause False premise	Make the judgment fairly.	Is it true based on inference?
False conclusion Either–or stand	Test the judgment:	Is it true based on values?
Selection of evidence that fits a claim	Does it apply to new cases?	Is it true based on reasons?
Generalization based on one case or inadequate evidence	What are the consequences if it is applied universally?	Is it true based on reliable evidence?
	Is it consistent with similar judgments? Is it fair?	Is it true according to experts?

Process Knowledge

Process knowledge is drawn from various disciplines and is adapted for presentation in current materials for students. Most recent textbooks include information on the work of geographers, historians, and other scholars that is related to such topics as world regions, history and geography of our country, and world cultures. Two important aspects of process knowledge examined here are the values and attitudes that are a part of inquiry and the models, methods, and materials used to study human relationships.

Values and Attitudes

The following values and attitudes are emphasized in current materials:

High regard for clear thinking, respect for differing views, and clear definition of problems and terms

Objectivity in gathering and reporting information, demand for evidence to support conclusions, awareness of how feelings can cloud thinking

Corroboration of findings by double-checking them, analysis of assumptions, biases, and possible errors, and continuing evaluation of study procedures to find ways to make improvements

Lasting curiosity about the causes and consequences of human behavior

Simple but important steps toward the attainment of these values may be made by posing such questions to students as

What is good about the idea? How can we use it? How can we improve it? [evaluating]

How can we restate the problem to make it clearer? What terms need clearing up? [analyzing]

Will we get the same result a second time? Why do we need to check that information? What other source can we use? [hypothesizing, comparing]

What is unfair in this statement? How is it biased? What changes are needed in it? [evaluating]

What evidence supports that idea? What evidence does not support it? [classifying]

What additional information do we need? Where can we get it? [analyzing, recalling]

How do feelings affect thinking about this issue? How can we control them? [analyzing]

Models, Source Materials, and Methods of Study

The models presented in Figure 6.1 are adapted from reports and recent social studies materials. Common phases of study are shown in the center and are surrounded by examples of models of study or inquiry used in various disciplines. Information on how geographers, historians, archaeologists, and other scholars conduct their studies may be found in social studies textbooks. The model given for anthropology may be useful when planning field trips and field studies. Social studies decision-making models are closely related to those presented for political science and economics (see chapter 9).

Source materials are shown in the last section. Many of the items listed are

MODELS OF STUDY OR INQUIRY

Geography

Identify and define the topic or the problem to be studied.

Consider all factors that may be related.

State questions or hypotheses related to each factor.

Gather data related to each hypothesis or question.

Evaluate and organize data to test hypotheses or answer questions.

Interpret findings and draw conclusions.

Suggest other needed studies.

Anthropology

Define objectives or questions for the field study.

Make a plan for gathering and recording data for each objective or question.

Make necessary arrangements.

Gather data by direct observation, interview, and participation (if feasible).

Organize and interpret data in light of objectives.

Summarize findings and draw conclusions.

Compare findings and conclusions with those of others.

History

Define the question or problem to be studied.

State hypotheses or questions to guide study.

Collect and evaluate sources of information.

Analyze and synthesize data in the sources.

Organize findings to answer questions and test hypotheses.

Interpret findings in relation to social, economic, and political developments.

Common Phases of Study

Define the problem and clarify objectives

State questions or hypotheses to guide study.

Make and use a plan to gather data.

Appraise, organize, and interpret data.

Make and check conclusions.

Consider further needs for study.

Sociology

Define the problem and relate it to existing knowledge.

State hypotheses to guide study.

Select an adequate sample.

Use appropriate techniques to gather data.

Organize and analyze the data to test each hypothesis.

Interpret findings and draw conclusions.

Suggest other studies.

Political Analysis

Define the problem and clarify related values.

Consider different choices or solutions.

Evaluate each choice or solution in terms of values, facts, and historical background.

Identify possible consequences of each choice or solution.

Evaluate the consequences in light of values.

Make judgments as to which choice or solution is best in terms of values.

Economic Analysis

Define the problem. Where are we and where do we want to go?

Identify goals, and rank them in order of priority.

Consider alternative ways to attain goals with usable resources.

Use concepts to explore the problem and the effects of alternative proposals.

Complete an analysis of each alternative in terms of goals.

Choose the best alternative to achieve goals.

Figure 6.1

available in media centers and in community resource centers, as described in chapter 3. Learning activities presented in children's textbooks and related activity booklets may be used to teach the recording, organizing, and presenting of data and to evaluate skills and other outcomes of study.

Methods of study are described in instructional materials for students along with suggestions for using them. Examples are examining artifacts, interviewing, polling, getting ideas from primary sources (letters, diaries, photos, and the like) and secondary sources (books and other items written or created by people not present during the event).

A helpful activity is to guide students in a planning discussion focused on the following: How shall we gather information? What sources shall we use? How shall we present information? The following examples shows how to summarize the discussion.

STUDYING OUR STATE

Ways to Gather Information	Sources of Information	Ways to Present Information
1.	1.	1.
2.	2.	2.

COLLECTING AND PROCESSING DATA

Source Materials

Written materials: textbooks, references, letters, diaries, minutes, newspapers, magazines, government reports and documents, business records, biographical materials, case studies

Art objects: paintings, murals, tapestries, vases, plaques, medals, jewelry, wall paintings, portraits, ornaments, sculpture

Orally transmitted materials: folklore, legends, sagas, ballads, anecdotes, stories, eyewitness accounts

Recorded materials: photographs, slides, films, tapes, records, maps, diagrams, graphs, charts

Inscriptions: monuments, plaques, buildings, coins, clay tablets, walls, grave markers, bridges, art objects

Physical remains: buildings, monuments, implements, tools, utensils, weapons, pottery, baskets, clothing, textiles, costumes, furnishings, musical instruments

Data bases: classroom, school, library, computer-linked

Methods of Study

Content analysis of printed materials, films, and other instructional media to gather data on meanings of terms, changes and trends, uses of resources, sex bias, treatment of minority groups, use of words to stir the emotions, underlying assumptions, and the frequency of occurrence of other items under study

Field trips to collect data on farming, business activities, conservation, transportation, communication, artifacts in exhibits, and other topics under study

Observation of activities of family members, construction workers, and other community workers; of the roles of police, fire fighters, and other public officials; of changes in the weather and seasons; of meetings of the city council, school board, and other groups

Interviews, polls, and questionnaires to gather data from fellow students, parents, community officials, business people, health workers, experts on conservation, and other experts on issues and questions under study

Role playing and simulation of activities and decision making in families, markets, banks, and other situations in which identification with others and involvement in decision-making processes are important

Experiments to determine what happens when different procedures or treatments are used, such as selecting and testing hypotheses about division of labor or presenting objects of varying sizes or colors to find out how one's perception of them changes

Analysis of proposals and activities in terms of benefits and costs, alternatives and consequences, stated goals and values, risks and rewards, and system analysis

Recording, Organizing, and Presenting Data

Make notes or record data obtained through interviews and on field trips.

Construct maps to show the distribution of homes, businesses, population, resources, and other phenomena; how such distributions as transportation networks and cities are related; and the flow of people, goods, and services between places.

Construct models, diagrams, graphs, tables, and charts of objects and processes under study to demonstrate and explain how they work and how they are used.

Prepare sketches, drawings, displays, and exhibits to illustrate processes, show the uses of objects, and highlight relationships between objects and human activities.

Prepare reports, oral or written, to share findings and conclusions with others.

Evaluating Inquiry and Materials

Keep logs, diaries, or other records for use in evaluating both individual and group activities.

Construct and use rating scales, charts, and checklists to appraise reports, maps, films, other sources of information, and individual and group activities.

Participate in discussions to appraise and improve the effectiveness of both individual and group inquiry.

Questions, Activities, and Evaluation

1. Examine a social studies textbook and note examples of the following:
   a. Concepts, concept clusters, themes, generalizations, and questions that include social science concepts
   b. Values and attitudes, models, materials, and methods of study
   c. Relative attention to material from core disciplines
2. Examine a course of study and do the same.
3. Examine a unit of instruction and do the same.
4. Which of the study guides, sample learning activities, and models presented in this chapter do you prefer? Discuss your choices with others and tell how you may use them.
5. Note how you might use several of the methods and materials in a unit.
6. Prepare five or six illustrative questions or study guides, using concepts, concept clusters, or themes.
7. Complete the following and discuss your responses with a colleague, exploring reasons for differences:
   a. A primary reason for basing the social studies program on content from the social sciences is _____
   b. The concepts from the following social sciences that I believe will be most useful in units I plan to teach are
      (1) Geography: _____
      (2) History: _____
      (3) Economics: _____
      (4) Political Science: _____
      (5) Anthropology: _____
      (6) Sociology: _____
      (7) Psychology: _____
   c. Models, methods, and materials most useful in elementary social studies are
      _____

References

Banks, James A., and Ambrose A. Clegg, Jr., *Teaching Strategies for the Social Studies* (4th ed.). White Plains, NY: Longman, 1990. Chapters on disciplines.

Beyer, Barry K., "What Philosophy Offers to the Teaching of Thinking," *Educational Leadership,* 47 (February 1990), 55–60.

Bohannon, Paul, "Spotlight on Anthropology," *Social Education,* 49 (February 1985), 135–38.

Bradley Commission on History in the Schools, *Building a History Curriculum.* Washington, DC: Educational Excellence Network, 1988.

California, *History—Social Science Framework.* Sacramento, CA: State Department of Education, 1988.

Checklist. New York: Joint Council on Economic Education, 1212 Avenue of the Americas, New York, NY 10036. List of materials for teaching economic concepts.

CIVITAS: A Framework for Civic Education. Project of the Center for Civic Education and the Council for the Advancement of Citizenship. Calabasas, CA: Center for Civic Education, 1990. Objectives, content, and activities for instruction on civic participation, knowledge, and virtue needed to be effective citizens.

Dowd, Frances, "Geography is Children's Literature, Math, Science, Art and a Whole World of Activities," *Journal of Geography,* 89 (March/April 1990), 68–73. How to integrate geography and literature; sample book lists.

Dynneson, Thomas L., "An Anthropological Approach to Learning and Teaching: Eleven Propositions," *Social Education,* 48 (September/October 1984), 410–18.

Egan, Kieran, "Layers of Historical Understanding," *Theory and Research in Social Education,* 17 (Fall 1989), 280–94. History as story, dramatic narrative, pattern seeking, and search for what actually happened.

Finn, Chester E. Jr., and Diane Ravitch, "No Trivial Pursuit," *Phi Delta Kappan,* 69 (April 1988), 559–64. Plea for structuring social studies around history and literature.

Gagnon, Paul, ed., *Historical Literacy: The Case for History in American Education.* New York: Macmillan, 1989. Recommendations from Bradley Commission and historians.

Genip News. Newsletter of Geographic Education National Implementation Project.

Geographic Education National Implementation Project, *K–6 Geography,* and *7–12 Geography,* Macomb, IL: National Council for Geographic Education, 1987; 1989. Themes, key ideas, learning activities.

Gilliard, June V., Chair, *Economics: What and When.* New York: Joint Council on Economic Education, 1988. Sequence of instruction for 22 concepts.

Gross, Richard E., and Thomas Dynneson, eds., *Social Science Perspectives on Citizenship Education.* New York: Teachers College Press, 1991. Chapters on disciplines.

"History and the Social Studies," *Social Studies and the Young Learner,* 2 (November/December 1989), 2–31. Special issue.

Jackson, Richard H., and Lloyd E. Hudman, *World Regional Geography.* New York: John Wiley & Sons, 1990. Comprehensive overview.

Johnson, Tony W., *Philosophy for Children: An Approach to Critical Thinking.* Bloomington, IN: Phi Delta Kappa, 1984. Description of program and materials for children.

Joint Committee on Geographic Education of the National Council for Geographic Education and the Association of American Geographers, *Guidelines for Geographic Education.* Macomb, IL: National Council for Geographic Education, 1984. Five themes and grade-level suggestions for development.

Levstik, Linda S., *History from the Bottom Up.* How to Do It, Series 5, No. 1. Washington, D.C.: National Council for the Social Studies, 1986. Tips on using primary sources.

Lipman, Matthew, *Philosophy Goes to School.* Philadelphia: Temple University Press, 1988. Suggestions for elementary school instruction.

Mehaffy, George L., "Oral History in Elementary Classrooms," *Social Education,* 48 (September/October 1984), 470–72.

"Moving Ahead With Geography," *Social Studies and the Young Learner,* 1 (November/December 1988), 3–29. Special issue.

Muessig, Raymond H., and Vincent R. Rogers, eds., *Social Science Seminar Series* (2nd ed.). Columbus, OH: Cha. E. Merrill, 1979–80. Volumes on history, geography, economics, political science, anthropology, and sociology.

Muir, Sharon Pray, "Time Concepts for Elementary School Children," *Social Education,* 54 (April/May 1990), 215–18, 247.

National Commission on Social Studies in the Schools, *Charting a Course: Social Studies for the 21st Century.* Washington, D.C.: The Commission, 1989. Available from National Council for the Social Studies; last section on disciplines.

Natoli, Salvatore J., *Strengthening Geography in the Social Studies,* Bulletin 81. Washington, D.C.: National Council for the Social Studies, 1988.

Sunal, Cynthia S., and Barbara A. Hatcher, *Studying History through Art,* How to Do It, Series 5, No. 2. Washington, D.C.: National Council for the Social Studies, 1986.

Thornton, Stephen J., "Should We Be Teaching More History?" *Theory and Research in Social Education,* 18 (Winter 1990), 53–60. Arguments against adding more history.

Update, National Geographic Society, 17th and M Streets, N. W., Washington, D.C. 20036. Get on mailing list; reports on geography learning activities.

Wilson, Everett K., "Spotlight on Sociology," *Social Education,* 51 (January 1987), 26–27.

Wronski, Stanley P., and Donald H. Bragaw, eds., *Social Studies and Social Sciences: A Fifty-Year Perspective.* Bulletin 78. Washington, D.C.: National Council for the Social Studies, 1986. Chapters on history and social sciences.

Incorporating Instruction on Topics of Special Concern

CHAPTER 7

Objective and Related Focusing Questions

To present guidelines and strategies for including instruction related to social concerns and demands:

- What general guidelines are helpful in planning and providing instruction on social concerns?

- What guidelines are helpful in incorporating instruction on multicultural, gender-equity, law-related, global, and environmental education?

- How are goals and objectives of various programs related to goals and objectives of the social studies?

- What conceptual components are included in different programs?

- How can concepts be used to generate focusing questions that guide study and move students' thinking to high cognitive levels?

- What are examples of teaching and learning activities to include in the social studies?

Guidelines

There are several guidelines for incorporating recommended programs in the social studies. The following apply to unit and lesson planning as well as to overall program planning.

Goals

The goals of each program should be clarified to identify their relationship to goals of the social studies and other subjects. For example, although multicultural education is strongly related to the social studies, aspects that deal with aesthetic expression can be included in art, music, and literature. And many aspects of environmental education are included in science education. After goals are clear, the teacher can decide whether to develop interdisciplinary units or to integrate instruction into appropriate subjects. This is far better than attempting to "do it all" in the social studies.

Integration of Instruction

Ideally, instruction should be integrated into units of study. For example, career education[1] has been incorporated in studies of workers in the community, state, and nation. Peace education may be included in global studies, which in turn may be a part of units on communities around the world, our country, and other lands.

Conceptual Components

To plan instruction on solid conceptual foundations, the teacher should identify key concepts, concept clusters, themes, and descriptive and prescriptive generalizations. These conceptual components serve as tools of study and schemata to structure or organize information, and help to generate focusing questions. They also help in preparing plans for developing main ideas, concepts, vocabulary, and the reading-language skills essential to effective learning.

Illustrative Questions, Study Guides, and Learning Activities

Focusing questions that link concepts and thinking processes should be generated along with study guides and learning activities. Those presented in this chapter may be used in regular units as task or activity cards and as study guides. Others may be generated by referring to the master list of activities in chapter 2.

Pitfalls to Be Avoided

When a special program is introduced, there is a danger of getting so involved in "our new program for the year" that the developmental social studies program is neglected. As one teacher said, "This year we are doing global studies. I'll get back to social studies next year, I hope."

Another pitfall is "drumming in the facts" about our ethnic group, environmental

---

[1]See the 1988 edition of this volume for a review of career education.

problems, or other topics. This approach is contrary to the recommendations of educators from various ethnic groups and experts on environmental education. Both of these dangers can be avoided if concepts, concept clusters, themes, and generalizations are used to organize information.

Slanting historical data to favor a group and the use of exhortation, polemics, scare tactics, and denigration of one group to play up another group must be avoided. Such techniques are self-defeating. Emphasis must be given to critical thinking in all phases of instruction, including topics of special concern.

Another problem is overemphasizing one aspect within a program, such as focusing on pollution problems and neglecting conservation and other aspects of environmental education, or dwelling on a single ethnic group to the exclusion of others.

Finally, there is the temptation to present ideas and concerns of interest to the teacher and other adults, but far beyond the comprehension of elementary students. Fascinating as they may be to the teacher, theories of race relations in ethnic studies, technical aspects of nuclear waste disposal in environmental studies, and diplomatic relations in global education are beyond the grasp of children. Such topics are better postponed until students have the background and the maturity to understand them.

Multicultural Education

In this section *multicultural education* is used in a broad sense to include multiethnic and ethnic heritage studies in a comparative culture context. The trend is to place the study of ethnic groups within the totality of human experience. High priority is given to developing an appreciation of one's own and other cultures and to eradicating racism, classism, sexism, ethnocentrism, prejudice, and discrimination. Value systems, lifestyles, cultural heritages, and current conditions are studied along with the cultural contributions of various groups. Knowledge of one's own and other groups is brought together to answer these questions: Who am I? Who are we? Who are they? What is special about each individual? Opportunities are provided for students to learn about their root culture, the derived culture of their ethnic group, and the common culture all of us share.

The reality of cultural and ethnic pluralism should be recognized and viewed as a source of cultural enrichment rather than as a divisive factor. All ethnic groups should have opportunities to participate fully in social institutions and still maintain their ethnic identity if they so desire.

Four approaches, not one, should be used: study of contributions of diverse groups; addition of multicultural topics to the curriculum; the transformation approach, whereby topics are viewed from various perspectives; and the decision-making/social action approach (Banks and McGee, 1989).

Goals and Illustrative Objectives

The following goals show the breadth of multicultural studies. Each goal is followed by an example of a related instructional objective that illustrates a desired student attainment.

1. To develop understanding of cultural diversity in our society, of diversity within and among ethnic groups, of ethnic heritage as a factor in lifestyle, and of the history, culture, and achievements of ethnic groups

   Describe gaps between the professed ideals of our society and current realities for native Americans; list three ways the gaps can be closed.

2. To apply thinking and decision-making processes to ethnic issues through such activities as interpreting events from various ethnic perspectives and evaluating proposals and actions

   Evaluate proposals for eliminating racism, prejudice, and discrimination by ranking them in order according to your judgment of their effectiveness.

3. To develop skills needed for communicating with both majority and minority groups, for resolving conflicts, and for taking action to improve current conditions

   Describe the steps of a procedure that may be used to clarify an issue in our school and make a plan to resolve it.

4. To develop attitudes, values, and behavior supportive of cultural diversity, ethnic differences, and the welfare of society

   State reasons why everyone in our society must be accorded justice, equal protection, and due process of law.

Conceptual Components

Concepts

Culture	Ethnicity	Ethnocentrism	Pluralism
Heritage	Race	Stereotype	Assimilation
Status	Discrimination	Prejudice	Social protest

Concept Clusters

Social interaction: cooperation, competition, conflict, assimilation, accommodation

Democratic values: justice, equality, liberty, concern for others, use of intelligence to solve problems, respect for human dignity

Americans: African, Cuban, Chinese, Japanese, Jewish, Puerto Rican, Italian, German, Greek, and so on

Themes

Cultural and ethnic pluralism	Unity and diversity in our society
Social protest and action	Discrimination against minorities

Descriptive Generalizations

Cultural diversity exists within ethnic groups as well as among ethnic groups.

American culture has been enriched by the achievements of members of many different ethnic groups and cultures.

What ethnic groups might you include in a unit to show contributions to cultural diversity in your community? San Francisco

Prescriptive Generalizations

All groups have a responsibility to take action that will eliminate racism, prejudice, and discrimination.

Civil rights guaranteed by the Constitution must be extended to all groups in our society.

QUESTIONS TO GUIDE STUDY OF GROUPS

How does the author define the terms *ethnic group, minority group,* and *race?* [interpreting]

Why do you suppose certain ethnic groups resisted *assimilation?* [inferring]

Why do you think some groups formed *ethnic* enclaves in cities? How can your idea be checked? [hypothesizing]

How can we organize and present our findings on the goals, actions, and achievements of *ethnic* groups? [synthesizing]

Which *actions* have been most effective in achieving goals? Why? Which have been least effective? Why? [evaluating]

(continued)

MULTIETHNIC DISPLAY OR FAIR

Make and display scrapbooks, drawings, murals, reports, movie box rolls, and other items related to topics in ethnic heritage and multiethnic units.

Have a multiethnic fair at which items such as those just listed are displayed and students give descriptions and explanations to visitors.

LESSON PLAN: THE FIRST AMERICANS

Objective:

To describe location and customs of five groups of First Americans

Materials:

Ann Sihler, "The First Americans," *Young America,* pp. 8–9.

Teaching/Learning Activities

Introduction

Ask students to tell who they think were the first Americans.

Direct students to read the article on the first Americans and be prepared to discuss these questions:

>Where did the first Americans come from?
>What five groups of first Americans are described?
>In what area of the country was each group located?
>What ways of living of each group are described?

Development

Discuss each of the above questions, including attention to the following:

>Location of each group
>Ways of obtaining food, shelter, and clothing
>Roles of men and women
>Unique or special features and contributions of each group

Conclusion/Evaluation

Ask students to summarize new ideas they discovered about the first Americans.

Have students make a retrieval chart that includes information on each group: location, food, shelter, clothing, special features

Use test items such as:

>Which group lived in a desert area?
>A. Cheyenne B. Hopi C. Iroquois D. Seminole

Follow-up

Have individuals or small groups investigate other groups of first Americans and share their findings.

Have individuals or small groups investigate the groups and find out where and how they are living today.

(continued)

Data Base Cards

Make data base cards and fact sheets for questions and topics under study, for example:

Data Card on Jewish Americans

Countries they left: _____

When they left: _____

Why they left: _____

Problems on arrival: _____

Ways of adapting: _____

Work they did at first: _____

How they helped each other: _____

Examples of achievements: _____

_____

IMMIGRANTS

See a filmstrip on immigrants, such as *Immigrants: The Dream and the Reality;* follow by discussing such questions as:

What dream did they have?
What problems did they have?
How did they solve the problems?
To what extent did their dream come true?
What still needs to be done to make their dream come true?

HISTORY QUIZ

Have students run the computer program *Black American History Quiz* to find out which black Americans they can identify. Follow up by having them investigate black Americans in the quiz.

WHO'S WHO

Make a *Who's Who* of notable men and women who have contributed to American culture.

(continued)

CREATIVE WRITING

Complete statements or write chain stories on topics under study.

When someone is name-calling I _____.

When I am caught name-calling I _____.

When someone prejudges others I _____.

When I am told I have prejudged others I _____.

Write about a special event with emphasis on how participants must have felt.

A person who has just beome an American citizen

A person who has been discriminated against in getting a job

A person who fled to the United States to gain freedom

PEN PALS

Write to pen pals and exchange scrapbooks with students of differing ethnic heritage. Use contacts set up by local schools or one of the following:

Correspondence Canada, 2695 McWillis, St. Laurent, Quebec H4R 1M5 Canada

International Friendship League, 40 Mount Vernon Street, Boston, MA 02108

Logo Exchange, ICCE, University of Oregon, Eugene, OR 97403

National Logo Exchange, P.O. Box 5341, Charlottesville, VA 22905

Student Letter Exchange, R R 4, Box 109, Waseca, MN 56093

World Pen Pals, 1690 Como Avenue, St. Paul, MN 55108

Sources of Strategies, Activities, and Materials

"Appreciating Diversity," *Social Studies and the Young Learner,* 1 (March/April 1989), 2–29. Special issue on multicultural education.

Banks, James A., and Cherry A. McGee, eds., *Multicultural Education Issues and Perspectives.* Boston: Allyn & Bacon, 1989.

Clark, Leon E., *Through African Eyes: Teaching Strategies.* New York: CITE Books, 1989.

Cullinan, Bernice E., *Literature and the Child* (2nd ed.). New York: Harcourt Brace Jovanovich, 1989. Chapter on social/ethnic groups.

"Educating Immigrant Children," *Phi Delta Kappa,* 70 (November 1988), 199–225. A special section.

Harvey, Karen D., Lisa D. Harjo, and Jane K. Jackson, *Teaching About Native Americans.* Washington, DC: National Council for the Social Studies, 1990.

Ramsey, Patricia G., Edwina B. Vold, and Leslie R. Williams, *Multicultural Education: A Source Book.* New York: Garland Publishing, 1989.

Rasinski, Timothy, V., and Nancy D. Padak, "Multicultural Learning Through Children's Literature," *Language Arts,* 67 (October 1990), 676–80.

Sigel, Roberta S., and Marilyn Hoskin, eds. *Education for Democratic Citizenship*. Hillsdale, NJ: Laurence Erlbaum, 1991. Guidelines for education in multiethnic societies.

Sleeter, Christine, and Carl A. Grant, *Making Choices for Multicultural Education*. Columbus, OH: Merrill Publishing Co., 1988.

Social Studies Review Committee, *One Nation, Many Peoples: A Declaration of Cultural Interdependence*. Albany, NY: State Education Department, 1991. Recommended multicultural perspectives.

Tiedt, Pamela L., and Iris M. Tiedt, *Multicultural Teaching: A Handbook of Activities, Information, and Resources* (3rd ed.). Boston: Allyn & Bacon, 1990.

Education for Gender Equity

The long and continuing struggle for social, economic, and political equality for women merits attention in all areas of the curriculum. Sexism and gender-role stereotyping are present in all realms of human activity, including the arts, law, education, medicine, industry, government, sports, family life, and politics. The progress toward gender equity that has been made in recent years needs to be accelerated so that the democratic ideas of equality, justice, and freedom for all will become realities.

Goals and Illustrative Objectives

The following are examples of goals and related objectives to emphasize in the social studies:

1. To develop understanding of the impact of tradition on views of the roles of males and females, the differences between views based on biological characteristics and views based on cultural beliefs, and achievements of women and men who have taken nontraditional roles

   Describe how traditions have limited the participation of women in the world of work and give two examples of recent changes.

2. To develop skill in detecting gender, stereotypes, bias, and inequalities in daily activities, current affairs, and various media

   List three biased statements (or stereotypes) found in reading materials or observed on TV and rewrite them to eliminate the bias.

3. To develop positive attitudes and an appreciation of freedom of choice as a basic right of both sexes

   Describe two examples of how freedom to choose has opened new fields of work for both men and women.

4. To participate in activities designed to provide equality of opportunity and fair treatment for both sexes

   Make, carry out, and evaluate a plan for assuring equity for girls and boys in classroom and school activities.

Conceptual Components

Concepts

Equity	Sexist language	Equality of opportunity
Gender roles	Reform movements	Nontraditional roles

Concept Clusters

Gender bias: males in active roles, women in passive roles; high status ascribed to males, low status ascribed to females; narrower interests assigned to females; less attention paid to females; females identified by male reference; males shown in figures and illustrations.

Freedom to choose: lifestyle, career, hobby, recreation, other activities

Themes

Women's suffrage movement	Struggle for equal rights
Elimination of discrimination	Equal pay for equal work

Descriptive Generalizations

Women have been leaders in major reform movements.

The roles of women have been limited by custom and tradition.

Prescriptive Generalizations

Men and women should work together to assure sex equity.

Boys and girls should participate equally in school activities.

Instruction should be provided in all grades. In early grades students may focus on the roles of boys and girls and men and women in the family, neighborhood, and community. In later grades the emphasis shifts to roles and events in the state, geographic regions, the country, and other countries. Approaches to instruction range from biographical and historical to descriptive and analytical in terms of roles, achievements, and discrimination.

Notable Women in United States History

The following examples are from U.S. history for grades 5 and 8. Recent textbooks and teaching guides include material on the achievements, roles, and activities of women in a framework of historical periods and movements, not as isolated episodes. A sound procedure is to plan ahead and identify women to be included in various units, as shown below.

1. Margaret Brent, Anne Hutchinson, Eliza Lucas Pinckney, Pocahontas, Mary Rowlandson, and others in the colonial period
2. Abigail Adams, Margaret Corbin, Lydia Darrah, Anne Catherine Greene, Mary Hays (Molly Pitcher), Mary Murray, Nanye'hi, Sacajawea, Deborah Sampson, Catherine Schuyler, Martha Washington, Phillis Wheatley, and others who helped in the United States's fight for independence and extension of country
3. Susan B. Anthony, Carrie Chapman Catt, Paula Wright Davis, Catherine Littlefield Greene, Belva Ann Bennett Lockwood, Esther Hobart Morris, Lucretia Coffin Mott, Elizabeth Cady Stanton, and others who worked for women's rights and suffrage

4. Angelina and Sarah Grimke, Rosa L. Parks, Harriet Beecher Stowe, Mary Church Terrell, Sojourner Truth, Harriet Tubman, Ida B. Wells, and others who worked to free blacks from slavery and extend civil rights

5. Jane Addams, Elizabeth Blackwell, Clara Barton, Theresa Cori, Dorothea Dix, Barbara McClintock, Florence Nightingale, Sally Ride, Anna Howard Shaw, Ellen Stern, Mary Edwards Walker, Rosalyn Yalow, and others in the fields of health, science, and welfare

6. Catherine Esther Beecher, Ruth Benedict, Angie Debo, Margaret Mead, M.J.B. Richards, Margaretha Schurz, Anna Garlin Spencer, Martha Carey Thomas, Laura Towne, Emma Hart Willard, and others in education and the humanities

7. Bella Abzug, Mary McCleod Bethune, Shirley Chisholm, Martha Collins, Elizabeth Dole, Millicent Fenwick, Ella T. Grasso, Barbara Jordan, Patricia Roberts Harris, Patsy T. Mink, Antonia Novello, Sandra Day O'Connor, Francis Perkins, Eleanor Roosevelt, Nellie T. Ross, Jeanette Rankin, Margaret Chase Smith, Catalina V. Villalpando, and others in government

8. Betty Friedan, Martha W. Griffiths, Coretta King, Gloria Steinem, Eleanor Smeal, Molly Yard, and other current workers for human rights

Illustrative questions, study guides, and learning activities follow.

FOCUSING QUESTIONS TO GUIDE STUDY

In general, what has been a basic goal in reform movements led by women? [generalizing]

Why do you think it took so long for women to get voting rights? How can we find out? [hypothesizing]

What stereotypes and sexist language are in your reading assignment? [analyzing]

What changes in the roles of boys and girls and men and women in the home are likely to occur in the future? Why do you think so? [predicting]

What should we include in a program to celebrate Women's History Month? [synthesizing]

Which of the books we have been using are fairest in their treatment of girls and boys and women and men? [evaluating]

INDIVIDUAL STUDY GUIDE

When did women win the right to vote in our country? What countries granted women that right before we did?

Who were the leaders of the following reform movements?
Women's suffrage   Abolition of slavery   Civil rights movement

Who were the first women to achieve the following?

Election to the House of Representatives   Election to the Senate

A solo airplane flight across the Atlantic   Graduation from medical school

Appointment to the Supreme Court   Appointment to the Cabinet

(continued)

HOW DID THESE MEN HELP?

To identify men who were involved in the women's rights movement, ask students to investigate and report on Frederick Douglass, William Lloyd Garrison, James Mott, and Theodore Weld. Ask students to look for current events reports on men currently working for sex equity.

Follow by having students find and report on gains for men that have resulted from reform movements led by women.

FINDING INFORMATION IN LEARNING CENTERS

1. *Reading center* that includes books and such references as Kane, *Famous First Facts;* Macksey, *The Book of Woman's Achievements;* Kulkin, *Her Story;* Webster's *Biographical Dictionary*

2. *Listening center* that includes reenactments of speeches and events on such recordings as *What If I Am a Woman?, Black Women's Speeches But the Women Rose . . . Voices of Women in American History, Side by Side: Reenactments of Scenes from Women's History, 1848–1920*

3. *Viewing center* that includes filmstrips, slide sets, and poster sets (posters available from TABS, 744 Carrol Street, Brooklyn, NY 11215)

FINDING INFORMATION IN OUR TEXTBOOK

1. Read pages 130–131 in *Our Country's History* and complete the following by writing a major achievement of each of these women:
   a. Anne Hutchinson _____
   b. Mary Rowlandson _____

2. Make a time line that shows the contributions and important dates for the following:
   Elizabeth Timothy   Abigail Adams   Mary Hays (Molly Pitcher)
   Elizabeth Seton   Phillis Wheatley   Deborah Sampson

3. Complete the following as you read about Margaret Chase Smith.
   a. In high school she worked as a _____.
   b. After her husband died she was elected to _____.
   c. Her stand on pay for men and women was _____.
   d. Her stand on funds for care of children was _____.
   e. Her stand on the right to criticize government was _____.

4. Use the index in your textbook to find the pages for "voting rights for women." Read and list the women who led the struggle, noting the contribution of each one.

(continued)

USING NONPRINT MEDIA

Have individuals and small groups gather data on women's activities presented in computer programs such as: *Women in History, Memorable Americans, Women of Influence.*

Show videos on *Women in American Life* and discuss activities of those presented in four historical periods.

Show the film *The American Parade: We the Women* and discuss the contributions of the following:

Sarah Grimke	Harriet Tubman	Elizabeth Cady Stanton
Sojourner Truth	Lucretia Mott	Susan B. Anthony

To demonstrate the power of Sojourner Truth's oratory, play the dramatization of her famous speech, "Ain't I a Woman," recorded on *Side by Side: Reenactments of Scenes from Women's History, 1848–1920.*

MAKING A RETRIEVAL CHART

Ask students to begin a retrieval chart as they watch the filmstrip *Notable Women of the United States,* noting the name, date, and contributions of each woman. Additions to the chart may be made later as various movements and periods are studied.

MAKING A DATA BASE

To guide students in making cards for a data base on key contributions of various men and women, provide an example such as the following:

Harriet Tubman, 1821–1913

Harriet Tubman escaped from slavery in 1849. She became known as "the Moses of her people." She risked her life as a conductor on the Underground Railroad, which took slaves to freedom. There was a reward of $40,000 for her capture, but she was never caught. She worked for the Union Army during the Civil War. She later started a school for old and needy blacks. The city of Auburn, New York, put up a bronze tablet to honor her.

WOMEN'S HALL OF FAME

To identify achievements of those in the National Women's Hall of Fame, have students investigate the following, guided by such questions as: What were her achievements? What obstacles were overcome? Was she first in her field? Why will her work be remembered?

Abigail Adams, Jane Addams, Marian Anderson, Susan B. Anthony, Clara Barton, Mary McLeod Bethune, Elizabeth Blackwell, Margaret Bourke-White, Gwendolyn Brooks, Pearl S. Buck, Rachel Carson, Mary Cassat, Willa Cather, Emily Dickinson,

> Carrie Chapman Catt, Dorothea Dix, Amelia Earhart, Alice Hamilton, Helen Hayes, Mary Harris Jones, Barbara Jordan, Helen Keller, Billie Jean King, Belva Lockwood, Juliette Gordon Low, Barbara McClintock, Margaret Mead, Lucretia Mott, Alice Paul, Frances Perkins, Sally Ride, Eleanor Roosevelt, Florence Sabin, Margaret Sanger, Mother Elizabeth Seton, Florence Seibert, Bessie Smith, Margaret Chase Smith, Elizabeth Cady Stanton, Lucy Stone, Harriet Beecher Stowe, Helen Brook Taussig, Sojourner Truth, Harriet Tubman, Ida B. Wells-Barnett, Mildred Didrickson Zaharias.

Follow with a discussion of women that students think should be added to the Hall of Fame. For information on activities and publications, have a committee write to National Women's Hall of Fame, 76 Fall Street, Seneca Falls, NY 13146.

FREEDOM TO CHOOSE ROLES

To highlight freedom to choose and nontraditional roles, provide such activities as

1. Showing films such as "Free to Be . . . You and Me" and "People Who Work."
2. Inviting women and men in nontraditional roles to share their experiences with the class.
3. Collecting and sharing photos, articles, and news reports on people in nontraditional roles.
4. Having students make panel presentations on women and men who have taken nontraditional jobs or have been appointed to unusual positions.

ELIMINATING BIAS AND DISCRIMINATION

To identify stereotypes, sexist language, and examples of discrimination, guide students to check textbooks, photos, news reports, and other materials. Ask students to suggest needed changes.

To identify current activities and people working to eliminate bias, ask students to find photos and articles for display on the bulletin board and discuss.

To identify and reduce sex bias in children's activities, ask students to survey such items as division of classroom jobs, composition of committees, choices of topics for reports, selection of current events, choice of roles in dramatic activities, use of sexist language, and extent of participation in different playground activities. Use the findings as a basis for discussions of ways to reduce bias.

CURRENT NEWS REPORTS

Have students find and share news reports on advances and setbacks for gender equity such as: court decisions, votes on ballot measures, state and federal laws, appointments to high offices, Emmy and other awards, demonstrations, admission to clubs, activities of NOW—National Organization for Women.

WINNING THE RIGHT TO VOTE

Study the map on page 69 of your textbook and write the dates that these states approved suffrage for women:

Wyoming ___ Colorado ___ Washington ___ California ___ Oregon ___ New York ___ New Jersey ___ Maine ___ Vermont ___ Virginia ___

Which area of the country led the nation in approving suffrage for women?

What reasons can you give for earlier suffrage in one area than in others?

FIND AND WRITE DEFINITIONS OF CONCEPTS

Gender	Aggression	Equity
Stereotype	Submission	Equality
Prejudice	Sexist bias	Equal pay for comparable worth
Discrimination	Equal opportunity	

SUMMARIZING FINDINGS

1. State main ideas about the leadership roles and activities of women in various reform movements.
2. Describe the most interesting women, activities, and events that they discovered.
3. State the most surprising accomplishments and activities that they discovered.
4. Select and place on a time line notable women and their accomplishments.

SELF-EVALUATION CHECKLIST

Rate your knowledge of each topic as follows:

1—Excellent   2—Good   3—Poor

___ Influence of women in colonial times

___ Activities of native women in early America

___ Unique roles of Pocahontas and Sacajewa

___ Lack of women's rights in early America

___ Anne Hutchinson's challenge to male religious leadership

___ Exploitation of working women

___ Main advocates of women's rights

___ Role of women in the Civil War

___ Leaders of the suffrage movement

___ Victory for women's suffrage in 1920

___ Importation of women to the colonies

___ Exploitation of indentured servants

___ Status of women in Europe and America

___ Women's roles in the Revolution

___ Changes in the rights and freedoms of women after the Revolution

___ Struggle for education of women

___ Seneca Falls convention in 1848

___ Women's roles in settling the West

___ Social reformers in urban areas

___ Continuing fight for sex equity

Use your textbook to find information on topics marked 3.

LESSON PLAN: CHANGES IN JOBS OF MALES AND FEMALES

Objective

To describe jobs males and females have now and to forecast jobs they will have in the future at home and at work

Materials

Film: "The Fable of He and She"

Introduction

Ask students to describe the jobs they do at home. Discuss similarities and differences between jobs of boys and girls.

Ask students to tell what jobs they will probably have as they grow older and to state why they think so. Discuss similarities and differences between jobs of boys and girls.

Development

Show and discuss the film.

Ask students to state the changes that may occur in the following jobs by the year 2000 and to give reasons why they think so:

> Jobs of boys and girls at home, after school, and in the summer
> Jobs of mothers and fathers (and other adults) at home and at work
> Jobs of men and women in business, factories, medicine, education, law, and other fields

Conclusion and Evaluation

Ask students to tell in general how they believe the jobs of males and females will change during the next 20 years.

Ask students to list jobs they may have 20 years from now (a) in the home and (b) at work.

Follow-up

Ask students to find and share news reports on jobs of men and women that show a break from tradition. Have them investigate the impact of such new technology as computers on jobs for men and women.

Ask students to brainstorm ways to speed up the achievement of equity in career choices.

Sources of Strategies, Activities, and Materials

Carelli, Anne O'Brien, *Sex Equity in Education: Readings and Strategies.* Springfield, IL: Charles C. Thomas, 1988.

Emeigh, Tanya H., "Native American Heroines," *Educational Forum,* 52 (Spring 1988), 255–68.

Janeway, Elizabeth, *Women: Their Changing Roles.* Salem, NH: Ayer Publishing, 1989. Reprints of *New York Times* items, 1880s–1970s.

Kirman, Joseph M., "Women's Rights in Canada," *Social Education,* 54 (January 1990), 39–42, 44. Sample unit; bibliography.

Styer, Sandra, "Sex Equity: A Moral Development Approach," *Social Education,* 52 (March 1988), 173–74.

Shelly, Ann C., and William W. Wilen, "Sex Equity and Critical Thinking," *Social Education,* 52 (March 1988), 168–72.

Shortridge, Barbara G., *Atlas of American Women.* New York: Macmillan, 1987.

Gibson, Anne, and Tompthy Fast, *Women's Atlas of the United States.* New York: Facts on File, 1987.

Seager, Joni, and Ann Olson, *Women in the World: An International Atlas.* New York: Pluto Press, 1986.

Stilt, Beverly A., et al., *Building Gender Fairness in Schools.* Carbondale, IL: Southern Illinois University Press, 1988.

"Theme: Women's Studies," *The History and Social Science Teacher,* 25 (Fall 1989), 5–28. Special section.

Women's History Curriculum Guide. National Women's History Project, P.O. Box 3716, Santa Rosa, CA 95402. Revised annually; activities, materials for students, references.

Law-related Education

The recognition that knowledge of basic aspects of law is a necessary component of civic competence and personal welfare has led to a rapid growth of law-related studies. This growth reflects current concerns about juvenile delinquency, justice for everyone in our society, rights of the individual, operation of the legal system, and citizens' obligations to the law. Law-related education emphasizes the knowledge needed for effective citizenship in today's society, including an understanding of Constitutional guarantees, individual and group rights and responsibilities, legal procedures to follow when help is needed, and how to hold authorities accountable.

In early grades, instruction is given on the rules and procedures needed to work, play, and live together at home, in school, and in the community. Instruction in later grades is extended to include both contemporary and historical events that highlight such concepts as justice, equal protection, due process, and civil rights. Special emphasis is given to aspects of law that touch the lives of students, such as rights and responsibilities, use of authority, and rules and regulations related to health, safety, recreation, and property.

Goals and Illustrative Objectives

1. To clarify the need for rules and laws designed to keep a balance between individual freedom and group welfare

   State three rules or laws for bicycle safety and give examples of how they promote individual and group welfare.

2. To develop understanding of such concepts as justice, equal protection, authority, responsibility, due process, property, civil liberties, and privacy

   State the meaning of property rights and describe ways to protect property rights in school.

3. To develop understanding and appreciation of the Constitution as the basis of our legal system and the roles and responsibilities of representatives of our legal system

   List civil liberties guaranteed by the Constitution and give an example of how each one is important in our daily lives.

4. To develop thinking processes and decision-making ability through activities that call for analyzing and evaluating legal issues and procedures

   Evaluate procedures for settling a dispute by stating whether all parties had a fair hearing, whether wrongs or injuries were corrected, and whether a fair decision was made.

5. To increase students' feelings of efficacy and reduce feelings of indifference and alienation related to laws and legal processes

   Describe at least three procedures that an individual or a group can use to challenge the misuse of authority.

Conceptual Components

The following are illustrative examples of conceptual elements drawn from political science and jurisprudence.

Concepts

Rules	Authority	Justice	Responsibility
Laws	Power	Privacy	Equal protection
Due process	Rights	Property	Legal system

Concept Clusters

Rights: of minors, women, accused, citizens; to public trial, bail, privacy, property, vote; due process, equal protection, protection from unreasonable search and seizure

Freedoms: religion, speech, press, assembly, petition

Themes

The need for rules and laws	Individual rights and responsibilities
The resolution of conflicts	Extension of civil liberties

Descriptive Generalizations

Rules and laws provide for individual and group welfare.

The Constitution serves as the basis of our legal system.

Prescriptive Generalizations

Individuals must exercise their rights and assume responsibilities to make our legal system work.

Equal protection must be given to everyone in our society.

Illustrative questions, study guides, and learning activities follow.

FOCUSING QUESTIONS TO GUIDE STUDY

How is *fairness* (justice) defined in this case study? [interpreting]

In general, how do *laws* help to promote *justice*? [generalizing]

How can we show on a chart the *freedoms* guaranteed by the *Bill of Rights*? [synthesizing]

What changes may be made in *laws* to improve the quality of *justice* for members of minority groups? Why do you think so? [predicting]

Which of the housing *regulations* suggested in this reading will best serve members of minority groups? Why? [evaluating]

WHAT AUTHORITY DO THEY HAVE?

Examine pictures of people in authority, such as parents, teachers, police, and judges, and discuss such questions as these:

> What authority does this person have? Why is it needed?
>
> What do we expect this person to do? Why is that important?
>
> What might happen to those who do not comply? Is that fair? Why or why not?

HOW DO RULES AND LAWS SERVE US?

Investigate and discuss how rules at home, in school, and in the community help people and how laws related to food, health, safety, housing, and other items close to the lives of students are designed to serve students, their families, and people in the community.

RULES, LAWS, AND PENALTIES

Make data base cards, fact sheets, or retrieval charts on rules and laws related to topics under study, following a format similar to this:

Topic	Rules or Laws	Penalties
Bicycle riding		
Dogs		
Trespassing		

JUVENILE COURT

Interview a resource person such as a judge, an attorney, or a police officer, or invite the person to come to the classroom, to obtain answers to such questions as these:

What is a juvenile court? Why do we have it? Who is in charge of it? How does it operate?

What rights do minors have? What legal assistance is available to minors?

EQUAL PROTECTION FOR ALL

Listen to recordings, reports, resource visitors, and material read by the teacher to get information related to such questions as these:

What does equal protection mean? How does it affect us?

What groups have been denied equal protection? What gains have been made? What steps still need to be taken?

ANALYSIS OF CASE STUDIES

Analyze case studies of events, incidents, and decisions related to sticking to rules and regulations, justice for members of minority groups, sex equity, freedom of expression, the trial of Peter Zenger, the Salem witch trials, and other historical events, following such procedures as these:

1. Identify the facts in the case.
2. State the issue(s) in the case.
3. Present arguments for and against the issue(s).
4. Make a decision.
5. State reasons for the decision.
6. Compare your decision and reasons with those made by a jury or a judge.
7. Discuss possible reasons for any difference between the student's decision and that of the jury or the judge.

Create and present case studies related to issues of concern to students, using stories, historical events, letters, current events, or information drawn from textbooks or other materials.

COLLECTION AND ANALYSIS OF NEWS REPORTS

Collect and analyze news clippings that deal with legal topics and issues such as vandalism, petty theft, disturbing the peace, accidents involving traffic violations, drug abuse, trespassing, and littering.

Make a scrapbook of news reports, organizing them into sections on civil rights, equal protection, authority, truth in advertising, and other topics.

SUMMARIZING FUNCTIONS OF LAW

Collect and analyze examples of incidents that occur in school and in the community and that are presented in learning materials to illustrate how law

1. Is a reflection of what people value.
2. Sets standards of behavior and related penalties.
3. Defines procedures for settling disputes.
4. Defines and sets limits of authority.
5. Provides a means of achieving justice.
6. Is changed to meet new conditions.

Sources of Strategies, Activities, and Materials

American Bar Association, Committee on Youth for Citizenship, 1155 East 60th Street, Chicago, IL 60637

Center for Civic Education, 5146 Douglas Fir Doad, Calabasas, CA 91302. Units on Authority, Justice, Privacy, Responsibility; booklets *We the People* on Constitution.

Constitutional Rights Foundation, 1510 Cotner Avenue, Los Angeles, CA 90025

Falkenstein, Lynda Carl, and Charlotte Anderson, eds., *Daring to Dream: Law and Humanities for Elementary School.* Chicago: American Bar Association, 1980.

Gallagher, Arlene F., *Living Together under the Law: An Elementary Education Law Guide.* Albany, NY: State Education Department, 1982 (ERIC ED 233 953) Activities, materials, and procedures for grades 1–6.

Greenawald, C. Dale, and Douglas P. Superka. *Evaluating Social Studies Programs: Focus on Law-related Education,* Boulder, CO: Social Science Education Consortium, 1982. Evaluation model, procedures, appraisal of programs.

Turner, Mary Jane, and Lynn Parisi, *Law in the Classroom: Activities and Resources.* Boulder, CO: Social Science Education Consortium, 1984.

Wheeler, Ronald, "Law-related Education," *Social Education,* 44 (May 1980), 381–97.

Newsletters and Journals

Center Correspondent, LRE Project Exchange, LRE Report, Street Law News, Bill of Rights in Action, CRF Newsletter, Children's Legal Rights Journal.

Global Education

The current emphasis on global education is part of the long-standing tradition in the social studies to develop world-mindedness and international understanding. In early grades children study families, schools, and communities around the world. Deeper understandings are developed in later grades through studies of other lands and peoples, relationships between our country and other countries, cultural interaction and borrowing, tightening interdependence among people in places throughout the world, and how we are all part of a global system of human interaction.

Students study environmental, energy, and economic problems, consequences of lifestyles, and our country's and other countries' role in world affairs. Opportunities are provided to identify basic human needs and diverse ways of meeting them; attention is given to explaining *why* differences exist as well as responding to questions of *what, where, when, why, who,* and *how.* Global connections among peoples and countries in a world of increasing interdependence, limited resources, cultural pluralism, and ethnic diversity are highlighted.

Goals and Illustrative Objectives

1. To develop understanding of human interconnections in a global system marked by cultural diversity, change, conflict, search for peace, and networks of communication and transportation

   Describe common human needs and concerns in one's own culture and in others and explain why ways of meeting needs differ.

2. To apply thinking and decision-making skills by exploring the impact on other people of personal decisions regarding the use of resources, lifestyle, and other matters

   Describe how decisions about lifestyle, use of resources, or ways to resolve conflicts may affect others here and in other places.

3. To apply and strengthen reading, study, and other skills by gathering, organizing, and reporting information related to global topics

   Locate and describe examples of how people depend on each other, as shown in the reading on the flow of goods, services, and ideas in and out of communities, states, and countries.

4. To develop attitudes and behavior that reflect respect for cultural diversity, appreciation of differences, understanding of why differences exist, and interest in exerting influence through appropriate activities

   Make a list of things one might do to help curb pollution and to influence others to do the same.

Conceptual Components

Concepts

Cross-cultural	Peace	Third World nations
Transnational	Communication	Developed nations
Global system	Interdependence	Developing nations

Concept Clusters

Interdependence: among families, communities, states, nations; in trade; use of resources; use of energy; improving the environment; worldwide transportation and communication; maintaining peace

Change: scientific, technological, social, economic, political, environmental

Themes

Cultural similarities and differences   Resolution of conflicts
Increasing interdependence of people   Interaction of cultures

Descriptive Generalizations

International networks of transportation and communication link communities and countries around the world.

All people are part of a global system in which change in one part may affect other parts.

Prescriptive Generalizations

All countries have a responsibility to cooperate in solving environmental, energy, economic, political, and other problems.

High priority should be given to equality, justice, and human rights here and in other lands.

Illustrative questions, study guides, and learning activities follow.

FOCUSING QUESTIONS TO GUIDE STUDY

What is positive peace? What is negative peace? How are they alike and different? [comparing]

How can we bring together and share our findings on *communication systems* that link communities around the world? [synthesizing]

What hypothesis can we state about relationships between developing and developed countries by using data in the computer programs *India* and *Latin America*? [hypothesizing]

Which of the proposals for improving the *food supply* in *developing countries* do you think is best? Why? [evaluating]

FAMILIES AROUND THE WORLD

How are our families alike? How are they different? [comparing]

How are families in Japan like ours? How are they different? [comparing]

What should we put in booklets about our families? About families in other lands? [synthesizing]

How are other families like ours? How are they different? Oakland, California

ME BOOKS

Make and share "me books," in which each child includes pictures and drawings that show "what is special (unique) about me," including age, height, weight, and skin color; liked and disliked foods; favorite toys, games, television programs, and other items; "things that make me happy and sad"; "size and composition of my family."

HE OR SHE BOOKS

Make and share books that show unique characteristics, customs, and behavior of a child in a different ethnic group or culture, similar in format to the "me books."

PICTURE CHARTS OR BOOKLETS

Make comparative picture charts that show what is unique or special about each child's family and a family from a different ethnic group.

Make picture charts or booklets of various ethnic groups here and in other lands to show how basic common needs for food, shelter, clothing, and security are met in a variety of ways.

OTHER WAYS OF LIVING

Find out about ways of living and learning of children in other lands, guided by such questions as these:

> What foods do they eat? What clothes do they wear? How are their homes like ours? How are they different? Why?
> What games do they play? What songs, poems, stories, and dances do they enjoy?

Collect information from exchange students, consular officials, and local persons who have visited places under study. Invite them to share slides, pictures, and objects and to answer questions.

INTERNATIONAL PEN PALS

Arrange for students to exchange letters and other materials with students in other lands. Use local school sources of pen pals or the list in the first section of this chapter on multicultural learning activities.

HOW ARE PEOPLE INTERDEPENDENT?

Make comparative analyses of human activities here and in other places, using pairs of questions:

> How do we depend on each other at home? How do they?
> How do we depend on each other at school? How do they?
> How do we depend on each other in the community? How do they?

OBSERVING COMMUNITY ACTIVITIES

Observe festivals, pageants, and commemorations of local groups that highlight customs, traditions, and values from other lands.

WHAT ARE THE ORIGINS OF FOODS?

Trace the origins of foods common to many countries, using encyclopedias and such references as Evans's *People Are Important,* Morris's *Dictionary of Word Phrases and Origins,* Sullivan's *How Do They Make It?* and Limburg's *What's in the Name of Fruits?* Then make a chart (or a world map) that shows where those foods we think of as American actually originated:

> *Asia:* wheat, rice, chickens, noodles, apples, apricots, other fruits
> *Central South America:* chocolate, gum (chicle), vanilla, potato, sweet potato, peanuts, tomatoes, pineapple
> *Europe:* ice cream, sausage, soda pop, gelatin, pretzels, beets, spinach
> *Middle East:* milk, butter, candy, olives, sherbet, melons
> *Native American:* cranberry, beans, corn, maple syrup, squash, pumpkins

INVESTIGATING INVENTIONS

Investigate where various objects were invented or first used, using encyclopedias and such references as Gekierc's *Who Gave Us . . .* and Waller's *American Inventions.* Then make a chart (or a world map) that includes such items as these:

> *China:* clock, ink, paper, printing, compass, gunpowder, porcelain dishes
> *England:* soccer, train, baby carriage
> *America:* rocking chair, safety pin, zipper, elevator, frozen food
> *Greece:* Olympic games, school system, kites (or China)

GLOBAL PEACE

Present and discuss such questions as:
> What is the meaning of peace? What is positive peace? What is negative peace? What are sound bases on which to build peace? What have the United States and the Soviet Union done to build positive peace?

WHAT DO THESE AGENCIES DO?

Have individuals or committees investigate the work of such international agencies as the UN, UNESCO, UNICEF, WHO, CARE, YWCA, YMCA, and the Red Cross.

SUMMARIZING AND CREATIVE ACTIVITIES

Interpret and make maps, charts, diagrams, graphs, and time lines—for example, maps of networks of air and sea tranportation; charts of food, clothing, shelter, and modes of travel; diagrams of the flow of people, products, and ideas between countries; graphs of population change and trade; time lines of events, showing the relationships between our country and other countries.

Make a retrieval chart of the ways in which our culture has been enriched by the achievements and contributions of immigrants, including medicine, inventions, politics, art, music, sports, education, and recreation.

Make murals, montages, and collages that highlight distinctive aspects of a country's culture, such as family life, modes of travel and communication, arts, crafts, ceremonies, costumes, utensils, and musical instruments.

Sources of Strategies, Activities, and Materials

Ad Hoc Committee on Global Education, "Global Education: In Bounds or Out?" *Social Education,* 51 (April/May 1987), 242–49.

Cogan, John J., and Donald O. Schneider, eds., *Perspectives on Japan: A Guide for Teachers.* Washington, D.C.: National Council for the Social Studies, 1983. Approaches to global instruction; background data, activities, and resources for instruction on Japan.

Fleming, Dan B., "Social Studies and Global Education," *The Social Studies,* 82(jan./Feb. 1991), 11–15.

Kniep, William M., guest ed., "Global Education: The Road Ahead, " *Social Education,* 50 (October 1986), 415–52. Special section

Nickell, Pat, and Mike Kennedy, *Global Perspectives Through Children's Games,* How to Do It, Series 5, No. 3. Washington, D.C.: National Council for the Social Studies, 1987.

Reardon, Betty A. ed., *Educating for Global Responsibility.* New York: Teachers College Press, 1988.

Reardon, Betty A., *Comprehensive Peace Education.* New York: Teachers College Press, 1988.

Redford, Staphanie M., guest ed., "Global Education," *The History and Social Science Teacher,* 22 (Winter 1986–87), 66–69. Special issue; guidelines, activities, resources.

Task Force on Global Education, National Council for the Social Studies, "Position Statement on Global Education," *Social Education,* 46 (January 1982), 36–38.

Traberman, Tama, "Using Microcomputers to Teach Global Studies," *Social Education,* 48 (February 1984), 130–37.

Tye, Kenneth E., ed. *Global Education.* Alexandria, VA: Association for Supervision and Curriculum Development, 1990. Guidelines and illustrative practices.

Organizations to Contact for List of Materials

American Forum for Global Education, 4500 John Street, New York, NY 10038

Center for Teaching International Relations, University of Denver, Denver, CO 80208

Global Perspectives in Education, 218 East 18th Street, New York, NY 10003

Institute for International Education, 809 United Nations Plaza, New York, NY 10017

Mid-American Program for Global Perspectives in Education, Social Studies Development Center, Indiana Univeristy, Bloomington, IN 47401

National Geographic Society, Educational Services, Washington, D.C. 20036

Population Reference Bureau, 777 14th Street, Washington, D.C. 20005

Environmental and Energy Education

Three major waves of concern about the environment have occurred in the past eight decades. The first, which took place in the early 1900s, was led by Gifford Pinchot and supported by President Theodore Roosevelt; it focused on expanding the public domain. The second, during the 1930s, stressed conservation and management of natural resources. The third, which began during the 1970s and continues in the 1990s, initially recognized the need to improve the environment, reduced air and water pollution, and conserve energy. Today there is concern about loss of parts of the public domain, wilderness areas, threatened species, destruction of rainforests and wetlands, oil spills, offshore drilling, acid rain, global warming, the ozone layer, nuclear and toxic wastes, energy conservation, and population growth.

Goals and Illustrative Objectives

Broadly conceived to include all the preceding concerns, the central goals and objectives of environmental and energy education are to develop

1. Awareness of environmental problems and conditions, causes and consequences of deterioration, corrective measures currently under way and needed in the future, and action that should be taken.

   Describe three environmental problems in our community and the steps that are being taken to solve them.

2. Understanding and appreciation of the impact of energy use on the environment and the economy, of the need for alternative energy sources, and of the consequences of high energy costs.

   State two or more effects on family life of increasing energy costs.

3. Thinking and decision-making processes by analyzing problems, taking and defending a position on issues, and evaluating proposals.

   Evaluate each suggestion listed on the chart for saving energy; tell how much energy each suggestion will save and estimate how many students will follow it.

4. Attitudes, values, and appreciations related to quality of life and a commitment to improve the human and physical environment.

   Demonstrate a commitment to conservation by carrying out a plan to reduce waste pollution at home and in school.

Conceptual Components

Concepts

Environment	Reclamation	Pollution
Ecosystem	Resources	Greenhouse effect
Balance of nature	Biodegradable	Industrialization

Concept Clusters

Conservation: human, water, soil, forest, wildlife, crop and grazing lands, wetlands, rainforests, minerals, public domain, recreational areas; wise use, restricted use, substitution, recycling

Quality of life: personal, social; physical, mental, emotional; rural, suburban, urban, inner city, state, regional, national, global

Themes

Interaction and interdependence	Variety and pattern
Adaptation and survival	Continuity and change

Descriptive Generalizations

People affect the environment and are affected by conditions, interactions, and changes in the environment.

Critical current problems are overpopulation, food supply, energy use, pollution, and preservation of endangered species, rainforests, and wetlands.

Prescriptive Generalizations

Industrialized nations, in cooperation with others, must devise programs that will restore and maintain the environment.

Immediate and long-range action should be taken by individuals and groups and by both public and private agencies.

Illustrative questions, study guides, and activities follow.

FOCUSING QUESTIONS TO GUIDE STUDY

How are population, environmental, and energy problems alike in the United States and Canada? How are they different? [comparing]

In general, what does the evidence show about progress in forest conservation in our country? [generalizing]

What are the main causes and effects of acid rain? Of ozone changes? [analyzing]

Which pollution problems are most serious in our country? How can we find out? [hypothesizing]

What do you think the main environmental and energy problems will be in the year 2000? Why? [predicting]

INVESTIGATING CONSERVATION PROBLEMS

1. Identify natural resources available in our country and natural resources that we get from other countries.
2. Define renewable, nonrenewable, and inexhaustible resources and list examples of each type.
3. Collect materials from local, state, and national organizations.
4. Interview local experts on conservation and take field trips to gather data.
5. Interpret physical and land-use maps of the United States to locate forest areas, mineral areas, and bodies of water and to identify the proportion of the nation's area that each occupies.
6. Interpret maps of other countries and regions of the world and compare them with areas of the United States, as noted in item 5.
7. Make data base cards on the estimated amount, location, and primary uses of such resources as coal, oil, natural gas, iron ore, and other minerals.
8. Make data base cards and report on the contributions of such conservationists as

George P. March	Fairfield Osborn	Paul B. Sears
J. Sterling Morton	Gifford Pinchot	Jay N. Sterling
John Muir	Theodore Roosevelt	Charles R. Van Hise

9. Have committees recommend action that can be taken to improve conservation of resources at home and in the community, state, and nation.

Should isolated areas such as this be used for offshore oil drilling? Why or why not? What might the benefits and the costs be? Social Studies Workshop, University of California, Berkeley

HOW CAN FORESTS BE CONSERVED?

Introduce the study by arranging a display of forest areas and discussing:

How many of you have been in a forest? Where is it located?

What was it like? What did you do? What fun did you have?

Was any timber being cut? Were new trees being planted?

Did you hear a lecture by a forest ranger? What was said about conservation?

Collect materials and gather information related to focusing questions:

1. Collect pictures, maps, graphs, newspaper and magazine clippings, and other materials to make booklets, reports, scrapbooks, and displays.
2. Write to the National Forest Service to obtain maps, folders, and other materials needed to answer questions, prepare oral and written reports, and make displays.
3. See films and filmstrips and read materials to identify practices that conserve forests, provide needed lumber, and protect the environment.

Organize, summarize, and present information through such activities as these:

1. Map major forest areas and national parks in the United States and identify those that students have visited.
2. Summarize steps that are being taken by the government and by private and commercial organizations to conserve forests.
3. Summarize steps that individuals who visit forest areas and vacation in national and state parks can take to conserve forests.
4. Prepare and share reports on how forest conservation helps to preserve wildlife, watersheds, soil wilderness areas, and lumber supply.

Express thoughts and feelings creatively:

1. Complete such statements as
   If I were in charge of forest conservation I would _____.
   If I owned a large forest I would _____.
   If I were in the lumber business I would _____.
   Three things everyone should do when in forests are _____.
2. Write haiku about some aspect of forests. (Haiku has five syllables in line one, seven syllables in line two, and five syllables in line three.)

LESSON PLAN: THE AMAZON RAINFOREST

Background

The Amazon Rainforest is one-third of the world's tropical rainforest. Scientists state that its destruction will have devastating effects on the ozone layer and will add to the Greenhouse Effect in addition to being harmful to Brazilians. The clearing of trees, burning of the forest, road building, cattle ranching, and settling of farmers for economic gain have hurt the ecosystem and had negative effects on Indians and rubber tappers. Chico Mendez, a leader of rubber tappers, and others have been killed because of their opposition to destruction of the Rainforest.

Objectives

To describe changes being made in the Amazon Rainforest
To identify the conflict of values related to changes in the Rainforest

Materials

Textbook, pages 367–371
News clippings
Jungle Stories: The Fight to Save the Amazon

Introduction

Ask students to tell what they know about the Amazon River. Explain that it is in a huge rainforest important to Brazil and the world. Write these questions on the chalkboard: What changes are being made in the Rainforest? What are the effects of these changes? What reasons are given for and against these changes? What values are in conflict?

Development

Ask students to read pages 367–371 in their textbooks to find answers to the listed questions.

Discuss responses to the questions. List the reasons for and against the changes.

Discuss the conflict of values due to desire for economic gain versus preservation of the Rainforest for the welfare of Brazil as well as for other countries.

Ask students to state why scientists are concerned about preserving the rainforest. What are effects on Indians? Others? The ecosystem? The ozone layer? The Greenhouse Effect?

On people in Brazil and other countries?

Conclusion/Evaluation

Ask students to summarize main changes and effects. Discuss positions on the conflict of values and ask: What should the government of Brazil do? Why? What should other countries urge Brazil to do? Why?

Follow-up

Request students to be on the lookout for news reports and TV programs such as *The Amazon Rainforest* and *The Decade of Destruction*. Urge students to read *Jungle Stories: The Fight for the Amazon* and clippings in the reading center on changes in rainforests in Central America, Africa, and Asia.

ENERGY SOURCES, USES, AND CONSERVATION

Introduce the study by discussing a display of pictures, pamphlets, and other materials on energy use, guided by such questions as

What forms of energy do we use every day?

What steps can we take to save energy?

What alternative energy sources should be considered?

What is the future outlook for safe sources of energy?

Have committees report on alternative sources: oil, coal, biomass, photovoltaic, nuclear, water, solar, wind. Include evaluation in terms of economic costs, environmental costs, advantages and disadvantages, and impact on quality of life.

Have individuals investigate and report on such new energy technologies as ceramic fuel cells, coal gasification, new-generation photovoltaic cells, lithium batteries, cogeneration, geothermal hot-dry-rock system, nuclear fusion, and superconductors.

Make a checklist of ways to save energy at home, in school, and in the community.

What are the pros and cons of nuclear power plants? How much better is second genera-tion nuclear technology? Will more nuclear plants cut dependence on foreign oil? Social Studies Workshop, University of California, Berkeley

INVESTIGATING VARIOUS TYPES OF POLLUTION

Introduce the study by showing pictures, a film, or a filmstrip describing pollution problems. Pose such questions as: Which problems are most serious in our community? State? Nation?

Organize committees to investigate different types of pollution and to con-tribute to the development of a retrieval chart:

Retrieval Chart on Pollution

Types	Pollutants	Effects	Prevention
Air			
Water			
Soil			
Food			
Solid wastes			
Toxic wastes			
Aesthetic			
Noise			
Acid rain			

Provide for class discussion and analysis of each type of pollution, as illustrated by the following examples of activities for air pollution:

1. Identify sources of air pollution in the community and surrounding area—motor vehicles, factories, burning dumps, power generating plants, and other sources.
2. Invite an expert to discuss causes and effects of air pollution, new techniques that are being developed to curb it, the economic costs, the human benefits, and current issues.
3. Interpret (and make) graphs of major sources of air pollution, such as the following:

WHAT DOES THIS GRAPH SHOW?

Major Sources of Pollution

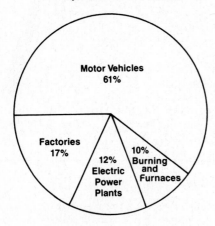

What is the main source of air pollution?
What is the second main source?
What percentage do other sources contribute?
What main idea can be stated about sources?
What sources are not shown?
How can we find out about them?

4. List common air polluting activities, such as smoking, burning trash and clippings, driving cars, using sprays, cooking outdoors, and burning oil and coal in furnaces; then discuss such questions as
   Which activities are necessary? Which are not?
   What substitutes might be used?
   What habits should be changed? Why?
   What habits probably will be changed? Why?
5. Complete a diagram that shows the causes and effects of air pollution, and discuss ways to remove the causes and minimize the effects:

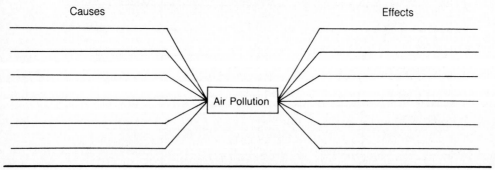

Sources of Strategies, Activities, and Materials

Alliance for Environmental Education, Box 1040, 3421, M Street, N.W., Washington, DC 20007.

Conservation Directory. National Wildlife Federation, 1412 16th Street, N.W., Washington, DC 20036. Check latest issue for list of agencies and organizations.

Directory of Environmental Education Resources. Available from the Center for Environmental Education, 624 Ninth Street, Washington, DC 20001.

EcoNet, Institute for Global Communications, 3228 Sacramento, San Francisco, CA 94115.

"The Environment: A Primer." *NEA Today,* 9 (April 1991), 15. List of sources of classroom materials.

ERIC Clearinghouse for Science, Mathematics, and Environmental Education, Ohio State University, 1200 Chambers Road, Columbus, OH 43212–6717.

National Energy Information Center, EI-231, Room 1F-048, Forrestal Building, Washington, DC 20585.

North American Association for Environmental Education, P.O. Box 400, Troy, OH 45373.

Otto, Robert, *Teaching Science-related Social Issues,* How to Do It, Series 5, Number 4, Washington, DC: National Council for the Social Studies, 1987. *Social Education* (April/May 1987).

Resources. Washington, DC: Resources for the Fugure, 1616 P Street N.W., 20036. Bulletin on resources and conservation; published four times a year.

State fo the World, Worldwatch Institute, 1776 Massachusetts Avenue N.W., Washington, DC 20036. See latest edition.

U.S. Environmental Protection Agency, 401 M St. N.W., Washington, DC 20460.

Local and State Sources

Agricultural agents; state agencies such as the Department of Natural Resources and others concerned with conservation, water resources, and pollution; some state agencies have local offices.

Incorporating Current Affairs, Issues, and Special Events

CHAPTER 8

Objective and Related Focusing Questions

To present guidelines and strategies for selecting and teaching current affairs, controversial issues, and special events:

- What are contributions of instruction on current affairs, issues, and special events to social studies objectives?

- What criteria are used to select significant events and issues that are meaningful to children?

- What are commonly used approaches to the teaching of current affairs?

- What guiding principles are helpful in dealing with controversial issues?

- What principles and strategies are helpful in providing instruction on holidays and other special events?

Students encounter a myriad of current affairs every day. The outpouring from the mass media includes some events and issues that are relevant to the social education of students. Teachers at all levels need to make a critical selection and plan ways to incorporate current affairs into the social studies and thereby enrich social understanding. The first step is to clarify contributions to social studies objectives.

Contributions to Social Studies Objectives

The study of current affairs and special events adds relevance, reality, and immediacy to the social studies program. Meaningful bridges can be built between life in and out of school and between the past and the present. Students' interests can be extended and deepened as they investigate events, issues, and holidays related to their own concerns, to long-term social trends, and to actions of individuals and groups. Units of study and material in textbooks, films, and other instructional media can be brought up to date. A beginning can be made in developing a continuing interest in the analysis of current affairs, the ability to evaluate the information that flows from the mass media, and an appreciation of the significance of holidays and other special events.

Study of current affairs and special events can deepen children's understanding of concepts and generalizations learned in units on the community, the state, the nation, or other lands. Thinking and study skills are applied as students collect, interpret, evaluate, and report on events. Attitudes and values are considered as students appraise actions and decisions in current affairs and develop new ideas on the environment, sex equity, civil rights, and other social concerns. The present, the past, and the future can be interrelated as students link current events to past developments and make projections for the future.

Selecting Current Affairs

The multiplicity of current events, issues, and problems makes the selection of those to be studied no simple task. Although help can be obtained by relying on children's weekly newspapers, problems still exist in selecting local and state events, adding events not included in such periodicals, and screening out some that have been included. These criteria should be used to select events for study:

1. *Educational value:* Will children learn something significant? What contributions can be made to conceptual, skill, and affective objectives?
2. *Appropriateness:* Is the topic appropriate in terms of the maturity of the pupils? Is it appropriate in terms of community conditions and feelings?
3. *Relatedness:* Is it related to past and future learning? Can it be related to basic units of study?
4. *Available information:* If needed, can background information be obtained? Are suitable teaching materials available?
5. *Available time:* Is there enough time to develop depth of understanding?

6. *Reliability:* Is accurate information available? Can facts be differentiated from opinions? Can any bias in it be detected and analyzed by students?

7. *Timeliness:* Is up-to-date information available? Is it related to basic trends?

Students as well as teachers should use those criteria to select significant events and to avoid trivial ones. An effective procedure is to discuss guidelines that students can use. Figure 8.1 shows examples that can be written on the chalkboard or on charts. Students may be directed to find news items related to such unit-related concepts and

REPORTING THE NEWS	GOOD NEWS ITEMS	FIND CITY NEWS
About parents' work	Is it important?	Activities of people
About our own work	Do I understand it?	Education
About trips we take	Can I report it well?	Recreation
About community activities	Is it interesting?	Special events
About changes in seasons	Is it related to our unit?	Other

FIND STATE NEWS	FIND NEWS ON REGIONS	FIND NEWS ON CANADA
Agriculture	Far Western states	Cities
Cities	New England states	Communication
Communication	North Central states	Conservation
Conservation	Rocky Mountain states	Education
Education	South Central states	Government
Government	Southeastern states	Mining
Industries	Southwestern states	Oil pipelines
People		Provinces
Transportation		U.S. relations
Other		Other

COMMITTEE AND INDIVIDUAL ASSIGNMENTS FOR ARTICLES

PROBLEMS COMMITTEE	TECHNOLOGY COMMITTEE	FUTURES COMMITTEE
Acid rain	Aerospace	Communication
Wetlands loss	Aquaculture	Education
Desert growth	Biotechnology	Health care
Droughts	Computers	Housing
Endangered species	Fiber optics	Population growth
Greenhouse effect	Lasers	Quality of life
Pollution	Maglev trains	Resource needs
Toxic wastes	Robotics	Transportation
Water supply	Superconductors	Telecommunications

Figure 8.1

topics as new families in our community, how our state and other states are interdependent, new roles of men and women, and relations between our country and others. Teachers may also arrange news learning centers, bulletin boards, panel discussions, and committees organized to find articles on topics; students are asked to collect relevant news items, pictures, and cartoons. Individuals and groups may make notebooks and scrapbooks on unit topics and thus improve the selection of significant events.

Approaches to the Study of Current Affairs

Each of the approaches to the study of current affairs described in the following sections has certain strengths and weaknesses. Many teachers use a combination of approaches, depending on the objectives to be achieved, the significance of the events involved, the units under study, and the materials available.

Relating Current Affairs to Basic Units

In general, the teacher should relate current affairs to basic units of instruction; then the problem of obtaining background material and giving perspective to current affairs becomes less difficult. As regional units, such as areas of our state, midwestern United States, and regions of South America, are studied, current events can be selected to highlight recent developments. As historical units, such as early times in our state and colonial life, are studied, current events can be selected to contrast then and now.

The greatest problem in relating current affairs to units of instruction is one of timing. As one teacher put it, "So many significant events occur either before or after I teach a unit." Many teachers meet this problem by using current events to launch units and, when possible, by timing the introduction of certain units to coincide with holidays, sessions of the state legislature and of Congress, and other scheduled events. They relate current events to past units and continue certain strands, such as transportation, communication, and conservation, from unit to unit. They assure their classes of a good supply of current materials by collecting clippings and having students collect clippings for the units to come and by filing copies of children's periodicals that pertain to units they plan to develop.

Weekly Study of Periodicals

Many teachers allot one period each week to the study of children's periodicals. It is convenient and relatively easy to assign the reading of articles, carry on discussion, and have students complete the activities and tests included in each weekly issue. But there are limitations to this approach. It may lead to routine reading and answering of questions, superficial learning caused by an attempt to cover too many topics, and failure to relate current events to basic topics and units. The suggestions presented later in this chapter in the section on weekly periodicals for children should help teachers to avoid these limitations and to get maximum benefit from the weekly study of current affairs. In addition, a sound procedure is to direct the study of weekly periodicals by stressing the points noted in Chart 8.1.

Studying Our Weekly Newspaper

Skim it first to get a general idea of the contents.
Study pictures, maps, charts, tables, and graphs.
Note articles related to topics we are studying.
Note articles on which background material is given.
Note articles on which background material is needed.
Look up the meaning of any words you do not understand.
Look for facts, opinions, and differing points of view.
Be ready to raise questions and make comments during discussion.
Check your understanding by completing the tests.

Chart 8–1

Miscellaneous Reporting

Reporting on news items may be done on a daily or a weekly basis or at irregular intervals. Teachers in primary grades and in some middle grades frequently use daily sharing. Some teachers prefer to have reporting on a weekly basis or at assigned times. Five minutes may be set aside for daily sharing; a full period may be scheduled if a weekly plan is followed.

The weaknesses in this approach include the reporting of trivial events, superficial learning because of a lack of depth of study, isolation of events from past experiences and basic units of study, and the tendency for discussion to wander. These weaknesses can be overcome in part by directing the selection of current affairs, suggesting better sources of news items, systematically relating current affairs to basic topics and units, holding to discussion standards, and providing for deeper study of more important current affairs. What at first may appear to be isolated events can sometimes be related to significant topics. For example, a bicycle accident may lead to a discussion of safety rules with emphasis on showing concern for others; a news item on minority groups may lead to a discussion of rights and responsibilities, fair play, and other democratic values in community living.

Because of television and discussions with adults at home, children may raise questions that are beyond their level of maturity. Such questions should be dealt with on levels of experience and understanding appropriate for the group. After adequate comment or discussion, the teacher should direct the group's attention to other, more appropriate questions, reports, or topics. At times, particularly in the primary grades, children may report personal family events that are not proper topics for group discussion. When this happens, the teacher should be prepared to make a tactful and unobtrusive shift to other topics. Sometimes a wise course is to suggest that a particular topic is one that the child may want to discuss later with the teacher.

Short Current Affairs Units

Current affairs of special significance cannot always be dealt with in the daily or weekly period, nor can they always be incorporated in units of work. An important community or state event or problem, a major election, activities related to commemorations, the coming of a nation to the forefront in international affairs, the study of an individual of current national and international importance—any of these may require an intensive short unit using current materials and related background material. Sometimes special units featured in children's weekly periodicals need a more extended period of study. By noting related materials and suggestions contained in the teacher's edition of the weekly newspaper and by collecting pamphlets, books, films, and other resources, a teacher can plan to achieve important objectives by introducing special units.

Whichever approach or combination of approaches is used, every effort should be made to have students attain the highest possible levels of thinking and understanding. Three levels may be quickly identified as one visits classrooms. The *first level* is the routine reporting of events. Each child has seen, read, or heard about an event and shares it with the group with little or no discussion and without analyzing its relationship to other experiences. At the *second level* the reporting of an issue or an event is followed by discussion of the most interesting points. This level requires more thinking by the class, may prove to be entertaining for those who participate in discussion, and may stimulate the interest of others. Usually it does not penetrate far beneath the surface to uncover basic concepts, trends, and relationships; it does not encourage any critical analysis of related issues and problems. At the *third level* students use problem-solving and critical thinking skills to explore the significance of the event or issue. They review supporting facts, consider differing points of view, and collect any additional data that are needed. To be sure, this third level cannot and should not be applied to all current affairs. When truly significant events are selected for study, however, children can usually be guided from the first to the third level, thus increasing the value of the experience.

Activities and Sources of Information

Many activities and sources are needed to develop a dynamic and interesting current affairs program. In selecting them, teachers should consider those that can be used by individuals and small groups as well as by the entire class. Here are some examples.

ILLUSTRATIVE LEARNING ACTIVITIES

Set up a news bulletin board; assign a group of four or five students to add current news items each week, and encourage other students to bring items on a voluntary basis. Be sure to alternate those in charge.

Make a *Who's Who in the News* bulletin board, on which students post names, photos, and articles of people related to topics of study.

View telecasts or listen to broadcasts of ceremonies, inaugurations, festivals, holidays, commemorations, and other special events at home or in school, then report and analyze highlights. Tape and discuss relevant parts of news, documentary, and other unit-related

---

programs. Have students use the Five *W*s and *H* to analyze and report news stories: Who? What? When? Where? Why? How?

Conduct mock television and radio newscasts with students taking such roles as anchorperson, on-the-spot reporter, editorial commentator, weather reporter, and sports reporter. Encourage use of audio and videotape equipment.

Conduct round-table and panel discussions, in which four to six students plan and present the topic (after critically reviewing news articles) and respond to questions from the class.

Analyze issues and problems in terms of the people involved, locale, causes or reasons, pros and cons, value conflicts, alternative solutions, consequences of alternatives, and feasible individual group action.

Analyze TV commercials in terms of the main message, health claims, scientific claims, other claims, use of athletes, use of notable people, use of *new* and *improved*.

Analyze types of proof or evidence for a position such as eye witness account, legal precedent, statistical evidence, historical events, personal experience, expert opinion, research findings, common sense, reference book facts.

Use students' periodicals or daily newspapers to develop special skills such as scanning headlines to locate items on a topic; using the index to find the editorial page, the travel section, or some other section; and finding the pros and cons on particular issues.

Ask students to find examples of bias—slanted views, derogatory terms, unfair opinions, and others—in news reports and articles by checking the following: ＿＿Headlines ＿＿Placement of Items ＿＿Photos and captions ＿＿Use of titles ＿＿Use of names ＿＿Use of statistics ＿＿Emotive words ＿＿Selection of facts ＿＿Omission of facts ＿＿Control of source

Find examples of "doublespeak," in which individuals and groups praise themselves and find fault in others. List examples in the space below.

Playing up their own good	Playing up the bad of others
Playing down their own bad	Playing down the good of others

Ask students to detect stereotypes—oversimplified and usually false representations of a person, place, or thing. Have them note favorable and unfavorable elements and how the sterotype can be corrected.

Analyze and evaluate news reports, editorials, and letters to the editor to identify point of view, positions on issues, bias, stereotypes, and prejudice.

Write editorials and letters to the editor on issues and topics of special concern to students.

Travel agencies and transportation companies have pictures related to new developments
How might such materials be related to the study of current events?

Plan and produce (duplicate) a newspaper for which students collect, write, edit, and proofread items related to (1) the unit under study. (2) other significant events, and (3) events of concern to students. Use available computer desktop publishing equipment.

Clip a unit-related article from the newspaper, duplicate and distribute it, and discuss it in terms of these questions:

> How important is this event? Locally? Nationally?
> What people are affected by it? How many?
> How important will it be ten years from now? Why?

Analyze the use of propaganda in news items and editorials, looking for such techniques as name calling, using generalities, naming great people, saying "plain folks agree," and urging everyone to get on the bandwagon.

Analyze ads for children by identifying "catch words" that are used, such as *latest, new, best, improved, bargain, free, hurry,* and *last chance.*

Ask students to project probable consequences of a trend or a development, as illustrated in the following lesson plan.

Lesson Plan: Futures Wheel

Objective

To make a futures wheel that projects consequences of a trend or an event

Materials

Diagram of a futures wheel for students to complete

Introduction

Discuss a trend or a major event that has been studied—for example, robots in factories, home computers, or solar power. Pose the question: What are possible consequences?

Development

Draw a futures wheel on the chalkboard and state that it is used to project consequences of events. Place the selected trend in the center of the wheel and ask students to give examples to place in the boxes around the center. Ask students what may follow from each of the consequences or effects. Continue to elicit other examples until students' ideas are exhausted. Discuss any questions students have about the procedure.

Pass out a diagram of a partially completed futures wheel and ask students to complete it. Discuss any questions they have.

Pass out a blank diagram of a futures wheel and ask students to complete it on a topic of their choice or on one of the following:

Smaller cars	Improved rapid transit	Increasing life span
Uses of robots	Solar-heated homes	Hydroponic farms

Conclusion and Evaluation

Share and discuss students' completed wheels, with attention to reasons for consequences, difficulties in projecting them, and additional suggestions of consequences. Assess participation and quality of reasoning.

Follow-up

Ask students to complete wheels based on other trends they select.

Complete this futures wheel

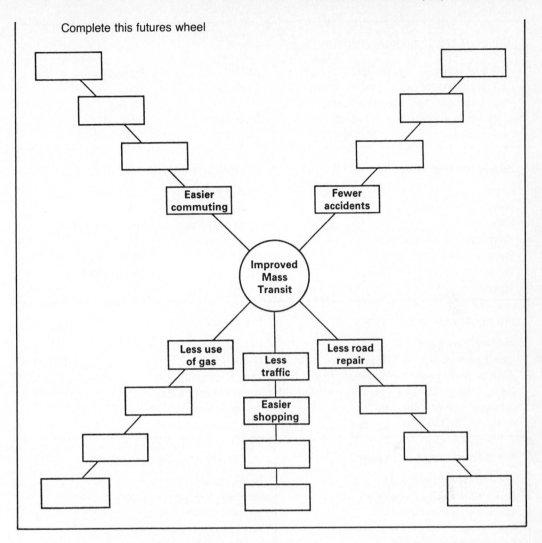

Students as well as the teacher should help select activities, and they should use a variety of sources and communication skills. Figure 8.2 shows specific suggestions that can be written on the chalkboard or placed on charts to direct students' attention to key points.

Weekly Periodicals for Children

Fortunately, well-prepared classroom periodicals are available for elementary school students. Examples are *My Weekly Reader, Scholastic Newstime,* and *NewsCurrents.* They are produced by experts and contain current affairs that meet the criteria discussed earlier. Properly used, they are an excellent resource. Guidelines for using them are:

WHICH OF THESE SHOULD WE USE?			
Individual reports	School intercom	Pictures	News maps
Committee reports	Bulletin board	Charts	Globe
Panel or debate	Quiz games	Murals	Models
Classroom newscasts	News files	Scrapbooks	Exhibits
Tape recorder	Picture file	Cartoons	Dramatizations

FINDING CURRENT EVENTS	PERIODICALS IN THE LIBRARY	
Bulletin board	*Current Events*	*The Times*
Interviews of experts	*Evening Star*	*Time*
News file	*Junior Scholastic*	*U.S. News & World*
Newspapers and magazines	*News Explorer*	*Report*
Radio and television newscasts	*Newstime*	*Weekly Reader*
School and neighborhood library	*Newsweek*	*Young Citizen*
Weekly newspaper		

PREPARING NEWS REPORTS	CHECKING REPORTS
Note the main ideas.	Is it accurate?
Select the most important facts.	Is it up to date?
Have pictures or other items to show.	Who reported it?
Be ready to locate it on a map.	How can facts be checked?
Be ready to answer questions.	Are there opinions in it?
If possible, relate it to a topic under study.	What do others say?

REPORTING CURRENT EVENTS	LISTENING TO CURRENT EVENTS
Is it important to the group?	Do I understand it?
Do I know it well?	Do I have questions to ask?
Can I give illustrations?	Is it related to my report?
Can I give it in my share of the time?	Is it related to topics we are studying?
Do I have the main ideas?	What other information is needed?
Can I relate to other topics or events?	Is it controversial? If so, are all sides given?

Figure 8.2

1. Select editions that fit students' reading levels. Editions on three or four levels may be needed for a class.

2. Include attention to developing readiness and understanding of purposes, building vocabulary, interpreting maps and graphs, and summarizing main ideas, as is done with textbooks and other learning resources.

3. Use each issue at the most appropriate time. For example, some teachers set aside an issue that is related to topics to be studied later.

4. Supplement the whole-class approach by providing for individual and small-group study of selected articles.

5. Discuss relationships to topics in units to place events and issues in a context that enhances learning.

6. Use both formal and informal evaluation, including tests in the periodicals and observation of students during sharing, reporting, and discussion.

7. In addition to a weekly periodical, include a critical selection of local, state, national, and international items related to topics under study.

8. Maintain files of back issues for reference on future topics.

9. Use maps, charts, graphs, tables, and diagrams to improve students' ability to interpret and make them.

10. Use other materials available in the school or local library, such as local and national newspapers, weekly news magazines, and supplementary resources provided by news magazines. Guides to the use of newspapers are available from American Newspaper Publishers Association, Box 17407, Washington, D.C. 20041. Copies of newspapers published on selected dates, such as Lincoln's assassination and the attack on Pearl Harbor, are available from PRIDE, 1310 Ann Avenue, St. Louis, MO 63104.

Controversial Issues

It is sometimes stated that "elementary school children have inadequate backgrounds to study controversial issues." Ordinarily the speaker means that children are unable to study critical issues currently being debated by adults and achieve adult levels of understanding. Certainly, many current issues are beyond a child's understanding; but controversial issues do come up in social studies, and experienced teachers wisely select some of them to study. Such study assumes that some issues will be approached as unanswered questions toward which there are differing points of view that should be studied in a thoughtful manner. Some may be handled briefly, others may simply be introduced as continuing problems that will be reviewed in the future, and still others may be studied in detail because of their importance.

In the primary grades, attention is generally given to issues and problems close to the lives of children—issues and problems that come up in school, in the neighborhood, and in the community. Examples of these are differences of opinion on ways of carrying out classroom activities, how to conserve resources, ways of using parks and playgrounds, fair play in the treatment of others, the contributions of others, and conflicts between individuals and groups. At times, the teacher may include issues raised by children—perhaps a labor dispute, a demonstration, housing problems, or ways of preventing discrimination against others. Problems growing out of community living should not be ignored, nor should they be handled in a way that is beyond the ability of children to understand. A simple answer, an explanation of the problem, a clarification of the issue, or a brief discussion may suffice. The important thing is to keep the way open for such questions, to discuss them on an appropriate level, and to begin to lay a foundation for ongoing study of issues.

In the middle and upper grades, more involved issues and problems are encountered as children undertake such units as our state, the United States, Mexico, Canada, countries of Latin America, the Middle East, or Africa, and growth of democracy. Current events periodicals raise issues that may be related to basic units of study. Children may be exposed to other issues through television and radio programs, newspapers, and discussion at home.

The board of education often sets policy governing the study of selected current issues and problems. The following statement is typical of the policies established in many school systems:

1. Only significant issues and problems understandable to children, and on which children should begin to have an opinion, should be selected for study in the elementary school.

2. Instructional materials must present differing points of view, discussion should include all points of view, and respect for the views of others should be shown.

3. Teachers must guide learning so as to promote critical thinking and open-mindedness, and they must refrain from taking sides or propagandizing one point of view.

4. Special attention must be given to a consideration of background factors, possible consequences of various proposals, the need for additional information, and the detection of fallacies of thinking, logic, and argumentation.

5. The importance of keeping an open mind—that is, the willingness to change one's mind in the light of new information—should be stressed.

Should more dams be built to provide water and electric power? What are the *pros* and *cons?* Social Studies Workshop, University of California, Berkeley

Generally, issues are not selected if they are offensive to individuals and groups in the community or if they will place the school in the center of a heated debate. Checking with other teachers and with the principal is a good idea when there is any doubt about the appropriateness of a particular issue.

Serious problems arise when a teacher becomes a crusader for a cause and pressures students to adopt the same point of view. Such behavior violates professional ethics and is a misapplication of the concept of freedom in teaching. When the teacher is asked to express an opinion, it should be given and noted as an opinion, and not as a final answer.

The behavior of teachers should be a model for students. Figure 8.3 contains points that teachers may demonstrate through their own behavior and emphasize in instruction for students.

WHICH ISSUE DO YOU PLAN TO INVESTIGATE?

Human rights	Acid rain	Ageism
Discrimination	Ozone layer	Sexism
Nuclear power	Rainforests	Drug abuse
Water supply	World hunger	Other

Defining an Issue	**Checking Materials**	**Discussing an Issue**
How shall we state it?	What is the author's background?	Define it clearly so that all sides are known.
Do we understand each term?	What group sponsors or publishes it?	Consider each position.
What are the subproblems?	What is the group's purpose?	Find facts related to all sides.
What parts are most important?	What are other points of view?	Verify and organize facts.
Do we have ideas about any part?	What materials present other points of view?	Make and change conclusions on the basis of facts.
Which parts need most study?		

Checking Points of View	**Working on Problems**	**Forming Conclusions**
What facts do I have?	Recall ideas related to it.	Wait until facts are checked and organized
How do I feel about It?	Think of possible ways to solve it.	Be sure facts are separated from opinions.
What do others believe?	Find information related to each possible solution.	Consider outcomes and consequences.
How do they feel about it?	Check and summarize information.	Test tentative conclusions.
What would I believe and feel if I were in their place?	Try out the best solutions.	Make final conclusions.
	Select the one that works best.	

Figure 8.3

Special Events

Special events—holidays, special weeks, and commemorations—are a vital part of every cultural heritage. They have been set aside as a time for celebration and the expression of treasured values, ideals, and beliefs. Special days and weeks call attention to significant events, institutions, documents, men and women, and customs. The study of special legal holidays can contribute to the development of patriotic attitudes and deeper appreciations of citizenship. The manner in which special days and weeks are presented, the depth and quality of understandings and appreciations that are achieved, the historical perspective that is developed, and the attitudes that result determine in large measure their meaning and significance in the lives of children. International understanding is increased as students learn about the significance of Pan-American Day, United Nations Day, and special days in other countries under study.

Although celebrations of religious holidays are a primary responsibility of families and religious institutions, learning about them may extend students' understanding and respect for cultural diversity. Care should be taken to respect differences in beliefs, activities, and modes of celebration. Sensitivity also must be shown to the feelings and views of those who do not participate in religious holidays. The right of all individuals and groups to religious freedom must be respected.

A Calendar of Selected Days and Weeks

Some school systems provide a calendar of special days, weeks, months, and ethnic holidays so that teachers may select and plan ahead for those their class will study. The following example should be modified to fit local and state requirements. Dates are announced each year for the undated days and weeks. Review the monthly calendar in *Instructor* magazine for dates and events and for teaching strategies.

Teachers should be alert to special days and events not shown on the calendar that are of importance to various groups. These may include German Day, Polish Bazaar, Mexican Independence Day, Cabrillo Day, and the Chinese Moon Festival in September; Madonna Del Lume (Italian), Irish Festival Week, Dia de la Raza, and Ohi Day (Greek) in October; Finnish Independence Day, Our Lady of Guadalupe, and Santa Lucia Day (Swedish) in December; Republic Day (India) and Chinese New Year in January; Our Lady of San Juan de Los Lagos (Mexican), St. Patrick's Day, and Greek Independence Day in March; Russian Easter, Cinco de Mayo (Mexican), Polish Constitution Day, Norwegian Constitution Day, and Asian-Pacific Heritage Week in May.

Grade Placement

Two policies are widely followed in determining the grade level at which special days and weeks will be included. First, certain holidays are studied in all grades, beginning in kindergarten and first grade. In succeeding grades opportunities are provided for more advanced learning through background studies, short units, relationships to basic social studies units, and varied activities. Second, certain special days and weeks

Calendar of Selected Days and Weeks

September, Labor Day, first Monday, Grandparent's Day, second Sunday, Citizenship Day, 17, Constitution Week, Native American Day, fourth Friday, Hispanic Heritage Week

October. Fire Prevention Day, 9, Columbus Day, second Monday, United Nations Day, 24, Halloween, 31, Social Studies Week

November. Veteran's Day, 11, American Education Week, Thanksgiving, fourth Thursday, Children's Book Week

December. Human Rights Day, 10, Bill of Rights Day, 15

January. New Year's Day, 1, Martin Luther King Jr.'s Birthday, 15, Franklin D. Roosevelt's Birthday, March of Dimes, 30

February. Black American Day, 5, Lincoln's Birthday, 12, Brotherhood/Sisterhood Week, Black History Month, Susan B Anthony's Birthday, 15, Washington's Birthday, 22

March. Luther Burbank's Birthday, 7, Conservation Week, Arbor Day, Women's History Month

April. Pan-American Day, 14, National Youth Week, Earth Day, Library Week

May. May Day, Loyalty Day, Law Day, National Teacher Day and Teacher Appreciation Week, International Goodwill Day, 18, Mother's Day, second Sunday, Armed Forces Day, third Saturday, Memorial Day, last Monday

June. Flag Day, 14, Father's Day, third Sunday

July. Independence Day, 4

August. National Aviation Day, 19, Women's Equality Day, 26, Nisei Week

Plan ahead to maximize learning during Black History Month and other special months and weeks. Richmond, California

are assigned to particular grades, when appropriate to the background and experience of children and units of study. State and local school district policies should be identified. These examples are illustrative.

> *Kindergarten and grade 1:* Halloween, Thanksgiving, Christmas, New Year's, Washington's Birthday, Lincoln's Birthday, Mother's Day, Father's Day, and Flag Day are included.

> *Grades 2 and 3:* The above are continued on higher levels, and Columbus Day, American Indian Day, Fire Prevention Day, Veteran's Day, Book Week, American Education Week, Arbor and Conservation Day, Memorial Day, Independence Day, and the day our community was founded are added.

> *Grades 4 through 6:* The above are continued on higher levels, and the following are added: Labor Day, United Nations Day, Constitution Week, Admission Day, Bill of Rights Day, Benjamin Franklin's Birthday; Susan B. Anthony's Birthday, Brotherhood/Sisterhood Week, Black History Month, Pan-American Day, Women's History Month, Women's Equality Day, International Goodwill Day, Armed Forces Day, other special days and weeks of significance in the community or state, and special days of importance in other countries that are studied.

Differentiating Experiences from Grade to Grade

Because many special days and weeks are given attention in each grade, overall planning is needed to make sure that children develop deeper appreciations and understandings as they progress through the grades. The following example on Arbor and Conservation Day includes activities that may be provided, beginning in kindergarten and continuing through the sixth grade. Notice how many of them can be made a part of such units as the family, our community, living in our state, and conservation.

Practices in Primary Grades

Major emphasis is given to introducing customs, traditions, ceremonies, rituals, the special meaning of terms, and the significance of selected special days and weeks. Activities and materials are matched to the children's maturity and their background of experience. Beginning with storytelling, simple art activities, and participation in classroom and school activities, the program moves to reading stories, reporting and sharing ideas, and more advanced activities.

Units of instruction in the social studies provide many opportunities for deeper study of special days and weeks. The home and family unit gives background to Mother's Day and Father's Day. The contributions of many different workers, a key aspect of Labor Day, takes on greater meaning as school and community workers are studied. Thanksgiving activities may be made a part of units on Indians or Pilgrims. Many teachers use Valentine's Day in the study of the post office. As communities in other lands are studied, attention may be given to ways in which New Year's, Christmas, and other holidays are celebrated. Arbor Day activities may be related to the study of conservation, a basic strand in many units from grade to grade.

Activities for Arbor and Conservation Day

Kindergarten through Grade 2

Take a nature walk in the neighborhood.

Learn about the many uses of wood.

Read and hear stories and poems about trees.

Write original poems and stories.

See films on forest animals.

Draw pictures of trees, flowers, and animals.

Take a study trip to see a house under construction.

Learn about synthetic fibers, paper, and other things made from wood.

Make picture books and scrapbooks.

Participate in a tree-planting ceremony.

Grades 3 through 4

Learn about commercial, recreational, and decorative values of trees

Learn about logging and other aspects of the lumber industry.

Make a collection of different kinds of wood.

Learn about the importance of trees in the conservation of water, soil, and animal life.

Learn about our state's watersheds and water supply.

Learn about new uses of wood in construction, industry, and hobbies.

See films on logging, lumbering, reforestation, and water resources.

Make charts, a mural, or a movie roll box to summarize basic concepts.

Grades 5 through 8

Invite conservation experts to discuss questions and problems raised by the class and to report on newer practices.

Learn about the consequences of poor conservation practices in ancient civilizations in China and the Middle East.

Discuss the balance in nature and how people must work in harmony with nature.

Read and report on contributions to the conservation movement of men such as Theodore Roosevelt and Gifford Pinchot.

Study and make maps of forest areas and state and national parks.

Create poems, pageants, and programs that highlight conservation needs, problems, and forward-looking practices.

See documentary films or television programs.

Plan and carry out a tree-planting ceremony.

Make scrapbooks containing pictures, clippings, and notes on conservation.

More Advanced Learning in Later Grades

Instruction in middle and upper grades should be planned to increase children's depth and breadth of understanding. Both the teacher and the class should search for new stories, poems, pictures, articles, and activities related to special days and weeks. After discussing what children have learned in earlier grades about a given day or week, some teachers use leading questions to guide the search for new ideas and materials: How did this special day originate? How was it celebrated in early times? What early customs have we kept for our own? How is it celebrated in other lands? What individuals worked to make it a holiday in our country? What are some famous stories and poems about this holiday?

More specific questions are used to guide the study of selected special days, as shown in these examples:

Veteran's Day: When was Armistice Day first proclaimed? Why was Armistice Day changed to Veteran's Day? Why is the unknown soldier honored each year at the National Cemetery in Arlington? What is meant by "preservation of fundamental principles of freedom"? What obligations should each individual assume for the peace, welfare, and security of our country?

Thanksgiving: What were harvest festivals like in ancient times? Why did people have them? According to various authorities, what was the first Thanksgiving like in our country? How was it different from earlier harvest festivals? Who was Sarah Josepha Hale, and what did she do to make Thanksgiving a national holiday? Which president issued the proclamation that made Thanksgiving a national holiday? How has the celebration of Thanksgiving changed?

Washington's Birthday: Where did Washington live as a boy? What was his home like? How was he educated? What are the main periods of his service to our country? What traits of leadership caused his countrymen to call on him to be the first president? Why is he honored as "the father of our country"? What is meant by "First in war and first in peace"?

Certain special days and weeks are explored in detail at a time when the class is studying a particular unit; this may be in addition to a short observance held as a part of classroom or school activities. For example, Constitution Day, Bill of Rights Day, United Nations Day, and the contributions of Franklin, Lincoln, Washington, and other historic leaders are included in units on the United States and the growth of democracy. Pan-American Day and International Goodwill Day take on deeper significance when tied in with such units as South America and other lands. Notable men and women and special days of importance in the child's state should be included in the unit on our state.

Short units are needed to give background on a certain special day or week. Examples are fire prevention, American Education Week, United Nations Day, and Red Cross Week. Short units on topics such as these give children the background they need to understand the purposes and activities of organizations and agencies that render services of benefit to both children and adults. Other short units may be developed on men and women, special weeks, or days of special importance in the community or state. Individual study and preparation of reports on related background information are used to develop greater depth of understanding. The following are examples of reports written by children in the fifth grade.

Harvest Festivals Before the Pilgrims Had Their First Thanksgiving

Long ago, before the Pilgrims landed, people had celebrations at harvest time. They were happy to have a good harvest. Some would make offerings to the spirits and gods that they thought made seeds fertile and made the crops grow.

The oldest known harvest festival, Succoth, was in Israel. The people gave thanks for finding a place to live and for the harvest.

In ancient Greece there was a celebration that lasted nine days. It was in honor of the goddess of the harvest, called Demeter. Demeter was also the goddess of corn.

The festival of the harvest moon was held in old China long ago. The Chinese would bake moon cakes. They also thought that a rabbit lived in the moon.

Some of our early settlers had learned about harvest festivals in England. The English would have feasts and share what had been raised. People in the villages would get together and each family would bring something.

The peasants in Old Russia had feasts and dancing. One custom was to place a wreath of grain by the house. A new one was put there each year. They thought it would help make a good harvest.

The Iroquois Indians had feasts at different times. One was in the spring at maple syrup time. Another was at planting time. Still another was at harvest time. They also had a bean and a corn festival. All together they had about seven festivals a year.

What Susan B. Anthony Did

Susan B. Anthony worked hard to get the right for women to vote. She also wanted equal rights for women in other things. She was a teacher once and only got paid $10 a month while men teachers were getting $40 a month. She said that this was not fair. She also said that women should choose their own jobs and take care of their own property. She also said that they should be able to go to college just the same as men.

I didn't know that women never used to have all these rights. It is a good thing that Susan B. Anthony came along. My mother says that some women take these rights for granted. They should remember what Susan B. Anthony did. I am going to remember her birthday on February 15.

Some teachers take time before the school year ends to consider special days that occur during summer vacation. For example, Independence Day and the events leading up to it can be studied as part of units on the United States. Children can be asked to watch for special reports and activities as celebrations take place during the summer. National Aviation Day, August 19, should not be overlooked as an opportunity for children to collect clippings and other materials for use in transportation and aviation units when school starts in the fall. Similarly, Labor Day celebrations and activities in early September are sources of experience and information that can be put to use at the beginning of the school year.

A variety of activities and materials for special days and weeks should be used to improve learning. Some examples follow.

Learning Activities for Special Events

Investigate origins of holidays, contributions of men and women, holidays in other lands, and customs brought from places around the world.

Have students run the computer program *Holidays and Festivals* to gather information on national holidays.

Interview workers at special agencies and organizations; experts on conservation, fire prevention and other topics; and writers and scholars who have studied special events and famous people.

Visit special exhibits, historic places, homes of famous people, and special agencies and organizations.

View films, filmstrips, slides, photographs, television programs, picture files, and exhibits that show special events.

Listen to stories, tapes, records, guest speakers, panel discussions, and individual and group reports.

Read stories, articles, poems, folktales, essays, biographies, autobiographies, diaries, documents, reference materials, and clippings.

Arrange bulletin boards, flowers for special occasions, room decorations, learning centers, and exhibits of book jackets and other items.

Design and make room decorations, greeting cards, costumes, hats, masks, puppets, gifts, gift wrappers, party favors, booklets, scrapbooks, shadow boxes, peep boxes, movie box rolls, dioramas, time lines, murals, and charts.

Create and share songs, poems, plays, skits, quiz games, and stories.

Make an international calendar of patriotic holidays and investigate their origins, purposes, and modes of celebration; discuss similarities to and differences from our patriotic holidays.

Participate in or witness role playing, pageants, festivals, ceremonies, parades, plays, and games.

Ask students to select one of the following and find its country of origin and its importance to the people who celebrate it:

Cinco de Mayo	Oktoberfest	Passover
Columbus Day	St. Patrick's Day	Hanukkah
Chinese New Year	Thanksgiving	Christmas

Plan ahead for special weeks and months. For example, ask students to help plan activities for Women's History Month. Consider topics to emphasize during various days and weeks of the month.

Major contributions of women	Contributions by women in various ethnic groups
Women in our city or state	Women in politics, government, and education
Leaders of reform movements	Women in the arts, sciences, and other fields

Sources of Information

Children's weekly newspaper and monthly magazines include stories and articles on great men and women, holidays, and special weeks. They contain stories and activities that may be used to provide fresh learning experiences. The teacher's guides that accompany weekly periodicals occasionally list related films, filmstrips, television programs, books, pamphlets, and other materials.

Children's encyclopedias are excellent sources of information. The background materials, stories, pictures, time lines, reading lists, dates of holidays, and other information they contain can be used for individual study and reference. *The World Almanac* lists the dates set for holidays each year and includes information on holidays observed in different states and on public days in Canada.

Professional magazines for teachers include stories, articles, units, bulletin board suggestions, construction activities, reading lists, bibliographies, and other material. Some articles are also useful to more able children who are pursuing individual studies or who wish to find directions for making things related to a particular holiday.

Television and radio program listings should be checked in newspapers, weekly program guides, and program bulletins issued by broadcasting companies and school systems. Newspapers and magazines for adults feature special reports and articles that can be read and shared by many children. Specific suggestions on special days and weeks are included in courses of study, units of instruction, and bulletins on special days available in local school systems.

Questions, Activities, and Evaluation

1. Select a current event from a local newspaper, using the criteria suggested in this chapter. Note objectives that might be achieved and make a plan for using the event, including a selection of learning activities from this chapter.

2. Select a holiday or some other special event and make a plan for teaching it, including objectives and learning activities.

3. Review several periodicals for children and identify articles, maps, charts, test items, and other material that you might use in a unit of instruction. Prepare an assignment for students similar to this example: "Look at the map of the Soviet Union on page 5 of your weekly news magazine. How many Soviet Republics are

shown? Which republic is largest in area? In which republic is Moscow? Which republics have voted to withdraw from the Soviet Union, according to the text below the map? Why?

4. Make a calendar of special days and weeks that are celebrated in your community. Indicate the grades in which certain days and weeks might be emphasized.

5. Which ideas in the figures in this chapter might you use in your teaching? What adaptations would you make to meet the needs of children in different grades?

6. Complete the following to indicate your point of view. Discuss your views with a colleague and explore reasons for any differences.

   a. The main contribution of current affairs study to achievement of social studies objectives is _____.

   b. The best approach to the study of current affairs is _____.

   c. The main criterion for selecting controversial issues for children should be _.

   d. A teacher's position on the study of religious holidays should be _____.

   e. The main criterion for choosing from the ever-increasing number of special days and weeks should be _____.

   f. When students ask the teacher to state what side should be taken on an issue, the teacher should _____.

References

Ellis, Arthur K, *Teaching and Learning Elementary Social Studies* (4th ed.). Needham Heights, MA: Allyn & Bacon, 1991. Chapter 15.

Goldstein, William, *Controversial Issues in Schools: Dealing With the Inevitable.* Bloomington, IN: Phi Delta Kappa, 1989.

Haynes, Charles C., ed., "Taking Religion Seriously in the Social Studies," *Social Education,* 54 (September 1990), 276–301, 306–10. Special section.

Harris, Jay J., *Celebrate Thanksgiving.* New York: Media Books, 1988.

Heitzman, William R., *The Newspaper in the Classroom* (2nd ed.). Washington, DC: National Education Association, 1986.

Kellman, Jerold L., and Nancy L. Kellman, *Birthday Bonanza.* Glenview, IL: Scott, Foresman, 1986. Seventy birthdays of notable people.

Kelly, Thomas E., "Leading Class Discussions of Controversial Issues," *Social Education,* 53 (October 1989), 368–70.

Lazar, Wendy, *Jewish Holiday Book.* Garden City, NY: Doubleday, 1977.

Livingston, Myra C., *Calloh! Callay! Holiday Poems for Young Readers.* New York: Atheneum, 1978.

National Council for the Social Studies, "Guidelines for Teaching Science-related Social Issues," *Social Education,* 47 (April 1983), 258–61; "Including the Study About Religions in the Social Studies Curriculum: A Position Statement and Guidelines," *Social Education,* 47 (May 1985), 413–14; "Science, Technology, Society and the Social Studies," *Social Education,* 54 (April/May 1990), 189–214, position statement and strategies.

Otto, Robert, *Teaching Science-related Social Issues,* How To Do It, Series 5, No. 4. Washington, D.C.: National Council for the Social Studies, 1987.

Passe, Jeff, "Developing Current Events Awareness in Chilren," *Social Education,* 52 (November/December 1988), 531–33. Approaches and strategies.

Personke, Carl R., and Dale D. Johnson, *Language Arts Instruction for the Beginning Teacher.* Englewood Cliffs, NJ: Prentice-Hall, 1987. Chapter on using newspapers.

Polon, Linda, and Aileen Cantwell, *The Whole Earth Holiday Book.* Glenview, IL: Scott, Foresman, 1983. Over 50 holidays around the world.

Developing Understanding and Thinking Skills

CHAPTER 9

Objective and Related Focusing Questions

To present guidelines and teaching strategies for developing conceptual components, modes, processes, and skills essential to productive thinking:

- What aspects of thinking are of central importance in the social studies?

- What modes, processes, and skills of thinking merit special attention? What are key features of each one?

- How can metacognition—thinking about thinking—be used by students to improve their thinking?

- What questions and strategies are used to develop concepts and generalizations—two key tools and outcomes of thinking?

- What questions and strategies are helpful to raise thinking to high cognitive levels?

- How can knowledge and thinking skills be unified in a model of teaching?

This chapter includes strategies for developing understanding and thinking ability—two goals of the social studies and two inseparable aspects of learning. Keep the following guidelines in mind as you read this chapter. Integrate instruction on content and thinking skills into each unit in accord with students' intellectual growth from the preoperational stage through the concrete operations stage and on to the formal operations stage. Adapt elements of various approaches (models of thinking, cognitive skills, logical reasoning), and help students transfer to the social studies skills that are taught in separate programs of instruction on thinking.[1] Stress critical thinking throughout instruction and recognize the differences among critical thinking, creative thinking, decision making, and problem solving. Guide students to use combinations of them as appropriate in terms of unit objectives. Pose questions, make suggestions, and provide activities that engage students in thinking about their thinking (metacognition), that fit different learning or cognitive styles, and that require use of the verbal and logical left hemisphere of the brain and the intuitive and creative right hemisphere. Stress the importance of such attitudes and behavior as respect for evidence, sensitivity to differing views, open-mindedness, control of feelings, and freedom to inquire and to express ideas. Remember that each student's background of understanding, self-concept, learning style, motivation, attitudes, interests, values, and skills affect thinking.

Overview of Selected Aspects of Thinking

Included among dimensions of thinking that instructional planners should consider are skills such as inferring, processes such as decision making and problem solving, critical and creative thinking, metacognition, knowledge, and level of cognitive development (Marzano et al., 1988). Chart 9.1 shows selected dimensions and other aspects of thinking stressed in current social studies programs.

Notice that thinking involves symbols—words, map symbols, numbers—that stand for objects and events. Thinking is sparked by questions, problems, and other stimuli. Facts, concepts, and other forms of knowledge are of key importance. Critical and creative thinking have widespread use, and decision making and problem solving are used at all levels. Specific skills are used in various modes and processes. Outcomes are as broad as social studies objectives and may include new questions and problems that initiate new rounds of thinking.

Modes, Processes, and Skills of Thinking

Figure 9.1 shows examples of selected features of modes and processes of thinking, with basic skills in the center to highlight their importance in all forms of thinking. Critical and creative thinking are used in decision making, problem solving and in-

---

[1] For a description of programs designed to develop thinking, see Marzano et al. (1988), Chance (1986), and Costa (1991). Be alert to differences in terms used. For example, critical and creative thinking may be referred to as *modes, ways,* or *forms* of thinking.

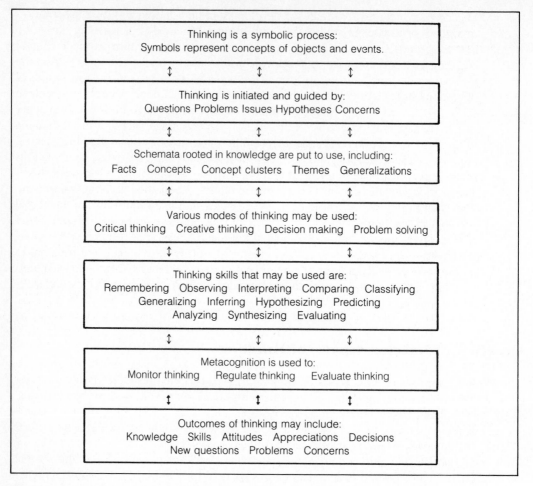

Chart 9.1

quiry, and a variety of learning activities. Decision making is focused on choosing among alternatives to achieve goals. Problem solving and inquiry are focused on finding solutions or answers, testing hypotheses, and arriving at warranted conclusions. The thinking skills are used in all forms of thinking as needed. The four forms of thinking have many common elements, but each has special features, as noted below.

Critical Thinking

Criteria or standards are clarified and used to analyze, evaluate, or judge ideas, statements, points of view, actions, behavior, discussion, committee work, and other activities.[2] Students are guided to examine critically ideas presented in instructional

[2] For various models and comparisons, see Beyer (1989), Costa (1991), and Marzano (1988).

EXAMPLES OF MODES, PROCESSES, AND SKILLS OF THINKING

Critical Thinking

Define what is to be judged, analyzed, or evaluated.

Clarify criteria or standards to use.

Gather data from reliable sources, determine their accuracy and relevance, and use them to determine how well the standards are met.

Detect bias, inconsistencies, stereotypes, and emotional appeals.

Distinguish facts from opinions and causes from effects.

Make judgment after considering relevant evidence and/or sound reasons.

Thinking Skills

Evaluating

Synthesizing

Analyzing

Predicting

Hypothesizing

Inferring

Generalizing

Classifying

Comparing

Interpreting

Remembering

Creative Thinking

Conceive a goal that stirs and guides creative thinking.

Imagine new uses of prior learning and build a rich background.

Identify forms, patterns, and elements and imagine new ways to synthesize them.

Decide on form, processes, and content and synthesize them.

Evaluate process and product in terms of goal.

Make changes in accord with insights gained from evaluation.

Contemplate possibilities for further refinement and enrichment of creative thinking.

Decision Making

Define the issue or situation.

Clarify goals and related values.

Explore alternative ways to achieve goals and support values.

Evaluate alternatives and consequences in terms of goals and values.

Prioritize the alternatives in terms of goals and values.

Decide on action to take.

Evaluate process, decision, and action.

Problem Solving and Inquiry

Identify and define the problem.

State questions or hypotheses to guide data collection.

Collect and appraise data.

Answer each question or test each hypothesis.

Base conclusions on verified data.

Evaluate and make needed changes.

State limitations and needs for further study.

Discuss ways to improve in the future.

Figure 9.1

materials—facts and opinions, positions on issues, cause-effect and other relationships, treatment of women and minority groups, bias, stereotypes, and propaganda. Beliefs and values such as fair play, justice, and equality of opportunity may be used as standards to appraise classroom and school activities and events studied in various units. Critical thinking enhances understanding of the significance of standards and values in human affairs and improves students' ability to use them to make appraisals and judgments.

Illustrative Questions

The following are examples of questions that focus attention on various aspects of critical thinking. Additional examples are presented in later sections of this chapter.

What is to be analyzed, evaluated, judged?

What criteria or standards should be used?

What information is needed to determine if standards are met?

How can facts be distinguished from opinions? Relevant information from irrelevant?

How can bias, stereotypes, and assumptions be identified?

How can cause-effect and other relationships be identified?

What weaknesses are there in reasoning? In use of analogies? In identifying alternatives? In other aspects?

How effectively have thinking skills been used in the making of our analysis, evaluation, or judgment? How can we improve?

In addition to using the above questions, the teacher should design specific unit-related questions that provoke critical thinking:

How are families alike? Different? Why should we respect families different from our own?

What rules are important in discussion? In the learning center? In group work? How do they help? Should any be changed? Why?

What services should communities provide for everyone? What should individuals have to provide on their own? Give reasons for your answers.

What plans should be made in our state to conserve resources? What should individuals be required to do?

Why did some settlers remain loyal to Britain during the American Revolution? What reasons were given for being a Loyalist? A Patriot?

To what extent should immigrants keep their ethnic and cultural heritage? To what extent should they be "Americanized"?

What problems faced by the country we are studying can be solved by outside help? By internal effort? By a combination of both?

What contributions of ancient civilizations do you believe to be most important in our lives today? Why?

The following examples of learning activities illustrate the variety that may be used in the social studies. Additional examples are presented in the following section and in later chapters.

Illustrative Learning Activities

Guide students to clarify the meaning of terms used in various contexts, as shown in this example:

To a general, *charge* means _____.
To a gas station worker, *charge* means _____.
To a store clerk, *charge* means _____.
To a _____, *charge* means _____.

Guide students to evaluate ways to gather and appraise information, using such questions as:

What procedures were used? Were they the best in terms of purposes?
How were personal feelings and point of view controlled? Is there any indication of personal bias? Is it admitted and explained?
How was information double-checked for accuracy?
What was done to compare findings with those of others?

Present a list of statements, of which half are facts and half are opinions. Ask students to mark *F* by each fact and *O* by each opinion. Ask students to explain how they distinguished between facts and opinions.

Use questions such as these to guide discussion of reasons for choices and decisions made by people under study:

What issue or problem did they face? What action did they take? What were the reasons for this action? What were reasons against this action? Do the reasons for the action outweigh the reasons against it?

Guide discussion of solutions to problems in terms of:

____ clarity ____ convenience ____ safety ____ practicality ____ durability
____ economy ____ ease of use ____ compatibility ____ comfort

Think out loud to show students the specific steps you used to solve a problem, make a decision, critically analyze an issue, or create something.

Arrange for pairs of students to think aloud. Have one student think aloud about a problem as the other student listens. Have the listener describe the steps taken and the procedures used. Have the students change roles.

Guide students to find and share examples of faulty thinking such as:

Causes: Identifying one cause when there are several
Weak generalization: not enough evidence to support a generalization
Selected evidence: using some facts and avoiding others to support a claim
Vagueness: Lack of definition of terms and use of confusing terms
Personal attack: attacking a person rather than focusing on an issue
Faulty assumption: an argument based on an unrelated or false idea
Appeal to authority: argument based on a reputed authority, not on evidence
Occurred together: two events are related because they occurred at the same time
Past as proof: it happened in the past so it will happen again
Popularity: people like it and believe it so it must be true

Ask students to group (classify) items and state the rule they used. For example, after reading a selection on natural resources and related products, students should list resources in one column and products in another and write the rule they used to group them.

Ask students to make and explain inferences, hypotheses, and predictions, using such questions as:

What inference can you make about their motives? Why do you think so?

What do you think we will find to be the best route to Oregon? Why do you think so?

What do you predict the population of our state will be 50 years from now? What is the basis for your prediction?

Have students explain, complete, create, and critique analogies as illustrated by these examples:

What common relationship is expressed in each analogy?

A mayor is to the city council as a governor is to the legislature.
Albany : New York : : Sacramento : California

Complete these analogies:

New : Hampshire : : West : _____
Brazil : South America : : Canada : _____

Create analogies:

City : state : : _____ : _____
Year : _____ : : _____ : _____

_____ : _____ : : _ _____ : _____

What is wrong with these analogies?

Shirt : clothing : : car : truck
Baker : bread : : carpenter : hammer

Have students find and correct false ideas, biased statements, and stereotypes about Africa, other countries, roles of women and men, minority and ethnic groups, and other topics.

Guide students to find and analyze cause-effect, part-whole, sequential, and other relationships, as suggested in chapter 11, and to make comparisons and infer associations while using maps, as suggested in chapter 12.

Creative Thinking

This mode of thinking emphasizes originality, divergent thinking, fluency, and production of new ideas. Teachers may stimulate creative thinking in the social studies by encouraging students to suggest new ways of doing things, to design work centers and displays, to organize information in new ways on maps and charts, to express thoughts and feelings through oral and written language activities, and to engage in art and music activities, construction, and other expressive activities, such as those suggested in chapter 10.

Creative thinking may begin with the building of a background of meanings, images, feelings, and expressive terms and phrases. In the next phase, known as the illumination stage, students discover new insights and relationships and new ways of expressing them. Students may then proceed to express their discoveries through a mural, a dramatic skit, creative writing, or some other creative activity. In this phase students may revise their projects and even start anew after evaluating the adequacy of expression of the original idea. Vital aspects of this process are the original conception of the idea, the perception of progress in expressing it, and the integration of elements into a harmonious whole.

Examples of questions that stimulate creative thinking are presented here and in later sections of this chapter. Sample learning activities are presented in the next chapter.

How can this problem be solved? How many ideas can we generate?

How can we use what we already know in new ways?

What do you see in this film (picture, slide, filmstrip) that is new? In what other ways might it be expressed?

How can we organize the ideas we have gathered in a new way? What form of expression should we use?

What new questions or hypotheses can we state to guide study of this topic?

What are some alternative ways to resolve this issue? How many can we brainstorm?

Which of these might be used to express new ideas learned in this unit: Program? Pageant? Mural? Quiz program? Other?

How may we evaluate the process? The product? What changes will help us achieve our purpose?

Decision Making

Decision making involves the making of intelligent choices by identifying objectives and alternative ways of achieving them. It is used in the social studies to make personal and group decisions about activities and procedures and to weigh options available to people studied in units and current events. Critical thinking and creative thinking may be involved in appraising alternatives and in making new proposals. Of key importance is clarification of both personal and social or group values that are used to make a decision.

Effective decision making involves several phases or steps. First, the relevant issue or situation is defined. Goals and alternative ways of achieving them are identified, and related values are clarified. The consequences of each alternative are then identified, appraised, and ranked in terms of the clarified values. Finally, the best alternative is selected, related action is considered, and the entire decision-making process is appraised. A helpful procedure for guiding the important task of analyzing consequences is presented in Chart 9.2.

Problem Solving and Inquiry

These processes of thinking involve the rational and objective study of questions, issues, and problems in the social studies. Their application ranges from investigating ways of living in families, communities, and cultures around the world to studying contemporary issues and global problems. Key objectives of problem solving and inquiry are to understand, explain, and predict human behavior. Creative thinking and critical thinking are involved in proposing and appraising various aspects of inquiry and investigation.

Investigation begins with defining the problem and posing questions or hypotheses to guide study. Then study procedures and sources of information are identified. Next, data sources are appraised, and information is collected, interpreted, and organized to answer questions or test hypotheses. Finally, conclusions are made and needs for further study are noted. Students must take special care to curb feelings and to prevent personal values from interfering with the making of conclusions based on evidence.

Chart 9.3 presents examples of guidelines that can be developed in class discussion.

A Cognitive Skills Model

Other models may be identified in social studies guides. For example, a model that includes problem solving and other aspects of thinking is shown in Chart 9.4 (Ontario, 1986, p. 12). A given lesson or unit may require use of only some skills, but extended units require use of all of them. The model should be used flexibly, and the skills should be introduced as needed to achieve lesson and unit objectives.

Analysis of Consequences

1. Clarify objectives and alternative ways to achieve them.
2. List desirable and undesirable consequences of each alternative.
3. Prioritize the alternatives in terms of optimum desirable consequences and minimum undesirable consequences.

Alternatives	Desirable Consequences	Undesirable Consequences

Chart 9.2

Using Problem-Solving and Inquiry Procedures

1. Define the problem. What question(s) should be researched? What are the main parts of the problem?

2. Establish tentative hypotheses or answers. What do we already know? What hunches do we have?

3. Clarify procedures and sources of data. What reading materials should be used? Who might be interviewed? What individual and group activities will be helpful? What else might we do?

4. Gather needed information. What information is relevant? Which ideas are facts and which are opinions?

5. Analyze and evaluate information. How should facts be classified? Which are most useful in answering research questions? Which facts are accurate? Which are not? How can we double-check?

6. Synthesize the information. What can we conclude? Which research questions can be answered? Which hypotheses can be confirmed?

7. Evaluate and project next steps. Which procedures and sources were most useful? Least useful? How can we improve? How well did we control personal feelings? What steps should be taken next?

Chart 9.3

Cognitive-Skills-Development Model

	Category	Description
1.	Focus	Limit, direct, or define a problem or issue.
2.	Organize	Select or develop a visual representation, chart, or organizer for the focus.
3.	Locate	Identify, find, and use reliable, relevant sources of information.
4.	Record	Summarize and translate information.
5.	Evaluate/ Assess	Determine the validity, appropriateness, significance, and accuracy of information.
6.	Synthesize/ Conclude	Observe relationships in and draw conclusion(s) from information.
7.	Apply	Predict, generalize, compare, and decide, basing these formulations on the conclusion(s).
8.	Communicate	Express information and ideas, and describe the cognitive processes involved.

Chart 9.4

Metacognition

In addition to using various modes of thinking, students need to be guided to "think about their thinking" (metacognition) and to find ways to monitor and improve it. The charts in preceding sections may be used to guide discussion of "How well did we

Thinking about Your Thinking	Biased Thinking	Thinking about Rule Making

What question(s) or purpose(s) did you have in mind?
 	
What plan, directions, or rules did you follow? What helped most?
 	
What materials were most useful?
 	
What difficulties arose? How did you handle them?
 	
What questions do you still have? How can you find answers to them?
 	
How can you improve?
	How can we avoid these?
	  Slanted definitions
	  One-sided statements
	  Sexist statements
	  Racist statements
	  Use of stereotypes
	  Withholding evidence
	  Hiding assumptions
	  Overgeneralizing
		Define the problem, situation, or need.
		
		Think of reasons why rules are needed.
		
		Propose rules you think will work and tell why.
		
		Discuss proposed rules and select ones to try out.
		
		Try them out, evaluate them, and make needed changes.

Thinking during Discussion	**Map Thinking**	**Thinking about Learning Style**

Think of the focus of discussion as the topic is introduced.
 	
Raise questions if any terms or other items are not clear.
 	
Think of the type of discussion and make contributions that fit it:
 	
  Contribute information during discussions of content.
 	
  State the pros and cons when issues are discussed.
 	
  Give reasons for your position on moral dilemmas.
 	
  Give original responses during brainstorming.
 	
  Give brief answers to questions raised in review discussions.
	What does the title tell you?
	
	What do the symbols represent?
	
	What do the colors show?
	
	How do you find directions?
	
	How do you measure distance?
	
	How do you locate places?
	
	What relationships between items do you infer?
	
	What mental map do you make when you close your eyes?
		I get a purpose by _____.
		
		I make a plan by _____.
		
		I begin work by _____.
		
		I proceed by _____.
		
		I get needed help by _____.
		
		I get answers by _____.
		
		I find main ideas by _____.
		
		I relate details to main ideas and concepts by _____.
		
		I summarize by _____.
		
		I check my progress by ____.
		
		I work best alone on _____.
		
		I work best in groups on ____.

Thinking about Questions to Ask	**Thinking about a Problem**	**Thinking about Events**
To recall an event: What happened? What did they do? To explain something: What does that word mean? What is an example? To apply an idea: How can we use that idea in our unit? To analyze something: What are the main parts? To synthesize parts: How can we put the parts together in a new way? To evaluate something: What standards should we use? To probe for more ideas: What are other reasons or causes?	How can it be defined? Why is it a problem? Is it a problem for everyone? For a group? For an individual? What are possible causes? How might the causes be removed? How might it be solved? If it cannot be solved, how might it be reduced? What help is available for solving it? How is it now being handled? What changes will help?	When did it happen? Where did it happen? How long did it last? Why did it happen? What were the causes? What were the effects? Who was affected? How was it related to other events? Was it part of a trend? How was it like and different from similar events? Will it be judged to be a major or a minor event? Why do you think so?

Figure 9–2

think" and to help students evaluate themselves.[3] In addition, the focus may be placed on thinking in a variety of situations, as illustrated in Figure 9.2. A helpful activity is small-group discussion in which students take turns "thinking out loud" about how to solve a problem, create something, or do some other task. Members of the group observe the student who is thinking out loud to note strong points related to defining the problem, suggesting procedures and sources to use, and other aspects of thinking about the problem. The teacher observes and guides the group to consider points that need special attention.

Generating, Organizing, and Interpreting Data

The foregoing modes of thinking call for a solid base of knowledge and the use of specific thinking skills. The development of knowledge and the development of thinking skills may be viewed as inseparable teaching-learning activities. This section gives procedures for developing knowledge by using thinking skills that are basic to those skills presented in later sections. Model questions are presented for improving students' ability to recall, collect, interpret, compare, and classify data (adapted from Taba et al., 1971; Hannah and Michaelis, 1977; and Bloom and others, 1956 and 1981).

Remembering

To remember is to retrieve pertinent information by recalling or recognizing cognitive and affective elements related to a topic. Students should be helped to develop memory frameworks, as shown in Chart 9.5. Questions such as these are used to focus attention on relevant information.

What do you recall about this topic? Question? Activity?

Who remembers the meaning of _____ (goods, services, specialization)?

Collecting Data

Data are collected by means of looking, listening, and using other senses and by reading, doing research, and gathering information from audiovisual material and other resources. Questions to guide data collection include

What can we find in this reading to answer our questions?

What ideas are presented in this filmstrip? Reference? Recording?

What data can we get directly from experts? From observing an activity?

With recalled and collected data in mind, the following skills may be used to process the data.

Interpreting

Interpreting includes explaining the meaning, stating the significance, and translating or illustrating the thoughts and feelings obtained from various sources. Students must

---

[3] See the section "Metacognition and Learning How to Learn" in chapter 11 for additional examples.

Wagon

Sailing ship

How did these technological developments change ways of living? (Social Studies Workshop, University of Calif., Berkeley)

exercise care in getting the intended meaning from a source so that further thinking is not clouded by misconceptions. Guiding questions are

What main ideas and supporting details did you find in this reading?

What relationships did you find between _____ and _____ (location of homes and schools, growth of cities and waterways)?

Can you explain the main idea in your own words?

Comparing and Contrasting

Comparing and contrasting are used to help students identify similarities and differences and to place items in a sequence. Guiding questions include

How are _____ and _____ (goods and services, exports and imports) alike? How are they different?

In what order should we place these _____ (items, events, cities)?

Classifying

Classifying is used to group or organize items by descriptive characteristics, uses, or relationships; it is also used to develop concepts, as shown in the next section. Guiding questions are

Which of these items belong together? Why?

How can the main uses of these resources be grouped?

Guidelines for using these various thinking skills are presented in Charts 9.5 through 9.9.

Remembering	Gathering Data	Interpreting
Retrieve what fits the topic.	Know what you are looking for and focus on it.	Clarify the meaning of terms and symbols.
Use key words, acronyms, visual images, rhymes.	Use a question or hypothesis to guide data gathering.	Find the main idea and related details.
Get clues as you listen.		Find cause-effect and other relationships.
Place items in ABC or 123 order.	Note major and minor items.	Get the intended meaning.
Use key dates, places, events, and concepts as organizers.	Take notes for future use.	State the meaning in your own words.
Take notes; make outlines and retrieval charts.	Check findings to be sure they are accurate.	Make a summary or a conclusion.
Use story grammar to note main character, problem, what happened, main point.	Look, listen, read, and ask questions.	Compare your interpretation with that of others.
	Use a variety of sources.	

Chart 9.5   Chart 9–6   Chart 9.7

Comparing and Contrasting	Classifying
Select a basis for comparison, such as size, shape, order, uses, behavior.	Select a basis for grouping items, as noted for comparing.
Describe the features or characteristics to be compared.	Examine each item to identify its features or characteristics.
Describe similarities and differences.	Identify similarities and differences.
Summarize the main similarities and differences.	Place items with common features in the same group.

Chart 9.8   Chart 9.9

Developing Concepts

Concepts and concept clusters are key elements of schemata, the knowledge structures that guide perception, categorize information, interpret experience, draw inferences, and evaluate information.[4] Concept development goes hand in hand with development of a knowledge base. Interpreting, comparing, and classifying are three important components of concept development. Students' understanding of concepts may be facilitated by providing both direct sensory experiences and vicarious experiences, ranging from observing activities and examining realia to reading and doing research on a topic. Literature, art, and music are used to develop qualitative shades of meaning. Reading about Daniel Boone, for example, adds meaning to students' conceptions of scouts, wilderness, and the adventures of explorers. Teachers should control the number and difficulty of concepts to be learned in order to develop depth of understanding and to avoid misconceptions and "word calling." Because words are the labels for concepts, meaningful vocabulary development requires concept development.

Types of Concepts

Three types of concepts may be identified as requiring a combination of attributes (Bruner and others, 1956). *Conjunctive* concepts, such as legislator and taxes, are based on characteristics that are additive. For example, taxes are a class of payments, and are levied according to law, and are paid to the government. *Disjunctive* concepts have either/or characteristics that need to be identified—for example, U.S. citizenship, which may be obtained by birth, or by passing an exam, or because one's parents were born here. *Relational* concepts, such as population density, per capita income, and area, are defined in terms of how one element varies in relation to another. Operational definitions may aid in understanding and working with relational concepts; per capita income, for example, is determined by dividing income by number of people.

Concepts may also be categorized by level of abstractness, comprehensiveness, and other features. At a low level of abstraction and difficulty are concepts of *concrete* items, such as lake, island, and goods. More abstract and difficult are *defined* concepts, such as interdependence, justice, and cultural exchange; these concepts require precise definition, a variety of examples, and identification of relationships—for example,

---

[4] For a discussion of schema theory see Lopach and Luckowski (1989) and Marzano (1988).

demonstration of interdependence among workers in a community. Instruction should also be designed to help students recognize the *specificity* and *generality* of concepts used in social studies. Land, resources, and nation are generally applicable to any culture, area, or time period. Concepts such as New England colonies, muckrakers, and caste system (in India) are applicable only in designated time periods, cultures, or places. *Value-neutral* concepts, such as resources, role, and communication, do not usually arouse feelings. In contrast, *value-laden* concepts, such as prejudice, discrimination, and justice, have preferential elements and stir feelings. Teachers should recognize that feelings associated with value-laden concepts are among the "facts to be considered."

Concept Development Strategies

Five strategies are used to develop concepts: defining, distinguishing examples from nonexamples, listing-grouping-labeling, problem solving or inquiry, and providing a series of learning activities.

Defining Learning definitions contributes to both concept development and vocabulary development. Students learn definitions from teachers and find them in textbooks, glossaries, dictionaries, and other sources. Several types of definition are used, as illustrated in the following examples:

> *Demonstrating:* Watch while I show a great-circle route on the globe.
>
> *Showing:* This picture shows a tropical rain forest.
>
> *Using analogies:* A governor is like a president except he runs a state.
>
> *Using synonyms or antonyms:* Being loyal means being devoted; the opposite is being a traitor.
>
> *Using glossaries or dictionaries:* The glossary says that *urban* means having to do with cities.
>
> *Stating behavior (behavioral definitions):* A legislator campaigns for office, writes bills, serves on committees, things like that.
>
> *Stating operations (operational definitions):* You figure population density by dividing the population of an area by the number of square miles in the area.

These model questions and Charts 9.10 and 9.11 may be used to focus attention on different types of definition.

> What do you mean by _____ (producer, goods, urban function)?
>
> What does _____ mean?
>
> What is a good way to clear up the meaning of this term? Using a picture or a model? Demonstrating the meaning? Other?
>
> Who can define _____ (carpenter, judge, scout) by telling what he or she does?
>
> Who can define _____ (average income per family, population density) by stating how it is figured?
>
> Which meaning(s) of _____ (bank, pollution, democracy) should we use? Which one best fits the context?

Questions to Guide Defining

What is to be defined (word, phrase, map symbol, behavior, operation, feelings)?

How is it like and different from others we know?

What is included? Not included?

What kind of definition (example, analogy, picture, demonstration, behavioral, operational) will be most useful?

Chart 9.10

Which Terms Arouse Feelings?	
Communism	Lobbyist
Demands	Majority
Democracy	Minority
Dictator	Police
Environment	Politician
Fair play	Pollution
Freedom	Poverty

Chart 9.11

An activity that is useful in defining concepts is the making of a semantic web or map. For example, print PUBLIC SERVICES in a circle on the chalkboard or a chart and draw lines from it to education, police, and other services

Distinguishing Examples from Nonexamples This is a deductive (general to specific) concept attainment strategy that begins with the name of the concept and moves to identification of examples; it is often used with the defining activities just noted.

1. State the concept to be learned or pose a question: "Today we are to learn about peninsulas. What is a peninsula?"

2. Identify defining characteristics (critical attributes): "Look at this example on the wall map. Which parts are surrounded by water?"

3. Present other examples of the concept: "Look at the map on page 22. See the peninsula at the bottom. Find the one on the next page."

4. Present nonexamples: "Look at the island on page 22. Why is that *not* a peninsula? Find others that are *not* peninsulas."

5. Have students state or write a definition: "A piece of land nearly surrounded by water and connected with the mainland."

Listing-Grouping-Labeling This is an inductive (specific to general) concept formation strategy developed by Taba et al. (1971) as one of three cognitive tasks. The classifying process is used to group items encountered in materials and activities:

1. Identify and list items to be grouped: "What did you see (hear, note)? What items are shown in this picture?"

2. Identify items that can be grouped together: "Which items seem to belong together?"

3. State characteristics of items that belong together: "Why do they belong together? How are they alike?"

4. Label the group: "What is a good name or label for the group? Why is that a good name (label)?"

How can you use displays such as these to develop concepts? San Diego Schools

Problem Solving and Inquiry Concept development, extension, and enrichment may be fostered through inquiry and problem solving, particularly when the concepts being considered are ones like justice, equality, democracy, prejudice, and others that grow in meaning as they are encountered in differing contexts. The meaning of concepts is clarified in ongoing activities, put to immediate use, and used to pose questions, gather and process data, and state conclusions, as the following example from a unit on prejudice illustrates.

1. Define the problem: "What is prejudice and how does it affect us?"
2. Pose questions (or hypotheses) to guide study: "What is prejudice? What causes it? What are different types of prejudice? What are the effects on oneself and on others? How can prejudice be reduced?"
3. Collect and process relevant information: "What information do we have on each question? How shall we organize it? Can we use the headings *causes, types, effects, and ways to reduce?*"
4. State a conclusion: "What can we conclude about causes, types, effects, and ways to reduce?"
5. Suggest needs for further study: "What new questions do you have? How can we find answers to them?"

Providing A Series of Activities This strategy beings with concrete activities and moves to pictorial and symbolic activities, as illustrated by the following examples for development of time concepts in early grades.

Clock Time

Use a metronome or clock with second hand to demonstrate the length of a second and seconds in a minute.

Synchronize the counting of seconds with a metronome or second hand by saying "one thousand one, one thousand two, etc."

Count the number of seconds or minutes it takes to complete such activities as walking around the classroom, writing one's name, reading an assignment, and drawing a picture.

Count the number of seconds it takes for a second hand to go around a clock face and a minute sand timer to empty.

Use a kitchen timer to demonstrate half-hour and hour and to set the amount of time allotted to varoius periods or activities.

Discuss and compare the number of minutes in class periods, recess, lunch period, favorite TV programs, and home activities.

Discuss and compare time needed to go from home to school and to places in the neighborhood and community.

Read and write time words and numerals such as minutes, hour, two o'clock, 2:00 p.m., and noon.

Calendar Time

Discuss hours in a day, major parts of a day including time in school, after-school, and sleeping, and time from noon to midnight and from midnight to noon.

Keep a record of a unit activity each school day and a personal activity over the weekend and arrange them in order to show activities for one week.

Expand the above to record activities for a month. Use the record to refer to yesterday, a week ago, three days ago, and so on.

Refer frequently to the classroom calendar posted on a bulletin board, using such terms as yesterday, today, tomorrow, last Friday, two weeks ago, and so on.

Teach and review names of days, months, seasons, major holidays.

Read and write such dates as June 1, 1987, and 6/1/87.

Make time lines that show events during a week, month, or year.

Chronology

Discuss sequence or order of the daily class schedule, days of the week, months of the year, the seasons, holidays, events in the lives of children, and changes in the neighborhood or community.

Arrange pictures of babies, toddlers, nursery and elementary school children, teenagers, and adults in order from youngest to oldest.

Arrange photos of changes in the neighborhood and community in chronological order.

Arrange drawings of events in a sequence and place events on a time line.

Use, read, and write such terms as first, second, past, present, future, before, after, next, later, sequence or order of events, yesterday, today, tomorrow, two years later, and time line.

Make time charts or lines of events in the community.

Checklist 9.1
WHICH TIME CONCEPTS DO YOU KNOW AND USE?

Clock time: hour ____ half-hour ____ quarter-hour ____ minute ____ second ____ morning ____ noon ____ afternoon ____ evening ____ midnight ____ a.m. ____ p.m. ____ time zones ____ prime meridian ____ International Date Line

Calendar time: ____ day ____ week ____ month ____ year ____ decade ____ score ____ generation ____ century ____ millennium ____ calendar year ____ fiscal year ____ school year ____ seasons ____ holidays ____ period ____ era ____ epoch ____ A.D. ____ B.C.

Chronology: ____ then ____ now ____ soon ____ before ____ after ____ next ____ yesterday ____ today ____ tomorrow ____ past ____ present ____ future ____ movement ____ trend ____ ancient ____ medieval ____ modern ____ prehistoric time ____ geological time ____ time line ____ time chart ____ chronology

---

Checklist 9.1 can be used by students for self-evaluation and by the teacher for diagnostic evaluation in middle and upper grades.

Developing Concept Clusters and Themes The strategies just described may be used to develop concept clusters and themes. Each concept in a cluster or in a theme must be given special attention. For example, the cluster of concepts included in *landforms*—plains, hills, plateaus, mountains—may be developed by identifying examples and nonexamples of plains, then hills, and so on. In addition, differences between plains and hills and between plateaus and mountains should be identified. Focusing attention on clusters of concepts allows meaningful comparisons to be made between pairs of concepts; moreover, meaningful examples and nonexamples are contained within the clusters. For instance, after identifying examples of plains, students may identify hills and plateaus as nonexamples. Another advantage is that relationships among the concepts in a cluster make for meaningful learning that promotes the ability to recall, recognize, and apply concepts. This may be illustrated by the comment of a student: "As you go across the plains you come to hills and then on to plateaus and finally to mountains—the Rocky Mountains."

Themes, such as ways of living on the frontier, the westward movement, equality for ethnic minority groups, and extending civil rights to all groups, call for concept development plus extending learning activities within a unit of instruction. For example, the theme of "extending civil rights to all groups" call for initial instruction on civil rights, followed by a series of learning activities on the struggles of various groups to achieve them.

Developing Generalizations

Generalizations are summarizing and concluding statements based on information and indicating the relationship among concepts. They have many uses in the social studies: to generate questions or hypotheses to guide study, to explain human behavior and relationships, or to build a model or a theory. For instance, students who comprehend the generalization "people use resources to meet basic needs" may then ask, "How do people in other countries use resources to meet their needs for food, shelter, and clothing?"

Generalizations range from limited statements that apply to a particular culture, time, or place to statements that have universal applicability. For example, a generalization about the causes of the Civil War is bound by time and place, but the law of supply and demand has universal application. Some generalizations are conditional and take an if-then form: "If the supply of an item increases, then the price will decrease (other things being equal)." A cause-effect relationship is implied in if-then generalizations.

Students should learn to distinguish between descriptive generalizations that are value-neutral and prescriptive generalizations that are valuative, just as they are expected to distinguish between statements of fact and opinion. Most generalizations in the social studies are descriptive, as they are in the social sciences. They take such form as "Population growth, industrialization, and urbanization are among the causes of environmental problems." Fewer in number but of equal importance are prescriptive, or value-laden, generalizations. They include a preference, demand, value, or value principle, such as "Population growth, industrialization, and urbanization must be controlled if the environment is to be improved." Notice that in descriptive generalizations the emphasis is on *what is;* in prescriptive generalizations the emphasis is on *what ought to be.* The implication is to clarify the basis or standards and related evidence for the prescription or recommendation.

Teachers may focus on the development of different types and levels of generalization by providing for three types of study. The descriptive and widely applicable (or universal) generalizations may be developed through studies that draw samples of data from selected times, places, or cultures. Students analyze the data to identify common elements that form a basis for generalizations. Descriptive and limited generalizations may be developed in units that focus on particular times, places, and cultures. Students bring together the particular features characteristic of such places as our community, Israel, or China, and they formulate appropriate time-, place-, and culture-bound generalizations. Prescriptive generalizations call for use of decision-making processes. Students consider alternatives and consequences and make a decision or a judgment regarding the best alternative in light of goals.

Teaching Strategies

Five teaching strategies for developing generalizations are presented in Charts 9.12 through 9.16. In all of them attention must be given to the meaning of the concepts that are included, the facts on which the generalization is based, and the relationship that is expressed. Useful guiding questions are

In general, what can we say about _____ (uses of transportation, causes of pollution)?

What are the main _____ (reasons for urban growth, effects of air pollution)?

What are the relationships between _____ and _____ (price and demand, price and supply)?

Basic Strategy for Generalizing

Procedure	Focusing Questions	Illustrative Application
Get the data (facts) clearly in mind and interpret them	→ What did you find? See? Hear? Read? Note?	→ What did you find to be major governmental activities at the local and state levels?
Identify common elements, relationships, or main ideas.	→ What common elements did you find? Which items are related?	→ What common activities (executive, legislative, judicial) did you find?
Make a tentative generalization.	→ What can we say in general?	→ What seems to be a sound conclusion about activities common at both levels?
Test the tentative generalization against other data.	→ Does our generalization hold up as we check other data?	→ What does this report (film, filmstrip, reading) show to be the main governmental activities at both levels? Is our generalization valid?

Chart 9.12

Inductive: From Data to Generalization

Collect, organize, and examine data.

Identify common elements, or what is generally true.

State a generalization based on common or general elements.

Check against the data to see if the generalization holds up.

Chart 9.13

Deductive: From Generalization to Data

Present the generalization to the group.

Present supporting data, cases, or evidence.

Refer students to sources of additional supporting data.

Ask students to find supporting data in the sources.

Chart 9.14

Problem Solving or Inquiry to Develop a Generalization

Define the problem to be investigated.

State a hypothesis or a question to guide study.

Collect, appraise, and organize related data.

Test the hypothesis or answer the guiding question.

State a generalization (conclusion) based on the data.

Chart 9.15

Decision Making to Develop a Prescriptive Generalization

Define the issue or the problem.

Clarify the values or the standards most important in the situation.

Consider alternatives for dealing with the problem.

Consider the consequences of each alternative.

Select the best alternative in terms of the values or standards.

State a prescriptive generalization based on the above.

Chart 9.16

TOKYO

OAKLAND

How are central business districts of large cities alike? In general, what features are common to all of them?

The basic strategy, in Chart 9.12, includes procedures and questions in a commonly used order. The other strategies illustrate inductive and deductive sequences and the use of problem solving and decision making to develop generalizations.

As noted for concept development, a series of learning activities may be provided to develop a generalization. For example, the generalization "All communities have laws and rules to protect and govern people" may be developed by such activities as:

Discussing familiar rules and laws everyone must follow in the students' community

Gathering information from reading materials on rules and laws in other communities

Seeing films and filmstrips on rules and laws in communities

Summarizing rules and laws designed to promote health and safety, maintain order, and protect individual rights

Stating a generalization in response to the question "In general, what can we say about rules and laws in communities?"

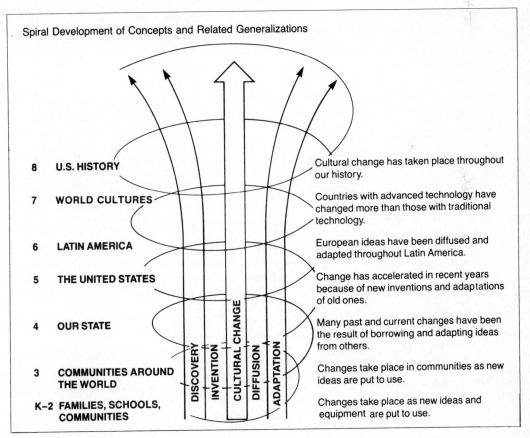

Spiral Development of Concepts and Related Generalizations

8	U.S. HISTORY	Cultural change has taken place throughout our history.
7	WORLD CULTURES	Countries with advanced technology have changed more than those with traditional technology.
6	LATIN AMERICA	European ideas have been diffused and adapted throughout Latin America.
5	THE UNITED STATES	Change has accelerated in recent years because of new inventions and adaptations of old ones.
4	OUR STATE	Many past and current changes have been the result of borrowing and adapting ideas from others.
3	COMMUNITIES AROUND THE WORLD	Changes take place in communities as new ideas are put to use.
K-2	FAMILIES, SCHOOLS, COMMUNITIES	Changes take place as new ideas and equipment are put to use.

DISCOVERY INVENTION CULTURAL CHANGE DIFFUSION ADAPTATION

Chart 9–17

Growth of Concepts and Generalizations

The meaning of concepts and generalizations should grow deeper and broader as students move from level to level and encounter them in new settings. For example, the concept of community may begin with one's own community, be expanded to include other communities, and eventually embrace the idea of national and world community. A generalization about using resources to meet human needs may begin with local uses and move to state, national, and worldwide uses of resources. Such spiral development of concepts and generalizations is illustrated in Chart 9.17, which shows how the four concepts in the cluster "cultural change" and related generalizations may be brought to higher levels of development in units at various levels.

Inferring, Predicting, and Hypothesizing

These three interrelated skills involve applying main ideas or principles to make inferences, predictions, or hypotheses. These skills are similar to one another in that they emphasize going beyond the data at hand to identify and consider consequences, cause-effect and other relationships, supporting data, reasons, principles, and conditions that have been assumed. Both similarities and differences are discussed in this section; they should be considered as plans are made to develop each skill.

To *infer* is to draw a possible consequence, conclusion, or implication from a set of facts or premises; often the inferences are not explicit in a source and students must read between the lines. Inferring is frequently used after interpreting a reading selection or some other source of information. Inferences should be logical, reasonable, and applicable in a given situation. Questions to ask students to guide inferring include

Why do you suppose _____ (that happened, they were surprised, they arrived at that conclusion)?

What do you suppose someone would do _____ (in that situation, if faced by that problem)?

Why do you think that _____ (they felt happy, the writer is biased)?

To *predict* is to forecast or anticipate what may happen under certain conditions. Like an inference, a prediction should be reasonable and supported by evidence, but one must usually wait to see if it is accurate—for example, a prediction about an election or a change in population. Students may be guided by such questions as

What do you think will happen if _____ (more people move to suburbs, acid rain is not reduced)?

What do you estimate the _____ (school enrollment, state population) will be in ten years?

What do you think they will do if _____ (the school budget is cut, the school day and the school year are extended)?

A hypothesis is usually more general than an inference or a prediction and should apply to all similar cases; it should also be testable. To *hypothesize* is to state a tentative

Dynamic lines and a red-silver color scheme made the 1937 *Super Chief* look fast, powerful, and glamorous. It was all of that, but Santa Fe realized that converting from steam to diesel also solved the desert water storage problem.

Which of these are trains of the future? Why do you think so? What are other possibilities? How about maglev trains? What sources should we use to find out? Social Studies Workshop, University of California, Berkeley

generalization or question that shows how two or more items are related. Hypotheses may be stated as questions, if-then statements, or declarative statements. The following are all examples of hypotheses: "What is generally believed to be a good location for cities?" "If a place has waterways, then it is a good location for a city." "Cities are usually located near waterways." Notice that each example indicates a condition (location of cities) and related items (near waterways), and that each may be tested by gathering data. Questions to guide students' hypothesizing are

What are the main causes of _____ (urban growth, air pollution)?

What are generally believed to be _____ (the advantages of division of labor, the reasons people moved westward)?

If people live in _____ (deserts, mountains, cities), what problems can they expect?

Strategy for Predicting and Hypothesizing

Procedure	*Focusing Questions*	*Illustrative Examples*
State prediction.	→ What will happen if _____?	→ What will our city be like in the year 2000 if urban growth continues?
or		
State hypothesis.	→ If _____, then _____? What usually happens when _____?	→ What usually happens to cities with high urban growth?
Give reasons or data that support the prediction or the hypothesis.	→ What is the basis for your prediction? Or for your hypothesis?	→ Why do you think our city will be like that? Why do you say that usually happens to cities?
State conditions for prediction to occur.	→ What conditions are necessary for your prediction to happen?	→ What conditions do you assume in saying our city will change that way?
or		
Identify needed data and data-gathering procedures to test hypothesis.	→ What data do we need to test the hypothesis? What procedures should we use?	→ What data do we need to show the usual effects of urban growth? How should we gather data?

Chart 9.18

The teaching strategy for predicting and hypothesizing presented in Chart 9.18 is adapted from one proposed by Taba et al. (1971). It is set up to show questions to ask when guiding students to predict or hypothesize.

The following plan illustrates how students can move to higher levels of thinking by predicting, then analyzing consequences.

Impact of Innovations

Objective

To project technological innovations and describe their possible consequences

Materials

Reader's Guide to Periodical Literature; magazines such as *The Futurist, Canadian Futures, Alternative Futures, Discovery,* and *Omni*; and books such as Christofer's *The Micro Millenium,* Didsbury's *Creating a Global Agenda,* Panati's *Breakthroughs,* and Toffler's *Third Wave.*

Introduction

Discuss past innovations such as radio and television. Ask students to describe what effects these innovations have had on them and on members of their families.

Development

Ask students to identify recent innovations. Guide discussion of such innovations as

Computers   Compact discs   Fiber optics   Lasers   Superconductors   Robots

Discuss each innovation in terms of (a) what it is and (b) its effects on human activities.

Divide the class into groups to research the innovations, with primary emphasis on their effects or consequences and future uses.

Ask members of each group to report to the class. Record findings on a retrieval chart with the following headings: "Innovation," "Uses in the Future," and "Consequences."

Conclusion and Evaluation

Ask students to summarize the future uses and consequences of each innovation.

Ask students to rank the innovations in terms of future usefulness and desirable consequences for human welfare, giving reasons for their ranking. If differences in ranking arise, organize teams to marshal evidence and present arguments for their position.

Evaluate students' learning by noting their contributions and the quality of their reasoning in projecting trends, noting consequences, and ranking the innovations.

Follow-up

Ask students to prepare individual reports on an innovation of their choice in which consequences are analyzed in terms of questions such as

What are possible benefits? What are possible negative effects?
How might the innovation affect family life? How might it affect you personally?
What effects might there be on the quality of life in our country? In other countries?
Will it lead to permanent or temporary changes in our lifestyles? Give reasons for your answer.
Finally, do you think the innovation is desirable or undesirable? Give reasons for your position.

Ask students to select an innovation or a trend and make a futures wheel.

Analyzing and Synthesizing Information

Analyzing and synthesizing are high-level intellectual processes that go beyond the development of information, concepts, and generalizations. They are used in the social studies to reorganize content and to bring it together in ways that are new to students. For example, students analyze environmental problems by breaking them down into causes and effects; they may then present the causes and effects in a new way, perhaps in a flowchart that relates each cause to its effects on people and other living things.

To *analyze* is to identify the parts, elements, relationships, or principles presented in reading materials, on maps, in audiovisual materials, and in other sources. Questions to ask students to guide analysis include

What are the main parts of this _____ (story, picture, map)? How are they related?

What _____ (concepts, activities, regions, time periods) are used to organize this material?

What is the central idea? What ideas are organized around it?

To *synthesize* is to bring parts together into a meaningful whole, to create a new product, or to form a unified structure around a concept, a theme, or some other element. The synthesis may take the form of a model, report, map, chart, story, display, or dramatic presentation. Such questions as the following may be used to emphasize creativity while guiding synthesis:

How can we show the main _____ (regions, types of work) in a new way?

What _____ (concept, theme, main idea) can we use to organize the parts?

What form of presentation should we use? Booklet? Chart? Map? Mural? Other?

To synthesize after an analysis has been made, one simply moves ahead to determine a new way to combine the parts identified in the analysis. For example, after major types of land use are identified, as shown in Chart 9.19, the teacher may ask: What are

---

Strategy for Analyzing and Synthesizing

Procedure	*Focusing Questions*	*Illustrative Application*
Identify useful ways to break the problem into parts.	→ How can we break the problem into parts? What main parts (types, reasons, causes) should be studied?	→ How can we break down our question on urban land use? What are the main types of land use in cities?
Define each part clearly.	→ What is the meaning of each part? What does each part include?	→ How can we define each type? Commercial? Industrial? Residential? Recreational? Other?
Identify and organize data related to each part.	→ What information do we have on each part? How are these parts related?	→ What data can we classify under each type of land use?
State summary, conclusion, or explanation based on the analysis.	→ What does our analysis show? What can we conclude?	→ Who can summarize the types of land use in order from greatest to least? How might we explain the differences?

If a synthesis is to be made, proceed as follows:

Identify organizing idea and form of presentation.	How can we present our findings in a new way?	How can we organize our findings on urban land use?
Decide on way to present findings and proceed.	What plan(s) do you think should be used? Why?	What organizing idea is best? What form of presentation is best? Why?

Chart 9.19

some new ways we can use to show major types of land use? After considering a map, diagram, mural, or other form of presentation, students may synthesize by making a new map combining themes or items from the material they analyzed. A clear understanding of the parts to be synthesized is prerequisite to combining them in a new way. The teaching strategy presented in Chart 9.19 illustrates how this may be done.

Evaluating, an Ongoing and Capstone Process

Evaluating is an *ongoing* (formative) process from the beginning of an activity through its culmination, as one asks: How well am I doing? How can I improve? Evaluating is also a *capstone* (summative) process that is on a higher cognitive level than the processes discussed earlier. In both processes, to evaluate is to make a judgment of the merit or worth of an activity or object in terms of selected criteria. Critical thinking is used to define criteria, apply them, gather related evidence, and make a judgment; otherwise an opinion is formed rather than a reasoned judgment.

Focusing questions are needed for two different types of evaluation. In the first type internal standards are used to appraise reports, reading selections, and other materials. Typical standards are accuracy, consistency in use of terms, soundness of arguments, and relation of conclusions to evidence. Guiding questions for internal evaluation are

How can _____ (our report, map; this graph, plan) be improved? Is it accurate? Well organized? Meaningful? Useful for our purpose?

How accurate (adequate, useful, consistent, biased) is this _____ (document, diagram, flowchart, report)?

To what extent are the _____ (conclusions, generalizations, inferences) supported by evidence? What logical fallacies are evident?

In the second type of evaluation external standards are used. These may be objectives, criteria, or a recognized standard of excellence. Examples of external evaluation are (1) using objectives of urban renewal as criteria to appraise plans, (2) using freedom of speech to judge the conduct of a meeting, and (3) using one model conservation program as a standard to appraise another. Guiding questions for external evaluation are

To what extent will this _____ (plan, program, type of action) lead to the stated goals?

Which of the alternatives is most desirable in terms of _____ (individual benefits, group benefits, objectives)?

To what extent were standards of _____ (justice, freedom, personal security) upheld during this period?

How does this _____ (report, antipollution proposal, airport, political system) compare with the model of an outstanding one?

The strategy presented in Chart 9.20 begins by identifying and defining what is to be appraised, then determining the standards or criteria that should be used. In

Strategy for Evaluating		
Procedure	*Focusing Questions*	*Illustrative Application*
Identify and define the focus of evaluation.	→	What is to be appraised? Why should _____ be assessed?	→	What are the proposals for recycling waste materials?
Identify and define standards of appraisal.	→	What standards (values, criteria) should be used?	→	What standards can we use to judge them? Goals? Benefits? Other?
Collect data related to each standard.	→	What is the evidence? What data can we find for each standard?	→	What evidence is available on the possible benefits or other standards used to judge them?
Identify possible outcomes (effects, consequences) of each proposal.	→	What are likely outcomes of each proposal? Which one will have the most desirable outcomes?	→	What effects or outcomes are expected?
Make a judgment, including suggestions for improvement.	→	Which one best meets the standards? How might it be improved?	→	In general, which proposal is best? Why? How can it be improved?

Chart 9.20

practice these phases may be joined together, providing students understand the focus of the evaluation. Next, evidence is gathered and interpreted to show the extent to which the defined standards are met. The next step is necessary if alternatives— different plans, materials, or proposals—are being assessed. Possible outcomes or consequences of each alternative are considered, and an attempt is made to identify the one that is most desirable in light of the standards. Finally, the quality or merit of the item(s) under appraisal should be judged and suggestions for improvement made as appropriate.

A Unifying Model of Teaching

The model presented in this section is useful in group work; it also provides a setting for generating individual activities. The various thinking skills are brought in as needed. Like any model, this one should be used flexibly, varying the steps or phases as appropriate to guide the creative study of selected topics and to avoid the pitfalls of a regimented, step-by-step procedure. The major phases are as follows:

1. Defining questions and problems to guide study
2. Recalling information and hypothesizing
3. Clarifying steps of procedure
4. Finding, interpreting, appraising, and classifying data
5. Generalizing and further processing of information as needed
6. Evaluating procedures and outcomes

Defining Questions and Problems

As new units are introduced and as different problems arise in a unit that is under way, questions and problems must be clearly defined. The objective is to get pupils to recognize and understand what is to be studied. During the initiation of a unit, materials may be selected to stimulate thinking. Pictures, maps, objects, and other resources can be arranged to highlight significant questions or problems. After the students have examined the materials, they should discuss the questions or problems to be attacked first. As initial problems are defined and clarified, they may be listed on the chalkboard or on charts, as illustrated in Charts 9.21 through 9.23.

Recalling Information and Hypothesizing

This phase should be both systematic and creative. As the teacher asks questions, students may recall both previous information and information introduced during the initiation of the unit: "What can you recall about this topic?" "What have you learned before that we might use?" "How is it like other topics we have studied?" The teacher may next ask questions designed to elicit hypothoses: "What ideas do you have on this topic?" "What do you think we will find?" "What answers might we find to the questions we have listed?" The objectives of these two sets of questions are to retrieve information related to questions posed by the group during definition of the problem, to get students to state hypotheses regarding what they may find, to identify misconceptions they may have, and to motivate the search for data. The following examples are given to indicate the nature of children's hypotheses:

> In a unit on the post office, the question under discussion was "What happens to letters that are put in mailboxes?" Children's comments were:
>> "A mail carrier picks them up. Then they are taken to the right place."
>> "Wait! They have to be sorted by somebody. I think they are taken downtown. Maybe they are sorted by workers or a machine."
>> "There must be a plan or a system. Then a mail carrier can deliver them."
> In a unit on the westward movement, the group was considering this problem on travel routes: Check the relief map of the United States and plan a route to

Work at Home	Boonesboro	Community History
What jobs are there?	Why was it built?	Who were the first settlers?
What skills are needed?	Who built it?	What were the first buildings like?
What can children do?	Where was it?	Where was the first school?
What do others do?	When was it built?	Where were the first streets?
	How was it built?	When was the railroad begun?
	How did people travel to it?	What changes have taken place?

| Chart 9.21 | Chart 9.22 | Chart 9.23 |

California from St. Joseph, Missouri; then check to see if your proposed route is the same as one of those used by early settlers. The children made the following hypotheses:

"Go straight across the plains and mountains to San Francisco. If you go this way, you have to find mountain passes through the Rockies and Sierras."

"Go along the Missouri to the Platte River and on to the coast across Utah and Nevada. If you would keep close to rivers, you could get water and there would not be many steep grades. I heard that some railroads and highways are built along water level routes."

"Go along south to Santa Fe and on to Los Angeles across New Mexico and Arizona. This would be a good route in the winter."

"Why couldn't we start our trip in St. Louis? Then we could use boats all the way to San Francisco."

Teachers sometimes ask, "Should hypotheses be proposed for every problem that arises?" No! When students lack the background for hypothesizing, the teacher should begin by studying the questions noted during definition of the problem.

Clarifying Steps of Procedure

This phase may be directed by the teacher or planned by the group. Ways to gather information, possible sources of information, and assignment of responsibilities are considered. Questions such as the following are raised: How shall we proceed? What are the next steps? How can we obtain needed information? What sources of information should be used? Should any jobs be assigned to individuals or small groups? Does everyone know what he or she has to do? A wide range of sources and procedures may be explored, as noted in Charts 9.24 and 9.25. The best possibilities are carefully selected, and children are urged to watch for others.

Finding, Interpreting, Appraising, and Classifying Information

With plans in mind, students proceed to gather and interpret data needed to answer questions, solve problems, or test hypotheses. Observation and related study skills are

Sources of Information	
Clippings	Newspapers
Encyclopedias	Pictures
Films	Slides
Filmstrips	Study trips
The library	Textbooks
Magazines	Visitors
Maps and globes	Find others

Chart 9.24

Procedures to Use	
Asking	Mapping
Collecting	Note taking
Constructing	Observing
Demonstrating	Outlining
Drawing	Reading
Experimenting	Writing for information
Interviewing	Find others

Chart 9.25

used to collect data. Terms are defined; pictures, maps, and other data sources are interpreted; comparisons and contrasts are made; and information is evaluated for accuracy and relevance. Different sources of information are used and cross-checked. If differences are noted in interpretations or if there is doubt about the accuracy of data, double-checking may be necessary. At times a film may need to be shown again, a section of a reference reread, or one reference checked against another. An expert may be interviewed to resolve a difference in fact or in interpretation of data.

As information is gathered it may be listed on the chalkboard or placed on retrieval charts for further use. If directions for making something or steps in a sequence of events are involved, they may be noted on a chart or on the chalkboard. An outline, a set of notes, or simply sharing and grouping information may be adequate. The objective is to organize information for generalizing and further processing as needed.

Generalizing and Further Processing of Information

Generalizing frequently follows the phases discussed in the preceding sections, although other processes may be used. For example, after interpreting data related to population growth in their city, students may draw and check inferences about possible environmental effects, state generalizations about the main causes of growth, make predictions about future growth and future ecological problems, and synthesize findings in graphs or maps to highlight growth during selected periods or in defined zones of the city. The following examples are illustrative:

> In a unit on our changing community, one group moved beyond interpretations and made the following generalizations and predictions:
>> "Changes have been faster in recent years. Some changes were made to take care of population growth. Some changes were caused by inventions."
>> "We predict that school enrollment will be 23,000 in ten years. Population will probably be around 112,000."
>
> In a unit on environmental problems, students proceeded to infer, generalize, predict, and synthesize as follows:
>> "Feelings about flood control and environmental problems seem to be high enough to get some action. Some people seem to be changing their ideas about what is important."
>> "The proposed legislation on environmental problems will be passed. If it is passed, the dam will probably be constructed at point A on the map, because it is best for preserving wildlife."
>
> Students then made a map to show location of flooded areas, points at which damage occurred to wildlife and to people, and possible sites for a dam.

Evaluating Processes and Outcomes

Evaluation is used during each phase of instruction. For example, as problems are defined the teacher may ask: Is the problem clear? Have main parts of the problem been considered? As procedures are discussed, the teacher may ask: Have good sources of information been noted? Does each individual know what to do? Similarly,

---

Appraising Sources

Is it related to the topic?

Is it recent enough for our purposes?

Is it reliable? Valid?

Is it published by a special interest group?

Does it contain enough information?

Can it be checked against reliable sources?

Chart 9.26

Appraising Information

Is it related to our questions?

Is the source reliable?

Is it consistent with related ideas?

Is it supported by evidence?

Is it too general to be useful?

Is it advanced for a worthy cause?

Chart 9.27

Appraising Reports

Is the title descriptive of the topic?

Does the introduction set the stage?

Are the ideas in good order?

Are main ideas supported by facts?

Are opinions distinguished from facts?

Do conclusions tie ideas together?

Chart 9.28

Fallacies of Thinking

Mixing up the real and the fanciful

Believing that there is only one way to do it

Thinking that one example "proves the rule"

Confusing facts and opinions

Believing that one thing caused another because they happened together

Letting our feelings hide some of the facts

Can you find others?

Chart 9.29

Good Thinking Guidelines

Get facts on all sides of the question.

Check facts from different sources.

Summarize information in usable form.

Check the meaning of unclear terms.

Compare your findings with others.

Make tentative conclusions and check them.

Consider alternatives and consequences.

Can you add others?

Chart 9.30

---

the following questions may be asked during the classifying, interpreting, and further processing of information: Are facts related to main ideas? Are relationships shown? Have we selected the best means of summarizing information? Using clues from observation, the teacher raises questions and makes comments that help students to appraise and to improve their work. Charts 9.26 through 9.30 contain points to consider in teacher evaluation and in student self-evaluation.

Questions, Activities, and Evaluation

1. Select a unit of your choice and note how you might encourage use of the following: (a) critical thinking, (b) creative thinking, (c) decision making, (d) problem solving or inquiry. Include specific examples of questions and activities to use that will emphasize the unique characteristics of each mode.

2. Review the section on generating, organizing, and interpreting data and note questions and activities you might use to build a solid base of knowledge. Which suggestions in the illustrative charts on remembering, collecting data, comparing, interpreting, and classifying might you use?

3. Select a concept of a concrete object, such as mayor, and a concept of an abstract quality, such as concern for others. Indicate the strategy you would use to develop each one. Explain why you selected the strategy.

4. Identify a main idea or generalization you wish to develop in a unit of your choice. Select a strategy for developing it and outline how you would use it. Explain why you selected the strategy.

5. Review the sections on analyzing, synthesizing, and evaluating and indicate how you might develop them in a unit. Use the suggested teaching strategies as guides to planning. What changes, if any, do you think might be made in the strategies? Why?

6. Present in outline form a plan for using the teaching model presented near the end of this chapter. What changes, if any, do you think should be made in it? Why?

7. Select any three charts presented in this chapter and modify them to fit a unit you plan to teach. Explain why you chose them over the others.

8. Write the following to get information on activity booklets to develop think skills: Research for Better Schools, 444 No. Third St., Philadelphia, PA 19123; Midwest Publications, P.O. Box 448, Pacific Grove, CA 93950

References

Bernard, Sister Matilda, "Association—A Key to Learning," *Social Education,* 53 (January 1989), 72–74. Sixty-five acronyms and clues to aid memory.

Beyer, Barry K., *Developing a Thinking Skills Program.* Needham Heights, MA: Allyn & Bacon, 1988. Specific skills and examples of programs.

Beyer, Barry K., "What Philosophy Offers to the Teaching of Thinking," *Educational Leadership,* 47 (February 1990), 55–60.

Blythe, Tina, and Howard Gardner, "A School for All Intelligencies," *Educational Leadership,* 47 (April 1990), 33–37. Seven intelligences discussed.

Bloom, Benjamin S., George F. Madaus, and J. Thomas Hastings, *Evaluation to Improve Learning.* New York: McGraw-Hill, 1981. Sections on analysis, synthesis, and evaluation.

Chance, Paul, *Thinking in the Classroom: A Survey of Programs.* New York: Teachers College Press, 1986. Descriptions of published programs.

Costa, Arthur L., ed., *Developing Minds: A Resource Book for Teaching Thinking* (Vol. 1), and *Programs for Teaching Thinking.* Alexandria, VA: Association for Supervision and Curriculum Development, 1991. Skills, models, strategies, metacognition, and programs.

Dewey, John, *How We Think.* Boston: D.C. Heath, 1910, 1933. Classic analysis.

Eggen, Paul D., and Donald P. Kauchak, *Strategies for Teachers: Teaching Content and Thinking Skills* (2nd ed.). Englewood Cliffs, NJ: Prentice-Hall, 1988. Strategies adaptable for use in many units.

Ellis, Arthur K. *Teaching and Learning Elementary Social Studies* (4th ed.). Needham Heights, MA: Allyn & Bacon, 1991.

Hannah, Larry S., and John U. Michaelis, *A Comprehensive Framework for Instructional Objectives: A Guide to Systematic Planning and Evaluation.* Reading, MA: Addison-Wesley, 1977. Examples of objectives, questions, and evaluation devices for each thinking skill.

Hyde, Arthur A., and Marilyn Bizar, *Thinking in Context: Teaching Cognitive Processes across the Curriculum.* New York: Longman, 1989. Guidelines and examples.

Jones, Beau F., and Lorna Idol, eds., *Dimensions of Thinking and Cognitive Instruction.* Hillsdale, NJ: Laurence Erlbaum, 1990. Metacognition, conceptualizing, reasoning, problem solving, and other dimensions.

Joyce, Bruce, and Marsha Weil, *Models of Teaching* (3rd ed.). Englewood Cliffs, NJ: Prentice-Hall, 1986. Chapters on information processing.

Kurfman, Dana, ed., *Developing Decision Making Skills* (47th yearbook). Washington, DC: National Council for the Social Studies, 1977.

Lopach, James J., and Jean A. Luckowski, "The Rediscovery of Memory in Teaching Democratic Values," *Social Education,* 53 (March 1989), 183–87. Discussion of schema theory, memory, and values.

McKenzie, Gary R., "The Importance of Teaching Facts in Elementary Social Studies," *Social Education,* 44 (October 1980), 494–98.

Manning, Brenda H., *Cognitive Self-Instruction for Classroom Processes.* Albany, NY: State University of New York, 1991.

Marzano, Robert J., et al., *Dimensions of Thinking.* Alexandria, VA: Association for Supervision and Curriculum Development, 1988. Processes and skills of thinking.

Marzano, Robert J., *Tactics for Thinking.* Alexandria, VA: Association for Supervision and Curriculum Development, 1988. Twenty-two tactics.

Muir, Sharon Pray, "Time Concepts for Elementary School Children," *Social Education,* 54 (April/May 1990), 215–18. Clock, calendar, and chronology activities.

Ontario, *Curriculum Guideline, History and Contemporary Studies.* Toronto: Ministry of Education, 1986.

Patriarca, Linda A., and Jan Alleman, "Studying Time: A Cognitive Approach," *Social Education,* 51 (April/May 1987), 273–77.

Paul, Richard, *Critical Thinking,* Sonoma, CA: Sonoma State University, 1990. Detailed analysis; handbooks also available for grades K–3, 4–6, 6–9.

Saskatchewan Education, *Understanding the Common Essential Learnings.* Regina, 1988. Chapter on critical and creative thinking.

Resnick, Lauren B., and Leopold E. Klopfer, *Toward the Thinking Curriculum: Current Cognitive Research.* 1989 Yearbook. Alexandria, VA: Association for Supervision and Curriculum Development, 1989. Chapters on reading.

Sternberg, Robert J. and Todd I. Lubart, "Creating Creative Minds." *Phi Delta Kappa,* 72 (April 1991), 608–614. Strategies and activities.

Taba, Hilda, et al., *Teacher's Handbook for Elementary Social Studies* (2nd ed.). Reading, MA: Addison-Wesley, 1971. Strategies for concept development, generalizing, and applying principles (predicting).

Tiedt, Iris M., et al., *Teaching Thinking in K–12 Classrooms.* Needham Heights, MA: Allyn & Bacon, 1989. Sample activities and lessons.

Torney-Purta, Judith, "Schema Theory and Cognitive Psychology: Implications for Social Studies." *Theory and Research in Social Education,* 19 (Spring 1991), 189–210. Procedures; concept maps.

Wadsworth, Barry J., *Piaget's Theory of Cognitive and Affective Development.* (4th ed.). New York: Longman, 1989. Detailed treatment.

Developing Creativity Through Expressive Experiences

CHAPTER 10

Objective and Related Focusing Questions

To describe teaching and learning strategies and activities that are used in the social studies to develop students' creativity:

- What expressive experiences are useful in developing students' creative thinking and their appreciation of creativity in our own and other cultures?

- How can creative writing be used to stimulate and nurture creative thinking?

- How can role-taking experiences—dramatic representaion, role playing, simulations—be used creatively?

- How can experiences in music, arts, and crafts be used in the social studies to foster creativity?

- What types of construction activities and processing of materials are useful in developing creativity?

This chapter focuses on two dimensions of creativity—creative thinking and appreciation of creativity in human behavior. Creative thinking is nurtured as students make plans, put information to new uses, and express their thoughts and feelings in new ways. Appreciation for the creativity of others is developed as students discover the richness of esthetic expression in their own and other cultures. Originality, initiative, and delight in discovery are highlighted in a variety of activities that add zest to learning. As a student exclaimed: "There really are a lot of ways to be creative!"

Creative writing, role playing, simulating, and other expressive activities bring the "doing" part of thinking into play. They also provide new insights into the hopes, aspirations, and feelings of others as students identify with people in their own and other cultures.

Expressive activities may be used to individualize and personalize learning. When students write stories, poems, and songs, when they paint pictures and construct objects, and when they take various roles and engage in simulation, they individualize their learning by expressing themselves in ways that fit their learning styles. And they personalize their learning by expressing their own thoughts and feelings.

Expressive experiences involve both *impression* and *expression*. Students form impressions as they learn about creative expression of the people being studied in a unit. They are then given the opportunity to express thoughts and feelings engendered by experiences in the unit. As a general rule, the richer the impression, the richer the expression.

Creative Writing

Opportunities to create and share poems, stories, and descriptions should be provided after children have established backgrounds of understanding. In the early grades, children may dictate their ideas to the teacher for recording on the chalkboard, charts, or a word processor, using a language-experience approach. A microcomputer with word processing capability allows young children to watch the display as the teacher enters their sentences; changes can be made easily, and a printout can be made for immediate use (Bradley, 1982). In later grades, students can write their ideas or use the word processor to express their thoughts and feelings directly, using such software as *Bank Street Writer, Compupoem, Story Tree, MECC Writer, LogoWriter, Word Vision, Word Perfect Jr., The Writing Workshop, MultiScribe, Write,* and *The Writing Connection.*

As children discover patterns in the poetry enjoyed by people in other cultures—such as haiku in Japan, with a five/seven/five pattern of syllables, and tanka, with a five/seven/five/seven/seven pattern—they can use the patterns to express their thoughts, as illustrated by these examples:

Lofty mountain peak,
   Rising above the plateau,
      With valleys below.
         The shimmering sea
            Extensive coral kingdoms
               Soft white sand shoreline

Blowing on our door,
   The westerly winds offshore,
      Blow forevermore.
         The rocky Maine coast
            Natural unspoiled splendor
               Magnificent views

Sea stars on the rocky reefs   A seascape panorama
      Nature's splendor everywhere.   Exhilarating delight.

Both teachers and students find the writing of a cinquain—a five-line stanza—to be an activity that sparks creative expression in units at all levels.[1]

Write a Cinquain!

First line—2 syllables   Small town,
Second line—4 syllables   Quiet, cozy,
Third line—6 syllables   A great place for living,
Fourth line—8 syllables   May it always be neighborly,
Fifth line—2 syllables   My home.

Students' creativity can be sparked by making puzzles, as shown here and in the next chapter. A variety of puzzles can be created by using such computer programs as *Puzzlemaster, Crossword Magic, Wordsearch,* and *Super Wordfind.* Authoring programs that do not require programming skills can also be used.

Make a Pyramid of States

1. First letter of leading dairy state   —
2. Abbreviation of Old Line State   — —
3. Abbreviation of the first state   — — —
4. Capital is Salt Lake City   — — — —
5. Capital is Austin   — — — — —
6. The island state   — — — — — —
7. The peninsula state   — — — — — — —
8. Capital is Lincoln   — — — — — — — —
9. Capital is Baton Rouge   — — — — — — — — —
10. Most populated state   — — — — — — — — — —

Make a Pyramid of States or Capitals

1.   —
2.   — —
3.   — — —
4.   — — — —
5.   — — — — —
6.   — — — — — —
7.   — — — — — — —
8.   — — — — — — — —
9.   — — — — — — — — —
10.   — — — — — — — — — —

---

[1] For a variety of other forms, see Padgett, Ron, ed., *Handbook of Poetic Forms.* New York: Teachers & Writers Collaborative, 1987.

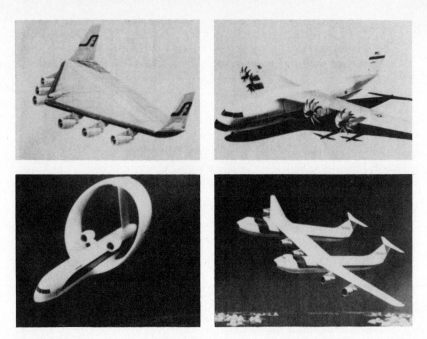

What alternative futures scenarios might students create for air transportation? What other technological innovations might be used to stimulate creative writing of futures scenarios? Social Studies Workshop, University of California Berkeley

Related art and music activities can be coordinated with writing activities. The results of creative expression can be collected and kept in individual or class scrapbooks, posted on bulletin boards, or used in the culminating activities for a unit. Creative writing suggestions are presented in Charts 10.1 and 10.2.

Ideas for Creative Writing

1. Stories and poems—topics, events, travel, people, activities
2. Descriptions—persons, places, things, events, activities
3. Futures scenarios
4. Booklets, scrapbooks, leaflets, charts
5. Quiz, television, computer programs
6. Television or movie box rolls

Chart 10.1

Finding Expressive Terms

1. Check the vocabulary chart.
2. Use the picture dictionary.
3. Listen as others discuss topics.
4. Look for them in our books.
5. Use the classroom dictionary.
6. Get ideas from pictures.
7. Get ideas from films.
8. Think of feelings as well as facts.

Chart 10.2

Role Taking through Dramatic Representation

Role taking enables students to identify with others in a variety of situations. Role-taking activities range from taking a role in a discussion to playing a role in a value-laden situation. This section focuses on role taking through dramatic representation.

Dramatic representation is an excellent substitute for firsthand experience with people, events, and situations far removed from the classroom. Although children cannot direct activities in a control tower at the airport, a railway classification yard, or a wagon train, they can participate in dramatic representation and thus gain insight into how such activities are directed. They cannot be fire fighters, post office workers, pilots, colonists, pioneers, scouts, or early settlers, but they can identify with such people through dramatic activities.

Children are familiar with dramatic representation. They have used it before entering school, make-believe and imaginary play—"being" a mother, father, teacher, bus driver, fire fighter, or airplane pilot. On entering school, children are eager to act out activities they are studying and to portray their impressions of people, events, and situations.

Dramatic representation in school, however, is different from make-believe play at home. At home children engage in dramatic play on their own; in school they are guided so as to achieve desired outcomes. At home children based their dramatic play on ideas and impressions they have gathered in an incidental fashion; in school they gather specific background information and make it the basis for dramatic representation of social studies experiences. At home make-believe play keeps children occupied; in school dramatic representation develops concepts, skills, attitudes, and appreciations.

Dramatic representation offers excellent opportunities to evaluate children's learning. As teachers observe children in dramatic activities, they can appraise how children use concepts, grasp main ideas, express attitudes, identify with others, and express themselves creatively.

Forms of Dramatic Representation

Dramatic representation takes a variety of forms in the social studies.

Dramatic play is used frequently in the early grades to portray activities in units on the home, school, neighborhood, and community. Dramatic play allows children to stage an informal and creative portrayal of experiences without a set pattern, refined staging, costumes, or memorization of parts.

Dramatic rhythms involve the interpretation of activities and events by means of rhythmic bodily movement. Dramatic rhythms differ from dramatic play in that rhythmic movement is emphasized. Dramatic rhythms differ from creative dance in that the child is interpreting something learned in the social studies. They are similar to creative dance in that children give their own personal interpretations, not those of others.

Role playing develops insight into human relations, problems of others, a main idea, or the feelings and values of individuals in a critical situation. After the role is portrayed in different ways, such questions as these may be discussed: Which role did you prefer? Why? Which role was least desirable? Why? How did each role make you feel? How might individuals feel in the actual situation? What might be done to improve the situation?

Dramatic skits are more formal than dramatic play; they involve the enactment of a selected event or activity in which assigned roles are taken and lines are learned to portray a significant incident—for example, the signing of the Mayflower Compact or the landing at Plymouth Rock.

Pageants are used to portray a sequence of incidents or activities related to such unit topics as the history of our community, the development of our state, the growth of America, and living in Mexico. Dramatic skits prepared by small groups within the class are easily arranged as a pageant.

Pantomimes may be used to portray simply and briefly such an activity as a plane landing, the movement of a boat into the harbor, or a scout on the lookout for Indians.

Dramatization may be employed to present a playlet or a play in which a script, costumes, and a stage setting are used.

Marionettes and puppets may be used for both creative dramatics and formal dramatization. Children may construct them, plan for their use, use them to present skits and plays, and use them in new situations by preparing new lines, staging, and costumes. Some teachers use them to build confidence in shy children as well as to provide a different form of dramatic expression for typical children.

Mock trials enable students to simulate courtroom activities, including the roles of the judge, plantiff and defendant and their attorneys, witnesses, and the jury.

Mock meetings may be planned and conducted in the upper grades to simulate New England town meetings, city council meetings, and legislative sessions.

Unfinished stories or *reaction stories* may be used to stimulate the enactment of situations in which children show what they would do if they were involved. After hearing a story about such problems as fair play, helping others, carrying out one's responsibilities, respecting property, or minority group relations, children act out a solution and evaluate the enactment.

In the following sections, attention is given to creative and informal dramatic activities, primarily because they are more difficult to plan and guide than are formal dramatics in which a script is followed. A teacher who has not observed or guided creative dramatic activities might first experiment with a play written for children. Next the teacher might plan with the class short skits related to topics under study. This may be followed by longer dramatic activities, until finally the group has moved to a creative and informal approach to dramatization.

Sometimes a teacher may decide that a play written for children—for example, a program for a special occasion or a dramatic activity related to the commemoration of a special event—is more appropriate than creative dramatics. If so, an appropriate play should be selected, rehearsed, and presented in a way that develops backgrounds of understanding, involves the students in planning and evaluation, and achieves other educational values.

Examples of Dramatic Activities

The following examples of activities that lend themselves to dramatization have been taken from different units of instruction. As you read them, note examples that you might use in a unit you are planning.

Families: cleaning, gardening, washing and ironing; taking care of the baby, taking care of pets; preparing and serving meals, having a tea party; enjoying leisure activities, telephoning friends

Supermarket: being a grocery clerk, a checker, a fruit and vegetable clerk, a customer; stocking shelves, making signs and price tags, weighing items, sweeping

Community workers: being a firefighter; working in the post office, receiving, sorting, and delivering mail; operating a filling station, cleaning trucks; broadcasting news; running the airport

Farms: pitching hay, feeding and watering animals, herding cows, milking cows; fixing the corral, plowing land, planting seeds, irrigating, harvesting; picking, washing, and bunching vegetables; loading, hauling, and distributing produce in trucks

Our State: early ways of transporting goods and communicating with others; hunting, trading, other life activities; outstanding episodes and personalities in the growth of the state; modern ways of transporting goods, earning a living, and communicating with others

Colonial Life: Pilgrims leaving Holland, the trip in the Mayflower, the Mayflower Pact, landing at Plymouth Rock, the first Thanksgiving; starting the first community, meeting Indians, getting food, cutting logs, planning the houses; playing games such as leapfrog, wood tag, spinning tag; a town meeting, a day in the colonial home, a visit with Indians, a quilting bee; reactions of Indians to the arrival of colonists

China: festivals such as New Year's, Festival of the Lanterns, Festival of the Dragon Boats, and the Mid-Autumn or Moon Festival

Dramatic Rhythms

Children are quick to respond to the rhythm in life around them. Grain swaying in the field, waves rolling in to shore, birds flying from tree to tree, people at work in the community, trains starting and stopping—all these will stimulate natural and spontaneous rhythmical expression. Similarly, rich experiences in the social studies lead to dramatic rhythms that are meaningful demonstrations of the children's impressions.

"Here comes a 747," said the child who demonstrated a long glide and finally stopped at the end of the "runway."

"Wait until the runway is clear," said the traffic controller as another "plane" gracefully circled the airport.

"I'm landing my Lear Jet now," said a third child, who glided in, stopped halfway down the "runway," and taxied away quickly.

Children often add rhythmic expression to many of the dramatic activities listed in the preceding section. From example, they may "catch the beat" and use rhythmic expression to portray such activities as digging, raking, and working in the garden; loading and unloading trucks, movement of freight trains as they start, gain speed, speed along, slow down, and stop; and activities of farmers as they ride horses, milk cows, and plow a field. When musical accompaniment is added, students bring together dramatic, rhythmic, and musical modes of expression to enrich their interpretations of activities, as noted later in this chapter.

In addition to interpretation through dramatic rhythms, folk games and folk dances have a place in the social studies. Many units would be incomplete if folk dances were omitted. For example, in units on Mexico the "Fandango," "La Cucaracha," and "St. Michael's Wheel" and in units on pioneer life "Old Dan Tucker," "Virginia Reel," and "Captain Jenks" are most appropriate. Other examples can be found in references listed at the end of this chapter.

Growth in dramatic rhythms progresses from simple interpretation of single episodes to more complete patterns of expression centered in a unifying theme. At first, children's responses to rhythm are short and simple. A single phase of an activity, such as the train starting, may be interpreted with real satisfaction. Other phases, such as gaining speed, slowing down, or going up a grade may be added later. Still later, several phases are brought together in a pattern of rhythm as the child portrays the complete activity. Finally, several children cooperate in rhythmic bodily expression of related activities, such as the train backing up to couple cars, starting up, traveling along, leaving cars at different places, and arriving at its destination. In this final stage, the group develops a unifying pattern that is a creative synthesis of individual interpretations.

Role Playing

Role playing may be used to develop empathy, concern for others, and other prosocial behaviors by having students enact an incident or a problem and propose desirable solutions. After a realistic incident has been chosen, students are asked to volunteer to play defined roles; the class observes and suggests other ways to enact the incident. Steps of procedure are illustrated in the following lesson plan (see Shaftel and Shaftel, 1982, for other examples):

Concern for Others

Objective

Select the value to be enacted and state the objective for the role playing. A sample objective in this case might be:

To demonstrate ways in which to show concern for others

Introduction

Warm up the group by presenting a story, a film, or another item that highlights concern for others (or some other selected value). For example, share an incident in which individuals showed concern for the ill or elderly by making things for them, providing entertainment, sharing books and magazines, and the like. Discuss other situations of significance to students in which they might show concern for others, selecting one in which they are interested for a role-playing episode.

Development

Select the role players either by choosing students in whom you have confidence or by asking for volunteers. Provide time for the role players to plan, guiding them by asking such questions as

1. What different roles are needed? Who will play each one?
2. How will concern for others be portrayed?

Prepare the class to observe by making such suggestions as these:

1. Pay particular attention to the ways in which concern for others is portrayed.
2. Think about how you would show concern for others if you were one of the role players.
3. Be prepared to answer these questions after watching the role-playing episode: How did each player show concern for others? In what other ways might they have shown concern for others? How would one actually feel in this situation?

Provide for the role-playing enactment by the selected students.

Conclusion

Discuss the enactment. Ask students the following questions:

1. How was concern for others shown? How realistic was it?
2. In what other ways might it have been portrayed?
3. Have you ever actually shown concern for another person in one of these ways? In another way? Describe what you did. How did the person react?
4. What are some other aspects of concern for others that we might role play? Who volunteers to enact them?

Provide for additional enactments and follow-up discussion as appropriate.

Evaluation

Use these questions to evaluate learning:

1. What new ways of showing concern for others were shown?
2. What ways of showing concern for others that we have used in the past were shown?
3. In what situations could you use both new and old ways of showing concern for others?

Mock Trials

Mock trials help students develop concepts of justice, learn key aspects of courtroom procedure, analyze issues, interpret facts, and evaluate decisions. To carry out a mock trial students must learn the roles of judges, jurors, attorneys, and witnesses. They also need to know courtroom procedures and rules of evidence. Visits to courts, interviews of judges and attorneys, study of materials for students, television programs, and films are useful sources of information (see Gallagher, 1977).

An inexperienced group should begin with a simple mock trial in which a judge hears the case and makes the decision with no attorneys present, as in small claims court. After students have built up a background of knowledge and experience, a civil court mock trial may be simulated. The main steps in a mock trial are briefing (preparation), conducting the trial (simulation), and debriefing (evaluation). Briefing should be thorough so that participants understand their roles, the issue, and the facts. The simulation should follow the steps outlined in Charts 10.3 and 10.4. Debriefing contributes much to learning as students evaluate the following: How were the roles played? How might they be changed? What was the issue? Which facts were relevant? How effectively were they presented? How sound were the arguments on each side? How might they be improved? Why do you agree or disagree with the decision? Can you think of sound reasons for an appeal?

Guiding Dramatic Activities

An essential first step in guiding dramatic activities is to develop adequate backgrounds of understanding so that children will dramatize events and activities authentically and creatively. Next, group planning is guided by such questions as

What shall we dramatize?

What space do we need?

What materials do we need?

What characters do we need?

Who should take each part?

By beginning with *what* to do, the children can open up many possibilities without undue concern about *who* will take each part. Decisions on who will take each part may well be left until the last stage of planning, after what is to be included in the dramatic activity is clear.

After plans are made, the group should try out the different suggestions, discuss them, and make changes as needed. During dramatic activity, the teacher should note needs, problems, and suggestions for improvement that may be used during follow-up discussion.

Group standards should be set up when needed to improve the value of the activity. For example, during a unit on the harbor, one group developed the standards

---

Small Claims Court
The plaintiff and the defendant appear before the judge.
The plaintiff states his or her case.
The defendant states his or her case.
The judge asks questions to clarify facts in the case.
The judge makes and explains the decision.

Chart 10.3

Civil Court
The court is opened and the jury sworn in.
Attorneys for the plaintiff and the defendant make opening statements.
Attorneys examine and cross-examine witnesses.
Attorneys present closing statements.
The jury receives instructions, deliberates, and gives a verdict.

Chart 10.4

in Chart 10.5 after a dramatic activity ran into difficulties because of "wrong boat sounds," "boats clogging the harbor," and "fire boats tugging liners in." Following a skit involving life in Boonesboro, another group listed the standards in Chart 10.6 because several children had failed to dramatize their roles authentically.

Continuous planning is needed to utilize dramatic activities effectively. Checklist 10.1 presents specific factors that may be used for planning, guiding, and evaluating dramatic activities.

Simulations

Simulations are scaled-down or simplified models of situations, problems, activities, or systems. Students assume roles and make decisions according to specified rules. Simulations are more restricted and patterned than typical role playing because of the rules and constraints that are imposed on them in order to portray the situation realistically. Simulation games currently being used in the social studies include *Dividing the Work, Market, The Barter Game, Making a Profit,* and *Roaring Camp.*[2] A variety of computer programs may be used to simulate decision making in economic, geographic, governmental, and Historic situations. Illustrative titles are *Sell Lemonade, Trading Post, President-Elect, Geography Search, Road Rally U.S.A., Oregon,* and *Lincoln's Decisions. Simulation Construction Kit* can be used to create simulations.

Teachers should anticipate and avoid problems that may offset the interest-building and motivating power of simulation games. Some simulations take so much time that other needed learning activities are neglected. Arguments may arise over rules and roles, or the desire to win may interfere with the attainment of stated objectives. Such problems may be avoided by following these guidelines:

1. Make a plan to clarify objectives, concepts to be used, roles and rules, time limits, space arrangements, and assignment of students to roles.
2. Make sure that the objectives, rules, and other elements of the plan are understood by the entire group.
3. Provide direction as needed during the simulation to help students keep the objectives in mind and follow the specified rules.

Running the Harbor

1. Share the boats with others.
2. Remember how each boat sounds.
3. Keep the harbor open for liners.
4. Let the tugs pull the liner in.
5. Listen to the captain's signals.

Chart 10.5

Protecting Boonesboro

1. Sentinels should keep a sharp lookout.
2. The gates should be closed on the signal.
3. Gun loaders should load guns and not shoot.
4. Scouts should sneak out through the little gate.
5. Get gunpowder out of the powder horns.

Chart 10.6

---

[2] See Muir, Sharon P., "Simulation Games for Elementary Social Studies," *Social Education,* 44 (January 1980), 35–39, for an annotated list of over 80 games.

Checklist 10–1
CHECKLIST FOR DRAMATIC ACTIVITIES

Teacher Preplanning

_____ What needs have arisen for dramatic activities?
_____ Are materials available? What space is needed?
_____ Are new ideas and information needed? How should they be introduced?
_____ Which children probably will wish to participate first? Which should?
_____ What will others do?

Group Planning

_____ Is attention given first to what to dramatize?
_____ Do the children select important aspects of living to portray?
_____ Are needs for materials considered?
_____ Do individuals suggest roles that are essential?
_____ Are new ideas and materials introduced to enrich the activity?

During the Activity: Children

_____ Are the children identifying with the person and the objects involved?
_____ Are important aspects of living portrayed?
_____ Are space and materials used effectively?
_____ Are the suggestions made during planning carried out in the activity?
_____ Are concepts being used accurately?

During the Activity: Teacher

_____ Are new needs emerging for the following?
_____ 1. clarification of ideas   _____ 3. group standards
_____ 2. authentic information   _____ 4. language expression
_____ Are concepts being expressed accurately in language and in action?
_____ Are any individuals confused or uncertain as to purpose, use of materials, or role?
_____ Are changes needed in space arrangements or materials?

Group Evaluation

_____ Does the group appraise the activity in terms of the roles discussed during planning?
_____ Are newly discovered needs and problems considered?
_____ Are inaccuracies and misconceptions clarified?
_____ Have leads developed to other group and individual activities that will extend and broaden interests and keep the unit moving forward?

4. Guide group debriefing and evaluation after the simulation, with attention to problems, effectiveness of strategies and decisions, needed modifications, and ways to make improvements.

Students may be guided to create their own simulations after they have gained experience with using simulations prepared by others. For example, a variety of simulations may be made using procedures similar to those in Monopoly®. The main steps in creating a simulation are: select an activity; choose the form of presentation; establish rules and define roles; plan a realistic portrayal; decide how and when a decision will be made; plan the debriefing/evaluation procedure. Authoring software is useful in creating computer-based simulations.

Music Activities

The world's musical heritage is a rich source of content and activities that help students understand people and their ways of living. People in cultures at home and around the world have expressed their customs, traditions, and values in music. Patriotic music has been written to stir feelings of loyalty, to highlight great events, and for festivals, ceremonies, and religious activities. Poems, stories, legends, and other literary works have been set to music. Folksongs and dances have evolved from everyday activities. Musical instruments have been invented to provide unique modes of expression. And as the music created in one part of the world has reached people in other parts of the world, cultural interdependence has increased.

Six types of music activity are used in social studies units of instruction: singing activities, listening activities, rhythmic activities, instrumental activities, creative expression, and research activities. By directing children's participation in each type of activity, a teacher can guide children to make meaningful cross-cultural comparisons, one of the main reasons for giving attention to music in the social studies.

Singing Activities

Singing is the most extensively used music activity in the social studies. Children's music books contain many songs related to topics in each unit of instruction. Children's identification with others is increased as they sing songs about human experience and activities—working and playing at home, working on the farm, living in a hogan, trekking westward across the plains, and living in other lands. Feelings about and appreciation of events in our country's history may be stirred as children sing "The Star-Spangled Banner," "America the Beautiful," "Battle Hymn of the Republic," and "Columbia, the Gem of the Ocean." A feeling of kinship with others may be kindled as children sing the folksongs of different regions of America and of other lands.[3]

In the social studies, special attention is given to the development of backgrounds of understanding of the songs included in each unit. The questions that follow may be used to guide study and discussion:

[3]For examples, See *Folksong in the Classroom,* a newsletter from John W. Scott, 229 Suffolk Street, Holyoke, MA 01040.

What thoughts and values are expressed?

What is the mood? The rhythmic pattern? The melody?

Is this a song of work, play, worship, adventure, nature, fantasy, or patriotism?

Is this song sung at festivals, ceremonies, or other special occasions?

Listening Activities

Through directed listening experiences children can learn much about the folksongs, dances, instruments, festivals, holidays, patriotic events, composers, and performing artists of greatest importance in each unit. Recordings of different types of music give realism and authenticity to children's learning. Radio and television programs, community concerts and folk festivals, individuals invited to school, and children's own recordings can also contribute to learning. Questions such as these may be used to guide listening and discussion:

What feelings were aroused?

Who can demonstrate the rhythmic pattern?

Who can name the instruments that were played? Have you heard them before?

What new tonal patterns did you hear?

How is this music related to customs and traditions?

What clues did you get about the cultural values behind this music?

Rhythmic Activities

Four types of rhythmic activity may be provided in the social studies:

1. *Informal rhythms* allow children to express rhythmic patterns without direction from the teacher.
2. *Formal rhythms* are directed by the teacher, and children move to the rhythm (skip, gallop, and the like) as music is played.
3. *Creative rhythms* encourage children to express their responses in original ways.
4. *Dramatic rhythms* stimulate children to use rhythmic expression to interpret experiences they have had.

As these activities are used in the social studies, special attention is given to the rhythmic patterns characteristic of the music, folk dances and activities included in units of instruction (see Charts 10.7 through 10.9). Rhythm instruments, recordings, native instruments, the piano, electronic keyboards, and the Autoharp are used to accompany rhythmic activities and to play rhythmic patterns.

Instrumental Activities

Musical instruments of various types may be used to extend children's learning. Rhythm instruments such as drums, sticks, blocks, bells, triangles, cymbals, gongs, rattles, and tambourines may be used to accompany rhythmic and singing activities, produce sound effects, and play rhythmic patterns. Chording instruments such as electronic keyboards, the Autoharp, and the harmolin may be used to accompany

Rhythms Around Us	Rhythmic Patterns		Finding Rhythms
Bells ringing	Gallop	Skip	Activities of people
Hammers pounding	Gavotte	Slide	Animals moving
Horns tooting	Hop	Swing	Folk dances
Horses trotting	March	Tango	Radio and television
Motors humming	Minuet	Trot	Recordings
People working	Polka	Walk	Songs and poems
Trees swaying	Schottische	Waltz	Trains, planes

Chart 10.7   Chart 10.8   Chart 10.9

various activities and to demonstrate harmonic and rhythmic patterns. Simple melody instruments such as melody bells, tuned bottles or glasses, song flutes, and recorders may be used to play tunes created by children as well as melodies discovered in the songs and recordings presented in units. Native instruments may be examined and played to give authenticity to music activities; examples are castanets, claves, guiro, maracas, cabaca, bongo, conga, antara or pipes of Pan, quena or flute, and chocalho in units on South America; and the bamboo xylophone, gong, temple block, and finger cymbals in units on oriental countries.

Creative Expression

Creative expression through music may be brought to high levels in the social studies as children develop insights and appreciations through activities in units of instruction. Poems and verse created by children may be set to music as children hum tunes or play them on simple melody instruments while the teacher records them on the chalkboard, a chart, or a tape recorder. Questions to guide students as they create a song are:

What moods or feelings shall we express?
What words or phrases fit the mood?
Shall we hum, play, or sing to create the melody?
What rhythms shall we use?
Shall we record the lyric and the melody?

Children can create accompaniments for songs, rhythmic movement, choral reading, and dramatic activities as they catch the mood and the rhythm of thoughts and feelings to be expressed. They can create special sound effects and background music for skits, plays, and pageants. They can make simple instruments from gourds, bamboo, bottles, glasses, and other materials. Creative expression through art, writing, dramatics, and rhythmic movement can be stimulated as children listen to recordings. A range of creative processes can be brought into play as children plan and develop concluding activities that include a script, lyrics and melodies, costumes, staging, musical accompaniments, and their own special effects. Computer programs such as

---

Investigating Music in Other Lands

What are some of their best-known songs?
What folk dances do they have? How are they related to festivals?
What costumes do they wear?
What music do they play at ceremonies and other activities?
What folk instruments do they have? How are they made?
What composers and artists live there?
What influences have others had on their music? How has their music influenced ours?
What customs, values, and beliefs are expressed through music?
What events, deeds, and activities have been set to music?

Chart 10.10

Music, The Music Machine, Music Shaper, Music Studio, Music Maker, and *Song Writer* extend students' opportunities to create songs, tunes, and rhythms.

Research Activities

Individual and group research activities may be undertaken to find background information on the music emphasized in units of instruction. A trip may be taken to a nearby museum to examine instruments and to see costumes used in folk dances. Experts may be interviewed or invited to come to the classroom to give demonstrations. Encyclopedias, library resources, and supplementary music books may be reviewed. Notebooks and scrapbooks may be compiled to summarize information. Illustrative questions to guide children's research activities are listed in Chart 10.10.

The diversity of the musical heritage among people in different cultural settings should be explored by the class. For example, in South America, Africa, Europe, Canada, and the United States, many different types of music are found, and as students study them they can discover the influences of diverse cultural backgrounds. Folk music, adaptations of music from other lands, music created by native composers, and famous performing artists may be studied as a part of units. For example, Argentina's music shows the Italian influence in "El Estilo," a melancholy song of the pampas. The tango shows Spanish influence, and the Indian influence is reflected in folk music. Well-known songs in children's music books are "Sí Señor," "Palapala," "Adiós Te Digo," "Chacerera," "Song of the Pampas," "The Gaucho," "Vidalita," and "Ay, Zamba."

Brazil's music shows the influence of the Portuguese, who sang the "Modinha" to drive away homesickness. The influence of Negroes is shown in the samba. Children's music books contain such songs as "The Painter of Cannahay," "My Pretty Cabacla," "Tutu Maramba," "Cantilena," "Sambalele," "Bambamulele," "In Bahia Town," "O Gato," and "Come Here, Vitu."

Arranging a Classroom Music Center

A classroom music center may be arranged and changed as different units of instruction are developed. Songbooks, instruments, other music materials, and pictures showing musical activities may be placed in the music center. The bulletin board in the music center might display news clippings about musicians in places under study, announcements of related programs on television and radio, a list of recordings for individual listening, and pictures showing native musical activities. The center might also include a listening post, maps showing the locale of songs and musicians, chording and rhythm instruments, and a flannel board for showing rhythmic and tonal patterns.

Arts and Crafts

From ancient times to the present, people have expressed their thoughts and feelings through various art forms. Artists and artisans of each generation have selected ideas and created forms that clarify, simplify, and interpret the ideals, beliefs, and customs of their times. Line, form, color, texture, space, and other elements have been unified in ways that are expressive of the artist's intentions. Touches of beauty have been added to dwellings, clothing, utensils, festivals, ceremonies, and other objects and activities.

Art activities enrich children's learning. Deeper insights and appreciations are developed as children discover the impact of art on homes, furnishings, cars, trains, airplanes, buildings, and other objects. Subtle shades of meaning may be brought out as children consider the work of artists who have portrayed great events, heroes, landscapes, poems, songs, everyday activities, ceremonies, festivals, and holidays. A feeling for modes of expression enjoyed by others may be kindled as children discover the concepts of nature in sand paintings of the Navahos, the simple beauty of the Puritan church, the delicate patterns in Japanese paintings, the search for harmony between people and nature in Chinese art, the recurring themes and patterns in Egyptian art, the stateliness of Roman architecture, and the desire for freedom boldly revealed in Rivera's murals. Cultural interdependence may be highlighted as the thunderbird, the cross, geometric forms, and other designs are discovered in the art of peoples in different lands. Charts 10.11 through 10.17 suggest ways to use art activities in units. Can you add others?

Which Should We Use in Our Unit?

Drawing, painting, sketching, illustrating

Making items out of paper, cardboard, metal, wire, wood

Weaving, sewing, stitching, embroidering, appliquéing

Modeling, carving, sculpting, whittling

Making dioramas, panoramas, shadow boxes

Chart 10.11

Planning a Mural

What main ideas shall we show?

What related ideas are needed?

How shall the ideas be arranged?

What materials shall we use?

What colors will be most effective?

What can we draw using *Dazzle Draw* and *Blazing Paddles* on the computer?

Chart 10.12

Learning How People Express Ideas in Arts and Crafts

Study pictures in our textbooks.

Look at reproductions of pictures and art objects.

See films, filmstrips, and slides.

Visit a museum or an art gallery.

Examine textiles, pottery, jewelry, and other objects.

Interview people who have visited other cultures or studied their art.

Read art books, reference materials, and current periodicals.

Collect pictures from magazines, newspapers, and travel folders.

Chart 10.13

Which of These Can You Find in Other Cultures?

Weaving mats, tapestries, cloth, rugs, and wall hangings

Making baskets from reeds and raffia

Creating designs on cloth, bark, woven raffia, parchment, skins, metal, stone, clay, wood

Embroidering or appliquéing on clothing, costumes, and textiles

Carving in wood, stone, ivory, and bone

Modeling and constructing objects out of clay

Making objects out of metal

Dyeing cloth, leather, bark

Making masks, costumes, and objects for use in ceremonies and festivals

Chart 10.14

How Are These Shown in Arts and Crafts?

Aspirations	Hopes
Beliefs	Ideals
Customs	Ideas
Events	Nature
Fears	Recreation
Feelings	Religion
Freedom	Superstitions
Heroes	Traditions

Chart 10.15

Which of These Do They Make?

Baskets	Leather work
Bead work	Mosaics
Blankets	Pottery
Containers	Rugs
Copperware	Shawls
Featherwork	Siverware
Figurines	Tiles
Instruments	Vases
Jewelry	

Chart 10.16

Which of These Art Concepts are Used?

Balance	Perspective
Color	Repetition
Design	Rhythm
Emphasis	Space
Form	Subordination
Integration	Texture
Line	Unity
Movement	Variation

Chart 10.17

As a general guideline, originality should be emphasized in both appreciative and creative activities. As the art of other people is studied, each individual, whether a child or an adult, will respond in unique ways. To be sure, children may have similar understandings of background ideas about the culture in which the art product was created and certain common understandings about the processes involved. But the individual's reaction, response, and feelings are always personalized.

But what if a child has misconceptions and erroneous ideas about the people or the activities portrayed? Misconceptions are corrected through additional study; simply telling or showing a child how to draw something is not a substitute for developing backgrounds of understanding of people and their ways of living. The ideas to be expressed and the media and processes used in an art activity may be enriched through directed study. But when children proceed to express the ideas, they must use their own techniques if the experience is to be called an art activity. Otherwise it is merely copying, illustrating, or reproducing the technique of another person. It is not art.

Types of Art Activity

Checklist 10.2 includes the main types of an activity used in the social studies. Each major type is followed by examples of items that may be made, designed, or arranged by children.

The Classroom Art Center

A work center for the arrangement of art materials facilitates pupils' work and makes possible more effective utilization of art activities in the social studies. Materials should be changed as new topics are studied. Related pictures may be displayed on the bulletin board, and selected art objects may be exhibited on nearby shelves, window sills, or tables. Space should be provided to display children's completed art work and to store unfinished work. Computer programs such as *Blazing Paddles, Delta Drawing, Paint, MousePaint, DeluxePaint, Easy 3D, AppleMouse II,* and various versions of LOGO may be used to create diagrams, sketches, posters, drawings, and other unit-related items. A Koala Pad can also be used for drawing.

Checklist 10–2
ART ACTIVITIES

Drawing and Painting: _____ Backgrounds _____ Borders _____ Cartoons _____ Decorations _____ Designs _____ Friezes _____ Greeting cards _____ Illustrations _____ Landscapes _____ Murals _____ Pictures _____ Posters _____ Sketches

Modeling, Sculpting, and Carving: _____ Animals _____ Beads _____ Bowls _____ Candlesticks _____ Dishes _____ Figurines _____ Jars _____ Jewelry _____ Jugs _____ Plaques _____ Pots _____ Tiles _____ Trays _____ Utensils

Designing: _____ Announcements _____ Backgrounds for collages _____ Booklets _____ Borders _____ Containers _____ Fans _____Greeting cards _____ Markers _____ Mats _____ Mosaics _____ Prints _____ Programs _____ Stage scenery

Arranging: _____ Cornucopias _____ Displays _____ Driftwood _____ Exhibits _____ Flowers _____ Fruits _____ Gourds _____ Textiles

Weaving, Sewing and Stitching: _____ Bags _____ Belts _____ Caps _____ Costumes _____ Curtains _____ Headbands _____ Mats _____ Rugs

Using Mixed Media: _____ Chalk and paper sculpture _____ Chalk, crayon, and paint _____ Combinations of discarded materials _____ Cut paper and tempera _____ Paint and yarn _____ Paper, cork, and wire

Printing and Stenciling: _____ Announcements _____ Borders _____ Decorations _____ Designs _____ Greeting cards _____ Programs

What objects might students construct for a tabletop map to show spatial relationships in a unit you are planning? Social Studies Workshop, University of California, Berkeley

Construction

Construction in the social studies usually involves the use of tools and materials to make authentic objects to promote the growth of social concepts and understandings. The value of construction lies in its contribution to learning, not in the products that are made. Lasting values may be achieved only if construction achieves significant objectives, shows students the connections between activities and objectives, and motivates students' learning—a primary outcome of carefully selected construction activities.

Examples of two types of construction are presented here to indicate the variety of items students can make in the social studies.

Paper and cardboard construction: albums, booklets, notebooks, scrapbooks; collages, montages, mobiles, stabiles; puppets, marionettes; dioramas, panoramas; shadow boxes, television and movie paper-roll programs; posters, graphs, maps; holiday decorations, containers, favors; table covers, wall hangings

Wood construction: playhouse furniture for home units; barns, trucks, silos, other items for farm units; oil tankers, tugboats, piers, other items for a unit on the harbor; covered wagon, churns, butter ladles, benches, brooms for units on colonial and pioneer life; planes, gliders, wind sock, control tower, model airport for units on air transportation

The following questions may be used as criteria to select activities and to guide planning:

What objectives can be achieved by this activity?

How practical is it in terms of available time, materials, and tools?

In what ways is it more effective than other activities?

How can it be used to develop accurate concepts and appreciations?

How can it be related to other activities in the unit?

Do students have the necessary backgrounds and construction skills?

Construction may be closely related to dramatic activities. Dramatic representation of activities in units on the home, the farm, the harbor, the airport, colonial life, Mexico, and other lands creates needs for objects, models, props, and scenery. Children can plan and make essential items and thus relate the making of objects to stated objectives.

Materials and tools are available in most schools for paper and cardboard construction activities. Materials for making items of wood can be obtained from crates, boxes, scraps of lumber, lumber yards, and hobby stores. Doweling of various sizes can be used to make masts, funnels, and other cylindrical items. Wooden buttons can be used for wheels, and an awning pole can be cut to make tank cars and oil and milk trucks. Students themselves will think of creative uses of materials and can obtain boards and make items at home—with the permission and assistance of parents! Simple tools such as saws, C-clamps to hold items, hammers, and a T-square are adequate for most activities.

Safety first is the motto in all activities! Proper use of scissors, saws, and other tools should be taught systematically, and close supervision should be provided during construction activities.

Processing Materials

Processing materials is similar in many ways to construction, in that similar values, selection criteria, techniques of planning, instructional procedures, and skills are involved. Processing materials in the social studies may be defined as changing raw or semiprocessed materials (yarn, for example) into finished products. Typical examples are making cottage cheese, processing wool and flax, dyeing fabrics, weaving, drying fruit, and making soap. As children engage in such processes, emphasis should be on the development of understanding and appreciation of creative ways in which people have met their needs without benefit of today's technological developments.

In early times, children helped to process a variety of materials. They helped with churning butter, collecting berries and making dyes, using tallow to make candles, and washing, carding, spinning, and weaving wool. Today children see finished products in stores and lack firsthand opportunities to carry out the processes involved in making them.

The social studies program offers many possibilities for processing of materials in study units:

Home and Family: making popcorn, applesauce, and cornstarch pudding

Dairy Farm: churning butter and making cottage cheese

Colonial and Pioneer Life: weaving, quilting, candle making, soap making, sewing, and drying fruits

Communication: making and using ink, parchment, clay tablets, and simple books

Mexico: grinding corn with a metate, making candles, weaving, cooking Mexican foods, making adobe bricks, and sewing

Making Butter

Materials: ½ pint whipping cream, ¼ teaspoon salt, a pint jar.
Pour cream into jar and seal it.
Shake until butter appears.
Pour off bluish milk.
Place butter in a bowl and add salt.
Add a few ice cubes and water; work with spoon to remove milk.
Pour off water and mold butter into a block.

Chart 10.18

Making Pumpkin Rings

Cut a pumpkin crosswise into halves.
Remove seeds and cut rings ½ inch thick.
Place rings on a pole to dry.

Chart 10.19

Making Apple Leather

Peel some apples and cook them in water.
After apples are cooked to a mush, spread them on a cloth to dry.
Let them stand for a day or two.

Chart 10.20

Steps to take in carrying out selected processing activities are presented in Charts 10.18 through 10.20.

The planning and guiding of construction and processing activities are similar in many ways to the planning and guiding of study trips, dramatic activities, and other "doing" activities in the social studies. Four basic steps are involved: (1) planning by the teacher, (2) planning with the class, (3) providing guidance during the activity, and (4) evaluating progress after the activity, as shown in Checklist 10.1.

Questions, Activities, and Evaluation

1. What two or three creative writing activities can you include in a unit of your choice?

2. Which forms of role taking through dramatic representation do you believe to be most useful in the social studies? Indicate ways in which you might use them.

3. Review a music book for a grade of your choice and identify songs, rhythms, listening activities, and instrumental activities that you might use in a unit.

4. Make a brief plan to show how you might provide for creative musical expression and for investigating the music of a culture under study.

5. Review the checklist of art activities and indicate specific ways in which you might use each major type in a unit.

6. Select one construction activity and one processing activity and note how you might use each in a unit.

7. Mark your position on the following by writing *A* if you agree, *D* if you disagree, and *?* if you are uncertain. Discuss your views with a colleague and explore reasons for any differences.

   a. Creative writing and other expressive activities are as basic as other social studies activities.

   b. Role-taking activities are among the best to help students identify with others.

What objectives might be achieved by constructing items or processing materials as shown here? Richmond and Los Angeles, California

    c. The many problems associated with stimulation games greatly limit their use in the social studies.

    d. Art activities should be given a prominent place in all social studies units.

    e. Music activities selected for use in the social studies should be closely related to those in the music education program.

    f. Many construction and processing activities can be given as homework and thereby improve home-school cooperation.

    g. Computer software greatly enhances creativity in social studies art, music, and simulation activities.

References

Anderson, W. M., and P. Shehan Campbell, *Multicultural Perspectives in Music Education.* Reston, VA: Music Educators National Conference, 1989. Music in world cultures.

Bradley, Virgina N., "Improving Students" Writing with Microcomputers," *Language Arts,* 59 (October 1982), 732–43.

Christopolus, Florence, and Peter J. Valluti, *Creative Thinking Through the Arts.* Bloomington IN: Phi Delta Kappa, 1990. Exploration, creation, and appreciation strategies for painting, music, dance and movement, and drama.

Ellis, Arthur K., *Teaching and Learning Elementary Social Studies* (3rd ed.). Boston: Allyn & Bacon, 1986. Chapter on games and simulations.

Gallagher, Arlene F., *The Methods Book: Strategies for Law-focused Education.* Chicago: Law in American Society Foundation, 1977. Chapters on role playing, simulations, and mock trials.

Grady, Michael P., *Whole Brain Education.* Bloomington, IN: Phi Delta Kappa, 1990. Hemispheric specialization; visual functioning; strategies.

Hickey, Gail M., "Mock Trials for Children," *Social Education,* 54 (January 1990), 43–44.

Jarolimek, John, *Social Studies in Elementary Education* (8th ed.). New York: Macmillan, 1990. Chapter on expressive experiences.

Keach, Everett T., Jr., and Nancy P. Kalupa, "Looking at China through Children's Art," *Social Education,* 48 (May 1984), 324–29.

Johnson, Charlie, *Word Weaving.* Urbana, IL: National Council of Teachers of English, 1990. Creative approach to poetry writing.

McCaslin, Nellie, *Creative Drama in the Primary Grades.* New York: Longman, 1987a.

McCaslin, Nellie, *Creative Drama in the Intermediate Grades.* New York: Longman, 1987b.

Morgenstern, Steve, "Goodbye, Old Paint—Hello, Computer Art," *Family Computing,* 5 (February 1987), 49–53.

Nelson, Murry R., *Children and Social Studies.* New York: Harcourt Brace Jovanovich, 1987. Chapter on computer simulations and games.

Personke, Carl R., and Dale D. Johnson, *Language Arts Instruction and the Beginning Teacher.* Englewood Cliffs, NJ: Prentice-Hall, 1987. Chapter on creative thinking.

Shug, Mark C., and Robert W. Beery, *Teaching Social Studies in the Elementary School.* Glenview, IL: Scott, Foresman, 1987. Chapter on simulations.

Seidman, Laurence I., "Folksongs: Magic in Your Classroom," *Social Education,* 49 (October 1985) 580–87.

Shaftel, Fannie R., and George Shaftel, *Role-Playing for Social Values* (2nd ed.). Englewood Cliffs, NJ: Prentice-Hall, 1982.

Social Studies Grade Five—The Western Hemisphere. New York: City Board of Education, 1985, 1987. Expressive activities for various countries.

Sternberg, Robert J., and Todd I. Lubart, "Creating Creative Minds," *Phi Delta Kappa,* 72 (April 1991), 608–614.

Sunal, Cynthia S., and Barbara A. Hatcher, *Studying History through Art,* How to Do It, Series 5, No. 2. Washington, DC: National Council for the Social Studies, 1986.

Using and Improving Communication Skills

CHAPTER 11

Objective and Related Focusing Questions

To describe principles, procedures, and teaching strategies for integrating language arts into the social studies:

- What strategies and learning activities are used to apply and improve reading, listening, speaking, and writing skills?

- What techniques and learning activities are helpful in developing social studies vocabulary?

- What techniques and learning activities are used to develop comprehension of social studies content?

- What reading–study skills need development to locate information, use references, and learn how to learn in the social studies?

- What guidelines and strategies are helpful in applying and improving listening, speaking, and writing skills?

A guiding principle is to integrate reading, listening, speaking, and writing skills in all subjects, thereby applying and improving basic skills and enhancing learning in each subject. A second principle is to use multiple approaches, not a single one. The whole-language approach may be used to integrate and interrelate applications of the language arts, to enable students to put language to functional use, and to increase use/enjoyment/meaning of literature related to social studies units. The language experience approach may be used after a field trip, film, or other experience to provide opportunities for students to dictate, record, and read their thoughts and feelings. The direct instruction approach may be used to build readiness, develop vocabulary, and transfer basic skills to functional uses in the social studies. Corrective/remedial instruction may be used to help students who have difficulties in applying communication skills to social studies topics. Learning centers may be used by including social studies resources and suggested activities in reading, listening, writing, reference, and computing centers. Unit-related library resources and a variety of literary materials should be provided for extensive independent reading.

Reading Skills

Three instructional tasks are essential to the improvement of reading in the social studies: building vocabulary, developing comprehension, and developing reading-study skills. The following examples of learning activities show how basic skills can be applied to social studies materials.[1]

Building Vocabulary

This section presents procedures and activities for developing concepts and the vocabulary used to express them. Attention is given to social studies vocabulary, meaning-building activities, sight vocabulary, and decoding skills.

Identifying Social Studies Vocabulary The following categories of words used in the social studies serve as overall guides to help identify vocabulary to be developed:

Core words, such as *role, values, interdependence,* and *adaptation,* are used in some textbook series to structure the program. They are found in different contexts, beginning with the home and community and moving to regions of our country and to other lands.

Technical social science words vary in use from unit to unit. Examples are *basic needs, peninsula, ethnic, landforms, frontier, goods, market, institution,* and *urbanization.* These words are usually defined in context or in the glossary of a textbook.

Unit words are found in particular units—for example, *city, town,* and *suburb* in readings on communities and *plantation, antislavery,* and *overseer* in readings on southern colonies.

[1]Acknowledgment is made to Dr. Ruth Grossman, City University of New York, Dr. Haig Rushdoony, California State College, Stanislaus, and Dr. Victoria Mui, California State University, Hayward, for comments on this chapter.

Names of particular people, events, times, and places are also found in certain units. Examples are *Lewis and Clark expedition, Sacajawea, Oregon Territory, Gold Rush,* and *Trail of Tears.*

Quantitative terms are found at all levels, ranging from *near* and *far* and *big* and *little* in materials for the early grades to *area, population, per person income, degrees of latitude and longitude,* and *decade, century,* and *millennium* in materials for later grades.

Similar-looking and -sounding words that may be confused include *when* and *where, role* and *roll, house* and *horse, conservation* and *conversation, principal* and *principle, alter* and *altar,* and *illegal* and *illegible.*

Figurative terms used in middle- and upper-grade materials include *rush hour, surging crowd, hat in the ring, cold war, hot line, closed shop, breadbasket of the country,* and *avalanche of votes.*

Multimeaning terms, such as *bank, belt, bill, cabinet, land, line, range, run,* and *set,* call for use of context clues and selection of the correct meaning in a dictionary.

Abbreviations and *acronyms* are usually defined in reading materials but should be called to the attention of students. Examples are A.M., P.M., B.C., A.D., U.S., UN, OPEC, TVA, N.Y., CORE, NAACP, AFL-CIO, NASA, NOW.

Several procedures are used to identify the vocabulary to develop in lessons and units. Check the teacher's manual that accompanies the textbook and note words to introduce along with ways to introduce them. Note the new concepts listed in units and plan meaning-building activities to develop them. Scan a reading selection ahead of time and list new or other terms to introduce. Keep a list of terms students ask about as they read, and encourage them to note any terms they do not know.

Examples of assessment activities and directions for building a word card file are presented here. Use them to focus attention on key words and to improve skill in identifying social studies terms to learn.

Watch as I show cards with words we will read as we study community workers. Raise your hand if you can tell the meaning.

worker	producer	services	baker	nurse
firefighter	manager	clerk	teacher	

Listed below are words we will be reading in our unit on colonial life. Mark each word as follows:

+ if you know what it means
? if you do not know it

_____ charter   _____ colonize   _____ colonialism

_____ plantation   _____ overseer   _____ indentured servants

Look in the glossary and write the meaning of each word that you marked with a ?. Be ready to state the meaning of each word you marked with a +.

Write a word in each blank space to make a sentence about the three branches of government: executive, judicial, and legislative.

The _____ branch makes laws. The _____ branch carries out laws. The _____ branch makes judgments about the meaning of laws.

Write new social studies words on index cards. After each word write the meaning as given by a picture clue, a context clue, some other clue, or the glossary. If necessary, use the dictionary and select the meaning that fits the context. If you are still not sure of the meaning, ask me.

Meaning-building Activities Activities that build meaning are a key part of vocabulary development; they may be used before, during, or after reading a selection. The meaning of concepts represented by words that are new to students should be developed prior to reading. Since no teacher can anticipate every concept that is unfamiliar to a child, it may at times be necessary to clarify the meaning during or after reading. Of key importance is reminding students to construct meaning as they read by using clues to meaning and meaning-building activities described below.

Three groups of meaning-building activities follow. The first group includes firsthand and visual concept development strategies used to build meaning prior to reading. The second group includes verbal concept development strategies and defining activites in building meaning during the reading experience. The third group includes interpretive concept development strategies and expressive activities that enable children to extend, enrich, and apply meanings in follow-up reading experiences.

Activities to Build Meaning

Firsthand and Visual Activities

Discuss pictures of objects in reading materials, such as *corral, silo,* and *stall* in dairy farm units.

Match pictures and related word cards prior to reading.

Observe people at work and see AV materials that show the *role* of *carpenters, nurses,* and other workers.

Examine models and realia to clarify the meaning of *canoe, kayak, carreta, Conestoga wagon, candle molds,* and other new terms.

Watch films or demonstrations that show such processes as *carding, spinning, weaving,* and *candle dipping.*

Guided Defining Activities

Group and label pictures or names of related items, such as *river, lake, gulf,* and *ocean* under *water bodies.*

State behavior—what people do—to clarify the meaning of *carpenter, mayor,* or other workers: A carpenter builds houses and makes other things out of wood.

State operations—what to do—to clarify the meaning of *harvesting, baking, mapping* or how to figure *area, population density, exact location* of a place: Figure *population density* by dividing the number of people in an area by the square miles or kilometers of the area.

Give examples and distinguish them from nonexamples:

Which are examples of *natural resources?* Which are not?

grassland	forests	houses	bricks	minerals	oil
suburb	mountains	water	soil	lumber	farm

Describe features or uses of an object or an activity: A *canyon* is a deep and narrow valley with steep sides.

Relate a new term to a known term, as in an analogy: A governor is like a mayor except he or she is the chief administrator of a state instead of a city.

Use synonyms and antonyms: *Interdependence* means depending on others for some things. It is the opposite of being on one's own.

Use the glossary and the dictionary to find definitions and the thesaurus to find synonyms and antonyms.

Discuss the meaning of words that contain the same word, prefix, suffix, or root: *courthouse, greenhouse, warehouse, statehouse;* and *coworker, cooperate, coexist.*

Discuss the meaning and note the spelling of homonyms: *air, heir; alter, altar; bail, bale; bazaar, bizarre; cannon, canon; fate, fete; hoard, horde; rain, rein, reign; serial, cereal; straight, strait; step, steppe; stationary, stationery.*

Listen to stories, poems, or songs that add meaning, stir feelings, or create a mood related to such terms as *courage, bravery, hardship, responsibility, cooperation,* and *concern for others.*

Discuss the meaning of figurative language, such as *cunning as a fox, did an about face, Trail of Tears, the Roaring Twenties, with an iron hand, square deal, winds of change.*

Interpretive and Expressive Activities

Make a pictorial map that shows a *school,* a *library,* a *hospital,* and other buildings. Place labels by each picture.

Make special interest maps that show regions, resources, travel routes, or other items, with appropriate words and symbols in the legend.

Draw or sketch the distinguishing features of an island, a peninsula, a terrace, a tableland, a mesa, and a butte. Then label them.

Create analogies based on unit words, such as: *county : state : : state : country.*

Create and label murals, dioramas, panoramas, and exhibits that highlight activities and events portrayed in reading materials.

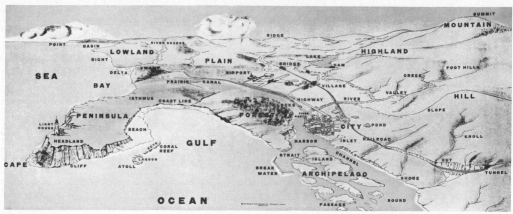

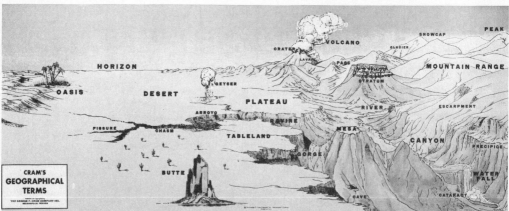

In what unit might you use a chart like this to build vocabulary? Can you find a similar one in a textbook? George F. Cram Company

Study guides such as the following may be provided to help students construct meaning on their own as they read.

CONSTRUCT MEANING AS YOU READ!

Get the meaning of each word and each sentence.

Get the meaning of each paragraph and each section in a selection.

Use new words in discussion and in other activities.

Construct semantic maps or webs and make visual models of key terms.

Find and use synonyms and antonyms.

Slow down to get the meaning of detailed and difficult paragraphs.

Make predictions and then check to see if you are right.

Use S Q 3 R: survey, question, read, recite, reread.

Be a critical reader and evaluate what you read and how well you get the meaning.

NOTE MAIN IDEAS AND RELATED DETAILS!

Keep your purpose in focus and look for related information.

Get clues from headings, subheadings, and topic sentences.

Group items into a scaffold, semantic map, or concept cluster.

Use self-questioning and questions in the text to check your grasp of ideas.

Note relevant details and ignore other information.

Review your notes to be sure no main ideas or significant details were missed, and that unimportant information was not included.

DO THESE BEFORE, DURING, AND AFTER READING!

Before Reading: ___*Preview introduction and headings.* ___*Recall related information and vocabulary.* ___*Clarify purpose or questions.*

During Reading: ___*Achieve purpose or answer questions.* ___*Clarify meaning of new terms, main ideas, and related details.* ___*Note information to include in a summary.*

After Reading: ___*Reorganize information and relate it to past learning.* ___*Apply information and use ideas in unit activities.* ___*Do self-evaluation of understanding of terms and main ideas.*

Building a Sight Vocabulary Directly tied to the meaning-building activities just noted is the development of a sight vocabulary that enables one to read without unnecessary pauses to recognize words. Activities should be provided to make sure that the basic words encountered in various reading materials become sight words. The whole-word method of building a sight vocabulary is emphasized in this section. Decoding skills or word recognition techniques presented in the next section should also be viewed as a means of building a sight vocabulary, not as crutches to use over and over on the same terms. As a child put it, "Once I know new words, I can really cruise along."

Activities to Develop Sight Vocabulary

Place cards with *fiord, inlet, river,* and other terms on them under pictures on the bulletin board that show what the words represent.

Match words with pictures: *shirt, skirt, raincoat,* or other clothing before reading a selection on clothing for a family: *grassland, farmland,* and *swampland* before a selection on farming: canal, harbor, and *pier* before a selection on water transportation.

Recognize labels on objects and pictures in the classroom: *north, south, east,* and *west* on the walls of the classroom; pictures of plains, hills, plateaus, mountains on the bulletin board; pieces of cloth made of wool, silk, cotton, nylon.

Recognize words on flashcards or the chalkboard prior to reading: *igloo, dogsled,* and *kayak* in a selection on Eskimos; *urban, suburban,* and *rural* before a selection on cities.

Distinguish similar terms presented on the board or on cards: *bake, cake, lake, take; thought, through; overflow, overthrow, overload, overland; govern, governor, governed, governing.*

Make picture dictionaries, booklets, charts, and scrapbooks of illustrations labeled with words to be used in reading.

Make a card file of basic words to be used in a unit—for example, *arctic, climate, deciduous, fiord, ice age, region,* and *taiga* for a unit on northern lands.

Make word banks consisting of large envelopes or word boxes with such labels as *weather words, food words, clothing words, transportation words, communication words,* and *law words.* Children write words and definitions on cards or slips of paper and deposit them in the word bank. Words are withdrawn and used at various times in sentences, stories, and other activities.

Discuss similarities and differences in the meaning of such words as *place, site, location, area, region.*

Make lists of compound words and then look for them in reading selections: *land* combined with *forms, slide, fill, owner.*

Separate and discuss the meaning of compound words: *drylands, wetlands, lowlands, highlands, inland.*

Match synonyms and antonyms: *hot* and *torrid, cold* and *frigid, equality* and *inequality, justice* and *injustice.*

Play word games, such as Fish or Word Baseball, using social studies terms.

Solve social studies word puzzles and use computer programs such as *Crossword Magic, Wordsearch, Wordtrix, Word Challenge,* and *Super Wordfind* to create word puzzles and lists.

Make a Hidden Word Puzzle

First, list social studies words to write in the puzzle. Second, write them in the puzzle across, down, or diagonally. Third, select letters at random and fill in the remaining spaces.

1.
2.
3.
4.
5.
6.
7.

8.
9.
10.
11.
12.
13.
14.

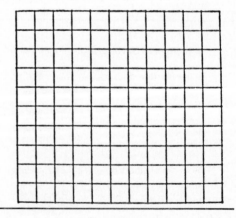

Find the Hidden Words

Draw a line around the economics words hidden in the puzzle.
You may go across or down.

BARTER   BUY   BUYER
CAPITAL   CASH   COMPETE   CONSUMERS
DEBT   DIVISION OF LABOR
DIVERSIFICATION   DUE
GOODS   INTEREST   INVESTOR   JOB
LABOR   LEASE   LEND   LOAN   LOSS
MARKET   MIXED ECONOMY   MONEY
NEEDS   OWE   PAY   PRODUCERS
PROFIT   RENT   RETOOL   SCARCITY
SELL   SELLER   SERVICES
SPECIALIZATION   TOOL   TRADE
VALUE   WANTS

```
I D I V E R S I F I C A T I O N
N E N S E L L L A B O R S A V E
V B T E B U Y W C A P I T A L E
E T E L U W A N T S A C O R E D
S N R L Y R G O O D S L O A N S
T Q E E E D B A R T E R L N D S
O F S R R E R E S O U R C E S P
R E T O O L D J O B O P A Y V E
D U E C L P R O F I T L O S S C
W A G E S F P S P F R I S K C I
M A R K E T S E R V I C E S A A
D I V I S I O N O F L A B O R L
C A S H X P R O D U C E R S C I
O W E Z C O N S U M E R S B I Z
M G M I X E D E C O N O M Y T A
P O V A L U E R T R A D E I Y T
E E N T E R P R I S E P A Y E I
T I N F L A T I O N M A R K E O
E L E A S E M O N E Y R E N T N
```

Applying Decoding Skills Four sets of techniques or skills are used in decoding. *Picture clues* are helpful because many illustrations in current materials are placed there to clarify basic terms. *Verbal context clues* are also helpful, with most new materials providing definitions, examples, and other clues. *Phonics* and *structural analysis* may be applied to many terms. When using phonics special attention should be given to exceptions; students should watch for them as they do in reading instruction. Such exceptions may well be anticipated by teaching them as sight words prior to reading, as noted in the preceding section. The various decoding skills are frequently used in combination. For example, using both context clues and phonics is usually more effective than using either one alone.

Picture Clue Activities

See films, filmstrips, or slides that clarify such terms as *broad grassy plains, towering redwoods, hot steamy jungle, glacier,* and *fiord.*

Prior to reading, direct attention to pictures in the selection and present the related terms on cards or on the chalkboard.

Show a picture as you present a new word, such as *lamp* or *fiord,* on a card or on the chalkboard.

Discuss a picture in a selection, then have children skim the text to find the related word.

Direct attention to pictures: Find the picture that shows *cooperation.* Find the one that shows *competition.* Find the one that shows *conflict.* Give an example of *cooperation, competition,* and *conflict* in our school.

Structural Analysis Activities

Compound Words

Break compound words into parts *playground, playhouse, plaything, playback, freeway, expressway, airway, driveway, seaway, waterway* and *overcoat, overcast, overbuild, overflow, overage, overgrowth*

Match two words that can be put together to make a compound word:

grand	way	air	ware	turn	basket
land	lord	class	way	waste	room
water	son	table	room	waiting	table

Match cards, each containing a single word, that can be combined to form compound words: *feed, lot; worth, while; book, store;* and *bath, room.*

Build word lists, make word charts, use word wheels, and play word games that call for making as many compound words as possible when one word is given:

How many words can you make by adding a word to *over?*
Who can make the most words by adding words to *land?*

Prefixes, Suffixes, and Roots

Recognize prefixes, suffixes, or roots in words selected from reading materials and presented by the teacher in a three-step teaching strategy:

1. The teacher explains the meaning of the prefix: The prefix *anti* means *against.* It is a part of such words as *antibusiness, antilabor,* and *antislavery.*
2. After discussing the meaning of a term, the teacher uses it in a sentence: The *antislavery* movement was strong in the New England states.
3. Students give or find additional examples and use them in sentences: His stand was both *antilabor* and *antibusiness.*

Use prefixes to derive the meaning: *im, il, dis, in,* and *un* meaning *not* in *impolite, illegal, irresponsible, dishonest, inactive,* and *unable; anti* meaning *against* in *antilabor, antibusiness, antislavery, antiwar,* and *anti-American; mid* meaning *middle* in *midday, midnight, midway, midstream, midweek, midwestern,* and *midwinter.*

Clarify the meaning of suffixes: *less* meaning *without* in *helpless, hopeless, fearless; ern* meaning *direction* in *eastern, western, northern,* and *southern;* and *ward* meaning *course* or *direction* in *forward, backward, toward, homeward, westward.*

Explore the meaning of roots: *act* meaning *do* or *move* in *react, activity, activate; civ* meaning *citizen* in *civil, civic, civilian; port* meaning *move* in *transportation, portable, export, import; gram* meaning *letter* or *written* in *telegram, diagram, cablegram; graph* meaning *write* in *autograph, biography, cartography; liber* meaning *free* in *liberty, liberate, liberal;* and *tele* meaning *distant* in *telegraph, telephoto, telephone, televise.*

Word Endings

Build word lists by changing the endings of words *serve, serves, serving, services, serviceable,* and *govern, governs, governing, governor, government, governmental*

Complete sentences in which an ending has been omitted:

Every community has producers of goods and serv(*ices*).
The workers were build(*ing*) a house.

Select endings from a list and use them to complete a sentence:

Choose the correct endings from the following and complete the sentence below: *s, ing, or, ment,* and *mental.*
A govern(*or*) is head of state govern(*ment*).

Syllabication

Look for words that make up a compound word and use them to break the word into syllables: *landform, landslide,* and *landlord.*

Use prefixes, suffixes, and roots to break words into syllables: *predict, prediction,* and *predictable.*

Recognize that "looking for little words in big words" does not work in such words as *somewhere, sloping,* and *station.* (Use of *me* and *her* in *somewhere, pin* in *sloping,* and *at* in *station* leads to errors.)

Find two consonants in the middle of a word and draw a line between them: *problem, support,* and *frontier.*

Verbal Context Clue Activities

Find and discuss the different types of verbal context clues in reading materials:

> *Definition in a sentence:* A *frontier* is the edge of an area where people live.
>
> *Definition in apposition:* They increased their *exports*—goods sent out of the country—during the past decade.
>
> *Definition by examples:* A *disaster* is a flood, a fire, or an earthquake.
>
> *Defintion by description:* A *freeway* is a highway with several lanes where people drive long distances without crossroads.
>
> *Comparison or contrast:* A *pagoda* is like a temple. A *stream* is much smaller than a river.
>
> *Synonyms or antonyms: Justice* means fairness to everyone. Being *prudent* is the opposite of being rash.
>
> *Statement of what a person does (behavior):* A *tax assessor* sets the value of property as a basis for taxation.
>
> *Statement of what to do (operation):* Find *latitude* by noting degrees north or south of the equator.
>
> *Explanation of word origin:* They put the horses in a *corral. Corral* comes from the Spanish word *corro,* a ring or a yard.

Solve word riddles, using as few clues as possible:

> What is it? It is found on a farm. They store hay in it. They milk cows in it. (*barn*)
> What is it? It is found in very cold regions. It is a huge mass of ice. It moves slowly. (*glacier*)
> (*Note:* The above may be combined with phonic clues by stating for the first one "It starts with a *b*," and by stating for the second one "It starts with *gl.*")

Find the sentence that tells how a *sphere* is round like a ball or a globe.

Find the paragraph that tells what people do when they *trade.*

Direct attention to definitions: According to the text, *adapt* means _____; *adopt* means _____.

State or write the missing term in a cluster of words that are usually used together:

> All people have basic needs for food, shelter, and (<u>clothing</u>).
> Major landforms are plains, hills, plateaus, and (<u>mountains</u>).

Use cloze procedure by filling in sentences from which words have been deleted:

> At night the people moving westward pulled their (<u>wagons</u>) into a circle. During the (<u>evening</u>) they gathered around a fire to talk and sing. Sentries stood watch through the (<u>night</u>) to prevent a surprise (<u>attack</u>).

State or write the meaning of a term with several meanings (for example, *fair* as right, just, equal, good, impartial, or unbiased) in such sentences as:

The judge made a *fair* decision.	(<u>just</u>)
Fair shares will be given to each one.	(<u>equal</u>)
The hearing will be *fair*.	(<u>impartial</u>)
The final report was *fair*.	(<u>unbiased</u>)
Paul did the *fair* thing.	(<u>right</u>)
Tomorrow will bring *fair* weather.	(<u>good</u>)

Phonics Activities

Name and label objects and pictures of things in various units that start with the same consonant or consonant digraph, such as *pot*, *pan*, *picture*, and *paint* or *plant*, *plumber*, and *playhouse* in a unit on homes and families; and *grow*, *growth*, *growing*, *grass*, *grain* and *granary* in a unit on farming.

Identify and list examples of consonants with more than one sound, such as *c* in *city* and *capital*, *s* in *increase* and *cause*, and *g* in *gold* and *general*.

Keep one chart of unit words having a long vowel sound signaled by a final *e*, such as *lake*, *space*, *time*, *scale*, *trade*, and *zone*, and contrast these with words on a separate chart of exceptions to the "final *e*" rule, such as *store*, *income*, *climate*, and *justice*.

Circle silent letters in such terms as *sack*, *might*, *lake*, *neighbor*, *know*, *house*, *horde*, and *steppe*.

Developing Comprehension Skills

Comprehension may be viewed as taking place on four levels. The first is the literal or factual level, which can be characterized as "reading the lines." The second is the inferential level—"reading between the lines." The third is the applicative level— "reading beyond the lines." The fourth level is the appreciative and creative level— "creating new lines."

All these levels are used in the social studies. The literal or factual level provides the foundation of movement to higher levels. The inferential level is used to draw inferences and implications, identify possible purposes and motives of an author, and explore assumptions that are not self-evident. The applicative level is used to solve problems, make predictions, evaluate what is read, and put ideas to other uses. The appreciative and creative level is reached as students respond by expressing new feelings, empathy, insights, and appreciations.

Activities to Develop Basic Skills This section presents examples of activities that can be used to apply and further develop comprehension skills as students read to achieve these purposes:

To interpret the meaning of the text and graphic materials

To find main ideas, to select details, to organize and summarize ideas

To follow directions, to find relationships, to derive generalizations

To draw inferences, to state and check hypotheses, to predict outcomes

To make critical evaluations, to form sensory impressions

Interpreting Activities

Interpret the text through such activities as these:

1. Stating the meaning in one's own words
2. Explaining the meaning of words, phrases, figurative terms, and paragraphs
3. Describing the feelings or mood created by a phrase, sentence, paragraph, or longer passage
4. Responding to such questions as

   How can this paragraph be summarized in one sentence?
   What are the three main points in this section?

Interpret pictures to clarify the meaning of terms used in the text, to visualize land scenes, objects, and activities, and to answer such questions as

   What is shown? What meaning does it add to the text?
   What word, concept, idea, or feeling does it illustrate?
   What scene, object, or activity is shown? Where is it? What is happening?

Interpret maps by noting the title; clarifying symbols in the key; identifying the location of what is shown; finding relationships between places and travel routes, products and re-sources, and other items; and describing the size and shape of places (see chapter 12 for detailed procedures).

Interpret the meaning of posters, guided by such questions as

   What is the purpose? What single idea is emphasized?
   How are lines, space, and color used to focus attention on the key idea?
   How convincing is it? What feelings does it arouse? Is it effective in stirring one to action? Why or why not?
   How is it related to events in the text?

Interpret cartoons, guided by such questions as

   What is the title? What event or issue does it highlight?
   What is the purpose? To ridicule? To explain something? To reveal an injustice? To present a point of view?
   What symbol is used? What is the meaning of it?
   What ideas are distorted or exaggerated? What is your reaction to the distortion?
   What are other points of view? How can they be used to counter the cartoonist's view?
   What meaning does it add to the text?

Interpret tables, guided by such questions as

   What is the title? Does it indicate what is presented?
   What questions can be answered by using data in the table?
   What changes or trends are shown?
   What are the largest, average, and smallest amounts that are included?
   What conclusion can be drawn?
   How is information related to the text?

Interpret graphs, guided by such questions as

> What is the title? What changes, trends, amounts, or predictions are shown?
> If symbols are used, what do they represent?
> If it is a bar or line graph, what is the scale?
> What is the source of information?
> What conclusion can be drawn?
> How is the information related to the text?

Interpret time lines, guided by such questions as

> What is the title? What time periods are included?
> What type of event is emphasized? Political? Economic? Social? Military? Other? How are events related?
> What key or pivotal dates are included? What changes follow them?
> What trends are shown in the sequence of events?
> What meaning does the time line add to the text?

Activities for Finding the Main Idea

Read a paragraph or a selection in the textbook, then state or write the main idea in your own words.

Read a paragraph and choose from a list of titles, phrases, or sentences the one that best expresses the main idea.

Answer questions that focus attention on the main idea:

> What is the main idea in the first paragraph on page 12?
> What is the topic sentence in the second paragraph on page 12? Is this sentence the main idea? If not, state the main idea in your own words.

Study the following in your textbook and write the main idea presented in each one:

> Cartoon, page 78: _____
> diagram, page 66: _____
> Table, page 73: _____
> Graph, page 81: _____
> Drawing, page 83: _____

Number (or list) in order the topic sentences that indicate the main ideas in three to five related paragraphs.

Use computer programs such as *Reading Comprehension: Main Ideas and Details* and *Interpreting What You Read.*

Activities for Selecting Details

Find and state the details that support a main idea identified in a paragraph or a selection.

Make a semantic map or web with a concept or main idea in a central circle from which lines are drawn to related details placed around the circle.

Make a chart on which details are placed under such headings as *food, clothing,* or *forms of transportation.*

Find and write main ideas and details in the three paragraphs on page 21.

> *First paragraph:* Write the main idea and two details under it.
> *Second paragraph:* Write the topic sentence. List two details under it.
> *Third paragraph:* List three details and write a conclusion based on them.

Read and list details that fit under headings listed on the board, such as *natural resources, uses of natural resources,* and *ways of conserving natural resources.*

Activities for Following Directions

Follow directions presented in the textbook for making a map, a graph, a chart, a diagram, or another object.

Follow directions for conducting an investigation, interviewing an expert, playing a game, or carrying out another activity.

Follow directions for using a computer program without "fouling up."

Answer questions that focus attention on directions:

> What are the steps farmer Jones followed to make butter?
> What directions for conducting a meeting are given on page 67?

Summarizing and Organizing Activities

Classify items identified in a reading selection under such headings as *food, furniture; resources, products;* and *physical traits, cultural traits.*

Arrange items in order by size, time of occurrence, or some other characteristic—for example, main events in the development of the community, the population of cities in a state from largest to smallest, and the area of states in a region according to size.

Make an outline, a chart, a graph, a table, or a map that summarizes and organizes information: an outline of steps in baking bread; a flowchart that shows the processing of steel; a graph that shows how much a family spends for food, shelter, clothing, recreation, and other items; a table that shows population growth; and a map that shows the location of major cities in a country.

Collect and organize information about a country, using the following topics as guides:

Major cities	Capital city	Population	Education
Climate	Landforms	Water bodies	Transportation
Regions	Resources	Industries	Recreation

Answer questions that focus attention on summarizing and organizing:

> Who can summarize the main idea in the first paragraph?
>
> Who can summarize in two or three sentences what was presented in today's reading?

Make a web or cognitive map that relates details to a concept or main idea. For example, place *contributions of ancient Rome* in the center of a chart and draw radiating lines to identify contributions in such fields as law, engineering, government, and literature.

Activities for Finding Relationships

Cause-Effect Relationships

Find and discuss causes and effects of individual behavior, group action, and historical events. Discover the relationship between family and community problems, seasons and climate, and economic and other problems.

Answer questions that focus attention on causes and effects:

> What causes were mentioned? What effects were described?
>
> Why did that happen? What reasons were given?
>
> Why are there usually several causes and several effects of human events?

Part-Whole Relationships

Find and discuss part-whole relationships: contributions of members of the family; the interdependence of neighborhoods, communities, states, and regions; relationships among parts of a transit system; relationships between lower and higher courts and their relationship to the total judicial system.

Answer questions that focus attention on part-whole relationships:

> How do members of the family depend on each other? How can each one help to improve cooperation in the family?
>
> How do people in neighborhoods depend on each other? How do people in one neighborhood depend on people in other neighborhoods?
>
> What are the main parts of our city transit system? What happens if one part breaks down?

Analogous Relationships

Find and discuss similarities and differences in family life in different cultures; in neighborhood and community activities; in the work of mayors, governors, and presidents; in the making of clothing and other items at home and in factories; and in modes of transportation and communication in different times and places.

Answer questions that focus attention on making comparisons and contrasts:

> How are they alike? How are they different?
>
> What is common in both activities? What differences are there?
>
> What are things that both mayors and governors do?

Quantitative Relationships

Find and discuss relative time and distance to various places, area and population of states and nations, duration of time periods in historical events, density of population, income per person, and value of resources, products, and services.

Answer questions that focus attention on quantitative relationships:

> How far is it from New York to Tokyo? How much time does it take by air? By sea through the Panama Canal?
>
> How much of the family budget is spent for housing? Food? Clothing? Transportation? Recreation? Health care? Other items?
>
> What is their most valuable natural resource? How much of it do they export?

Sequential Relationships

Find and discuss the order in which a series of events occurred or the steps of procedure for an activity—for example, steps in processing iron ore or making steel; main periods in the history of a community, state, or nation; and steps taken to get a bill passed.

List terms or phrases in a sequence to indicate the order in which events occurred in a reading selection:

1. Religious persecution
2. Decision to leave
3. Long voyage
4. New colony started

Answer questions that focus attention on sequential relationships:

> In what order did the events occur? How are they related?
>
> What are the main steps in baking bread? Making silk?
>
> Why was that event called a turning point? What preceded it? What followed it?

Place Relationships

Find and discuss relationships between the location of the school and the homes around it, between shopping centers and homes or main streets, between large cities and waterways or other transportation systems, between farms or industries and land, water, or resources, and between elevation or distance from the equator and climate.

Answer questions that focus attention on place relationships:

> Why was our school located in a residential section of the city?
>
> Why are so many large cities near waterways?
>
> Why are there so many farms in that location?
>
> Where is Buffalo in relation to New York?
>
> How is the climate of Denver related to its elevation, nearness to the Rockies, and distance north of the equator?

What are the main steps in making lumber—from forest to boards? How can we find out?
Social Studies Workshop, University of California, Berkeley

Activities for Deriving Generalizations

State or write in one's own words what can be said in general about a topic discussed in a selection—for example, "All members of a family are consumers of goods and services."

Complete statements after reading a selection:

How people use resources is determined primarily by _____.

Select from a list of generalizations the one that best fits a reading selection the class has just finished.

Distinguish factual statements from general statements:

> Mark *F* by each statement that is a fact and *G* by each statement that is a generalization.
>
> _____ Our city has a central business district.
>
> _____ The business district in our city is in a central zone.
>
> _____ Cities have central business districts.

Answer questions that focus attention on forming generalizations:

> What general statement can we make about causes of the event described in this selection?
>
> Based on facts presented in this chapter, what can we say in general about the climate of the North Central states?
>
> What conclusion can you draw from the facts in today's reading selection?

Activities for Drawing Inferences

Read a selection and examine pictures in it, then state how the characters portrayed may feel, what motives they may have, or what they may value.

Select from several inferences presented by the teacher the most reasonable one, based on information in a selection that has just been read.

Read between the lines to state implications, consequences, or reasons: "They seem to believe it is better to give than to receive."

Answer questions that focus attention on the drawing of inferences:

> What do you think the effects or consequences will be? Why do you think so?
>
> What motives might the author have had? What reasons can you give for your answer?
>
> Why do you think that happened? What makes you think so?

Activities for Stating and Checking Hypotheses

Complete a statement presented by the teacher: If the work is divided, production is usually (increased).

State a hypothesis in your own words after reading a selection:

> I think I will find that all North Central states have hot summers and cold winters.

Examine a map that shows water bodies and landforms, then state hypotheses about the location of cities, travel routes, agricultural areas, and manufacturing centers:

> We will find that cities were located near harbors or rivers.

Select from several statements presented by the teacher the one that is the best hypothesis, given the information in a selection.

Answer questions that elicit the stating of hypotheses:

> Do you think that all fathers have the same role as the one in today's story? Why or why not? How can we find out?
>
> Do you think that all communities depend on other communities for many things, as described in our reading? Why or why not? How can you find out?

Activities for Predicting Outcomes

Predict how a story is likely to end after reading the first part or listening as the teacher tells the first part.

Predict what may happen next after reading a current news report, then keep track of the event to find out what actually happens.

Answer questions designed to elicit predictions:

> How do you think this story will end? Why do you think so?

> Based on trends described in this chapter, what is the probable future of the central business district? Why do you think so?

> After examining the figures on population growth in this chapter, what do you predict the population will be ten years from now? What is the basis for your prediction?

Activities for Making Critical Evaluations

Distinguish facts from opinions, the real from the fanciful, observations from interpretations and inferences, true statements from false ones, and generalizations based on data from inferences, hypotheses, and predictions that go beyond given information.

Distinguish fact from opinion by writing *F* for fact and *O* for opinion:

_____ The population doubled in 10 years.   _____ Too many people moved here.
_____ More people mean more jobs.   _____ Unemployment is up to 11 percent.

Critique materials for ethnic, racial, sexual, and national stereotypes, looking for catch words, slogans, bias, and prejudice.

Evaluate illustrations, maps, graphs, and selected passages in terms of such criteria as clarity of presentation, provision of meaning clues, usefulness or relevance, and treatment of the sexes and ethnic groups.

Check the qualifications of the author, the currency of material, the accuracy of the sources of information, and the completeness of information.

Discuss the use of such persuasion or propaganda techniques as name calling, glittering generalities, getting on the bandwagon, common folks, testimonials, playing up the good aspects of one group and the bad aspects of other groups, downplaying the bad aspects of one group and the good aspects of other groups.

Answer questions that focus attention on critical evaluation:

> Which family in today's story would you most like to visit? Why?

> Which pictures in this chapter are fair representations of activities of women? Which are not? Why do you think so?

> Is this generalization based on adequate information? If not, what additional information is needed? Where might we find it?

Activities for Forming Sensory Impressions

Discuss the feelings, images, sounds, and other impressions evoked by the material.

See pictures, films, and other media that illustrate verbal descriptions in the selection.

Discuss the feelings evoked by sentences taken from the selection—for example, "The hard journey over the pass left them exhausted," and "There were shouts of joy as they approached the water hole."

Answer questions that focus attention on sensory impressions:

Have you ever seen a roaring river? Where? What was it like? How was it similar to the one in our story? How was it different?

Can you find a picture of a windswept plateau? A dense jungle?

How would you describe a gushing spring? A trickling spring?

How might we show grassy plains, golden wheat fields, or rolling hills in a drawing or a mural?

Reading on Your Own

Before reading: Preview introduction and headings. Clarify your purpose. Recall related ideas.

During reading: Achieve your purpose. Clarify meaning of terms. Note ideas for a summary.

After reading: Review and relate ideas to past learning. Evaluate: How well was your purpose achieved?

Chart 11.1

Concentrating As You Read

Focus your thinking on what you are reading.

Have note-taking and other needed materials ready for use.

Keep the purpose or the question in mind and search for related ideas.

Use headings for clues to what is coming next.

Do not let noise or activity of others distract you.

Focus on building meaning of terms and ideas.

Chart 11.2

Finding Purposes

Does the title suggest a purpose?

Do main headings suggest purposes?

Do you have questions of your own?

Are questions to guide reading listed?

Can questions listed during group discussions be answered?

Can you find purposes by skimming?

Chart 11.3

Finding Word Meanings

Look for
    Definitions
    Context clues
    Picture clues
Use
    The word box
    The glossary
    The dictionary
Ask
    When you have tried but cannot find the meaning

Chart 11.4

Speed of Reading

How does speed vary when reading:
    Main ideas?
    Specific details?
    Directions?
    Familiar ideas?
    Graphs? Tables?
    Flowcharts
    Definitions?
    Time lines?
    Maps? Diagrams?
    Stories?

Chart 11.5

Using Reading Aids in Books

Do you check headings to get an overview?

Do you use pictures to clarify words and ideas in the text?

Do you get the main ideas from graphs and tables?

Do you follow the steps in charts and diagrams?

Do you use the table of contents and the index to locate material?

Chart 11.6

Reviewing What You Have Read

Can you recall ideas related to your purpose for reading?

Can you recall ideas related to headings in the chapter?

Can you answer questions at the end of the chapter?

Can you answer questions listed during group discussion?

Can you think of questions about main ideas to ask others?

Chart 11.7

Metacognition and Learning How to Learn. Metacognition, discussed in chapter 9, can be extended to reading and other skills to help students "learn how to learn." For example, students can "think about" their reading if asked such questions as: Do I have a clear purpose? Do I find main ideas? Do I use headings and other aids? Do I distinguish important from trivial details? Do I find the meaning of new terms and unclear sentences? Do I review and summarize main ideas? Charts 11.1 through 11.7 contain specific skills for students to consider in order to be independent learners.

Developing Reading–Study Skills

No subject offers better opportunities to develop and apply reading–study skills than does the social studies. The following examples of activities and procedures not only sharpen basic reading–study skills but also help students "learn how to learn."

Locating Information in Books

Learn the parts of social studies textbooks through such activities as these:

1. Examine the table of contents, guided by such questions as What are the main units or sections? What chapters are in the first unit? the second unit? On what page is the glossary? On what page is the index?
2. Examine the list of maps, charts, diagrams, and other aids: On what page is the map of Alaska? On what page is the map that shows the population of the United States and Canada? On what page is the map that shows great-circle air routes?
3. Use the index to locate specific topics and to clinch the learning that people are alphabetized by last names and places by first name: On what page can we find George Washington Carver? Are first or last names of people placed first in the index? On what page can we find New York? Is the first or last name of a place given first?
4. Use the glossary to find the meaning, spelling, and pronunciation of terms.

Use study guides to familiarize students with textbook organization:

Which of the following should be used to locate the information noted below?

A. Title   C. List of Maps   E. Glossary
B. Contents   D. List of Charts and Graphs F. Index

To find the pages on which deserts are described: _____
To find main parts or units in the book: _____
To find an illustration of a Corn Belt farm: _____
To find the pronunciation of a word: _____
To find the titles of chapters: _____
To find the location of major mining areas: _____

Using References

Use encyclopedias to find maps, tables, diagrams, pictures, graphs, and written material related to topics under study, with particular attention to such understandings as the following:

1. Articles are in alphabetical order by title, with articles beginning with *A* in volume 1, *B* in volume 2, *C–Ch* in volume 3, and so on.
2. Guide words at the top of pages tell what is presented on each page.
3. The last names of people are placed first.
4. The first names of places like Latin America and New York are placed first.
5. The index lists all articles and gives some facts not included in articles.
6. The index also lists maps, charts, pictures, tables, and graphs.
7. Study guides, questions to answer, articles to read, and related books to read are given for topics in our social studies units.

Use dictionaries to find a variety of information in addition to meaning, spelling, and pronunciation of terms, such as

Antonyms	Charts	Weights	Maps
Synonyms	Tables	Measures	Foreign terms
Word origins	Diagrams	Drawings	Abbreviations

Use the *World Almanac* to find the following:

1. Scan the "Quick Index" on the last page and list the pages on which the following appear:
   Canada _____   Environment _____   Maps _____   States _____

2. Scan the "General Index" in the front and list the pages on which these appear:
   Population, U.S. _____   Illinois _____   Israel _____

Use other references and library materials to locate information on questions and topics in units of study:

Card catalog	Atlas	*Junior Book of Authors*
Reader's Guide	Directories	Maps
Vertical file	*Who's Who*	*Statesman's Yearbook*
Dictionary	Encyclopedias	Other yearbooks

Use the computer program *How Can I Find It?* to improve library skills. Summarize on charts the skills involved in using library materials as shown in this example on using the card catalog (use microfilm if it has replaced the card catalog):

1. Use the guide letters on each drawer to locate cards.
2. Cards are in alphabetical order by author, title, and subject.
3. Find the author card if you know the author's name.
4. Find the title card if you know the title.
5. Find the subject card if you do not know the author or the title.
6. Note the call number on the upper left hand corner of the card.
7. Look for cross-references, which are indicated by *see* and *see also*.

Use computer programs such as *Using an Index, Dictionary Skills, The Atlas, The Encyclopedia, The World Almanac, Thesaurus, Card Catalog.*

Skimming and Scanning

Use the ability to skim to preview and select material for further study, to get an overview, to find how a chapter is organized, or to decide if a selection can be used to answer a question or to identify details, as shown by the activity that follows.

HOW MANY INDUSTRIES CAN YOU FIND?

Skim pages 224–258 and mark an X by each industry that you find.

_____ Agriculture	_____ Transportation	_____ Tourism
_____ Manufacturing	_____ Dairying	_____ Mining
_____ Communication	_____ Trade	_____ Electronics
_____ Fishing	_____ Publishing	_____ Smelting
_____ Food processing	_____ Forestry	_____ Building

Other: _____

Use the ability to scan to find a topic in an index; to find a name, a date, or another specific item; or to find a particular map, chart, table, or diagram. Use questions such as the following to guide you:

Are you trying to find a date, a name, or the answer to a specific question?

Have you scanned the index or the list of maps to locate it?

Do headings give clues to the location of the item?

If it is a number, have you checked the tables?

Listening Skills

Listening skills are used to participate in discussion, to get directions for activities, to clarify concepts, to get ideas from reports, to get a feeling for the mood or tone of expression of others, to evaluate statements of fact and opinion, and to achieve other objectives. Examples of uses, skills, and standards that students should understand and apply are shown in Figure 11.1.

IMPROVE LISTENING SKILLS

Pre-Listening: Clear purpose? Speaker's purpose clear? Materials ready to take notes?

During Listening: Verbal meaning clear? Gestures and other nonverbal clues add meaning? Main points and key details clear?

Post-Listening: Purpose achieved? Questions to ask on unclear points? Notes adequate for future use? Any ways to improve?

NOTE IDEAS AS YOU LISTEN	LISTENING FOR INFORMATION	LISTENING TO EVALUATE
What is the topic? What are the main ideas? Which ideas are new? Which ideas are most useful? With which ideas do you agree? Disagree? Why? What conclusion can be made? What ideas support it?	Have a question or a purpose in mind. Get ideas in order. Relate details to main ideas. Ask questions about parts that are not clear. Summarize the main ideas.	What is to be appraised? What standards are to be used? What is the evidence? Which statements are facts? Which are opinions? What conclusion or judgment can be made? Which standards are met?
LISTENING TO REPORTS	**EVALUATION OF LISTENING SKILLS**	**CRITICAL LISTENING**
Focus attention on the reporter. Note subject and aspects to be reported. Note main ideas in order. Note relevant details under each main idea. Note the conclusion and summary of reasons for it. Note questions to ask the reporter.	—I have a clear purpose. —I pay close attention. —I note ideas in order. —I note relevant details. —I visualize descriptions. —I get meaning of terms from the context. —I listen critically. —I take notes or summarize key points.	Clear purpose in mind? Facts distinguished from opinions? Stated and unstated assumptions identified? Bias, stereotypes, and clichés identified? Reasons and soundness of reasoning checked? Basis for conclusions evaluated?

Figure 11.1

Many of the learning activities presented in the preceding sections can be adapted for use as listening activities. The guiding principle is to shift instruction from reading to listening as shown by these examples:

Listen as I read this paragraph. What is the main idea?

Here are the directions for completing the outline map. Listen carefully!

Listen to this tape recording of our class discussion. Note how we can improve.

Listen to this description of the Amazon jungle. What feelings does it arouse?

Listen as I read a list of items that are in our textbooks. Should you use the table of contents, the index, or the glossary to find the following? (1) definition of a word; (2) chapter titles; (3) page on which a subject appears.

The taping of material can be used to improve listening skills and learning by listening. For example, a listening center can be used to present material on audiotapes for individual and small-group use. Taping a discussion and playing it back may be used to demonstrate the need for careful listening. As students listen to the tape, they should note repetitious statements, failure to follow up on questions, and other points in need of improvement. The same activity can be used to appraise and improve speaking skills, discussed in the next section.

Speaking Skills

Extensive use is made of speaking skills to express thoughts and feelings aroused by listening, observing, using a variety of audiovisual media, and reading. Speaking activities range from show-and-tell, sharing information on a topic, and telling about people observed at work in the community to reporting current events, describing objects and activities, giving oral reports, and discussing topics and problems. Examples of activities and guidelines are presented in Figure 11.2.[2]

There are several points to keep in mind for effective use of speaking skills in the social studies. Maintain a supportive and positive atmosphere in which students feel free to speak without fear of ridicule. Help students build a speaking vocabulary, using activities presented in the section on reading skills. Have students use pronunciation aids in dictionaries and textbooks for such terms as oasis (ō ā' sis) and adobe (uh-DOH-bee). Have small-group conferences to help students prepare oral reports. Encourage use of pictures and other items to illustrate points and to add interest to reports and other speaking activities. Emphasize students' strengths during evaluation and guide students to use standards such as those in Figure 11.2 for self-evaluation.

---

[2]For specific guidelines, see these sections in preceding chapters: Discussion in 4, Oral Reports in 5, and Role Playing and Dramatizing in 10.

SHOW-AND-TELL	OUR RULES FOR SPEAKING	WHICH DO YOU ALWAYS DO?	WHICH CAN YOU REPORT ON?
Pictures Drawings Models	One at a time! Take turns! Raise your hand to be recognized!	Speak so all can hear. Stay on the topic. Give others a turn.	A topic in our unit A current event A holiday or a notable person

HOW CAN YOU USE THESE IN ORAL REPORTS?

Photograph	Drawing	Postcard
Chalk talk	Puppet	Movie roll
Globe	Map	Time line
Graph	Chart	Diagram

WHAT DO THESE WORDS MEAN?

goods	services
produce	consume
barter	exchange
supply	demand

WHICH ROLES CAN YOU DESCRIBE?

Teacher Librarian Nurse
Police Fire fighter
Stenographer Store clerk
Mayor City Council member

DESCRIBE THESE COMMUNITIES:

A mountain community
A desert community
An arctic community
A tropical community
A mining community
A lumbering community
A fishing community

ORAL HISTORY REPORTS ON OUR COMMUNITY

Early Explorers
First Settlers
First Buildings
First Newspaper
First Radio Station
First School

TOPICS FOR ORAL REPORTS ON OUR STATE

Early Explorers	Resources
Early Settlers	Agriculture
Famous People	Industries
Population Growth	Trade
Our Capital	Transportation
First Cities	Communication
First Governor	Recreation

TOPICS FOR ORAL REPORTS ON OTHER CULTURES

Foods	Art
Shelter	Music
Clothing	Education
Occupations	Religions
Transportation	Government
Communication	Recreation
Rituals	Holidays
City life	Rural life

BE READY TO DESCRIBE THESE SURFACE FEATURES:

Mountain	River
Plateau	Stream
Mesa	Tributary
Valley	Lake
Prairie	Delta
Desert	Gulf
Steppe	Bay
Taiga	Inlet

CAN YOU TELL HOW TO DO

Find books in the card catalog
Find articles in *Reader's Guide*
Use an index to locate subjects
Conduct an interview
Chair a meeting
Give a book review

INDIVIDUAL ORAL REPORTS

Speak so all can hear.
Follow your plan and state ideas in order.
Point to pictures or other items to illustrate points.
Read quotations from cards in order to state them correctly.
Answer questions after the report.

GROUP ORAL REPORTS

Divide the topic into main parts or subtopics.
Each member collects and organizes ideas on one part.
Review notes to be sure there is no repetition.
Set time limits for each member's report.
Give the reports and answer questions raised by the audience.

PROBLEM-SOLVING DISCUSSIONS

State the problem and discuss the main parts.
Define unclear terms and any questions that are raised.
State possible solutions to the problem.
Discuss evidence that supports each solution.
Choose the best solution.
Discuss ways to test the solution.

Figure 11.2

Writing Skills

Writing activities improve learning and sharpen thinking in addition to extending and developing writing skills. Expecially useful in the social studies are the following:

> Making word lists, captions for pictures, box dictionary cards, game materials, greeting cards

> Preparing booklets, scrapbooks, fact sheets, files, data bases, simulated newscasts, newsletters, class newspapers

> Creating poems, stories, plays, songs, charts, diagrams, word puzzles, word pictures of places, "you are there" scenes, simulations, programs, pageants

> Labeling items on bulletin boards, events on time lines, features on maps

> Completing unfinished sentences and stories, outlines, charts, diagrams, maps, tables, graphs, forms

> Listing and defining new terms, main ideas and related details, synonyms and antonyms for key words

> Taking notes, outlining, summarizing, editing, revising, proofreading

> Writing reports, letters, summaries, book and other reviews, directions, annotations, articles, editorials, commentaries, scenarios, case studies, biographical sketches and vignettes of people, thumbnail sketches of places and events, story frames

> Keeping records, diaries, logs, journals, notebooks, minutes of meetings

> Making plans for interviews, field trips and surveys, recording data, transcribing and reporting data

Guidelines and Techniques

Develop social studies writing vocabulary by making word charts, listing terms on the chalkboard, and guiding students to make word cards and individual word lists. Use brainstorming and word games to build lists of terms, synonyms, antonyms, and colorful terms.

Encourage students to use a picture dictionary, a standard dictionary, and a thesaurus to find useful terms. Have students use computer programs in school and at home that contain a dictionary and a thesaurus.

Explore with students the variety of ways they can use writing in the social studies, as noted at the top of Figure 11.3.

Ask questions and make comments that stimulate thinking and serve as springboards to writing: "Describe three things you like best about _____ (our community, our state, social studies)." "If you had been _____ (a colonist, pioneer, wagon train leader), what would you have done to _____ (assure safety, get food, establish friendly relations with Indians)?" "Describe the kinds of transportation you think there will be in our state 50 years from now." See Figure 11.3 for other examples.

Encourage writing by giving helpful and constructive feedback, with emphasis on good features of each student's writing. Have students share their writing and find good features. Display reports and other written materials and arrange word cards, files of fact sheets, and other materials for reference use.

WHICH OF THESE CAN YOU WRITE FOR OUR UNIT?

Story	Song	Notes	Captions	Diary	Diagram	Directions	Article
Poem	Riddle	Outline	Word list	Log	Chart	Questions	Editorial
Play	Limerick	Summary	Fact sheet	Journal	Checklist	Main ideas	Interview
Scenario	Speech	Report	Data base	Letter	Description	Conclusions	Case study

WRITE DIRECTIONS

For an activity, a game, finding a place, making something, using a road map or a reference.

Directions for _____

Needed materials ____
_____

List steps in order.

WRITE A DESCRIPTION

A community worker you admire

Role of the mayor

An exciting event

The first school in our community

A place you want to see

WRITE CONCEPT CLUSTERS

Goods: _____

_____

Services: _____
_____

Resources: _____
_____

Landforms: _____
_____

Water bodies: _____
_____

WRITE A JOURNAL

Crossing the Atlantic on the Mayflower

Starting a colony in New England

Trekking west on a wagon train

Building a cabin in Oregon

DESCRIBE FEELINGS

A child moving to a new community

A new immigrant from China

A slave on a southern plantation

WRITE ENDINGS

Pioneers felt happy when _____.

Pioneers felt sad when _____.

The scout was surprised when _____.

COMPLETE THE FOLLOWING

Responsibility is _____
_____.

Freedom is _____
_____.

Cooperation is _____
_____

MAKE UNIT WORD LISTS

List and define new terms.

_____

_____

_____

USE THE COMPUTER

To write outlines, reports, letters, poems

To make data bases

To make captions, greeting cards, and banners

To make a class newspaper

USE THESE PROGRAMS

Bank Street Writer for word processing

Hometown to make a community database

Crossword Magic and *Wordsearch* to make word puzzles

Newsroom to make a class newspaper

MAKE A DATA BASE

Our community and others

Our state and others

Our country and others

Notable women and men

Biographical sketches of presidents

COMPARE TWO COUNTRIES

Population Location

Area Climate Terrain

Resources Products

Industries Trade

Imports Exports

Relations with U.S.

Problems and Future Prospects

CREATIVE WRITING

Stories, poems, plays

Songs, limericks, metaphors

Haiku, cinquain

Simulations, games

WRITE HAIKU

Five syllables in the first line

Seven syllables in the second line

Five syllables in the third line

WRITE ANALOGIES

Family is to home as class is to _____.

House is to shelter as coat is to _____.

_____ is to _____ as _____ is to _____.

WHAT IF?

You lived in a desert region

Russia had not sold Alaska

Women had not gained the right to vote

Figure 11.3

Linking The Process:

Problem-Solving Process	Report-Writing Skills	Writing Process
1. Define a problem.	• Develop the question(s) to be researched.	• prewriting
2. Establish a tentative hypothesis.	• Review what is already known.	
3. Interpret the information available.	• Develop further questions to guide the research.	
4. Gather additional information.	• Gather facts.	
5. Analyze the information.	• Sort facts. • Place facts in sequence to make an outline.	
6. Synthesize the information.	• Choose a form of presentation (e.g., report, persuasive letter, diary, autobiography, stories).	
	• Draft, edit, proofread, present answer to the question(s)	• drafting (putting the ideas on paper)
	• Use ideas creatively.	• editing (improving the ideas) • proofreading (checking the mechanics) • publishing/presenting (sharing)

Chart 11.8

Link reporting and writing skills to problem solving, as shown in Chart 11.8 (British Columbia, 1986, p. 227).

Have individual and group writing conferences, some with a focus on content and others with a focus on various kinds of writing, specific skills, or evaluation. Arrange small groups to meet special needs such as organizing notes, paragraphing, sequencing ideas, and using computer programs such as *Publish It!, Bank Street Writer, Kidwriter, Story Tree, Storymaker, First Draft, Multiscribe, Children's Writing and Publishing, Once Upon a Time,* and *The Write Connection* for writing reports, story and poetry writing, desktop publishing, and other writing activities.

Have individual and group writing conferences, some with a focus on content and others with a focus on various kinds of writing, specific skills, or evaluation. Arrange small groups to meet special needs such as organizing notes, paragraphing, sequencing ideas, and using computer programs.

Provide for cooperative writing, in which two or three students work together on a writing project. Have a writing conference to select a topic, clarify roles, and make decisions about form and other matters.

Use cloze procedure (fill in blanks) and maze procedure (select best answer) to focus on selected terms. For example:

Write a Report

Prewriting: Define the topic; gather, check, and organize information.

Writing: Make a first draft that includes main ideas and related details in this order: introduction, development, conclusion.

Revising: Read the draft critically and make changes that clarify meaning and improve the flow of ideas.

Editing: Polish the revised copy, proofread, correct mistakes, and be sure it is in proper form.

Evaluating: Think of ways you can improve each of these steps.

Chart 11.9

Mountains and plateaus are major (<u>landforms</u>). (<u>Hills</u>) and (<u>plateaus</u>) are also major (<u>landforms</u>).

Farmers build terraces in (mountain, prairie, desert) regions.

Provide guidelines as shown in Chart 11.9 to help middle- and upper-grade students write reports.

In the early grades reports may be dictated by children and recorded by the teacher or taped at the listening post. If microcomputer equipment is available, children can dictate reports as the teacher records them, view each sentence as it is displayed, make changes, and get a printout of their dictation. In later grades students can use word-processing skills to prepare written materials. A challenging project is a social studies newspaper that includes students' reports on selected topics, historical events in a "you were there" style, or social studies activities to report to parents. Creative thinking can be nurtured by having students write futures scenarios, as illustrated in the following lesson plan.

Writing Scenarios

Objective

To write scenarios related to a future event

Materials

Paper and pencil

Introduction

Explain that a scenario is used by futurists, military personnel, policy planners, and others to help them think about the future and various alternatives. Although it is an imaginary account, efforts are made to project situations as the writer thinks they will happen.

Development

Ask students to respond orally to a question of this nature: If you were to advise a writer of scenarios on what to include about schools 50 years from now, what would you say?

After discussion of contributions and any questions about scenarios, ask students to write a scenario for one of the following or for a topic of their choice:

A twenty-hour workweek	Education by television and computer
New energy technologies	Robots replace factory workers
Underwater cities	Cooperation replaces competition
Living in a space colony	Ideal city of the future

Conclusion and Evaluation

Ask students to share and discuss their scenarios, encouraging them to give reasons for their views.

Evaluate written scenarios, with emphasis on imaginative thinking and projection of alternative views.

Follow-up

Encourage students to write other scenarios and to get ideas from the following sources: Dickson, *Future File;* Kahn, *The Next Two Hundred Years;* and such journals as *The Futurist, Canadian Futures, Science News,* and students' news periodicals.

Have students rewrite scrambled words and complete and make word lists and puzzles.

Rewrite the Scrambled Words

First, rewrite each of the following scrambled words. Second, write sentences in which each rewritten word is used correctly.

urbbus	owtn	trycoun	antion	muntycomi	agevill
malceti	anri	erhwate	nidw	returapmete	leevation

MAKE A SCRAMBLED WORD LIST

First, select 10 or 12 words from the social studies textbook. Second, scramble them and write directions as shown above.

Complete This Geography Puzzle

Write the words in the blanks so that they cross one of the given words. The word NORTH has been done for you.

CLIMATE   OCEAN
COLD   RAIN
EAST   SOUTH
ELEVATION WEATHER
EQUATOR   WEST
NORTH   WIND

					T							
					E							
					M					N		
P	R	E	C	I	P	I	T	A	T	I	O	N
					E					R		
					R					T		
					A					H		
					T							
					U							
					R							
					E							

Make A Word Puzzle

Select 10 or 12 words from our textbook. List the words and print two of them in blank spaces, as shown above. Write directions and give an example, as shown above.

Focus on writing to learn as evaluations are made. Use holistic evaluation to appraise overall expression of ideas. Use analytical evaluation to identify specific improvements each student can make. Encourage self-evaluation by students in which they adapt and apply standards developed in class discussion, as illustrated by the following:

Summaries: Brief and to the point? Main ideas included? Clear concluding statement?

Social studies reports: Subject related to unit? Clear title and introduction? Main ideas and related details in meaningful order? Related maps, pictures, or other items included to clarify points? Clear conclusion? Sources noted? Correct spelling and grammar?

Creative writing: Original and novel expression of thoughts and feelings? Imaginative portrayal of people, events, and situations? New and alternative proposals to achieve goals? New solutions to problems? Concepts or skills used in a new way? New descriptions, interpretations, inferences, metaphors, or figures of speech?

Questions, Activities, and Evaluation

1. Read a chapter in a social studies textbook for children and the notes to the teacher in the accompanying manual.
   a. List the vocabulary that should be developed.
   b. Note techniques for vocabulary development suggested in the manual.
   c. Review the vocabulary development techniques suggested in this chapter and add useful ones to those noted in the manual.
   d. Note examples of questions and activities that you might use to guide students to (1) interpret the meaning of a section, a graph, a table, or some other item; (2) find main ideas and related details; (3) find relationships; and (4) formulate a generalization, draw an inference, state a hypothesis, predict an outcome, or form a sensory impression.
2. Plan an activity that students might do in a unit to find needed information and develop the following reading–study skills:
   a. Locating information in a textbook index
   b. Using an encyclopedia
   c. Using a glossary, a dictionary, or a thesaurus
   d. Finding up-to-date information in *The World Almanac* or another library resource
3. Select one of the charts in this chapter and adapt it to fit a unit for a grade level of your choice.
4. Note examples of ways you might use the following in a unit:
   a. Listening to evaluate or to achieve another objective
   b. Oral reports, buzz sessions, or some other speaking activity
   c. Questions and comments to guide discussion of a topic
   d. Three of the writing activities noted in this chapter
5. Make a plan for a writing activity similar to the one in this chapter on "Writing Scenarios."
6. Make a word puzzle you can use in a unit of your choice.

References

Abel, Frederick, James G. Hawviler, and Nancy Vandeventer, "Using Writing to Teach Social Studies," *The Social Studies,* 80 (January/February 1989), 17–20. Prewriting, composing and postwriting suggestions.

Anntonacci, Patricia A., "Students Search for Meaning in the Text through Semantic Mapping," *Social Education,* 55 (March 1991), 174–5, 194.

British Columbia, *Resource Manual Social Studies 4–7.* Victoria, Canada: Ministry of Education, 1986.

Chenfeld, Mimi B., *Teaching Language Arts Creatively.* San Diego: Harcourt Brace Jovanovich, 1990. Activities adaptable for use in social studies.

Cornett, Claudia E., and Lesley A. Blankenship, *Whole Language = Whole Learning.* Bloomington, IN: Phi Delta Kappa, 1990. Guidelines and sample practices.

Dupuis, Mary M., et al., *Teaching Reading and Writing in the Content Areas.* Glenview, IL: Scott, Foresman, 1989. Specific activities.

Gall, M. D., et al., *Tools for Learning: A Guide to Teaching Study Skills.* Alexandria, VA: Association for Supervision and Curriculum Development, 1990.

Gee, Thomas C., and Steven J. Rakow, "Helping Students Learn by Reading," *Social Education,* 54 (October 1990), 398–401. Strategies and activities.

Gold, Lillian, *The Elementary School Publishing Center.* Bloomington, IN: Phi Delta Kappa, 1989.

Hennings, Dorothy G., *Teaching Communication and Reading Skills in the Content Areas.* Blomington, IN: Phi Delta Kappa, 1988. Specific procedures.

The Horn Book Magazine. Articles and reviews of children's books.

Marzano, Robert J., et al., *Reading Diagnosis and Instruction.* Englewood Cliffs, NJ: Prentice-Hall, 1987. Chapter on schema and metacognition; chapter on thinking skills.

"Notable Children's Trade Books in the Field of the Social Studies," annual review, *Social Education* (April–May issue).

Rubin, Dorothy, *Teaching Elementary Language Arts.* Englewood Cliffs, NJ: Prentice-Hall, 1990. Chapters on listening, reading, and writing.

Standal, T. C., and R. E. Betza, *Content Area Reading.* Englewood Cliffs, NJ: Prentice-Hall, 1990. Chapters on readability, vocabulary, and comprehension.

Stewig, John W., and Sam L. Sebasta, eds., *Using Literature in the Elementary Classroom.* Urbana, IL: National Council of Teachers of English, 1989. Essays with emphasis on whole-language instruction.

Stotsky, Sandra, ed., *Connecting Civic Education and Language Education.* New York: Teachers College Press, 1991. Uses of communication activities to develop civic mindedness.

Tompkins, G. E., *Teaching Writing: Balancing Process and Product.* Columbus, OH: Charles E. Merrill, 1990. Activities useful in social studies.

Wiseman, Donna L., *Reading Instruction: A Literature-based Approach.* Englewood Cliffs, NJ: Prentice-Hall, 1991. Chapters on comprehension, vocabulary, other subjects, and independent reading.

Zarnowski, Myra, *Learning About Biographies: A Reading and Writing Approach for Children.* Urbana, IL: National Council for Teachers of English, 1990. Activities for middle and upper grades.

Developing Globe and Map Concepts and Skills

CHAPTER 12

Objective and Related Focusing Questions

To present guidelines, strategies, and teaching/learning activities for developing the concepts and skills essential to effective use of globes and maps:

- What concepts and skills are emphasized in current programs in primary, intermediate, and upper grades?

- What general guidelines are useful at all levels of instruction?

- What types of practical teaching/learning activities can be used to teach concepts and skills related to the globe, symbols, location, orientation and direction, scale, distance, comparisons and inferences, and map projections?

- What principles and procedures should be used in mapping and map-making activities?

Primary responsibility for developing globe and map concepts and skills is placed on teachers in elementary and middle schools in social studies programs throughout the country. The sequence of instruction is geared to students' developmental stages, experiences, and capabilities, provides for cumulative development of concepts and skills, and is tied closely to topics of study in each grade.

Overview of Concepts and Skills

Examples of key concepts and skills are summarized in Figure 12.1 by blocks of grades. Those introduced in the K–2 block are tied closely to children's daily experi-

---

SYMBOLS: WHAT IS IT?

K–2: models; pictorial and semipictorial symbols for familiar features; lines for streets and roads; colors for land and water; direction labels and arrows

3–4: symbols for towns, cities, and other features; letter-number coordinates, such as A–3, on road maps; how symbols differ on maps; map legend; compass rose

5–6: symbols on special-feature maps; colors to show relief, elevation, and other features; uses of hachures, shadings and dots, contour lines, legend

7–8: variety of symbols on maps in atlases and other sources; international color scheme; isobars, isotherms, and other isolines; legend

LOCATION: WHERE IS IT?

K–2: familiar places in neighborhood and community; nearby communities; land and water areas; state, country, continents, and oceans on globe

3–4: communities studied in other lands; main cities and capital in state; resources, cities, and other features in regions studied; current events

5–6: regions of United States; countries in North America; explorers' routes; colonies; westward expansion; countries studied in other lands; latitude and longitude; high, middle, and low latitudes; relative to selected places

7–8: Prime Meridian; International Date Line; time zones around the world; historical and current events; natural and cultural features in places studied; analysis of distributions of population, resources, and other features

ORIENTATION AND DIRECTION: WHICH WAY IS IT?

K–2: left, right; up, down; north, south, east, west; to familiar places; sunrise in east, sunset in west; shadow at noon; orientation of community map

3–4: cardinal and intermediate; relation to poles and equator; grid lines as direction lines; orientation of maps; directions to places by compass rose

5–6: parallels as east-west lines; meridians as north-south lines; habit of orienting maps correctly; directions to places studied

7–8: directions on various map projections; changes in directions on great-circle routes; systematic orientation of maps in atlases and other sources

---

SCALE AND DISTANCE: HOW BIG IS IT? HOW FAR IS IT?

K–2: larger, smaller; scale on classroom and neighborhood/community maps; globe as small-scale model of earth; near, far; blocks to familiar places; miles and kilometers; relative distance to familiar places

3–4: inch to block and mile; centimeter to kilometer; graphic scale to measure distance; scale on highway, textbook, and state maps; distance/travel time

5–6: comparison of maps of a given area on different scales; selection of scale to make a map; distance on great-circle routes and in degrees from equator

7–8: interpretation of fraction and graduated scales; analysis of large- and small-scale maps of the same area; relative and exact distance to places

COMPARISONS AND INFERENCES: WHAT RELATIONSHIPS ARE THERE?

K–2: comparison of pictures and symbols for features; distance and time between familiar places; relative size of neighborhoods, continents, and oceans

3–4: relative size of communities, states, and regions; comparison of size and shape of areas on maps and globes; relationships between location and climate, between land use and terrain, and between other features

5–6: relative size of countries; climate in relation to latitude, elevation, coastal location, and wind currents; industries in relation to resources and technology

7–8: comparison of old and modern trade routes; distortion of areas on various map projections; factors related to location and growth of urban centers; distributions of resources, population, and other features

Figure 12.1

ences, familiar landscape features, and neighborhood/community studies. Those in the 3–4 block are embedded in studies of communities, the state, and regions. Those in the remaining blocks are related to studies of our country and other lands. Shifts may be made between blocks to accommodate individual differences, provide needed review and reteaching, and take account of available learning resources. The sequence of concepts and skills is similar to the sequence found in current social studies textbooks and curriculum guides.

There is much overlap among the preceding concepts and skills, and they may be used in various combinations. For example, symbols must be used to locate places, find distances between and directions to places, and make comparisons and draw inferences. Direction and distance may be used to state the relative location of a place as "ten miles north of Albany."

Instructional Guidelines

Emphasize the usefulness of globes and maps as sources of information for answering questions related to spatial relationships, such as Where is it? In what direction is it? How far is it? How big is it? What is there with it?

Guide students' interpretation and use of the variety of content contained in maps in textbooks and other sources as noted in the following list and in Charts 12.1 and 12.2.

Community: streets, buildings, parks, zones, neighborhoods, airport

Travel: highways, state and national parks, cities, railroads, resorts

Political: cities, states, regions, countries, alliances, boundaries

Physical: landforms, water bodies, terrain, elevation, vegetation

Climate: precipitation, temperature, wind and ocean currents, types

Population: distribution, density, migration, rural, urban

Economic: resources, products, crops, industries, land use, trade

Historical: explorations, colonization, territorial changes, events

Special: parks, monuments, literary works, religions, languages

Develop the concepts essential to effective use of globes and maps. Included among concepts related to content are natural or physical features such as landforms, water bodies, terrain, and climate and concepts of cultural features such as urban and rural areas, population density, and transportation networks. Included among cartographic concepts are symbols, direction indicators, reference systems for locating items, cardinal and intermediate directions, scale, and distance. Remember that con-

---

Find Information on Maps

Streets and places in cities

Roads and cities in states

Highways, railways, airways

Cities, countries, continents

Resources, industries, products

Distance, direction, elevation

Mountains and other landforms

Oceans and other water bodies

Precipitation and temperature

Climate in various regions

Population density and migration

Transportation and communication networks

Farming, religion, culture regions

Landform, coastal, physical regions

Can you add others?

Chart 12.1

Maps in Our Encyclopedias

Location of cities, states, countries, continents, and water bodies

Maps of major cities that show famous landmarks

Physical relief maps that show surface features

Political maps showing cities, states, provinces, and countries

Regional maps of the United States, Central America, and other places

Historical maps of notable events

Interesting places such as parks and monuments

Comparison maps that show relative size of states and countries

Pictorial maps that show plants, animals, products, and resources

Chart 12.2

cept development is needed to build readiness for map reading, as it is for other types of reading.

Use maps and globes to deepen understanding of the five geographic themes noted in chapter 6: *location* as communities, states, and other areas are studied; *place* as human and physical characteristics of areas are identified; *human/environment interaction* as adaptations to and modifications of the environment are studied; *movement* as transportation networks, trade routes, and movement of people, goods, and ideas are noted; and *regions* as desert, mountain and other physical regions, and Corn Belt, mining, farming, industrial and other human (cultural) regions are identified.

Guide students to apply thinking skills as they use the globe and maps. For example, comparisons can be made of size, location, population, distance, and other factors. Inferences and hypotheses can be made regarding location of cities, transportation routes, resource use, and rural and urban areas. Analyses can be made to divide a city into zones or a country into regions. Syntheses can be made by completing outline maps that bring together distributions of features in a given area, reveal associations between features such as cities and transportation routes, and highlight interconnections within and between regions. Evaluations can be made of travel routes, land use, advantages and disadvantages of various map projections, and maps made by students and by others. Examples of questions to pose and errors to discuss are presented in Figure 12.2.

Guide students in making maps related to topics of study. Floor, tabletop, and sandbox maps are useful in representing the location of features concretely and realistically. Use models, blocks, and pictures to represent objects in early grades, and use standard symbols as students develop an understanding of them and discover their uses in textbook and other maps. Include attention to map scale, grid system, and direction indicators such as the compass rose. Have students use standards for evaluating their own maps, as noted in the later section on mapping activities.

Provide instruction in a sequence that begins with familiar features and concrete activities and gradually moves to unfamiliar features and abstract learning. For example, instruction on symbols should begin with models and pictures to represent familiar objects, move to pictorial and semipictorial symbols, and then move on to standard symbols in accord with students' mastery of underlying concepts.

Provide two types of learning activities: (1) those that include systematic instruction on specific concepts and skills, and (2) those in which reference is made to the globe or to a map during the study of topics in a unit, current events, and other subjects. Reference activities are needed to develop competence in applying concepts and skills, to appraise students' ability to make applications, and to nurture the habit of referring to the globe and maps as appropriate.

Provide instruction on specific concepts and skills at a time when students can put them to use. Supplement textbook instruction with computer programs, filmstrips, and films. An effective pattern is *demonstration* followed by *practice* and *application*. For example, use of scale to measure distance can be demonstrated on a wall map, practiced on textbook maps, and applied as questions about distance arise in units of study. Keep this pattern in mind as you read the following examples of activities for developing specific concepts and skills.

Arrange maps and globes for ready reference to aid mapping activities and to identify distortions on map projections. Social Studies Workshop, University of California, Berkeley

THINKING AS YOU USE GLOBES AND MAPS

USING THE GLOBE	INTERPRETING MAPS	ERRORS IN THINKING
What do the colors represent?	What does the title tell you?	Symbols stand for the same features on all maps.
How do you tell directions?	How do you identify the meaning of symbols?	
How do you find the shortest distance between two points?	How do you find directions and orient the map?	North is always at the top of maps.
How do you find the distance north or south of the equator?	How do you measure the distance between places?	Up is north and down is south.
How do you measure distance on great-circle routes?	How do you find and state the location of places?	The shortest distance between two points is along a parallel.
How can you identify the approximate location of time zones?	What relationships between features do you infer?	Areas colored the same are at the same elevation
How do you use the globe to identify distortions on maps?	How do you find distortions?	Size and shape of areas are the same on globes and maps.

Figure 12.2

Illustrative Teaching–Learning Activities

Presented in this section are examples of activities that are widely used to develop concepts and skills. Activities for use in initial instruction are presented first. These are followed by activities for advanced instruction in middle and upper grades. Those that meet students' learning needs should be used, regardless of the grade in which they have been placed.

The Globe: A Model of the Earth

Use a globe in early grades to develop concepts of the roundness of the earth and major land and water areas. Present the globe as a model of the earth after clarifying the concept *model* by discussing toy cars and other models familiar to children. Point to the land and water areas and ask children to tell the colors that show them.

Show the area on which we live. Point to North America and state that this is the large land area called *North America*. Point to the location of the United States and the home state.

Use a globe to show the location of places encountered in the study of families and communities in other lands, in reading instruction, and in other subjects.

Identify the North Pole and demonstrate that north is toward the North Pole. Use a washable crayon to draw lines from the home state and from other places to the North Pole to the north-south lines (meridians) and describe how they converge at the North Pole. Do the same for the South Pole. Explain that the directions north and south must not be confused with *up* and *down*. Show that up is away from the globe and down is toward the globe.

Point to the equator, show that it encircles the globe, and explain that it is midway between the poles and divides the globe into *hemispheres*. Show the Northern Hemisphere and explain that in includes the area north of the equator. Do the same for the Southern Hemisphere. Have students point to continents in the Northern and Southern Hemispheres. Discuss the following questions: Where is the most land? Why is the Northern Hemisphere sometimes referred to as the land hemisphere? Why is the Southern Hemisphere sometimes called the water hemisphere?

Show the Western and Eastern hemispheres. Ask: What continents are in the Western Hemisphere? What continents are in the Eastern Hemisphere? In which hemisphere is the continent on which we live? In which hemisphere is the largest continent? The smallest one?

Demonstrate day and night by shining a flashlight on the globe in a darkened room and slowly turning the globe from west to east. Place a piece of plasticene on the home state and ask students to tell when day begins and ends as you turn the globe. Stop rotating the globe and ask students to point to the day and night hemispheres.

Demonstrate directions north and south along the meridians (lines of longitude) and east and west along the parallels (lines of latitude). Ask students to point to places in response to such questions as, What north-south line crosses British Columbia, Washington, Oregon, and California? What states are south of Montana? Which states are directly west of Ohio? Which states are east of Texas? What is the first country east of New York across the Atlantic Ocean?

Demonstrate how parallels and meridians form a grid that can be used to locate places. Have students locate places in response to such questions as: What state is approximately 40° N, 90°W? What city is located at 30° N, 90° W? What is the approximate location of Washington, DC?

Develop the concept *great circles* by showing that the equator and the meridians are circles that divide the globe into hemispheres. Demonstrate that a great circle is the shortest distance between places and compare the distance on great-circle and other routes. For example, hold a tape along the 30° N parallel and measure the distance from New Orleans to Cairo. Hold the tape tightly against the globe and measure the great-circle distance. Ask students to describe the areas over which an airplane would fly on each route. Ask them to describe the shortest route by ship. An illustrative lesson plan follows.

PLAN FOR TEACHING GREAT CIRCLE DISTANCE

Objectives:

To demonstrate understanding of great circles as the shortest distance between two points.

To show the great circle distance between selected places.

Materials:

Globe

World wall map

Textbook that shows great circle distances

Introduction:

Direct attention to a wall map of the world and ask students to state the shortest distance from New York to Tokyo. Repeat the activity, using a globe.

Development:

Ask students to look at the section in their textbook that describes and shows great circle routes. Ask:

> What are great circle routes? How can they be shown, using a string or tape on a globe?
> Why are they shown as curved lines on world maps? Why are they shown as straight lines on polar projections? Why are they the shortest distance between places?

Demonstrate how to use a tape on a globe to show great circle distance.

Conclusion:

Ask a student to show great circle distance from New York to Tokyo on a globe. Follow by having a student point to the route on a world wall map.

Follow-up:

Ask students to find great circle routes on a globe between Atlanta, Denver, Los Angeles, and other cities to Delhi, Moscow, Singapore, and other foreign cities.

Have students draw freehand sketch maps to show the above.

Point to the Tropic of Cancer and the Tropic of Capricorn. Turn the globe slowly and explain that these parallels are 23½° N and 23½° S, respectively, and that places between them on each side of the equator are in the low latitudes and most have tropical climates. Identify the middle latitudes, which include places with temperate climates, by pointing to the area between the Tropic of Cancer and the Arctic Circle in the Northern Hemisphere and the Tropic of Capricorn and the Antarctic Circle in the Southern Hemisphere. Point to the high latitudes, which include places with polar climates, between the Arctic Circle and the North Pole and between the Antarctic Circle and the South Pole. State that these are sometimes referred to as *torrid, temperate,* and *frigid zones,* but that the preferred terms are *low, middle,* and *high latitudes.* Give students a worksheet on which lines are drawn to represent the parallels just described and ask them to complete it by labeling each of the following: equator, Tropic of Cancer, Tropic of Capricorn, Arctic Circle, Antarctic Circle, low latitudes, middle latitudes, high latitudes.

Demonstrate revolution of the earth around the sun; explain changes in the seasons and the meaning and dates of the solstices and the equinoxes. Follow with a discussion of diagrams in students' textbooks that show earth-sun relationships on June 21 or 22, September 22 or 23, December 21 or 22, and March 20 or 21. Use such questions as: When are the sun's *direct* rays north of the equator? On the equator? At the Tropic of Cancer? South of the equator? At the Tropic of Capricorn? When is there sunshine all day north of the Arctic Circle? South of the Antarctic Circle? When do summer and winter begin in the Northern Hemisphere? In the Southern Hemisphere?

Compare time zones on a map to meridians on a globe and explain why each zone represents about 15 degrees of longitude ($360° \div 24 = 15°$). Point to the Prime Meridian and explain that it is in the center of the zero time zone. As one goes westward, time is one hour earlier in the next zone, two hours earlier in the following one, and so on. Rotate the globe to show how time changes, why noon is one hour later at 15-degree intervals, and that when it is noon in places on one side it is midnight in places on the opposite side. Discuss the time zones in the United States, beginning with eastern standard time at 75° W longitude. Have students describe deviations from meridians. Point to the International Date Line and explain that this is where each new calendar day begins. Travelers add a day crossing it to the west and subtract a day crossing it to the east.

Guide students to summarize key concepts and skills, beginning with first learning in early grades and advanced learning in later grades, as illustrated in Figure 12.3.

Symbols: What Is It?

Have students in early grades use models, pictures, and blocks to stand for real things on floor maps. Ask them to tell what is represented and how the models, pictures, and blocks differ from what they stand for. As the broader community is studied, have students use semipictorial symbols to show houses, the school, a hospital, and other objects. Show aerial photos, pictures, and slides to help students visualize what symbols represent. Have students find pictures that show what symbols stand for.

Show a globe; point to the use of blue to show water and other colors to show land. Discuss colors that students may use to show a nearby lake, a city park, the

OUR GLOBE	COLORS AND LINES	POLES AND EQUATOR
It is a model of the earth. It is round like a ball. It shows land and water bodies.	Blue shows water bodies. Other colors show land. Lines show directions, boundaries, and rivers.	The North Pole is the farthest point north. The South Pole is the farthest point south. The equator is midway between the two poles.
THE EARTH	LARGE WATER BODIES	LARGE LAND MASSES
It is a large sphere. It turns once each day, causing day and night. It has more water than land on its surface.	The large water bodies are called oceans. We live on land between the Atlantic and Pacific oceans. Two other oceans are the Arctic and the Indian.	The large land masses are called continents. We live on North America. Six other continents are South America, Europe, Asia, Africa, Australia, and Antarctica.
UP, DOWN, NORTH, SOUTH	DIRECTION LINES	HIGH, LOW, MIDDLE LATITUDES
Up is away from the earth. Down is toward the earth. North is toward the North Pole. South is toward the South Pole.	The equator and other lines of latitude, called *parallels*, are east-west lines. The Prime Meridian and other lines of longitude, called *meridians*, are north-south lines.	The high latitudes, near the poles, have cold climates. The low latitudes, near the equator, have tropical climates. The middle latitudes, between the high and the low latitudes, have temperate climates.
HEMISPHERES	KEY PARALLELS	LATITUDE AND LONGITUDE
Northern and Southern Eastern and Western Land and Water Day and Night	Arctic Circle, 66½° N Antarctic Circle, 66½° S Tropic of Cancer, 23½° N Tropic of Capricorn, 23½° S	Latitude is the distance in degrees north or south of the equator. Longitude is the distance in degrees east or west of the Prime Meridian.
TIME ZONES	KEY MERIDIANS	GREAT CIRCLES
There are 24 time zones. Each zone covers about 15 degrees of longitude. There are 7 zones for the 50 states; Eastern, Central, Mountain, Pacific, Yukon, Alaska-Hawaii, Bering. As you move between zones, the standard time changes one hour: an hour earlier to the west, an hour later to the east.	Prime Meridian: 0° line of longitude, from which time and east-west distances are measured. International Date Line is drawn close to 180° longitude and determines date change: one day later going west, one day earlier going east—Tuesday on west side is Monday on east side.	Great circles divide the globe into hemispheres. The meridians and the equator are great circles. Hold a tape tightly to the globe to make and measure great circles. A great-circle route is the shortest distance between two points. Note changes in direction along great-circle routes.

Figure 12.3

parking area around a shopping center, and other familiar features. Have students use arrows to show directions on floor and other maps.

Discuss three perspectives from which features can be viewed: ground-level or profile view, combination of profile and aerial view, and consistent aerial view as used on maps and globes. Take students on a walking trip and have them compare the ground view with that of an aerial view of the same area or to the view from a high building. Discuss the shape of objects as seen from the ground and as seen from above—for example, from the front of a house and from the roof. Have students place tissue paper on an aerial photo and trace a map of selected features, such as streets and buildings. In middle and upper grades compare maps of specific areas with aerial and satellite photos and to Landsat maps of the same areas.[1]

Develop concepts of features represented by symbols. Begin with familiar landscape features in the neighborhood and community. Show pictures of hills, lakes, and other features. Direct attention to wall charts and to drawings or pictures in textbooks that show specific features.

Direct attention to textbook and other maps students are using. Discuss new uses of symbols and colors and guide interpretation of the legend or key. Point to examples of the use of symbols on the map. Check students' understanding by asking them to explain the meaning of symbols and to point to examples on the map. Compare symbols on new maps with those on familiar ones and discuss differences in the use of symbols, such as dots for communities of differing size on one map and dots for population density on another. Stress the importance of always examining the legend! As a student said, "The legend is really a key. It opens the door to maps."

Explain that elevation and altitude refer to height above sea level and may be shown by colors and by contour lines. Discuss the shades of color used to show elevation on maps in textbooks and atlases. Show a map with contour lines and point to the highest and lowest elevations, the steepest area with lines close together, and gentle-sloping areas with lines farther apart.[2] Have students make a model of a mountain with one steep side out of layers of clay or balsa wood and color each layer. Direct them to view the models from above and draw contour lines on graph paper. Follow by having students draw a simple contour map of a hill 600 feet high, using a contour interval of 100 feet.

Compare the use of colors to show elevation on a relief map and on a wall map. Point out that gradual changes in elevation are shown on the relief map in contrast to seemingly abrupt changes on the wall map. Ask students to identify sloping areas on the relief map and then point to the same areas on the wall map.

Guide students' interpretation of maps that show special conditions or features. For example, as students in upper grades encounter isolines that show where temperature, rainfall, water depth, and other items are the same, have them describe and trace with a finger the area over which the same condition or feature is shown.

[1]Kerman, Joseph M. "A Hundred and One Satellite Map Bargains," *Social Education,* 45 (October 1981), 470–72; "Use of Black-and-White Landsat Images in the Elementary School," *Journal of Geography,* 80 (November 1981), 224–28. Landsat maps may be obtained from Educational Programs Office, NASA Goddard Flight Center, Greenbelt, MD 20771. U.S. Geological Service, EROS Data Center, Sioux Falls, SD 57198, has 2″ × 2″ slides of major metropolitan areas.

[2]A topographic map, of a desired area can be obtained from National Cartographic Center, 507 National Center, Reston, VA 22092.

Make arrangements for pairs of students to use such computer programs as *Unlocking the Map Code, The Language of Maps, MapMaker, Atlas*Draw,* and *World Atlas Action.*

Have students summarize information on symbols and uses of colors for placement on charts or in students' notebooks, as illustrated in Figure 12.4.

CHECK THE LEGEND	SYMBOLS ON TEXTBOOK MAPS	HOW ARE THESE SHOWN?	
What do colors stand for?	Straight lines show roads on level land.	Airports	Population
What do lines represent?		Boundaries	Products
What do symbols represent?	Curved lines show roads on hilly land.	Capitals	Railways
What do shadings represent?	Black squares show houses.	Cities	Rainfall
What date is given?	Clusters of squares show towns.	Lowlands	Resources
What other information is given?		Mountains	Rivers
What questions do you have?	Blue lines winding between hills show rivers.	Plains	Roads
		Plateaus	Seaports

WHICH DO COLORS SHOW?	ELEVATION BY SHADES OF COLOR		ANNUAL RAINFALL	
Elevation of lands?	Red	10,000 and up		Less than 5 inches
States and countries?	Dark brown	5,000–10,000		5–10 inches
Distribution of resources?	Light brown	2,000–5,000		10–20 inches
Density of population?	Yellow	1,000–2,000		20–50 inches
Land use and crops?	Light green	500–1,000		over 50 inches
Natural vegetation?	Dark green	0–500		
Westward expansion?	Grayish green	Below sea level		
Federal lands?				

SYMBOLS TO USE ON OUTLINE MAPS

⌂	School	★	Capital	═══	Freeway	∼	River
⌂	Church	●	City	━━	Main road	⊣	Dam
+	Hospital	•	Town	──	Minor road	⋎	Swampland
▱	Factory	+++++	Railroad	⟩⟨	Pass	⬭	Lake
✈	Airport	—·—·—	Boundary	⟩--⟨	Tunnel	≋	Sea coast

Figure 12.4

Location: Where Is It?

Ask students in early grades to describe the relative location of objects in the class-room and of buildings around the school by using such terms as *to the right, to the left, next to, in front of,* and *behind.* Ask such questions as, Is my desk to your right or to your left? What building is in front of our school?

Have students locate streets, the school, and homes around the school on floor maps and simple neighborhood maps. Have them locate the airport, factories, and other features as the broader community is studied.

Distribute worksheets with lines that form a grid and ask students to mark the location of their desks and other objects in the classroom. Repeat the activity for rooms in the school and for buildings around the school.

Have students make simple sketch maps that show streets and buildings around the school and in the neighborhood around their homes.

Point to the location of the community, state, and country on the globe and on hemispheres and world maps. Do the same for oceans and continents.

In studies of the state, ask students to use the number-and-letter system to locate places on road maps. Direct attention to the index of places and guide students to find the point on the map where the given numbered and lettered lines meet. Later, this skill can be transferred to the use of the index in atlases.

If the community is shown on an insert on the road map, use the opaque projector to make an enlargement of it. Eliminate unnecessary detail and thus obtain a large map that can be used to refine skill in locating places in the community.

As regions and countries are studied, extend the concept of relative location of places by discussing the impact of mountains, terrain, and waterways on accessibility to places. Point out how improvements in transportation and the construction of roads and canals have helped to overcome barriers—for example, polar flights on great-circle routes, tunnels through mountains, the Panama Canal.

Show that parallels are east-west lines and meridians are north-south lines that form a grid that can be used to locate places. Guide students to use parallels to identify places north or south of their community or state and to find places nearer to or farther from the equator. They can use meridians to identify places east or west of their community or state and to describe the location of places on the same meridian as directly north or south of each other.

Show middle- and upper-grade students how to use degrees of latitude and longitude to locate places. For example, after indicating that Denver and Philadelphia are on or near 40° N, ask: How can we use degrees of longitude to indicate the location of these cities? Show that Philadelphia is 75° W and Denver is 105° W (30° farther west). Combining degrees of latitude and longitude, we have these approximate locations: Philadelphia 40° N, 75° W, and Denver 40° N, 105° W.

After finding the latitude and longitude for given places, reverse the procedure and have students find places when latitude and longitude are given. For example, ask students to find the capital of a country located 20° N and 100° W (Mexico City) or to find the city located 30° N and 90° W (New Orleans). Use the following activity in a lesson or as an individual task card to refine skill in locating places by latitude and longitude.

What national park has huge domes of rock and long waterfalls? Where is it located? When was it made a national park? (Social Studies Workshop, University of California, Berkeley)

Have students use available computer programs such as *Game of the States, Uncle Sam's Jigsaw, Road Rally U.S.A., Journey into the Unknown, World Atlas Action, One World Countries Database, The Medalist—Continents, European Nations & Locations, Where in the (USA, World, etc.) is Carmen Sandiego?*

Location by Latitude and Longitude

      Directions.　Use the map of North America in your textbook or desk atlas to complete the following:

  1. Write the latitude and longitude in approximate degrees for:

    Boston _____ _____　　Toronto _____ _____　　Anchorage _____ _____

    Oahu _____ _____　　　Houston _____ _____　　Montreal _____ _____

  2. Write the name of the city at each of the following approximate locations:

    33N, 87W _____　　33N, 97W _____　　40N, 112W _____

    52N, 97W _____　　48N, 122W _____　　40N, 77W _____

  3. Write the name of the city that is closest to a ship that sends an SOS from 30N and 120W. _____

  4. Write the name of the gulf that is located between 20N to 30N and 80W to 100W. _____

  5. Use the index in your desk atlas or the list of latitude and longitude for cities in *The World Almanac* to check your answers to the first two items.

Follow the preceding activity by having students locate other places, such as Athens, Rome, Rio de Janeiro, Tokyo, and Sydney. In addition, show upper-grade students the division of degrees into minutes and seconds, as is done in some atlases and in *The World Almanac*. Follow by directing students to note the precise location of cities for which they have noted approximate locations.

Direct students to show the location of features being studied on outline maps— for example, cities, states, countries, routes of explorers, colonies, westward expansion, high, middle, and low latitudes, climate regions, landforms and water bodies, resources and products.

Identify time zones on maps of the United States and the world, and explain how they are related to longitude, the Prime Meridian, and the International Date Line. Provide systematic instruction, as illustrated in the following lesson plan.

LATITUDE, LONGITUDE, AND TIME ZONES

Objectives

To state how latitude and longitude are numbered
To describe how latitude and longitude are used to locate places
To identify time zones and state how they are determined

Materials

Film, *Latitude, Longitude, and Time Zones*
Textbook, pages 20–21

Introduction

Ask: Who can tell what the lines that circle the globe from east to west represent?
   Who can tell what the lines that circle the globe from north to south represent?
   Who knows how time zones are determined?
Watch as the film is shown and be ready to discuss each question.

Development

Show the film and discuss each question, including attention to the following:
What is the heavy dark line around the center of the globe? How are degrees of latitude numbered, starting with the Equator?
What are the lines that circle the globe and run through the North and South Poles? What is the Prime Meridian? How are degrees of longitude determined, starting with the Prime Meridian?
How can places be located precisely by using latitude and longitude?
How are time zones determined? What time is it in New York when it is 4:00 in the afternoon in London?

Conclusion

Have students point to lines of latitude on the globe and on a large wall map. Do the same for lines of longitude.
Discuss the map of time zones on page 21 of the textbook.

Follow-up

Have students read pages 20–21 of their textbook.
Have students note the latitude and longitude of New York, Miami, Denver, Seattle, and Los Angeles on a globe or wall map.

Orientation and Direction: Which Way Is It?

Review and use concepts of directions to objects and directions from one's position, such as *over, under, in front of, in back of, toward, away from, left* and *right*. Ask such questions as: What is over the book shelves? Who is sitting in front of Ben? Is Bill's desk to the right or to the left of Mary's? Watch while I walk. Am I going toward or away from the classroom door? What street is in back of our school? Direct students to: Point to the object under the picture on the wall to your left. Take one step to your right. Turn left and describe what is in front of you.

Clarify *up* and *down* by asking students to respond to the following: Point directly over your heads. What do you see when you look up in our classroom? Outdoors? Now, point to the floor. What do you see when you look down in our classroom? Outdoors? Is up always away from the earth? Is down always toward the earth?

Use a globe to demonstrate *up* and *down* and *toward* the earth. Call on students to show up and down from various positions on the globe. Conclude by asking: Is up always away from the earth? Is down always toward the earth?

Have students stand with their backs to the sun at noon. Explain that they are facing north. Ask: In what direction is your shadow pointing? What direction is to your right? What direction is to your left? What direction is behind you? Explain that where we live the sun is always in the south at noon.

Place signs NORTH, SOUTH, EAST, and WEST on classroom walls. Ask: What do you see when facing north? East? West? South? Direct students to do the following: Take one step north. Take one step south. Point east. Point west. Turn to face toward the east. Turn to face south. Point north.

Print the cardinal directions on the sides of a large piece of paper. Draw lines on it to represent rows of desks. Ask students to state how the paper should be placed on the floor or on a table so that each side is in the correct position. Next, have students place either pictures they have drawn of themselves or name cards in the correct position. Ask: Whose desk is north of Betty's? Whose desk is east of Ben's? Is Sue's desk west or south of Paul's?

Distribute worksheets with direction arrows that form a cross with NORTH labeled. Direct students to print EAST, WEST, and SOUTH by the correct points of the other arrows. Have students orient their worksheets with the NORTH arrow pointing toward the NORTH sign on the classroom wall.

Make a floor or tabletop map of the area around the school and place direction arrows on it. After a walking trip have students name the streets around the school, guided by such questions as: What street is north of our school? What street is east of our school? What street is south of Elm? What street next to our school should we take to go west?

Ask students to name familiar places that are north of the school. Follow by asking them to name places that are east, south, and west of the school.

Show students how to use a compass outdoors to identify cardinal and intermediate directions. Ask them to tell the direction to various objects on the playground and near the school as you point to them.

Direct attention to a compass rose on a textbook map. Ask students to state the direction from one place to another on the map, referring to the compass rose as needed to identify the direction. Follow by having students state the direction to various places as you point to them on a wall map.

Play a game called "What Direction Am I Going?" Make statements such as those listed here, and after each one ask: What direction am I going? Students may refer to a wall map.

1. I am walking toward the rising sun.
2. I am walking north and turn left.
3. I am flying from Denver to Chicago.
4. I am flying from St. Paul to Miami.
5. I am flying from Los Angeles to Tokyo on a great-circle route.

Review with middle- and upper-grade students how to find directions by using a compass and their shadows at noon. Explain that their shadows at noon show north because places north of the Tropic of Cancer (where the sun's rays are overhead only on June 21 or 22) the noonday sun is always to the south.

Demonstrate how to use parallels and meridians to identify places east and west and north and south of each other. For example, Los Angeles is east of San Francisco and Reno, the southern tip of Ontario is south of the state of Washington, and nearly all of South America is east of the United States. Show that places on the same parallel are east or west of each other because parallels are true east-west lines, and that places on the same meridian are north or south of each other because meridians are true north-south lines. Show how the pattern of grid lines differs on Mercator, polar, and other projections. Use a globe to show directions on great-circle routes.

Provide practice in orienting maps correctly as students complete outline maps and interpret maps in textbooks and other sources.

Make arrangements for pairs of students to use computer programs such as *Direction and Distance* and *Latitude and Longitude*.

Scale: How Big Is It?

Have students describe relative size of objects as larger or smaller, compare the size of models, photos, and drawings with the large objects they represent, and draw pictures to represent trees, houses, and other large objects.

Have students use blocks or boxes of varying size to make a floor map that represents the school, houses, and other buildings on the streets next to the school. Discuss how small objects are used to stand for large ones.

Discuss the following as representations of large objects: maps of the classroom, neighborhood, and community; the globe as a model of the earth; and drawings and maps in textbooks.

Ask questions such as these: How high is a building if a model of it is ten inches high and the model is made to a scale of one inch to twenty feet? What is the scale if a rowboat eighteen feet long is shown in a drawing as three inches long? If one inch is used to stand for one block, how many inches should be used to show a street that is eight blocks long?

Demonstrate how an inch or a centimeter can be used to represent a block, a mile or a kilometer, or some other distance. Have students use one inch to stand for a yard, or one centimeter to stand for a meter, and draw a map of the classroom. Repeat the activity later by having students use one inch or one centimeter to stand for a block on a neighborhood map and for a mile or a kilometer on a community map.

Direct attention to the scale on textbooks and other maps and discuss the following: graphic or bar scale with segments numbered to show miles and kilometers, and a statement of inches-to-miles and centimeters-to-kilometers, as illustrated in Chart 12.3.

Have students compare an area shown on maps with different scales—for example, a textbook map and a wall map of the United States. Also, compare maps of a given area with different scales as students use atlases, encyclopedias, periodicals, and other sources.

Have students complete outline maps of the community, the state, and other areas, using maps with different scales.

Direct attention to the use of small-scale maps to show large areas and large-scale maps to show small areas in textbooks, atlases, and other sources. Have students describe the features and greater detail shown on large-scale maps that cannot be shown on small-scale maps. As a student stated: "The larger the scale, the more detail."

Discuss profile drawings of mountains, plains, and other landforms. Point out that the vertical scale is different from the horizontal scale and that elevation is distorted; for example, mountains are shown to be relatively higher than they really are. Do the same for relief maps, which show mountains to be higher above sea level than they would be shown if the horizontal scale were used.

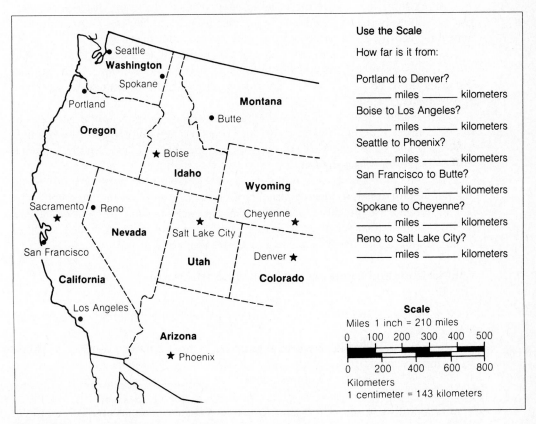

Chart 12.3

Explain the representative fraction scale (1 : 1,000,000) and graduated scales as students in grades 7 and up encounter them. For example, on a scale of 1 : 1,000,000 one unit on the map represents the given number—1,000,000 units on earth. Explain that a graduated scale is used to show how the scale varies with latitude and is important on air age or polar maps and on some world maps.

Distance: How Far Is It?

Have students use the terms *nearer* and *farther* to describe relative distance to objects in the classroom and familiar places near the school.

Have students use centimeters, inches, yards, and meters to measure short distances between objects in the classroom and on the playground.

Ask students to count and report the number of blocks from home to school and to familiar places in the neighborhood. Follow by having them count the blocks between the same places on a neighborhood map.

Take students on a walking trip of one mile (or one kilometer) around the school, and have them count the blocks and record the time it takes. Trace the route and count the blocks on a school-neighborhood map. Show students how the scale can be used to measure distance between familiar places.

Demonstrate how to use the scale on other maps to figure the distance between places. Follow by having students figure the distance, as illustrated in Chart 12.3. Repeat the activity, using state, highway, country, and other maps.

Ask students to compare distances between places on great-circle routes and other routes, using a globe and illustrations in their textbooks. Have them estimate distances north and south of the equator, using 1 degree of latitude to represent approximately 69 miles.

Have students use the globe and appropriate maps to estimate the distances to places being studied in units and current events. Have them compare the distance across selected states, countries, and continents, and relate distance to travel time by various modes of transportation.

Show students how to use parallels to identify places farther north or south of one another and meridians to identify places farther east or west of one another. Follow by having students use the globe or a map to answer such questions as: Which is farther north, Seattle or Toronto? Which is farther east, Los Angeles or Reno? Which is farther south, Hawaii or Florida? Which is farther north, Spain or Mexico?

Comparisons and Inferences: What Relationships Are There?

Compare distance and time between familiar places in the neighborhood and community.

Compare the relative size of communities, states, countries, continents, rivers, lakes, and oceans.

Compare area, surface features, climate, products, and other features of places studied.

Compare two maps of the same area and describe relationships. For example, compare a map of the United States that shows landforms to one that shows population and discover that few people live in mountainous areas. Later, find out if this is true in other areas.

Infer conditions in an area on the basis of knowledge one has. For example, what conditions would one expect to find in a desert area? In a tropical rainforest?

Infer the relationships that exist between various features, such as elevation and growing season in areas located in high, middle, and low latitudes; ocean currents, winds, and location on a continent and weather and climate of a particular area; highlands and grazing; lowlands and farming; travel routes and surface features; industries and natural resources and level of technological development; natural vegetation and rainfall, type of soil, and elevation; temperature at places near the equator and temperatures at high and low elevations; location of cities and access to oceans and large rivers; industrial centers and natural resources and transportation systems.

Make a habit of double-checking inferences by consulting other sources of information, analyzing cause-effect and other relationships, and using critical thinking skills, as suggested in chapter 9.

Map Projections

The globe shows land masses and water bodies accurately in terms of area, shape, distance, and direction. Distortion is introduced when the surface of the globe is transferred to a flat map. Students in middle and upper grades should become aware of different projections, and distortions within them. To do this without presenting technical cartographic details, provide activities such as the following:

Demonstrate how difficult it is to flatten a sphere by peeling an orange and flattening the peeling.

Place tissue paper on a globe and trace a small area, such as a state, and a large area, such as North America. Discuss how much more the paper is distorted when a large area is traced.

Examine and discuss the illustrations in textbooks and other sources that show how distortion is introduced when the globe is flattened to make a map.

Compare the size and shape of large areas on world maps with the same areas on the globe—for example, Alaska and Greenland on a Mercator projection and on a globe.

Compare the shape and area of North America and other continents as shown on various projections and on the globe. Have students describe where the distortion is greatest on different projections.

Compare recent National Geographic world maps based on the Robinson projection to earlier ones based on the Van Der Grinten projection. Direct attention to how much more the size of Alaska, Canada, Greenland, and the U.S.S.R. is exagerated on the Van Der Grinten.

Discuss the purposes for using different projections as students encounter them in textbooks and other sources: equal-area and interrupted projections to compare size and shape of areas; Mercator projection, which shows correct directions and is used in navigation; polar projections, which show shortest distance or great-circle routes and are used to plan long flights.

Individual Activity Cards

The globe, wall maps, and the variety of maps in textbooks and atlases can be made the focus of individual learning activities. Write clear directions and questions on cards, as illustrated by these examples:

Direction from the School

Look at the map on page 30 that shows things around a school. The arrows show the directions north, south, east, and west. Write answers to these questions on a separate sheet of paper.

1. What is the name of the street north of the school?
2. What is the large building south of the school?
3. What direction is it from the school to the lake?
4. What is the name of the park three blocks east of the school?
5. How many blocks west is it to Walnut Street?

Physical and Cultural Features

Look at the map on page 60 of your textbook. Complete the following:

Four physical features shown on the map are:
1. _____ 2. _____ 3. _____ 4. _____
Four cultural features shown on the map are:
1. _____ 2. _____ 3. _____ 4. _____
The cultural feature that is farthest north is a _____.
The physical feature in the southwest corner is a _____.

Location of Continents in Hemispheres

Use the globe in the social studies learning center to answer these questions.

1. Which continents are completely or partly in the Northern Hemisphere?
2. Which continents are completely or partly in the Southern Hemisphere?
3. Which continents are completely or partly in the Eastern Hemisphere?
4. Which continents are completely or partly in the Western Hemisphere?
5. Which continents are crossed by the equator?

What large water bodies touch on North America? What harbors are along the coasts? Where are the main rivers and lakes? How are they used?

Where are the mountain ranges? What regions do they border?

What climates have been identified in North America?

What are the main natural regions of North America? Which are best for farming? For grazing? For lumbering? For industry? Where do most of the people live? Where is population the densest? Social Studies Workshop, University of California, Berkeley (Map from Rand McNally & Co.)

INTERPRETING A TIME ZONE MAP

Objective:

To name the time zone in which selected places are located

Procedure:

Study the time zone map on page 266 and write the zone in which the following are located:

Delaware, Maryland, Indiana, Iowa, Kansas, Colorado, New Mexico, Arizona, California, Alaska, Hawaii

INTERPRETING A HISTORICAL MAP

Look at the map on page 289 and write the names of the states that became part of the United States during these time periods:

1. 1810–1819   2. 1820–1839   3. 1840–1859
4. 1860–1869   5. 1870–1919   6. after 1920

COMPLETE A PARAGRAPH ABOUT THE GLOBE

A globe is an accurate representation of land and water areas of the _____.
The line that circles the globe midway between the poles is the _____. The
east-west lines are lines of _____. The north-south lines are lines of
_____. The north-south line from which degrees of longitude are figured is the
_____ _____. Degrees of latitude are computed north and south of
the _____.

CLIMATES IN REGIONS OF THE UNITED STATES

Use the map on page 18 to answer the following: In what regions of the United States are these climates?
1. Cold and dry year-round _____
2. Hot and dry year-round _____
3. Hot and rainy year-round _____
4. Hot summer and cold winter _____
5. Dry summer and mild rainy winter _____

FIND THE WORLD'S MAJOR DESERTS, MOUNTAINS, OCEANS, AND SEAS!

Use the *Physical Map of the World* on the bulletin board by the map center to complete the following:

a. List the deserts located in the following:
North America _____ West Coast of South America _____ Africa
_____ India _____ Mongolia _____

2. List the names of mountain ranges located in the following:
North America _____ South America _____ Africa
_____ Europe _____ U.S.S.R. _____ Asia
_____

3. List the oceans located as follows:
West of North America _____ East of North America _____ West
of South America _____ East of South America _____ West of
Africa _____ East of Africa _____ West of Europe
_____ East of Australia _____ East of Japan _____
North of Europe _____

LOCATION OF MOUNTAIN RANGES, GREAT BASIN, AND GREAT PLAINS

Refer to the map of landforms on page 22 and answer these questions:
1. What mountain ranges are in Alaska?
2. What mountain range extends from Canada, through the United States, and on into Mexico?
3. Between what mountain ranges is the Great Basin?
4. Between what mountain ranges are the Great Plains?

LOCATION OF PEOPLE AND PLACES IN SPECIAL ATLASES

Refer to these special atlases to find the location of people and places in our units of work:
Third World Atlas   State of the World Atlas   Women in the World

Mapping Activities

Concepts and skills are applied and extended as students are involved in making maps related to topics of study. The focus in early grades is on familiar features in the immediate environment. In later grades the focus shifts to topics related to studies of the state, regions, the country, and other lands. The variety of maps that may be made are noted here.

Floor or table maps with blocks, models, and drawings to represent objects.

Maps on wrapping paper, with objects represented by paper cutouts or drawings made by pencil, crayon, or tempera paint

Pictorial maps of objects in the neighborhood and community, resources and products in selected areas, and other features

Specimen maps that show the location of real items such as wheat, corn, and cotton

Mural maps with strips of paper or tape for streets and drawings or cutouts for buildings, parks, and other features

Relief maps made of papier-mâché, clay, moistened sand, or other modeling material

Large wall maps made by projecting a small map or by using a pantograph or proportional squares to enlarge a map

Jigsaws puzzle maps of states, countries, and continents

Maps made on slated globes and flat maps and on outline maps to show air routes, trade routes, early explorations, and other items

Transportation maps with line and dot patterns to show air, railway, interstate highway, and major pipeline routes

Historical maps of exploration, early settlements, colonization, westward movement, and territorial expansion

Special interest maps of national and state parks, major cities, seaports, river systems, and states in the Sunbelt, the Frostbelt, and the Heartland

Transparent maps of resources, population, transportation networks, and other distributions to project and to place over base maps to show relationships

The following sample lesson plan for making a classroom map can be adapted for making neighborhood, community, and other maps:

Lesson Plan for Making a Classroom Map

Objective

To make a map that shows the location of objects in the classroom

Materials

Large piece of wrapping paper to represent the classroom
Construction paper cutouts to represent desks and other objects
Drawing paper without a grid for students' use
Drawing paper with a grid for students' use

Introduction

State that today we are going to make maps that show the location of desks and other objects in the classroom.

Development

Place the wrapping paper on the floor or on a table and explain that it represents the classroom.

Show the cutouts and explain that they stand for objects in the classroom.

Show the cutout that represents the teacher's desk and place it in the proper position.

Show the cutouts that represent students' desks and ask where they should be placed. Begin with those nearest the teacher's desk and ask each student to show where the cutout for his or her desk should be placed.

Show the cutouts for other objects and call on students to show where they should be placed.

Hand out the drawing paper without a grid and tell students to make a drawing that shows the location of objects in classroom.

Discuss any difficulties students had in locating objects accurately.

Hand out the drawing paper with a grid on it and ask students to make a drawing that shows the location of objects.

Conclusion

Discuss the advantages of using paper with a grid to map objects.

Follow-up

Give students paper with a grid and ask them to make a map of a room at home and bring it to class on the following day.

Outline Maps

Outline maps are useful at all levels to map features related to topics of study. For example, a simple outline map of the streets around the school can be used to locate features as students take a short walk or "mapping trip." Outline maps of the neighborhood and community are used to locate students' homes, the school, the central business district, and other features. Outline maps of the state, the country, and other areas are used extensively in middle and upper grades.

When the need arises for an outline map that is not furnished by the school district, several procedures are used to make one. The opaque projector can be used to make large outline maps from those in textbooks, newspapers, and other sources. Maps on slides and filmstrips can be projected and traced. Proportional squares can be used to enlarge small maps. Draw small squares over the small map, draw the same number of squares on wrapping paper, and mark the outline in the matching squares on the wrapping paper. The outline of a desired map can be traced on a sheet of paper or stencil and duplicated. Students should use the foregoing techniques to make outline maps needed for individual and small-group projects.

Guidelines for students to follow as they complete outline maps are as follows:

Collect and check information on features to be mapped.

Select symbols and colors and note them in the legend.

Use the grid to locate features accurately.

Print the names of places in parallel form.

Make a north arrow or a compass rose to show directions.

Print the title in capital letters at the top.

Print the date under the title.

Print your name in the upper right-hand corner.

Modeled Relief Maps

Modeled relief maps are helpful in many ways. They can help show why people settle in certain places, why highways are built in certain places, where mountain passes are located, how mountain ranges cause certain areas to be dry and other areas to receive much rainfall, how climate is affected by terrain, how areas are drained by rivers, and a host of other questions related to distance, travel, elevation, and topography. Relief maps enable children to visualize surface features and conditions in the areas being studied.

Remember that the vertical scale on relief maps is different from the horizontal scale. For example, Pike's Peak, which may be prominent on a relief map, is only a tiny pinpoint on the earth's surface when its elevation (under 3 miles or 4.8 kilometers) is considered in relation to the circumference of the earth (25,000 miles, or 40,225 kilometers). Nevertheless, one child who had seen it said, "It was no pinpoint from where I saw it," thus indicating that relief on smaller areas stands out dramatically and realistically. By mapping a smaller area, less distortion is introduced. When large areas are mapped, however, considerable distortion is introduced and should be considered as children grow in their understanding of map scale. One technique is to draw a long line on the chalkboard to represent the distance across the area being mapped. Then draw vertical lines to show the relative height of mountains, plateaus, and other features to be shown. Thus, if a mountain approximately 3 miles high is located in an area 300 miles long, the vertical line would be 3 inches, while the baseline would be 300 inches. (Corresponding metric measurements would be mountain, 4.83 kilometers high; length of area, 483 kilometers; vertical line, 7.6 centimeters; and baseline,

How might you use aerial views to improve map making and map reading in a unit you are planning? Find examples in a textbook. Social Studies Workshop, University of California, Berkeley

760 centimeters.) After such a demonstration, one fifth grader said, "That mountain isn't so high when you think of how long the ground is." When distortion exists, the teacher should explain that features are relatively higher than they should be to show them more clearly.

The outline on which the relief map is made should be carefully prepared. A wise procedure is to make two outline maps and to use the second one as a working guide while the modeling material is being placed on the relief map. Then, when one area is covered or one layer is on, the second outline map is available for easy reference. Make a list of the features that are to be shown, show pictures illustrating them (the jagged Rockies, long flat praries, great valleys), and guide children to find them on physical maps, either wall maps or maps in atlases.

Make the map outline by means of a projector or one of the other methods discussed under outline maps. Sketch in rivers, mountains, other features, and contour lines. After the outline is mounted on a base board, drive in brads and small nails to show relative height and position of peaks, mountain ranges, and hills; these serve as guides during the modeling process. Anticipate and discuss common errors, such as gross distortion of features (hills and mountains too large), omission of significant features (lakes, valleys, dams), inaccuracy of slope (rivers running uphill), and errors in relative height of features (Appalachians and Rockies same height). Plan for gradual inclines from plains to hills to mountains where appropriate. Some teachers also find it helpful to show and discuss relief maps made by classes of preceding years.

Many relief maps can be made and used without coloring them in any way. The features will stand out clearly and the surface will speak for itself as children use the map. In other instances, the surface can be painted to highlight features and to show contrasts. Tempera water paint works very well; the surface can be protected by shellacking after it has dried. Enamel can also be used if the surface is first shellacked. Another effective technique is to place sawdust in a can or jar of powdered paint and to shake thoroughly. After coating the areas to be colored with glue, sprinkle the sawdust on and allow the glue to dry. Brush off any loose particles. Clean sand can be used in a similar manner. Be sure to plan carefully for the use of different colors on appropriate sections of the map so that they will be clear in contrast and consistent with standard uses of color on maps. See Charts 12.4 and 12.5 for guidelines.

Clay Relief Maps

Have a map to guide modeling.

Mix clay or use ready-mixed clay.

Spread the clay over an outline map.

Build up mountains, hills, and valleys.

Trace rivers with a pencil.

Use tiny sticks to show trees and other items.

Chart 12.4

Papier-Mâché Maps

Have a map to guide modeling.

Put one layer of paper-mâché on outline map.

Add other layers as needed for hills and mountains.

Form valleys and river channels.

Allow the map to dry.

Paint with enamel or water paints.

Chart 12.5

Recipes for Modeling Material

Several different materials can be used to model relief maps. If the maps will be used for only a short time, use simple and inexpensive recipes: finishing the surface with paint and shellac is unnecessary. If the maps are used often, they should be well made and shellacked to protect the surface.

paste and paper

Tear paper towels or newspapers into one-and-one-half-inch pieces. Put paste on one piece at a time, wad it or shape it with your fingers, and stick it on the map outline. Build up hills and mountains as desired. Paint with tempera paint after the paste has dried.

paper strips and paste

Begin with crumpled paper to build up terrain, holding it in place with string or masking tape. Dip half-inch strips of paper towels into wheat paste and place them on the crumpled paper form. After two layers have been placed on the map, coat the entire surface with paste and allow it to dry, secure the base of the map so that it cannot buckle. After the map is dry, paint with calcimine paint.

sawdust and paste

Mix any sawdust, except redwood or cedar, with wheat paste (from wallpaper store); spoon paste into sawdust until it is well moistened and of good modeling consistency. Good proportions are 5 cups of sawdust to 1 cup of wheat paste. The mixture may be applied directly to wood or cardboard. Paint it after it is dry.

papier-mâché

This is one of the most popular modeling materials. Tear twenty to twenty-five newspaper sheets (or paper towels) into fine shreds and soak them for 24 hours. Pulverize the soaked paper by rubbing it over a washboard or by kneading it. Add wheat paste (or 4 cups of flour and 2 cups of salt) until mixture is of the same consistency as modeling clay. Build up mountains, plateaus, and hills by applying papier-mâché mixture to the surface. After three to six days of drying, paint elevations, water, and other features.

salt and flour

Mix equal parts of salt and flour, using only enough water to hold the ingredients together. Apply to map outline, modeling the terrain according to plan. (Keep out of humid places because salt attracts moisture.)

plaster and sawdust

Mix one pint of plaster, one pint of sawdust, and one-quarter pint of paste that has been dissolved in water. Knead and apply to map outline. Paint after the mixture has set for fifteen to thirty minutes.

plaster and papier-mâché

Add two pints of plaster, one-half tablespoon of LePage's glue, and one-half pint of water to prepared paper mâché. Be sure that the mixture is of modeling consistency. Paint after mixture has set for thirty to forty-five minutes.

Questions, Activities, and Evaluation

1. Which of the examples of map and globe use presented in this chapter might you incorporate in a unit you are planning? Can you think of additional uses of maps and globes in the social studies program?

2. Study a recently published map and check the legend, the use of colors, and the information presented. Can you find related pictures to illustrate items on the map?

3. Prepare a list of questions you can use with children to direct their attention to symbols and features on a map you plan to use.

4. Study the charts presented in this chapter nad note ways you can adapt them for use in a unit.

5. Examine two or three social studies textbooks that contain maps and notice how they are discussed in the text. Note questions that can be answered by children as they use the maps. Refer to the accompanying teacher's manual for suggestions. Make an activity card based on one of the maps.

6. Select one of the map-making activities and indicate how you might use it in a unit.

7. Review a local course of study or a textbook for a grade of your choice, or both, and make a summary of the suggested map and globe concepts and skills.

8. Visit a nearby media center and preview computer programs, filmstrips, and films on globe and map concepts and skills. Note how you might use them in a lesson or a unit.

9. Make a large chart of symbols for classroom use. Include three columns with commonly used symbols in the first column, pictures of what each symbol represents in the second column, and the name of the feature represented by the symbol in the third column.

References

Ellis, Arthur K., *Teaching and Learning Elementary Social Studies* (4th ed.). Needham Heights, MA: Allyn & Bacon, 1991. (Chapter 9)

Fernald, Edward A., and Rodney F. Allen, "Great Circles and Distance," *Social Education,* 53 (January 1989), 71–72. Specific teaching suggestions.

Forsyth, Alfred S., Jr., "How We Learn Place Location: Bringing Theory and Practice Together," *Social Education,* 52 (November/December 1988), 500–3. Current methods; computer software programs.

Frazee, Bruce, ed., "Teaching Map Reading Skills," *Social Education,* 50 (March 1986), 199–211. Special section with articles on concepts, skills, and learning activities.

Garvey, John B., "New Perspective on the World," *National Geographic,* 174 (December 1988), 911–13. Examples of distortions on various projections.

Hovinen, Elizabeth L., *Teaching Map & Globe Skills.* Skokie, IL: Rand McNally, 1982.

Kelly, Joseph T., and Gwendolyn N. Kelly, "Getting in Touch with Relative Location," *Social Education,* 86 (May/June 1987), 127–29. Tactile and visual activities.

Metz, Howard M., "Sketch Maps," *Journal of Geography,* 89 (May/June 1990), 114–18. Uses of freehand drawn maps.

Morse, Frances K., "Junior Mapmakers," *Teaching and Computers,* 4 (May/June 1987), 17–20. Using Logo or graphics arts package to make maps.

Muessig, Raymong H., ed., "Building Map Skills to Advance Geographic Understanding," *Social Education,* 49 (January 1985), 20–46. Special section with articles on techniques, topographic maps, literary geography and mapping, and map functions.

Muir, Sharon P., "Understanding and Improving Students' Map Reading Skills," *Elementary School Journal,* 86 (November 1985), 207–16. Piagetian tasks; Bruner's sequence; practical suggestions.

Rice, Gwenda H., "Teaching Students to Be Discriminating Map Users," *Social Education,* 54 (October 1990), 393–97. Various map projections shown and reviewed.

Rushdoony, Haig A., *Exploring Our World through Maps.* San Francisco: David S. Lake Publishers, 1988. Activities for grades 1–6.

Werner, Robert, and James Young, "A Checklist to Evaluate Mapping Software," *Journal of Geography,* 90 (May/June 1991), 118–120.

Winston, Barbara J., *Map and Globe Skills: K–8 Teaching Guide.* Macomb, IL: National Council for Geographic Education, 1984.

Developing Affective Elements of Learning

CHAPTER 13

Objective and Related Focusing Questions

- What affective elements—interests, attitudes, appreciations, values, related behavior—are included in many programs?

- What are core societal values? How do they differ from personal values?

- What strategies and teaching/learning activities can be adapted and used to achieve affective objectives in the social studies?

- What strategies from various approaches to values education can be used to develop values and valuing processes?

- What strategies and activities can be used to develop democratic behavior that is consistent with core societal values?

Affective elements of learning are being given greater attention for several reasons. Democratic citizenship requires understanding of and commitment to such core societal values as human dignity, justice, equality, general welfare, minority protection, respect for people and property, regard for privacy and diversity, and freedom of speech, religion, press, and assembly. Core values are essential to participation in sociocivic affairs. Personal values are different and must be respected; they are used by each of us to make individual choices and decisions related to recreation, purchases, and other personal preferences. Demands for ethics in government highlight the significance of such virtues as honesty, fairness, integrity, respect for rule by law, avoidance of favoritism, self-discipline, regard for the public good, humility, morality, rectitude, and diligence. Resurgent concerns for strong programs of character education include attention to self-discipline, self-control, respect for self and others, feelings of self-esteem, constraints of pursuits of self-interest, ways to find peaceful solutions to problems, cooperation, acceptance of responsibilities, and other basic traits. Programs designed to attain gender equity and eliminate prejudice and discrimination against minority groups underscore the importance of equality of opportunity, willingness to act to achieve equality and justice, fair application of laws and moral principles, eradication of stereotypes, counterstereotyping to show examples contrary to stereotypes, and a commitment to complete and unrestricted application of democratic values. The demands for democratic government by peoples in countries long dominated by communist regimes signal the importance of core values that must never be taken for granted.

Reflective of core values and typical of the democratic person are these behaviors, which each unit should stress: cooperation, responsibility, concern for others, open-mindedness, and creativity. As one teacher stated, "These behaviors are capstone outcomes of instruction." Their development contributes to the nurturance of prosocial behavior (Oliner, 1983) and to learning and living the related beliefs and values that make democracy work. Their extension to the hidden curriculum—learning acquired concurrently with the planned curriculum—helps students apply what they learn in the social studies.

Various strategies may be used to achieve outcomes, as illustrated in later sections of this chapter. An encompassing strategy similar to the decision-making model includes the following phases:

Identify attitudes, values, or appreciations to be developed as issues and topics are studied.

Consider alternative ways to resolve issues or handle problems.

Explore consequences of various alternatives and identify those most beneficial in terms of desired attitudes, values, and appreciations.

Make a judgment in terms of desired outcomes and appraise it in terms of its applicability to other cases.

Integrate the above into basic instruction, as shown in the next section.

Integration of Learning Activities in Basic Instruction

Identifying Objectives

A first step is to note affective objectives in unit and lesson plans, as shown in these examples based on procedures suggested in chapter 1.

> To list and demonstrate ways to show concern for members of one's family
>
> To show appreciation of the contributions of community workers by describing goods and services they produce.
>
> To identify the attitudes and the values of women and men who led the struggle to obtain civil rights
>
> To explain the meaning of values in the Bill of Rights and give examples of their significance in current affairs.
>
> To demonstrate interest in learning about human affairs by finding and sharing current events related to topics of study

Objectives may be written on various degrees of internalization of the affective domain (Krathwohl et al., 1964). For example:

> *Receiving:* to listen to a report on ways to show concern for others
>
> *Responding:* to state feelings aroused while listening to a story
>
> *Valuing:* to state why showing concern for others is important
>
> *Organization:* to show concern for others consistently
>
> *Characterization:* to show concern for others in all situations habitually

Illustrative Learning Activities

Checklist 2.1 in chapter 2 should be used to select learning activities. The selected activities should be used in ways that evoke positive emotional overtones, because attitudes, appreciations, and values are rooted deeply in feelings. The cognitive elements of affective learning need development because understanding the meaning and significance of attitudes and values is essential to effective application of them to human affairs. The following may be adapted for use in various units of study.

Introductory Activities Show a filmstrip, arrange a display of pictures, or call attention to sections in reading center materials that highlight attitudes, appreciations, or values. Discuss a story, dilemma, incident, or news report related to affective objectives. Pose questions or elicit questions from students to focus attention on affective elements, as shown in these examples: How can we show respect for each other in discussion? What attitudes toward work do outstanding workers have? How were equality and justice extended by Martin Luther King, Jr.? What individual responsibilities go along with freedom of speech and press?

Developmental Activities The following examples illustrate how affective and cognitive elements are related, the variety of activities that may be used, and the importance of the teacher's role.

Build a knowledge base that includes understanding of the concepts, beliefs, and appropriate behavior in situations selected for study. For example, justice as fairness and the belief that individual rights must be respected may be clarified and used to develop standards of behavior for use in discussion and in other activities. Knowledge of actions that harm others, the effects of discrimination, and denial of civil rights, along with information on needed corrective measures, may be used to make and weigh proposals for improvement. A desired outcome is reflected in such statements as, "Knowing that, I must act differently," and, "Is that so? Then we must do this."

Use questions that stimulate students to explore reasons for actions and to think about related feelings. Examples are:

Why must rules for discussion be followed? What happens when they are broken? How do you feel when they are broken?

Why was the Underground Railroad started? Who ran it? How must the "passengers" have felt? Why?

How did you feel when you heard the recording of Sojourner Truth's famous speech? Why was it so powerful?

Why was the bus boycott started in Montgomery, Alabama? What did Rosa Parks do? How must she have felt? Why?

A series of questions may be used to move students to a higher level of commitment (Hannah and Michaelis, 1977). For example, after the students have read a selection or have seen a film that highlights responsibility (or some other behavior), group discussion may be guided by questions on these levels of commitment:

Responding level: What examples of responsibility did you find?

Complying level: Why should you carry out responsibilities?

Accepting level: Why should you carry out responsibilities on your own?

Preferring level: Why is it always better to carry out individual responsibilities than not to do so?

Integrating level: Why should you consistently be responsible in all home and school activities?

The discussion may be concluded by having students list specific home and school responsibilities and suggest ways to improve in carrying them out consistently.

Provide role models that students regard highly and can emulate. Teachers, students, community leaders, notable women and men, or significant others may serve as role models. Of key importance is the model provided by teachers. For example, references to minority groups should be made in positive terms, and facial grimaces, jokes, or other indicators of negative attitudes must be avoided. As students move from unit to unit they may be guided to analyze role models that typify exemplary students, community workers, members of minority groups, and present and past individuals who worked for gender equity, civil rights, and fulfillment of other values.

Provide experiences that kindle the imagination and arouse positive feelings. Stories, legends, folk tales, poetry, and other unit-related literature are very helpful in stimulating desirable emotional responses and giving insight into the feelings of others (Stewig and Sebasta, 1989). Also helpful are art and music activities, creative writing, and the making of murals, collages, and displays that reflect values and behavior related to topics of study. Guide students to find and share values and character traits reflected in unit-related art, music, and literary activities.

Provide dramatic activities and role playing in which students take defined roles, identify with others, express positive attitudes, and demonstrate desirable behavior. Guide students to try *new* attitudes and demonstrate ways to handle critical situations. Provide opportunities for analysis of incidents illustrative of negative attitudes, followed by portrayals that demonstrate positive attitudes.

Use community resources and provide for observation of relevant community activities or participation in unit-related events. For example, members of minority, ethnic, or affirmative action groups may be invited to discuss: (1) values of special concern to them, (2) basic values they have in common with others, and (3) actions they are taking to achieve equality and justice for themselves and for others. Holidays, festivals, and commemorations may be observed to clarify customs, traditions, values, achievements, and contributions that are highlighted and the reasons why they are important and should be respected. Explore the significance of flag ceremonies, codes of ethics, the Bill of Rights, the Pledge of Allegiance, pageants, historical shrines and monuments, and special TV and radio programs. Discuss items to include in a code of ethics for public officials, such as honesty, integrity, fairness, humility, no payment for speeches, open-mindedness, respect of all groups, and self-control.

Guide students to discover positive expression of attitudes and appreciations in daily activities and in instructional media. Direct their analysis of situations in which there is marked disparity between the real and the ideal, noting ways to move toward the ideal. Help them identify beliefs and ideals that were and still are important in daily living in the community, the state, the nation, or other lands. For example, students may analyze reasons for immigration in the film *America-Huddled Masses* or in other media, comparing them to reasons for immigration today.

Have students find and discuss both positive and negative attitudes of characters in stories related to unit topics. Discuss the impact of attitudes on interaction with others.

Explore the impact of religious beliefs and values on ways of living in our own and in other lands from early times to the present (Haynes, 1990). For example, students may find and discuss the meaning of the Noble Eightfold Path that includes right views, right resolve, right speech, right action, right livelihood, right effort, right mindfulness, and right concentration. Be descriptive, not prescriptive, in guiding discussion of religions and their impact on behavior; emphasize the point that instruction is *about* religion; and avoid imposition of any beliefs and other actions inconsistent with freedom of religion and separation of church and state.

Provide directed study activities that focus students' attention on affective elements in instructional media, as shown in Charts 13.1 and 13.2.

Guide students to find, discuss, and apply values as they engage in class activities and study topics and issues. For example, equality of justice and opportunity may be considered as fairness in all activities, in case studies and current events that focus on individual and group needs and actions, and in discussions of the contributions of individuals from various ethnic groups who were guided by the ideal of equality for everyone.

Find and Share Examples of These!		
Values	Attitudes	Appreciations

Standards of
  Worth
  Utility
  Quality
	Dispositions to act
	  Positively
	  Neutrally
	  Negatively
		Feelings of
		  Admiration
		  Esteem
		  Respect

Chart 13.1

Define and Give Examples of These!		
Individual Freedoms	Individual Responsibilities	Individual Rights
Expression, worship, conscience	Respect for freedoms and rights of others	Life, liberty, pursuit of happiness
Thought and inquiry	Honesty, tolerance, helpfulness	Dignity, privacy, justice, equality
Assembly, political participation	Self-control and compassion	Due process, private property

Chart 13.2

Encourage students' self-evaluation by asking students to check the following that they *always* do:

___ Disagree courteously

___ Show concern for others

___ Help others

___ Insist on equality for everyone

___ Help resolve conflicts

___ Respect others

Guide students to demonstrate democratic behavior in group activities, to observe examples in school and community activities, to find examples in textbooks and other materials, and to be creative and think of other examples. Have them record their findings on a worksheet such as the one shown in Chart 13.3

Discuss negative examples and have students propose actions that are consistent with high standards; for example, irresponsible behavior in group work should lead to a clarification of rules to guide future activities. Analyses of a lack of teamwork and concern for others can pinpoint specific ways to improve. Reviews of prejudice and bias can reveal the importance of being open-minded and fair in the treatment of individuals and groups.

Provide time for discussion of value conflicts such as environmental needs versus economic goals, individual rights versus the common good, comparable pay for com-

Find and Record Examples of Democratic Behavior				
Democratic Behavior	*Examples of what you do*	*Examples you observe*	*Examples you find in materials*	*Think and add other examples*
Cooperation				
Responsibility				
Open mindedness				
Concern for others				
Creativity				

Chart 13.3

parable worth versus pay based on supply and demand. Also helpful are discussions of such topics as responsibilities that go along with individual freedoms, ways to eliminate stereotypes from our thinking, hardships and satisfactions of civil rights leaders, and the significance today of values expressed in the Declaration of Independence and other basic documents.

Develop understanding of the nature of prejudice and ways to avoid it. Consider stereotypes as they are encountered in units of study, instructional media, and students' experiences. The following illustrative plans may be used to guide individual, small-group, or class study.

Prejudice

Objective:

To define prejudice and state ways to avoid it

Focusing Questions:

What is prejudice? How can it be avoided?

Materials:

Dictionary, textbook *People in the Americas*, filmstrip *Exploding Myths of Prejudice*

Activities:

Complete the following on a separate sheet of paper.

1. Write the meaning of *prejudge* as given in a dictionary.
2. List three prejudgments you have made in the past—for example, a person, a food, or an activity you prejudged.

3. Write the meaning of *prejudice* as given in a dictionary. Note how prejudging is a part of prejudice.

4. After seeing *Exploding Myths of Prejudice,* complete the following:
   Examples of prejudging are _____.
   Myths about prejudice are _____.

5. List three things you can do to avoid prejudice.

6. You meet someone for the first time. List what you want to learn about this person while deciding whether or not to become friends. What prejudgments should you avoid? Why?

7. A person meets you for the first time. List what you want this person to learn about you while deciding whether or not to become friends. What prejudgments should this person avoid? Why?

8. List rules you and other students can follow to avoid prejudice in the future.

Stereotypes

View a film such as *Stereotypes: African Girl Malabi* after listing students' responses to these questions:

> What do you think Africans look like? What do they eat? How do they dress? What are their houses like?
> Where did you get your images or ideas of Africans?

After showing the film, ask students to compare their responses to what they actually saw in the film. Which comparisons are radically different? How could such false ideas about Africans have been learned?

Conclude by discussing how oversimplified mental images of others can lead to wrong ideas. Ask students to think of ways they can find out if their images of other people are accurate—for example, seeing films, reading about them, looking for individual differences, and evaluating statements for bias.

Which Statements are Biased? What Stereotypes Can You Find?

Evaluate these statements in terms of fairness, equality, and concern for others. Which ones are fair? Which are not? Why? Be prepared to discuss the stereotypes you identify.

> Members of *that* group are not cooperative.
> Members of any group are not all the same.
> People in *that* country are not industrious.
> Housework should be done by women.
> Their standard of living would be higher if they worked harder.
> Some teachers like male principals better than female principals.
> Male principals handle discipline better than female principals.

Have students investigate and report on actions of women and men to advance civil rights and achieve gender equity; reasons people from diverse lands have come here and contributions they have made to our culture; and how human dignity and rights have been negated through discrimination, persecutions, the Holocaust, and apartheid. Include attention to discrimination related to age, ethnicity, national origin, race, and sex; the impact of discrimination on employment, housing, voting, and education; and progress that has been made and steps still needed to eliminate discrimination. Guide students to make booklets or scrapbooks that contain pictures, drawings, reports, and news items related to holidays, notable persons, issues of special concern, and other value-laden topics.

Use individual and group guidance techniques to help individuals overcome negative attitudes and to redirect their behavior into positive channels. Individual counseling and small-group discussion of ways to abide by class standards and demonstrate respect for others should be used as needed without hesitation. Direct attention should be given to behavior that is expected and how the student must proceed to meet the stated expectations.

Concluding Activities Desired affective outcomes should be highlighted as students share reports, make summaries, complete booklets, present programs, and discuss main ideas. For example, new interests expressed by students, attitudes and values of civil rights leaders, helpful services provided by public and private agencies, progress in reducing discrimination, and ways to eliminate stereotypes and prejudice are key learnings to clinch in concluding activities.

Provide activities that focus attention on affective outcomes. For example, involve students in the making of summary charts with such titles as Contributions of Community Workers, Rights and Related Responsibilities, A Comparison of Values in Our Country and China, and Values Held by Notable Women and Men. Have students prepare entries for a dictionary of attitudes, appreciations, and values that include definitions and examples. Ask students to dramatize or role-play selected incidents to demonstrate desirable attitudes, application of core values, and democratic behaviors.

Interrelate concluding and evaluating activities by asking students to complete sentences that express desirable attitudes and appreciations, as shown by these examples:

We are dependent on farmers for _____.

A responsibility I must assume to assure others' property rights in school is ____.

The customs of students who are refugees from other lands must be respected because _____.

I can promote gender equity in school by _____.

Evaluating Activities Observe students' comments, questions, expression of feelings, and participation in learning activities, using Checklist 13.1 as a guide.

Conduct evaluative class and small-group discussions, posing such questions as:

What topics were most interesting? Why? Least interesting? Why?

Which topics should be given further study?

Checklist 13–1
CHECKLIST FOR OBSERVATION OF AFFECTIVE OUTCOMES

Interests

_____ Expresses a desire to _____. (learn more about a topic, continue an activity, do an individual project, etc.)

_____ Raises questions about _____. (where to find more on a topic, a project to undertake, a person to investigate, etc.)

_____ Volunteers and participates actively in _____. (discussion, small-group activities, preparation of reports, etc.)

Attitudes

_____ Demonstrates a disposition to act positively toward _____. (social studies activities, members of minority groups, etc.)

_____ Frequently and consistently states _____. (preferences for learning activities, likes and dislikes, opinions, etc.)

_____ Responds consistently to such statements as _____. (I am for _____, I am against _____, I favor _____, etc.)

Appreciations

_____ Expresses high esteem, regard, or gratitude for _____. (contributions of civil rights leaders, Bill of Rights, etc.)

_____ Shows appreciation by spontaneously making such statements as _____ ("That was really important!" "She worked hard to get voting rights for women." "I'm glad they didn't quit!" etc.)

_____ Describes in detail the contributions of _____. (notable women and men, early civilizations to our culture, etc.)

Values

_____ Defines in own words the meaning of such values as _____. (equality, justice, privacy, minority protection, etc.)

_____ Uses values in decision making and gives reasons for _____. (choices, decisions, judgments, rating of alternatives, etc.)

_____ Describes adherence or nonadherence to values in _____. (current and past events, topics of study, etc.)

Character Traits

_____ Finds and shares examples of such traits as _____ (self-discipline, self-control, etc.)

_____ Consistently demonstrates such traits as _____ (honesty, fairness, concern for others, etc.)

_____ Urges others to act in accordance with such traits as _____ (kindness, diligence, humility, etc.)

Democratic Behavior

_____ Defines and gives examples of such behavior as _____. (cooperation, responsibility, concern for others, etc.)

_____ Demonstrates democratic behavior in _____. (class discussion, committee work, group projects, etc.)

_____ Finds and describes examples of democratic behavior in _____. (school and community activities, instructional media, etc.)

What ideas did you find on ways to obtain gender equity in school and community activities? How will both girls and boys benefit?

What attitudes are needed to assure success?

What contributions did civil rights leaders make to the protection of minority rights? To general welfare? To extension of equality and justice?

Provide rating devices such as the following and those discussed in the next chapter.

HOW DO YOU RATE YOURSELF ON THE ITEMS BELOW?

Write A for very good, B for good, C for fair, D for poor, F for very poor.

___ Respect for others	___ Sensitive to others' needs	___ Being honest
___ Interest in others	___ Fair judgment of others	___ Being frank
___ Listening to others	___ Cooperating with others	___ Helping others
___ Sticking to the job	___ Thinking before acting	___ Admitting errors

---

Strategies for Developing Values

Several guidelines are followed to nurture the growth of key values. Valuing strategies are embedded in regular instruction as decision-making and critical thinking skills are applied to issues that students comprehend. The meaning of value concepts and the significance of values in human behavior are clarified. Indoctrination, imposition of values, and one-sided interpretation are avoided. A reflective stance and an open atmosphere are maintained to stimulate students to think freely and critically about conflicting choices.

Multiple approaches are used so that instruction can be adapted to fit issues and individual and group needs. For example, direct instruction may be used to teach core democratic values. Clarification strategies may be used to help students explore personal values and positions on issues in past and current events. Moral reasoning may be used to analyze what should be done by one facing conflicting choices. Rational analysis may be used when information can be gathered and used to make judgments, choices, or decisions. Action learning may be used to enable students to undertake projects designed to implement value decisions.

Direct Instruction

Modeling, reasoned persuasion, behavior modification, and specific suggestions are illustrative of direct approaches to values education.

Modeling Models are presented and discussed to provide good examples of such valued behavior as fairness, responsibility, respect for others, and courage in the face of adversity. Members of the community, exemplary students, or the teacher may serve as models. Also used as models are outstanding athletes, film and TV stars, characters in stories, notable women and men, and individuals from ethnic and minority groups. Students are asked to find and share good examples and to criticize poor ones. Commendation is given to students who follow good examples and who set good examples for others. Study guides may be used to guide students' search for character traits and virtues in literary and other sources, as shown by the following example.

WHICH VIRTUES WERE DEMONSTRATED BY PEOPLE IN OUR UNIT?

___ Self-discipline	___ Cooperation	___ Open-mindedness	___ Morality	___ Faith
___ Self-control	___ Fairness	___ Kindness	___ Loyalty	___ Hope
___ Self-respect	___ Honesty	___ Civility	___ Rationality	___ Charity
___ Respect for others	___ Integrity	___ Humility	___ Fortitude	___ Modesty
___ Concern for others	___ Patience	___ Empathy	___ Rectitude	___ Fidelity
___ Responsibility	___ Diligence	___ Perseverance	___ Temperance	___ Piety
___ Other: _____				

Reasoned Persuasion Valid reasons for accepting and living by such values as human dignity, justice, and concern for others are analyzed with students. Class discussions of issues are held to reveal how consideration of underlying value conflicts improves the making of sound decisions and judgments. Small-group discussions are held to consider how such values as respect for others and fairness can be applied to specific problems that have arisen in committee or other activities. Individual conferences are held with students who need specific help in behaving in accord with such values as respect for others and group welfare. Films, stories, and other materials are used to explore the importance of accepting and living by such democratic ideals as individual dignity, the general welfare, and equality for all.

Behavior Modification The following illustrate procedures for developing behavior that is consistent with desired values.

State an objective: Ben is to show respect for others in discussion by listening to others and not ridiculing their comments.

State a criterion: Respect must be shown in all discussions.

Select a procedure: Use praise for reinforcement of positive behavior and removal from discussion to inhibit negative behavior.

Clarify and apply the procedure: Discuss these procedures with Ben so that he fully understands his role in discussion. Give praise or remove Ben as warranted by his behavior.

Evaluate and repeat procedure if necessary: Discuss improvement in behavior and ways to make further improvement, giving praise as it is earned and repeating the procedure as needed to achieve the objective.

Specific Suggestions At times students may be told directly to adhere to standards, behave in accord with values, and consider the consequences of not doing so. Appeals to conscience and following the Golden Rule may be suggested to get students to think more deeply about what is right or wrong in a given situation. Students may be directed to limit choices to those that are consistent with stated values.

Planned Questioning Strategies

Three strategies from the Taba Curriculum Project are closely directed by the teacher (Wallen and others, 1969). The first one (Chart 13.4) helps students to clarify feelings of others and to identify with them. The second one helps students identify values in events and the reasons that underlie action in events. The third one is action-oriented and focuses on what should be done to deal with a problem. All three can be adapted for use in units at various grade levels. They can be applied to past and current events, incidents in stories, case studies, and problems faced by people under study.

What people and events are honored here? What values are reflected by the building of monuments such as these? Social Studies Workshop, University of California, Berkeley

Clarifying Feelings

Procedure	Focusing Questions	Illustrative Application
Recall and clarify the event.	→ What is the problem? What happened? What did they do?	→ What promises did treaty signers make to the Indians?
Infer possible feelings.	→ How do you think they (he, she) felt? Why might they feel that way?	→ How did the Indians feel when the promises were broken? Why?
Infer the feelings of other persons.	→ How did others feel about it? The same? Differently? Why?	→ How did settlers feel? Why? How did others feel? Why?
Relate to experiences of students.	→ Has something like that ever happened to you? How did you feel? Why?	→ Have promises to you ever been broken? How would you have felt if you had been an Indian? Why? A settler? Why?

Identifying Values in Events

Procedure	Focusing Questions	Illustrative Application
Clarify the facts.	→ What is the situation? What happened?	→ What did the film show was happening to Indian lands?
Identify main reasons.	→ Why did it happen? What reasons can you think of?	→ Why were settlers moving into Indian territory?
Infer values from the reasons.	→ What do the reasons indicate is important to them?	→ What was most important to the Indians? To the settlers?
Identify possible student action and reasons.	→ What would you do in the same situation? Why?	→ What do you think should have been done? Why?
Identify student values from reasons.	→ How does this show what is important to you?	→ How does your view show what is important to you?

Analyzing Problems

Procedure	Focusing Questions	Illustrative Application
Clarify the problem.	→ What is the problem? Issue? Difficulty?	→ How can we save energy at home and in school?
Identify alternative solutions and reasons for them.	→ What should be done? Why? What else might be done? Why?	→ What should be done? How can waste be prevented?
Identify strengths, weaknesses, and possible reactions.	→ Which is the best solution? What might the reaction be to each one?	→ Which proposals are best? Which will be supported?
Relate to students' experiences.	→ Have you ever had a problem like this one? What did you do?	→ Which have been tried before? What did you do to help?
Evaluate past experience.	→ As you look back, was that a reasonable thing to do? Why?	→ What worked best? Would you do it again? Why or why not?
Consider alternatives and reasons for them.	→ Is there anything you would do differently? Why?	→ What might be done differently? What might work better? Why?

Chart 13.4

Value Clarification Strategies

Strategies in this approach are designed to help students clarify personal values in an atmosphere that encourages students to respond freely. Students have the right to pass and are encouraged to respond honestly and to avoid comments that inhibit the expression of others. A *value* is defined as something chosen freely, prized and affirmed, and acted on repeatedly (Raths et al., 1978).

Many of the strategies can be adapted for use in social studies units to move beyond the clarification of personal values. The guiding principle is to apply them to value-laden topics in units and current affairs. In all strategies, taking the role of teacher-therapist, giving the impression that all values and views are of equal worth, and taking moral relativism to an extreme should be avoided. The following examples are adapted from Raths et al. (1978), Simon (1972), and Hendricks (1984).

Clarifying Questions Nonjudgmental questions are posed to stimulate students to think about values they hold and why they hold them:

> Why do you feel (think, act) that way? How long have you felt that way? How do others feel about it? Why might some feel differently?

> Can you tell what you mean in other words? How might you explain your decision to others? Is this what you mean? (The teacher repeats or rephrases a student's comment.) Can you give an example?

> What alternatives have you considered? What are possible consequences? What may happen if you do that? What might others do in your situation? Why?

> Why is it so important? How does it compare in importance with other actions you might take? How much do you really value it?

> What might you do if you were in their (her, his) situation? Why? What other actions might you take? Which would be most desirable? Why?

Value Sheets Value sheets provoke thinking about value concepts, such as cooperation, friendship, concern for others, and fairness, or about value-laden topics that arise in units of study. They range in content from a single provocative statement to a paragraph or two on a problem, an issue, or an incident. Sometimes a picture, cartoon, part of a film, or some other resource is presented to stir thinking. The presentation is followed by directions or questions that call for choosing, prizing, or acting, as shown in these examples:

A Word to the Wise Is Enough! (Benjamin Franklin)

What does this saying mean to you? What do you think it meant to patriots during the Revolutionary War? What do you think it meant to Tories? What do you think it meant to those who were not sure which side to choose? In what situations can it be used today? How can you use it in school and at home?

If You Were a Colonist

Imagine you were living in New England during colonial times. How important do you think the items listed below would have been? Rate each one from 1 to 5, with 1 for the most important, 2 for the next, and so on.

_____Health	_____Wealth	_____Hard work
_____Patriotism	_____Peace	_____Strict laws
_____Religious freedom	_____Education	_____Family life

Circle the one you think would be most important of all. Write a reason for choosing it: _____
_____

Underline the one you think would be least important. Write a reason for choosing it: _____
_____

A value sheet is useful in instruction designed to develop democratic values and behavior. An objective is noted and questions and activities are planned to attain it, as shown below.

Open-mindedness

Objective

To define open-mindedness and identify ways to be open-minded in social studies activities

Introduction

Ask students to read the following value sheet.

Open-Mindedness

Read these definitions and be prepared to ask any questions you have about their meaning.

"Showing fairness and impartiality."
"Considering others' points of view."
"Being broadminded and reasonable."
"Weighing the *pros* and *cons* of proposals."

Development

Respond to students' questions to clarify the meaning of each definition.
After discussing each definition, ask: What should we include in a definition that we can use in class activities?

Conclusion

Have groups of four to five students prepare definitions. Ask each group to report its definition. Discuss good ideas in each one and guide the class to make a definition that includes the best elements.

Discuss how the definition can be applied to the following:

Committee work	Preparing reports	Analyzing issues
Discussion	Making decisions	Planning a project

Evaluation

Ask students to note how they will be open-minded when

1. discussing current events.
2. choosing a committee.
3. giving a report.
4. discussing reports of others.

Rankings and Ratings Values may be identified, surveyed, and compared, as shown in these examples.

How Do You Rank English Settlements in These Places?

Write 1 for the settlement you think was best, 2 for the next best, and so on. Write a reason for your first and last choices.

_____Boston	_____Charleston	_____Jamestown
_____New York	_____Providence	_____Savannah

Reason for 1: _____

Reason for 6: _____

How Important Were These to Early Settlers in Our State?

Mark each item as follows: 3, most important; 2, important; 1, least important.

_____Food	_____Health	_____Family life
_____Clothing	_____Wealth	_____Education
_____Shelter	_____Happiness	_____Law and order

How Important Are These in Our State Today?

Mark each item as follows: 3, most important; 2, important; 1, least important.

_____Food _____Health _____Family life
_____Clothing _____Wealth _____Education
_____Shelter _____Happiness _____Law and order

Which ones did you rate the same in early times and now? Why?
Which did you rate differently in early times and now? Why?

How Do You Rate Yourself?

Mark each item as follows: 5, very good; 4, good; 3, fair; 2, poor; 1, very poor.

_____1. Showing respect for all students
_____2. Considering new ways to do things
_____3. Contributing ideas during discussion
_____4. Being a helpful committee member
_____5. Being the chairperson of a committee

Logs and Diaries These devices are useful for recording valued activities, learning, or other items. They may be used throughout a unit or for a single activity. They are most useful when students' attention is directed to specific items, as shown in these examples:

My Social Studies Learning Log

Name: _____Date: _____

I learned _____.
I was puzzled by _____.
I liked _____.
I disliked _____.
The next thing I need to do is _____.
I rate my performance to be _____.

Items for Your Diary on Our State Unit

_____Contributions of notable women and men, past and present
_____Values and concerns of ethnic and minority groups
_____Main ideas about key events, geography, and government
_____Current changes and possible consequences of them
_____Roles and responsibilities of officials and other adults
_____Plans for the future and action needed to implement them
_____Other items you believe to be important

Other Strategies Other activities range from defining value concepts and putting one-self in the place of others to taking a stand on issues and weighing alternatives. All of the following may be adapted to fit various topics of study:

Cooperation

Cooperation means _____.

I can cooperate in discussion by _____
_____

I can cooperate better on committees by _____
_____

WHICH DO YOU ALWAYS DO?

___Show respect for others ___Work for equality for everyone ___Correct bias and prejudice

___Show concern for others' welfare ___Seek justice for all ___Enjoy helping others

___Carry individual and group responsibilities ___Keep promises ___Do fair share of group work

___Display virtues: ___honesty ___fairness ___self-control ___cooperation

___diligence

What Do These Value Concepts Mean?

Concern for others means _____.

Being a good friend means _____.

Justice under law means _____.

Gender equity means _____.

If I Were, of If I Had Been

If I were governor of out state, the first thing I would do to assure gender equity is
_____

If I had been one of the first settlers in our state, three wishes I would have made and reasons for them are:

1. _____

Reason: _____

2. _____

Reason: _____

3. _____

Reason: _____

Feeling Best

I feel best in discussion when _____.
Children in colonial times felt best when _____.
Teachers feel best when _____.

Make a Shield for a Notable Person

Draw a shield and divide it into six spaces. Print the following in the spaces: (1) the person's name, (2) field of work, (3) main contribution, (4) two wishes the person might make today, (5) one quotation, and (6) a fitting motto.

Make Three Wishes

For our community: _____

_____

For our state: _____

_____

For our country: _____

_____

Where Do You Stand on These Issues?

More Wilderness Area in Our State

Yes . . . . No

Stopping Acid Rain

Act now . . . . Do more studies

Listing and Weighing Alternatives

List alternatives	Should try it	Should study it	Should forget it
1. _____	_____	_____	_____
2. _____	_____	_____	_____
3. _____	_____	_____	_____

Moral Reasoning

The goal is to foster moral development by guiding students to develop progressively higher levels of moral reasoning based on a growing conception of justice (Kohlberg, 1984; Galbraith and Jones, 1976). Conceptions of justice and types of reasoning have been structured in terms of these levels and stages of moral development:

Preconventional level: Most 4- to 10-year-olds base reasoning on consequences of action. Stage 1 is characterized by a punishment and obedience orientation. Physical consequences determine goodness or badness, and justice may be viewed as "an eye for an eye." Stage 2 is characterized by an instrumental orientation, an exchange of favors, and "you scratch my back and I'll scratch yours."

Conventional level: Most 10- to 18-year-olds and many adults base reasoning on conformity and loyalty. Stage 3 is characterized by an interpersonal concordance orientation, conforming to get approval, and "being a good boy or a nice girl." Stage 4 is marked by a law-and-order orientation, respect for authority, loyalty to family and country, and "doing one's duty."

Postconventional level: Some adults base reasoning on ethical principles. Stage 5 is marked by a social contract and legalistic orientation. Right action is judged by adherence to contracts, general rights, and "a legal point of view." Stage 6 is marked by a universal ethical principle orientation and is achieved by very few. Moral reasoning is based on self-chosen universal principles of justice that "respect the dignity of all human beings as individuals."

Teaching Strategy A moral dilemma is presented to students orally or through a reading, a filmstrip, or another medium to highlight conflicting value choices. Here is an example.

What Should Jed Do with the Nuggets?

Jed's father has had poor luck prospecting for gold. They have no food and all their money is gone. Another prospector has "hit it rich." As he hurriedly loads a bag of nuggets on his horse, he does not notice that a few nuggets fall from the bag. *Should* Jed take the nuggets to his father or return them to the owner? Why or why not?

After brief discussion of the dilemma, students are asked to take a position and give reasons for it. If there is little disagreement, more information may be given. For example, other miners will ask where the nuggets were obtained or Jed's father will repay the rich prospector as soon as possible.

Small-group discussion (four to five students) is provided next so that students can analyze reasons and prepare questions about reasons, both for and against, for use in class discussion.

Finally, reasons are critically examined in class discussion, guided by such questions as:

What are reasons for keeping the nuggets? For returning them?

What questions does each group have?

Which is more important—helping one's family or not taking something that belongs to others?

What if Jed's father had "struck it rich" and lost the nuggets?

What might the consequences be if Jed keeps the nuggets? What if everyone kept things that someone lost?

Follow-up activities may be provided—for example, finding related examples, writing a solution that resolves the dilemma, or creating a dilemma story on the same issue or another one.

Group Discussion Emphasis must be placed on what the central character or group *should* do, not *would* do. A discussion of what a person *would* do shifts the focus from moral reasoning to an analysis of factors involved in predicting behavior. Students' moral reasoning can be improved by posing probe questions such as these:

Perception-checking questions to clarify the issue and identify points of agreement and disagreement: Are there questions about what is happening? What choice(s) does the person have?

Issue-related questions to clarify the issue: Should property rights be respected? Why or why not? What family obligation does Jed have? Why?

Interissue questions to focus on value conflicts: Which is more important—family welfare or property rights? Why?

Role-switch questions to consider various points of view: What if Jed's father had lost the nuggets? Should the finder return them? Why?

Universal consequences questions to consider broad implications: What if everyone did this? What might the consequences be? Why?

Creating Dilemmas Teachers and students may prepare dilemmas after several have been analyzed. Identify issues that require an individual or a group to make conflicting value choices: telling the truth versus shielding a friend, sharing with others versus maintaining one's property rights, individual freedom versus obedience to authority, self-interest versus the good of the group, and keeping promises versus changing one's mind for personal gain.

Realistic issues may be identified in a unit, current event, or school activity, For example:

Should May tell on her friend who took an extra cup of water after the wagon train leader ordered everyone to a set limit until they reached the next water hole? Why or why not?

Should Susan join a demonstration to demand comparable pay for comparable worth at the factory where her mother works and may be laid off if the demand is met? Why or why not?

Should June, who is on probation because of being late to school, take time to help a blind person cross a busy street? She has been told that she cannot serve as class president if she is late again. What should June do? Why?

Alterations or additions to the preceding list may be prepared to get a division of opinion that will stimulate group discussion. Finally, probe questions are prepared to guide discussion and improve reasoning.

Rational Analysis

A primary goal of rational analysis is to apply critical thinking and decision-making skills to value-laden issues. This approach is used by many teachers because it employs skills that are used on many social studies topics. It is especially useful when information can be collected to support a value judgment or decision.

Teaching Strategy The following steps are adapted from the model presented by Metcalf (1971):

Clarify and define the problem or the issue: What is the problem? What is the main issue? What values are in conflict? What terms need to be defined? What is to be judged?

Gather information: What facts are available? What other facts are needed? Which are facts and which are opinions?

Assess the information: How can the facts be checked? Which are based on evidence? Which are unsupported? What do experts say?

Sift out relevant information: Which facts are related to the problem or the issue? Which are needed to make a value judgment or decision?

Make a tentative judgment or decision: What is a reasonable judgment or decision? Is it adequately supported by the facts? What are sound reasons for it?

Appraise the judgment or decision: Does it apply to other cases? Is it consistent with similar judgments or decisions? Does it apply to everyone, including ourselves? What are possible consequences if it is adopted universally?

Action Learning

A primary goal of this approach is to enable students to act on their values in the classroom, the school, and the community. It is most useful when students can be involved in such projects as making collections for the needy, helping the elderly, sharing scrapbooks with housebound children and adults, making holiday cards for absent students, and undertaking other activities that show concern for others or some other basic value. As with rational analysis, action learning puts basic thinking and decision-making skills to use.

Teaching Strategy The main difference between this and other strategies is the special emphasis on deciding whether or not to act; if the decision is to act, *action and evaluation follow,* as shown below.

Clarify the need or the problem: What is the problem? What, if anything, should we do about it?

Consider information and take a position: What are the facts? What additional facts are needed? What is our position on taking action?

Decide whether or not to act: How can we help? Will our involvement be a contribution? What are possible consequences?

Plan and carry out the action: What steps should we take individually and as a group? What materials are needed? Carry out the plan, making revisions as needed.

Evaluate action and project future steps: Which procedures were most effective? Which were least effective? How can they be improved? What should we do in the future?

Notice that the action learning strategy is similar to the problem-solving and decision-making models. Action learning is not limited to school and community projects; it can take place in the classroom as students take action to secure gender equity, promote adherence to group rules, and demonstrate democratic behavior in group activities.

Questions, Activities, and Evaluation

1. State two affective objectives for a unit of your choice and list activities you might use to achieve them. Refer to the activities noted in this chapter and in the checklist of activities in chapter 2.

2. Examine a textbook and note examples of values, appreciations, and other affective elements. What questions might you use to guide study and discussion of them? What teaching strategy might you use? Make a plan to show how you would use it.

3. Prepare a list of ways to develop democratic behavior in a unit of your choice. Make a worksheet similar to the one presented in this chapter, including examples for each behavior of: (a) what students can do, (b) what students can observe, (c) what students can find in materials.

4. Check your position on the following and discuss it with colleagues.

	Yes	No	?
a. The schools should leave instruction on values to the family and the church.	___	___	___
b. The schools must develop core democratic values, such as justice and equality.	___	___	___
c. The schools should teach students *how* to value, not *what* to value.	___	___	___
d. The social studies program should help students progress to higher levels of moral development.	___	___	___
e. If programs of character education are to succeed, basic values and virtues must be taught in school.	___	___	___
f. All of the above should be rejected.	___	___	___
g. A better point of view is _____			

References

ASCD Panel on Moral Education, "Moral Education in the Life of the School," *Educational Leadership,* 45 (May 1988), 4–8.

Benninga, Jacques S. *Moral, Character, and Civic Education in the Elementary School.* New York: Teachers College Press, 1991.

Butts, R. Freeman, *The Morality of Democratic Citizenship.* Calabasas, CA: Center for Civic Education, 1988. Chapter 4, twelve core values.

"Citizenship and Ethics," *Social Studies and the Young Learner,* 1 (September/October 1988), 3–21. Special section; articles on ethics, economic reasoning and values education, and citizenship.

Ellis, Arthur K., Teaching and Learning Elementary Social Studies (4th ed.). Needham Heights, MA: Allyn & Bacon, 1991. Chapter 13.

Galbraith, Ronald E., and Thomas M. Jones, *Moral Reasoning.* Minneapolis: Greenhaven Press, 1976. A handbook with sample dilemmas and techniques.

Haynes, Charles C., ed., "Taking Religion Seriously in the Social Studies," *Social Education,* 54 (September 1990), 276–301, 306–10. Special section.

Hannah, Larry S., and John U. Michaelis, *A Comprehensive Framework for Instructional Objectives.* Reading, MA: Addison-Wesley, 1977. Chapter on attitudes and values.

Hendricks, William, *Values.* Stevensville, MI: Educational Service, 1984. Activities for values clarification.

Jarrett, James L. *The Teaching of Values.* New York: Routledge, 1991. Key values and attitudes.

Kohlberg, Lawrence, *Psychology of Moral Development.* New York: Harper & Row, 1984. Detailed treatment.

Metcalf, Lawrence E., ed., *Values Education* (41st yearbook). Washington, DC: National Council for the Social Studies, 1971.

Nucci, Larry, ed., *Moral Development and Character Education.* National Society for the Study of Education. Chicago: University of Chicago Press, 1989. Essays on various approaches.

Oliner, Pearl M., "Putting Compassion and Caring into Social Studies Classrooms," *Social Education,* 47 (April 1983), 273–76. How to develop prosocial behavior.

Raths, Louis E., Merrill Harmin, and Sydney B. Simon, *Values and Teaching* (2nd ed.). Columbus, OH: Chas E. Merrill, 1978. Concrete suggestions.

Simon, Sidney B., Leland W. Howe, and Howard Kirschenbaum, *Values Clarification.* New York: Hart Publishing, 1972. Collection of practical strategies.

"Special Section: Reducing Prejudice," *Social Education,* 52 (April/May 1988), 264–91, 302–3.

Stewig, John W., and Sam L. Sebasta, *Using Literature in the Elementary Classroom.* Urbana, IL: National Council of Teachers of English, 1989.

Superka, Douglas, Christine Ahrens, and Judith E. Hedstrom, *Values Education Sourcebook.* Boulder, CO: Social Science Education Consortium, 1976. Chapters on approaches.

Wallen, Norman E., et al., *Final Report: The Taba Curriculum Project in the Social Studies.* Reading, MA: Addison-Wesley, 1969. Valuing strategies.

Evaluating Students' Learning

CHAPTER 14

Objective and Related Focusing Questions

To present guidelines and specific procedures for evaluating cognitive and affective outcomes of instruction:

- What guidelines are used to evaluate learning in the social studies?

- What informal techniques and devices are useful in appraising cognitive and affective outcomes of instruction?

- How can student self-evaluation and peer evaluation be guided to improve learning?

- How can charts and checklists be prepared and used to appraise performance and products?

- What principles and procedures can be used to prepare test items and use published tests?

A primary function of evaluation is to make decisions about ways to provide instruction that enhance the achievement of social studies objectives. The evaluation process includes stating objectives in measurable form, collecting related evidence, and using the evidence to make instructional decisions. Diagnostic evaluation is used to identify individual and group needs. Formative evaluation is done during instruction to appraise ongoing progress. Summative evaluation is done at the end of a unit or term to appraise the attainment of stated objectives.

Students' learning may be appraised at local, state, and national levels. Local assessment is most useful to teachers because it is directly related to the program of instruction. State assessment programs stress basic skills, although a few include social studies or citizenship. The National Assessment of Educational Progress has included U.S. history, civics, and geography.[1] Information on state and national assessments, available in local school districts, may be checked for sample objectives, illustrative test items, and relative achievement of students.

Criterion-referenced measurement is used to determine the extent to which defined objectives have been met. Norm-referenced measurement may be used to compare the achievement of students with that of a large sample in terms of percentile, grade-equivalent, or other scores. Emphasis has been given to criterion-referenced measurement in recent years.

Guidelines for Evaluation

Plan and conduct evaluation systematically. First, determine the purpose. Second, select the technique(s) to be used. Third, collect assessment data and judge the results. Fourth, use the results to make a decision on what to do to improve teaching and learning. Fifth, implement the decision and continue the evaluation process.

Consider all objectives. Knowledge, skills, attitudes and values, and participation may vary in emphasis, but none of them should be neglected. For example, specifications for assessment of unit outcomes might include test items on knowledge and skills, a brief questionnaire on attitudes, and a checklist on participation—all related to unit objectives.

Evaluate continuously. Use diagnostic or preassessment to identify individual and class needs. Make a needs assessment by determining the gap between current status of students and the desired status. Use formative assessment during instruction and make adjustments. Use summative assessment to determine whether objectives have been achieved.

Integrate evaluation and instruction. This is vital in the social studies because the many different learning activities provide useful evidence of achievement. For example, discussion, reporting, and committee activities can be observed to assess use of concepts and expression of attitudes. Curriculum alignment should be checked systematically to be sure there is a match between what is taught and what is evaluated.

[1]National Assessment of Educational Progress, Educational Testing Service, Princeton, NJ 08541. Request *NAEP Newsletter* and the list of available reports. For a summary of findings for 20 years, see *America's Challenge: Accelerating Academic Achievement,* 1990.

Select appropriate techniques and devices. Observation, discussion, charts, portfolios of students' work, and checklists are helpful. Computer testing, teacher-made tests, and test items in textbooks and workbooks are related to instruction and can be modified to fit unit objectives. Self-reports such as attitude questionnaires and value scales, logs or diaries and videos of activities, completed task cards, learning progress charts or maps, quality circles, and anecdotal records or behavior journals that focus on a student are appropriate at times.

Provide for student self-evaluation and constructive peer evaluation in addition to teacher evaluation. Skill in self-evaluation is essential to the development of increasing self-direction needed for effective citizenship and lifelong learning. Constructive peer evaluation adds a valuable dimension to the appraisal of students' learning. Checklists, rating forms, and other devices may be used to develop students' evaluation skills. Differences among self-evaluations, peer evaluations, and teacher evaluations should be discussed to find ways to improve evaluation procedures.

Use assessment data constructively. Observation, discussion, charts, and checklists yield data that can be used immediately to modify instruction, provide feedback, and enhance learning. Summaries of data from tests, portfolios of work samples, observation, and other appraisals should be used to determine grades, report to parents, and implement the accountability program in accord with school district policies.

Assessment Techniques and Devices

Observation by the Teacher

A most useful technique is daily observation of students as they participate in discussion, committees, and other social studies activities. Assessment may be made of interests, attitudes, work habits, acceptance of responsibility, and other behavior. For example, information on students' attitudes can be obtained by looking for the following:

1. Positive or negative statements about a person, a group, an activity, an object, or an organization
2. Number of times reference is made to the above in positive or negative terms
3. Willingness or unwillingness to work or interact with an individual or a group or to defend or help others in time of need
4. Expressions of likes, dislikes, preferences, and opinions regarding individuals, groups, and activities

Checklists are used to focus observation (and student self-evaluation). For example, Checklists 14.1 and 14.2 contain specific behavior to observe and are easy to use in a variety of situations. Columns containing students' names may be added to the right to keep a record of the behavior of members of a committee, other groups, or the class. Other examples are presented later in this chapter.

Items to include in checklists and charts may be identified through teacher observation. For example, after observing the use of sexist language in discussion, one

---

Checklist 14–1
APPRAISAL OF OPEN-MINDEDNESS

Rate as follows: 1, good; 2, fair; 3, poor.

____ 1. Considers differing ideas
____ 2. Tries new ways to do things
____ 3. Puts facts before feelings
____ 4. Seeks all sides of issues
____ 5. Willing to change views
____ 6. Judges others fairly

Checklist 14–2
APPRAISAL OF WORK IN SMALL GROUPS

Rate as follows: 1, good; 2, fair; 3, poor.

____ 1. Keeps the task in mind
____ 2. Cooperates with the leader
____ 3. Does not disturb others
____ 4. Is courteous to others
____ 5. Does a fair share of the work
____ 6. Helps find ways to improve

---

teacher guided the class to develop a chart for future evaluation that included these items: (1) Use terms such as *active* and *strong* to describe both women and men; (2) give examples of both men and women when discussing notable people; (3) describe roles and contributions of both women and men in discussions of historic events; (4) use terms such as *fire fighter, chairperson,* and *homemaker* instead of *fireman, chairman,* and *housewife;* and (5) include examples of women in leadership positions along with those of men.

Several guidelines may be followed to improve the quality of observation. First, focus on a few students, looking for specific behaviors, as illustrated in the checklists and charts in this chapter. Second, do not be influenced by overall impression of a student (the halo effect). Third, look for both positive and negative instances of behavior, being sure not to be caught in the trap of fault finding. Fourth, note reactions later so that observation will not be obscured by personal feelings and data may be interpreted as objective as possible.

A point to keep in mind when interpreting observations is that similar types of behavior may not be indicative of similar learning. For example, some students may help others because of concern for others; other students may help because they want to move in on the activity. Some students may carry out a responsibility because it is line with group plans, while others may do it merely to obtain approval of the teacher. By and large, however, most observed behavior can be interpreted at face value when students are engaged in meaningful activities.

Group Discussion

Discussion is widely used to assess daily activities, unit projects, use of concepts, attitudes, thinking and reporting skills, and other aspects of instruction. Standards can be applied and revised, all students can be involved, students' self-evaluation can be improved, and the teacher can direct attention to key objectives. Outcomes for both the students and the teacher include knowledge of progress, strengths and weaknesses, and next steps to take.

Questions that focus attention on unit objectives are needed to guide discussion. For example, questions for community studies are: What special features make our community different from others we have studied? Why do you think so many early communities were located near waterways? Who can describe the different zones in a city? In which of the cities we have studied would you most like to live? Why? Sample questions for a unit on regions are: How are regions defined? What characteristics might be used to define regions of our country? Which regions are best for agriculture? Why? Which ones are most densely populated? Why? Other examples may be found in the lists of focusing questions presented in chapters 6 and 7.

Also helpful are questions that require students to state what comes next and what is missing:

Cover part of a map, a picture, or a diagram and ask, "What is covered?" or "What is missing?"

Cover part of a time line, give part of a demonstration, or tell part of a story and ask, "What comes next?"

Give incomplete directions for going somewhere, conducting a meeting, or doing an activity and ask, "What is missing?"

Another activity to use or to introduce during discussion requires students to arrange items in sequence or in proper position:

Show pictures, or cards with phrases or sentences on them, and ask students to arrange them in order.

Ask students to arrange, in proper position, parts of maps or large pictures that have been cut to show special features, relative size or location of features, or other items.

Show pictures that belong in a scene (farm, airport) and ask students to arrange them to show relative position.

An important use of discussion is to devise evaluation standards for selected activities, as shown in Checklist 14.3. Discussion may at times be the focus of evaluation, as shown in Checklist 14.4.

Checklist 14–3
WHICH DO YOU DO?

__Use questions to guide study
__Get ideas from reading materials
__Get ideas from AV materials
__Take and organize notes
__Share ideas during discussion
__Help to plan next activities

Checklist 14–4
DISCUSSION STANDARDS

__I wait to be recognized.
__I give others their turn.
__I make a contribution.
__I stick to the topic.
__I listen to others.
__I help find ways to improve.

Quality Circles

Quality circles include four or five students whose task is to make an evaluation and identify ways to make improvements in learning activities. They give attention to difficulties, needed changes, ways to improve, and progress in making improvements. General questions to guide appraisal of an activity are: What strong points should be continued? What weak points should be eliminated? What difficulties arose? How can they be overcome? What specific recommendations should be made to improve the quality of our work?

Specific questions may be used for evaluation of a selected activity. For example, one group used the following to find ways to improve the quality of map work: What changes are needed in (1) use of symbols, (2) use of color, (3) printing of place names, (4) accuracy of location of items, and (5) clarity of the legend? Another group was guided by these questions as they appraised the quality of committee work: What can the chairperson do to get each member to contribute? How can each member do a fair share of the work? What changes are needed in work standards? What should be done to get all members to follow work standards? Which standards are most difficult to follow? Why? What should be done to meet them?

Committee procedures may be used, with a chairperson as leader and a recorder to report recommendations for improvement. Student involvement in devising questions, identifying needed changes, and making recommendations keeps responsibility on students for the continuing improvement of learning activities. A desirable spinoff is growth in self-direction, a key element in lifelong learning.

Charts and Checklists

These devices are helpful in student self-evaluation and peer evaluation as well as in teacher evaluation of students' achievement. Students' performance can be appraised as shown in Charts 14.1 through 14.3 and in Checklist 14.7. Products can be appraised as shown in Checklists 14.5 and 14.6. Also useful in both self-evaluation by students and teacher evaluation of students' learning are experience charts dictated by students after an activity such as a field trip.

Is the Meaning Clear?	
Needs	Producer
Wants	Consumer
Goods	Buyer
Services	Seller
Price	Supply
Profit	Demand

Chart 14.1

Analyzing

Are the main parts identified?

Can you tell why each part is important?

Can you tell how the parts are related?

Chart 14.2

Evaluating

Is the focus of evaluation clear?

Have you defined evaluation standards?

Do you have evidence for each standard?

Chart 14.3

Checklist 14–5
CHECKLIST FOR OUTLINE MAPS

____ Title descriptive of content?

____ Compass rose drawn accurately?

____ Needed data double-checked?

____ Symbols defined in legend?

____ Neat and legible printing?

____ Places located accurately?

____ Source(s) of data given?

Checklist 14–6
SOCIAL STUDIES REPORTS

____ Significant topic selected?

____ Social studies concepts used?

____ Main ideas supported by details?

____ Main ideas in proper order?

____ Effective use of maps and illustrations?

____ Clear title, introduction, and summary?

____ Sources of information noted?

Checklist 14–7
CHECK ITEMS ON WHICH YOU NEED HELP!

Defining Terms and Issues

_____ Identify clear and unclear definitions.

_____ State similarities to and differences from other issues or problems.

_____ Identify appropriate and inappropriate questions.

_____ Identify relevant and irrelevant ideas.

_____ Recognize individual and group values.

_____ Express issue, problem, or terms in own words.

Judging and Using Information

_____ Identify evidence related to problem.

_____ Identify inconsistencies and contradictions.

_____ Identify facts, opinions, and reasoned judgments.

_____ Identify assumptions, bias, stereotypes, clichés, propaganda, and doublespeak.

Drawing Conclusions

_____ Base conclusions on evidence.

_____ Draw implications and inferences.

_____ Distinguish inferences from generalizations.

_____ Use conclusions to formulate hypotheses and make predictions.

_____ Recognize overgeneralizing and conclusions not based on evidence.

Various scales are used in rating devices designed for evaluation by the teacher and for self-evaluation and peer evaluation by students. Shown here are graphic, numerical, grading, and ranking scales.

Participation in Group Work

|————————————|————————————|————————————|————————————|

Very often works   Sometimes works   Rarely works
with others   with others   with others

|————————————|————————————|————————————|————————————|

Very effective   Fairly effective   Not effective in
in group work   in group work   group work

How Good Is Your Work on Committees?

Mark each item as follows: 5, very good; 4, good; 3, fair; 2, poor; 1, very poor.

_____Making plans for work   _____Sticking to the job

_____Being a helpful member   _____Following work rules

_____Chairing a committee   _____Doing a fair share of work

_____Respecting all members   _____Finding ways to improve

Rate Yourself on Media Literacy!

Grade yourself as follows: A, always; B, frequently; C, sometimes; D, rarely; E, never.
Which of these do you analyze and evaluate to detect good and bad features?
___ Newspapers ___ Magazines ___ Radio ___ TV ___ Video ___ Film ___ Trade
books ___ Textbooks ___ Computer programs ___ References ___ Other? _____
Which of these do you use to analyze and evaluate media?
___ Purpose ___ Motive ___ Point of view ___ Assumptions ___ Values ___ Facts
___ Opinions ___ Emotional appeals ___ Persuasion techniques ___ Other? _____

Skill in Social Studies Activities

Rank the following in order, beginning with 1 for the activity you do best. Write reasons
for no. 1 and no. 8.

_____Committee work   _____Making maps

_____Group discussion   _____Reading books

_____Individual reports   _____Reporting events

_____Interviewing   _____Self-evaluation

Reason for 1: _____
Reason for 8: _____

These guidelines are used to prepare charts and checklists for use in evaluation:

1. Identify specific items to include by checking teaching guides, relevant chapters in this volume, and other pertinent materials.
2. Observe students and analyze products of their work to note specific needs and to modify items you have identified.
3. Vary the number of items from three to seven for students to use in self-evaluation to as many as needed for adequate teacher evaluation of a defined achievement domain.
4. Involve students in discussion of those you make and in the designing of those based on observed needs so that they will understand how and why to use them.

Questionnaires and Inventories

These self-report devices are used to assess feelings, interests, attitudes—affective outcomes of instruction. Forms of response vary from marking a smiling or non-smiling face and yes-no to five- and seven-place scales, as shown here. Attitude scales often have five places, ranging from strongly agree to strongly disagree, strongly favor to strongly disfavor, or other appropriate terms.

Mark the Face that Shows How You Feel

1. Studying our community
2. Reading about communities

Are You Interested in These Hispanic Unit Activities?

1. Reading about leaders   Yes   No
2. Interviewing leaders   Yes   No
3. Giving a report   Yes   No
4. Making a booklet   Yes   No

Social Studies Attitudes

Mark as follows: SA, strongly agree; A, agree; U, uncertain; D, disagree; SD, strongly disagree.

_____1. Students learn how to be good citizens in the social studies.
_____2. More time should be given to history of our country.
_____3. Students learn more from individual study than from group work.

Preference for Group Work

Rank in order your preference for working on the following committees, beginning with 1 for your first choice.

_____Crafts   _____Dioramas   _____Interviewing

_____Mapping   _____Murals   _____Quality circle

HOW DO YOU RATE SOCIAL STUDIES INSTRUCTION?

1. Rank these in order of importance. Use 1 for the most important, 2 for the next most important, to 5 for the least important.
   ____Art ____Arithmetic ____Reading ____Science ____Social Studies
2. Should we have *more* or *less* of the following in social studies?

Library books	More	Less	Films and videos	More	Less
Field trips	More	Less	Individual reports	More	Less
Role playing	More	Less	Arts and crafts	More	Less
Committee work	More	Less	Class discussion	More	Less
Simulations	More	Less	Computer projects	More	Less
Ethnic studies	More	Less	Gender equity	More	Less
Futures studies	More	Less	Law studies	More	Less
Geography	More	Less	History	More	Less
Civics	More	Less	Economics	More	Less

3. What is the best part of social studies instruction?

   _____

4. What is the worst part of social studies instruction?

   _____

The semantic differential is used to assess attitudes toward a group, a person, an activity, a place, an object, or an event (Osgood et al., 1957). Students mark their position on a scale between bipolar adjectives, as shown in Chart 14.4. Examples of other adjectives are brave–cowardly, bright–dull, calm–agitated, clean–dirty, clear–hazy, fair–unfair, high–low, honest–dishonest, nice–awful, relaxed–tense, sweet–sour, useful–useless, and valuable–worthless.

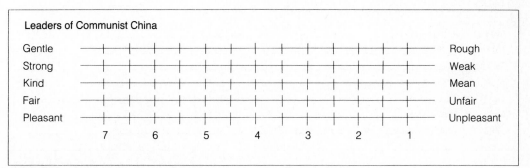

Chart 14.4

Examples of titles of scales to prepare for use in the social studies are: Living in Our Community, Fire Fighters, Using Computers, Veteran's Day, Early Settlers in Our State, Living in a Desert Region, Our Country's Future, Pioneer Life, Moving West in a Covered Wagon, Achievements of Harriet Tubman, The Japanese, Life in China, Contributions of the Romans, and Life in the Middle Ages. Feelings about social studies activities may be assessed by scales with such titles as Working on Committees, Preparing Individual Reports, and Group Discussion.

Students may participate in the preparation of useful scales by suggesting topics and proposing or adding adjectives. For example, one group proposed the following bipolar terms for a scale on Our Public Transit System: bright–dull, cheap–costly, easy–hard, fast–slow, and good–bad. Another group planned a scale entitled The Gold Rush and used the dictionary and the thesaurus to double-check antonyms included in the following: bold–timid, excited–calm, gritty–smooth, lucky–unlucky, peaceful–warlike, wealthy–poor, and wild–tame.

Logs and Diaries

Both individual and group logs or diaries contain information for use in evaluation. The group-made log contains material dictated by the class, may be in experience chart form, and is related to daily activities. Individual logs or diaries are kept by each child. A helpful recording form is shown in Chart 14.5.

Anecdotal Records

Brief notes on a student's behavior are made to gather data on interests, learning difficulties, misbehavior, and special needs. Teacher comments are added later to indicate steps to take to improve learning. The excerpts in Chart 14.6, from a behavior journal on a student who had been doing poorly in social studies, illustrate how anecdotal records may be used. Because of the extra time and work involved, such records should be limited to situations of special importance for which needed evaluation data are not available.

Daily Learning Log

Name _____Unit _____Date _____

New concepts learned _____

Other learning _____

Difficulties _____

Most interesting activity _____

Least interesting activity _____

Most valuable activity _____

Other comments _____

Chart 14.5

EXCERPTS FROM BEHAVIOR JOURNAL ON MAE R.

Date	*Incidents*	*Comments*
10/4	Did not volunteer for an individual project.	May be interested in making a study of a notable woman.
10/6	Asked if materials were available on black women.	Must check with librarian.
10/7	Asked if anyone was reporting on Sojourner Truth.	Great! Materials available.
10/11	Volunteered to make a booklet.	Must give help as needed to assure success.

Chart 14–6

Portfolios of Students' Work

Students' reports, map work, social studies art work, semantic maps, and other materials may be examined to appraise learning and identify points to clarify in instruction. Samples gathered at the beginning and the end of a term or a unit may be compared to appraise students' progress and to report to parents. Tape recordings of discussions and oral reports may be used by students as well as by the teacher to appraise verbal skills and use of concepts. Emphasis should be given to positive ways to improve so that students benefit without embarrassment.

Individual Conferences

In serious cases a conference with a student helps to identify needs, difficulties, interests, and reasons for behavior. Special care should be taken to be a good listener, focus on specific examples of behavior, elicit suggestions from the student, and maintain rapport throughout the conference. Specific appraisals may be made by having a student think aloud while interpreting a map or table, using an index or table of contents, or engaging in another activity in need of evaluation.

Peer Evaluation

Students' evaluation of each other goes on constantly and should be put to constructive use. Benefits to students are development of skill in making positive comments and constructive suggestions, improvement of self-appraisal by comparing one's own work with that of others, and development of skill in applying standards objectively and fairly. Students also benefit from immediate feedback that is expressed in terms they understand, is grounded in learning activities, and is representative of perceptions of fellow students.

GOOD EVALUATORS

_____ Have clear standards in mind and use them to make an appraisal.
_____ Apply the standards fairly and honestly to everyone.
_____ Find good points that should be developed further.
_____ Find needs for improvement and make constructive suggestions.
_____ Double-check to ensure accuracy and fairness of the evaluation.
_____ Reserve judgment when there is lack of evidence or uncertainty.

RATING EACH OTHER IN COOPERATIVE WORK

Name of member _____ Name of evaluator _____

1. Listens to the chairperson	Always	Usually	Rarely
2. Listens to other members	Always	Usually	Rarely
3. Sticks to the job	Always	Usually	Rarely
4. Follows committee rules	Always	Usually	Rarely

Strongest point: _____
Needed improvement: _____

Chart 14.7

Constructive peer evaluation requires the use of guiding principles and rating forms such as those in Chart 14.7.

Constructing and Using Tests

Criterion-referenced and norm-referenced tests are used in the social studies. Criterion-referenced tests are designed to assess achievement in such defined domains as knowledge of state historical events and development of map skills. Norm-referenced tests provide percentile, grade-equivalent, or other scores that are used to compare the achievement of local students and classes with the achievement of a large sample of other students in the same grade or age group.

Criterion-referenced tests are being used with increasing frequency because they fit local instruction, reveal what each student has mastered, and provide data needed to individualize instruction. They are used in the operation of competence-based programs and the accountability system. For example, mastery of map skills may be assessed by items that require students to interpret the legend, use the scale, identify directions, and locate places. The ability to use thinking skills may be assessed by items that call for generalizing, analyzing, and evaluating, as shown in the next section. The guiding principle is to note the competencies in a given domain of instruction and to prepare related test items.

Computerized testing may be done by arranging items in a format that provides feedback. Tests can also be adapted to students' responses so that the next item is related to the response on the preceding one (Bracey, 1990).

Items on Levels of Cognitive Complexity

The following items are designed to assess the use of thinking skills and mastery of selected concepts on six levels of cognition: knowledge, comprehension, application, analysis, synthesis, and evaluation (Bloom, 1956). The items are based on thinking skills presented in chapter 9 and on concepts from a unit on Our State.

Knowledge Level

Recalling

Which ocean is on the western edge of North and South America?

    A. Arctic B. Atlantic C. Indian D. Pacific

Observing

Write the names of three resources shown on the map on page 72 in our textbook.

_____

Comprehension Level

Interpreting

The graph on page 76 shows that population growth was greatest from

    A. 1910–1930 B. 1930–1950 C. 1950–1970 D. 1970–1990

Generalizing

Which statement best expresses the main idea in the section on "Location of Cities"?

    A. The largest cities are near productive resources.
    B. The largest cities are near natural waterways.
    C. The largest cities are near scenic areas.

Application Level

Inferring

What seems to be the purpose of the author of the report on "The Coming Water Shortage"?

    A. To urge dam construction   C. To cut industrial use
    B. To urge use of rivers   D. To promote recycling

Hypothesizing

Complete the following to state a hypothesis that can be tested by gathering evidence:

The area of our state that would be hurt the most by a water shortage is _____.

A good source of evidence to test the hypothesis is _____.

Predicting

Based on trends shown in the graph on page 78, what do you forecast the population of our state to be in 2010?

_____

Analysis, Synthesis, and Evaluation Levels

Analysis

Use an outline map to divide our state into major landform regions.

Synthesis

Make and illustrate a tourist map that shows at least four scenic attractions in our state.

Evaluation

If you could choose, where would you most like to live in our state? _____

Write two reasons for your choice:

_____

_____

Items for Affective Objectives

Most units include objectives related to desirable attitudes, appreciations, interests, or values that involve students' feelings. They may be assessed by items that require students to give ratings, make rankings, or respond on a continuum such as strongly agree to strongly disagree. Various levels may be assessed, ranging from receiving and responding to valuing and holding a system of values (Krathwohl and others, 1964; Hannah and Michaelis, 1977). The examples presented earlier in the section on questionnaires and inventories are illustrative of self-reports that are useful. The following examples are designed to assess seriousness of problems, preferences, degree of importance and interest, and willingness to act on values.

How Serious Are These Problems in Our State?

Mark each item as follows: A, very serious; B, serious; C, fairly serious; D, not serious; E, not sure.

_____1. Acid rain   _____3. Air pollution   5. Mass transit

_____2. Toxic waste   _____4. Urban blight   6. Water pollution

Which State Do You Prefer?

Rank the following in order of your preference as a state in which to live, beginning with 1 for your first choice.

_____Alaska   _____California   _____Florida   _____Hawaii

_____Illinois   _____New York   _____Oregon   _____Texas

Reason for first choice: _____

Reason for last choice: _____

Rate the Following Topics

Directions. Mark an X on the lines below each topic to show how important and how interesting it is to you.

1. History of Our State

Very important   Not important

Very interesting   Not interesting

2. Contributions of Ethnic Groups

Very important   Not important

Very interesting   Not interesting

3. Living in Mexico

Very important   Not important

Very interesting   Not interesting

What Should All Students Do? What Do You Do?

1. Everyone should show respect for minority group members.
    Strongly agree   Agree   Undecided   Disagree   Strongly disagree
2. I show respect for minority group members.
    Always   Most of the time   Sometimes   Seldom   Never
3. Everyone should find and correct unfairness to minority groups.
    Strongly agree   Agree   Undecided   Disagree   Strongly disagree
4. I find and correct unfairness to minority groups.
    Always   Most of the time   Sometimes   Seldom   Never
5. Everyone should use proper language when discussing minority groups.
    Strongly agree   Agree   Undecided   Disagree   Strongly disagree
6. I use proper language when discussing minority groups.
    Always   Most of the time   Sometimes   Seldom   Never

Items Based on Instructional Materials

Useful criterion-referenced items can be based on material presented in textbooks and other media as illustrated here. Notice the increasing levels of complexity, beginning with remembering in the first item and moving to interpreting in the second, analyzing in the third, and evaluating in the last.

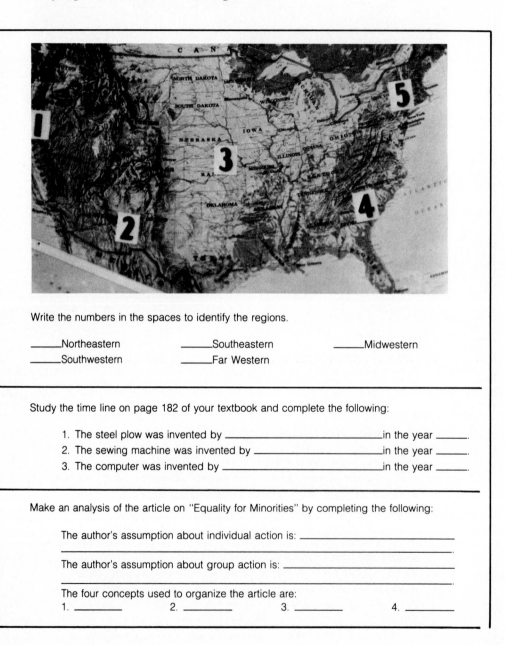

Write the numbers in the spaces to identify the regions.

_____Northeastern   _____Southeastern   _____Midwestern
_____Southwestern   _____Far Western

Study the time line on page 182 of your textbook and complete the following:

1. The steel plow was invented by _____in the year _____.
2. The sewing machine was invented by _____in the year _____.
3. The computer was invented by _____in the year _____.

Make an analysis of the article on "Equality for Minorities" by completing the following:

The author's assumption about individual action is: _____
_____.

The author's assumption about group action is: _____
_____.

The four concepts used to organize the article are:
1. _____   2. _____   3. _____   4. _____

Rate the film on *Sex Discrimination* as follows:
    A, fair to both sexes; B, fairer to women; C, fairer to men; D, unfair to both sexes.

Rate the following and write a reason for each rating.

_____1. Sex equity in all activities
      Reason: _____

_____2. Freedom to make career choices
      Reason: _____

_____3. Sex stereotypes
      Reason: _____

_____4. Responsibility for work at home
      Reason: _____

Situation and Problem Items

The ability to apply concepts and main ideas can be assessed by items that present a situation or a problem, as shown in the following examples.

A problem of pioneers moving westward was selecting food to take in their covered wagons. Mark a + by each item that they would take.

_____Apples	_____Carrots	_____Dried beans	_____Lettuce
_____Bacon	_____Cereal	_____Eggs	_____Milk
_____Bread	_____Cheese	_____Flour	_____Rice
_____Cake	_____Cookies	_____Hamburger	_____Salt

Members of a committee have had trouble working together. Suggestions for improvement are listed below. Mark each item as follows: A, agree; D, disagree.

_____Ask the teacher to step in when a problem arises.
_____Ask the chairperson to straighten out problems.
_____Each member should ignore troublemakers.
_____Any troublemaker should be removed by the chairperson.
_____Members should go to their seats if trouble arises.
_____Ask the troublemaker to stick to the job.

Realistic and challenging situations and problems of two types may be presented. The first is based on instruction provided in units of study, as shown in the first example. The second is based on situations or problems that have arisen during social studies instruction, as shown in the second example. A situation or a problem that could be a topic of discussion is satisfactory. Plausible responses can be obtained from teaching materials and from observation of students in discussion or other activities.

The range of answers can be extended by adding a free response item: Write an additional answer that you think is a good one.

The following general model can be used to assess a variety of problems in depth. Notice that it goes beyond the above examples to include key aspects of problem solving and decision making.

PROBLEM, SOLUTIONS, CONSEQUENCES, DECISION, REASON(S)

Complete the following by stating a problem, listing possible solutions and consequences, making a decision, and noting the reason(s) for it.

The problem: _____

_____

Solution 1: _____

Consequences: _____

_____

Solution 2: _____

Consequences: _____

_____

Solution 3: _____

Consequences: _____

_____

Decision: _____

_____

Reason(s): _____

_____

Guidelines for Item Construction

Two main types of test items need to be prepared to fit units of study. Selection-type items, such as multiple choice, binary choice (true-false, yes-no), and matching, are objective and relatively easy to score. Supply-type items, such as short-answer (completion) and essay, are useful when students should respond by noting the answer rather than choosing one.

A sound procedure is to begin by preparing multiple-choice items, followed by preparing others as needed to assess desired outcomes. For example, true-false items may be used when there are only two alternative responses. Matching items may be used to assess the ability to associate or relate two sets of information. Completion and essay items may be used when students should be able to construct the answer.

Characteristic of all well-prepared test items are clear directions, appropriate reading level, and correct sentence structure. No items should be trick questions, contain double negatives, or suggest unintended clues to answers. Textbook wording should be avoided because it tends to foster rote memorization. Items of the same type (multiple-choice, matching, and so on) should be grouped in separate sections in a test.

The examples that follow include items for assessing knowledge, skills, attitudes, and participation. The first two examples in each set illustrate items used in early grades. The guidelines that conclude each section contain specific rules for item construction.

Multiple-choice Items

These items consist of a question or an incomplete statement (called a *stem*) followed by three or more plausible responses. The correct one or the best one is the answer; the others are distractors that are useful in diagnosing errors and identifying areas in need of review or reteaching. Sometimes, variations on selecting the correct response are used, such as selecting the incorrect answer and selecting two or more correct answers. Such optional responses as *all of the above* and *none of the above* should be used rarely if at all, because they confuse many children.

Draw a line under the best word to end the sentence.

1. A person who buys goods and services is a
   consumer.   producer.   worker.

Draw a circle around the best answer.

1. What are food, shelter, and clothing?
   A. basic needs   B. human wants   C. three wishes

Directions. Write the letter of the correct answer in the blank space by each item.

___ 1. Who helped to survey and plan Washington D.C.?
       A. Banneker   B. Franklin   C. Jefferson   D. Washington

---

Directions. Circle the letter by the best answer.

1. Which nation has the largest population?
   A. China   B. India   C. U.S.A.   D. USSR

Directions.   Mark the space on the answer sheet to show the answer you select.

1. What is the Ring of Fire?

   A. volcanoes around the Pacific Rim
   B. volcanoes that created Hawaii
   C. volcanoes around Mexico City
   D. volcanoes in the Andes

Directions.   Write a + in one of the blank spaces below each item to show how you feel.

1. What is your position on the plan to involve students in the anti-litter project?

   _____Strongly   _____Agree   _____Not sure   _____Disagree   _____Strongly
   agree   disagree

Guidelines

1. The stem should present one question or one problem and should contain most of the item's content.

2. Avoid negatively stated items if possible and be sure that one alternative is the correct or the best answer.

3. Select plausible alternatives, make them about the same length, distribute them evenly among answer positions, and keep all choices in the same category—that is, do not mix persons, places, and things.

4. Be sure that each alternative is grammatically consistent with the stem, as in the preceding examples.

5. Avoid alternatives that overlap or include each other as in this example:

   Over the past decade the employment of women in executive positions has increased

   A. less than 10 percent.
   B. more than 30 percent.
   C. less than 20 percent.
   D. more than 40 percent.

6. Avoid clues, such as words in the stem that are also in the answer, or the use of *a* or *an* at the end of the stem when the alternatives do not all begin with a vowel or a consonant. For example, note how the use of *an* gives a clue in this item:

   A strait is an

   A. hilly area.
   B. inlet of water.
   C. small bay.
   D. strip of land.

Matching Items

These items are a space-saving modification of multiple-choice items. They are used to assess students' ability to associate terms and meanings, persons and events, causes and effects, and other related items. Matching pictures with descriptions or names and matching word pairs or parts of sentences are widely used in early grades. A variety of items may be used in later grades.

Draw a line to show the provider of each service.

Provider	*Service*
Clerk	Education
Nurse	Protection
Police	Business
Teacher	Health

Draw a line between the following to make correct sentences.

Carpenters work to produce	clothing.
Farmers work to produce	shelter.
Tailors work to produce	food.

MATCHING PEOPLE AND CONTRIBUTIONS

Write the letter by the contribution in the space by the persons who made it.

____1. Jane Addams
____2. Susan B. Anthony
____3. W. E. B. DuBois
____4. Booker T. Washington

A. founded Tuskegee Institute, a school for blacks
B. helped to found the NAACP
C. founded Hull House to help the poor
D. worked for women's right to vote
E. worked for reform in politics
F. worked to end monopolies

Time Periods

Match the following by writing the letter by each time period on the right in the correct space on the left.

____1. Before 3500 B.C.
____2. Greek civilization
____3. Roman Empire
____4. Babylonia
____5. Holy Roman Empire
____6. Time of feudalism
____7. Renaissance
____8. Reformation

A. Prehistoric times
B. Ancient times
C. Middle Ages
D. Modern times

Guidelines

1. Place related material, such as people and events or causes and effects, in each item; do not include unrelated content.
2. Keep the number of items small (three to seven), provide extra responses in one column or permit some responses to be used more than once to minimize guessing by middle- and upper-grade students.
3. Arrange the items in one column in alphabetical, chronological, or some other logical order and those in the other column in random order.
4. Keep the columns on the same page so that students will not have to turn the page to match items.

Binary-choice Items

True-false, yes-no, right-wrong, and other two-choice items should be used only when two plausible answers are possible. A variety of formats may be used, ranging from the typical true-false item to the cluster format, as shown below.

True	False	1. Cooking and sewing are examples of goods.

T	F	1. Opportunity cost is the best thing one gives up to get something else.

Yes	No	1. Are tools, materials, and equipment productive resources?

Y	N	1. Division of labor occurs when Joe dries dishes washed by May.

Mark N by items that are part of the natural environment
Mark C by items that are part of the cultural environment

_____1. Lumber	_____4. Steel	_____7. Minerals	_____10. Animals
_____2. Gardens	_____5. Plants	_____8. Pollution	_____11. Zoos
_____3. Dams	_____6. Rivers	_____9. Forests	_____12. Air

Mark a + by items that describe features of the Great Plains.

_____1. Farming	_____5. Desert	_____9. Hot summers
_____2. Grazing	_____6. Highland	_____10. Little rain
_____3. Manufacturing	_____7. Lowland	_____11. Mild winters
_____4. Mining	_____8. Tableland	_____12. Long spring

Guidelines

1. Include an equal number of true and false items of equal length and arrange them in random order.

2. Avoid use of *all, none, always, never,* and other specific determiners that are usually false, and *generally, should,* and *may,* which are usually true.

3. Make each item definitely true or false; avoid use of *few, many, important,* and other ambiguous terms.

4. Place the key element in the main part of the statement or the question, not in a phrase or a subordinate clause. Do not use double negatives.

5. Simplify marking by placing the answer column as shown in the preceding examples. Make a stencil to place over the answers. If students are required to write the answers, ask them to write + for true and 0 for false, which are easier to score than *T* or *F* or + and −.

6. Extensions to use with students in upper grades are: if an item is false, rewrite it to make it true; if an item is true, explain why; find proof for each answer by checking the textbook or other source; add a third column *O* to be marked if the item is based on opinion or *E* to be marked if more evidence is needed.

Short-answer Items

These items require students to complete sentences, give examples, define terms, state analogies, write main ideas, and supply other answers to unit-related questions. A broad range of cognitive and affective outcomes can be assessed. In the examples that follow, a model item format is presented first and is followed by a sample item.

An example of _____ is _____ Other examples are _____, _____, and _____.
An example of a *service* is *health care*. Other examples are _____, _____, and _____.

A _____ is _____.
A *producer* is _____.

Read pages _____ and list _____.
Read pages *78–81* and list *three of our state's natural resources.*

_____   _____   _____

_____ is to _____ as _____ is to _____.
Farm is to *rural* as *city* is to _____.

Classify the _____ by writing their names in the correct column.

_____   _____   _____

Classify the *cities included in today's reading* by writing their names in the correct column.

Banking Centers	*Trade Centers*	*Resort Centers*
_____	_____	_____
_____	_____	_____

_____ means _____.

To consume means _____.

Complete the following outline of _____.

Complete the following outline of *main ideas* and *supporting details* as you read pages *40–43.*

A. _____

   1. _____

   2. _____

B. _____

   1. _____

   2. _____

Study the _____ (map, graph, table, time line) on page _____ and _____

Study the *table* on page 54 and *rank the countries in order,* beginning with 1 for the country largest in land area. Next, rank them in order by population.

Country	Land Area	Population
Brazil	_____	_____
Canada	_____	_____
China	_____	_____
USSR	_____	_____
U.S.A.	_____	_____

We should _____because _____.

We should *support equal rights for others* because

_____

Keep a _____ (daily, weekly) record of _____

Keep a *daily* record of *ways you helped others.*

Activities in _____ (school, community) in which I like to participate are _____

Activities in *school* in which I like to participate are _____

Guidelines

1. Omit only key words, phrases, or dates, not minor details. Do not write such a statement as "The role of mayors is _____." Many different responses are acceptable.

2. Use blanks of uniform size and do not use *a* or *an* before a blank so that no clues are given.

3. Use definite statements with omissions that call for one correct response. Give students credit for other acceptable responses.

4. Do not omit so many words that meaning is obscured, as in "The Puritans left _____ to settle in _____ because _____."

5. Provide blanks as shown in the preceding examples to facilitate writing by students and scoring answers.

Essay Items

Two types of essay items may be used with students who have the needed writing skills to assess complex learning at the application, analysis, synthesis, and evaluation levels. Restricted-response items set clear limits for the response. Extended-response items provide for greater freedom of response. Both types provide evidence of complex learning not obtained from objective tests made up of the items noted previously. However, scoring is more difficult and time-consuming.

The first two items listed are restricted-response items designed to assess learning at the application and analysis levels. The last two are extended-response items designed to assess learning at the synthesis and evaluation levels.

Describe the land, climate, and resources of Mexico. Next, describe the resources that are used to make products for foreign trade.

Summarize the key ideas in today's reading selection. Be sure to place them in the order in which they were presented.

Write a plan for litter cleanup in our school. Note rules and procedures that all students should follow.

Describe three different map projections. Write a critique of each one that includes attention to recommended use, distortion of land areas, distortion of water areas, and distortion in polar areas.

Another form of essay text is a writing assignment that is similar to a learning exercise or an independent study project. Students are required to write and edit a report and to double-check it for accuracy of content, spelling, and grammar. Examples follow.

The Middle Colonies

1. Write the names of the colonies that were between the New England and the southern colonies.
2. Write a paragraph about each middle colony that includes the following:
   a. Name of the colony
   b. Founder of the colony
   c. Why it was founded
   d. Name and date of the first settlement
   e. Country of origin of settlers
   f. A distinctive feature of the colony
3. Proofread your report and make needed changes to ensure accuracy of content, spelling, and grammar, which will be used to grade your report.

Accomplishments of Ancient Greeks

1. Write a paragraph about each individual listed below. Describe the accomplishment for which each one is recognized.
   a. Homer   c. Sappho   e. Aesop   g. Herodotus
   b. Anaxagoras   d. Socrates   f. Plato   h. Aristotle
2. Proofread and revise each paragraph to be sure that content, spelling, and grammar are accurate. Grading will be based on clarity of expression and accuracy of content, spelling, and grammar.

Individual Reports

1. Choose a person, an event, or another topic related to our unit of study.
2. Write a two-page report that includes the following:
   a. Title, introduction, development, conclusion
   b. Sources of information
3. Your report will be graded in terms of originality, clarity of expression, and accuracy of content, spelling, and grammar.

Guidelines

1. Prepare questions or statements that clearly define the task, require the use of high-level skills, and do not call for long answers beyond the writing competence of students.

2. Write model answers and use them to check the intent and the clarity of each item; make any needed revisions.

3. Use model answers to score essay items that do not call for divergent responses. For items with divergent answers use criteria such as completeness, organization, originality, use of examples, and use of key concepts.

4. Score papers anonymously to avoid the halo effect. (Have students write their names on the back of the test paper.) Score all students' answers to one question before going to the next one so that scoring standards will be applied consistently.

5. Inform students when spelling and grammar are to be scored. Give separate scores for them and do not let their scoring influence the scoring of content.

Test Item Banks

A teacher can create a bank of test items by writing items for each unit on a 3 × 5 card. Items may be swapped with fellow teachers and thus increase the size of the test bank. Examples of useful computer programs are *Examwriter, QuickTests, Test Quest, Testmaster, Test It!, Quiz Program, Test Factory, Test Generator,* and *All of the Above.*

Some school systems maintain test item banks from which teachers select items. If the item bank is computerized, teachers can locate useful items, run a printout, and use the items in their own tests.

Published Tests

Tests available from organizations and commercial publishers contain a variety of items that are useful in the social studies. Specimen copies of tests from organizations are available—for example, from the following:

> National Council For Geographic Education, Western Illinois University, Macomb, IL 61455. (Intermediate level)

> Joint Council on Economic Education, 1212 Avenue of the Americas, New York, NY 10036. (Primary and intermediate grades)

Standardized tests with sections on the social studies contain items on skills and concepts that are useful and suggestive of items that teachers can construct. See the following in the college or school district library: *California Achievement Tests, Iowa Tests of Basic Skills, Metropolitan Achievement Test, Sequential Tests of Educational Progress, SRA Achievement Series, Stanford Achievement Test.*

Test makers use items such as those shown in Figure 14.2 to assess commonly taught concepts and skills.

Money to pay for the cost of roads comes from

    A. contributions.

    B. dividends.

    C. dues.

    D. taxes.

Which map is best for locating state capitals?

    A. highway map

    B. political map

    C. population map

    D. relief map

Which one of these workers provides a service?

    A. farmer

    B. home builder

    C. manufacturer

    D. store clerk

The area with letter C on it is

    A. part of Europe.

    B. North America.

    C. the Atlantic Ocean.

    D. the Pacific Ocean.

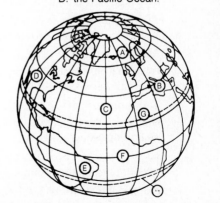

Figure 14.2

Pitfalls to avoid when using published tests are (1) expecting all students to be "at or above the norm," (2) failing to interpret students' achievements in light of capabilities, (3) not taking time to diagnose individual needs, and (4) making a self-fulfilling prophecy by setting low expectations for low achievers.

Guiding principles for effective use of standardized tests are: (1) select a test that fits what has been taught; (2) interpret achievement levels in terms of each student's background and capabilities; and (3) follow up by providing instruction to meet individual needs.

Test-taking Tips

Tips such as these should be discussed with students to help them develop effective test-taking procedures:

Ask, if directions are not clear. Do the sample items and ask if you have any questions.

Concentrate as you read each item, then choose the best answer. Work rapidly, but carefully. Skip an item if you do not know the answer. Return to it later.

Do try to answer all items. Choose the answer you think is best. Be sure the number of each item matches the number on the answer sheet.

Clearly mark the space on the answer sheet. Erase all of it if you make a change.

Start immediately when told to begin. Do not let anything or anyone distract you!

Questions, Activities, and Evaluation

1. Consider practical ways to use each of the basic guidelines to effective evaluation presented in the first section of this chapter. Which do you believe to be the most difficult to apply? Which do you believe now need greater emphasis?

2. In what ways can you provide for student self-evaluation in a unit you are planning?

3. Examine a cumulative record currently being used in a school system in your area. What provision is there for recording progress in social studies? What additional provisions, if any, are needed?

4. Note ways in which you might use each of the following in a unit of your choice: observation, examination of samples of work, interviews, discussion, charts, checklists, rating scales, and questionnaires.

5. Prepare several test items in each form discussed in this chapter. Plan items for assessing both affective and cognitive objectives.

6. Examine the teacher's edition of a social studies textbook and note the suggested evaluation activities. What additions and changes can you make to improve them?

7. What is your position on the following? Check your position and discuss it with others, and then change each statement so that it reflects your views.

	Yes	*No*	*?*
a. Priority should be given in the social studies to evaluation of such lasting outcomes as concepts and skills.	___	___	___
b. Teachers at all levels should emphasize self-evaluation by students.	___	___	___
c. Observation of students is one of the most useful and practical ways to evaluate learning in the social studies.	___	___	___
d. Charts and checklists are among the best devices for teacher appraisal of students and for self-evaluation by students.	___	___	___
e. Teachers should make their own test items for each unit.	___	___	___
f. Teachers should be held accountable for achievement in social studies as well as in reading and arithmetic.	___	___	___
g. The best way to appraise teacher effectiveness is by the amount of pupil gain as shown by tests.	___	___	___

References

Airasian, Peter W., *Classroom Assessment*. New York: McGraw Hill, 1991.

Bloom, Benjamin S., ed., *Taxonomy of Educational Objectives, Handbook I: The Cognitive Domain*. New York: D. McKay, 1956.

Bracey, Gerald, "Computerized Testing: A Possible Alternative to Paper and Pencil?" *Electronic Learning,* 9 (February 1990), 16–17.

Conoley, June C., and Jack J. Kramer, eds., *Tenth Mental Measurements Yearbook*. Lincoln, NE: University of Nebraska Press, 1989. Reviews of tests.

Ebel, Robert L., and David A. Frisbie, *Essentials of Educational Measurement* (5th ed.). Englewood Cliffs, NJ: Prentice-Hall, 1991. Chapters on test items.

Ellis, Arthur K., *Teaching and Learning Elementary Social Studies* (4th ed.). Needham Heights, MA: Allyn & Bacon, 1991. Chapter 8.

ERIC Clearinghouse on Tests, Measurement, and Evaluation. American Institutes for Research, 1055 Thomas Jefferson Street N.W., Washington, DC 20007-3893. Write for list of materials.

Gronlund, Norman E., and Robert L. Linn, *Measurement and Evaluation in Teaching* (6th ed.). New York: Macmillan, 1990. Detailed treatment.

Hannah, Larry S., and John U. Michaelis, *A Comprehensive Framework for Instructional Objectives*. Reading, MA: Addison-Wesley, 1977. Sample items, charts, and checklists on various levels for cognitive and affective assessment.

Krathwohl, David H., Benjamin S. Bloom, and Bertram B. Masia, *Taxonomy of Educational Objectives, Handbook II: The Affective Domain*. New York: D. McKay, 1964.

Kubiszyn, Tom, and Gary Borich, *Educational Testing and Measurement*. Glenview, IL: Scott Foresman/Little, Brown, 1990. Test design and use; test software.

Osgood, Charles E., et al., *The Measurement of Meaning*. Urbana, IL: University of Illinois Press, 1957. Semantic differential.

Popham, W. James, *Educational Evaluation* (2nd ed.). Englewood Cliffs, NJ: Prentice-Hall, 1988. Detailed treatment.

Salvia, John, and James F. Ysseldyke, *Assessment* (5th ed.). Boston: Houghton Mifflin, 1991.

Sparzo, Frank J., *Preparing Better Teacher-made Tests*. Bloomington, IN: Phi Delta Kappa, 1990. Practical tips and examples.

Stiggins, Richard, et al., *Measuring Thinking Skills in the Classroom*. West Haven, CT: NEA Professional Library, 1989. Assessment techniques.

Vavrus, Linda, "Put Portfolios to the Test," *Instructor,* 100 (August 1990), 48–53. Tips for using portfolios to evaluate learning.

Wise, Naomi, and Jane H. Kon, "Assessing Geographic Knowledge with Sketch Maps," *Journal of Geography,* 89 (May/June 1990), 123–29. Use of freehand maps drawn from memory.

Index